Media Coverage
of Crime and
Criminal Justice

Media Coverage of Crime and Criminal Justice

Matthew B. Robinson

CAROLINA ACADEMIC PRESS
Durham, North Carolina

Library of Congress Cataloging-in-Publication Data
Robinson, Matthew B.
  Media coverage of crime and criminal justice / Matthew B. Robinson.
    p. cm.
  Includes bibliographical references and index.
  ISBN 978-1-59460-943-5 (alk. paper)
  1. Crime in mass media. 2. Mass media and crime. 3. Mass media and
criminal justice. 4. Criminal justice, Administration of. I. Title.
  P96.C74R63 2010
  364--dc22

                          2010038573

CAROLINA ACADEMIC PRESS
700 Kent Street
Durham, North Carolina 27701
Telephone (919) 489-7486
Fax (919) 493-5668
www.cap-press.com

Contents

Preface

Every citizen, every day, has contact with the media in some form. Whether it is in the form of advertising, news or entertainment, and whether it is television, Internet, newspaper, radio, or some other form of media, the media are inescapable. As a result, the media impact our world in very important ways.

For many Americans today, relatively new forms of media have even greater impacts on our lives. For example, we often rely heavily on websites, social network sites, blogs, and so forth for both news and entertainment.

From the very founding of the press in America, crime and criminal justice have held a prominent place in the media. Today, news about crime and criminal justice and entertainment centering on it are widespread. Thus, crime and punishment are often on the forefront of Americans' minds.[1]

Unfortunately, images of crime and criminal justice in the media tend to diverge from reality in important ways. This explains why people who rely on media for their information about crime and criminal justice tend to hold misconceptions about crime, criminals, and criminal justice practice. *Media Coverage of Crime and Criminal Justice* critically examines media coverage of crime and criminal justice to help correct these misconceptions and shed light on important realities of crime and criminal justice in the United States.

While there are other texts on the market focused on the impact of mass media on criminal justice, this text is the only one that starts with the issue of corporate ownership of the mass media as a potential problem for gaining an accurate understanding of the realities of crime and criminal justice. Further, this text presents basic information about the media in the introductory chapters and then applies this information to specific issues of crime and criminal justice in the rest of the book, thereby focusing on the same issues and themes throughout the book.

In this book, the reader will learn what is meant by the terms "media" and "mainstream media" and also will learn about alternative sources of media information. Topics analyzed include how the media are organized, how they operate, and to what degree citizens are exposed to the media. Additionally, the book analyzes competing explanations of media coverage of crime and criminal justice, using examples from the real world to show why the media cover topics (and ignore others) the way they do.

The book deals with media coverage of law-making and crime, policing, courts, and corrections. There are separate chapters of media coverage of each branch of criminal justice, with reviews of the literature focused on the most recent and influential research on these topics. The book also examines how the media both help and hinder effective crime control and crime prevention efforts. The book concludes with a summary of the book as well as suggestions for media reform, based on major findings of the book.

The book focuses mostly on images of crime, but an additional chapter is also devoted to how terrorism and the war on terrorism are covered in the media; the chapter is offered online as a supplement to the book for those who are interested in expanding their examination beyond crime and criminal justice. This material is relevant for the book because of the overlap and parallels between the war on crime and the war on terror.[2] Recent laws and policies aimed at reducing and preventing terrorism (e.g., the USA PATRIOT Act) have actually been more widely used to pursue ordinary, everyday street criminals, and serve as evidence of the increasingly punitive nature of criminal justice in the United States.[3]

Most of the book deals with media that are aimed at providing information to citizens (the news, for example). Yet, the book also analyzes literature on entertainment media and how issues of crime and criminal justice are depicted on television, in movies, music, and so forth. This is important for at least two reasons: First, crime is very popular in modern entertainment; and second, most U.S. citizens spend more time interacting with entertainment media than with news media.

In my teaching and writing about criminal justice reform in the United States, I've learned that little criminal justice reform is possible without considering needed reforms in the way American media are organized and operate. One goal of this book is to provide the information necessary to understand how to achieve such reform. While the book can thus be considered "activist" in nature in that it clearly has an agenda, the material is presented in a fair and objective manner. First and foremost, the goal of the book is to tell the truth about the media.

I start with this important point: It is impossible to fully understand criminal justice—the law, crime, police, courts, corrections—without studying the media. This is because the media play such an important role in criminal justice policy. The media impact criminal justice policy directly (e.g., by featuring criminal justice officials in stories) and indirectly (e.g., by impacting public perceptions of crime, justice and injustice). Ray Surette agrees, writing "crime, justice, and the media have to be studied together because in twenty-first century America they are inseparable, wedded to each other in a forced marriage. They cohabitate in an often raucous, sometimes riotous, but ultimately unavoidable relationship."[4]

Given the numerous interrelationships between the media and criminal justice agencies, it is not possible to fully understand criminal justice practice without understanding the media. If you are a student of criminal justice, reading this book will not only teach you about the media but will also help you gain a more complete understanding of the realities of criminal justice practice.

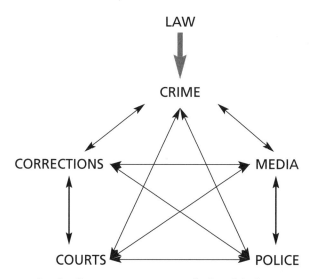

Each arrow in the figure represents a relationship between some aspect of criminal justice and the media. For example, when crimes are committed—especially certain types of crimes (e.g., random, violent crimes against innocent victims)—they are often broadcast in the news media. The media also rely on police personnel for information about crimes after they occur as well as allow the police to appear in their stories. At each stage of the criminal justice process, the media play an important role, as when the media cover a high profile criminal trial or an escape from a prison.

Finally, it is important to note that there are new examples of media coverage of crime, criminal justice, and related topics literally every day. For this reason, it is important that you pay attention to the news and entertainment media as you read this book. By doing so, you will see the most current examples of issues and topics raised in this book. It is also recommended that you visit the website related to this book. Here you will find many more examples of media coverage of crime, criminal justice and related topics, as well as links to media organizations and groups working to change the media. You will also find links to blogs about the media, crime, criminal justice, and related topics. Look for this symbol throughout the book.

 ⌐⊖ This symbol will alert you to additional information on various topics that have been placed on the website: www.pscj.appstate.edu/media/

Part I
The Organization and Goals of the Media

Chapter 1

Introduction to the Media, Part I: Who Owns the Media and What Are the Goals of the Media?

Learning Objectives

After reading this chapter, you will be able to:

1) Define the *media*.
2) Define the *mass media* or *mainstream media*.
3) Differentiate between the three major kinds of media.
4) Explain which forms of media are more objective and realistic and which are less objective and realistic.
5) Define and differentiate between the *inner ring*, *middle ring*, and *outer ring* news sources.
6) Explain why the inner ring media have the most influence in society.
7) Identify from where people get their information about crime and criminal justice policy.
8) Identify who owns the most important media in the United States.
9) Define *media consolidation, horizontal integration, vertical integration, synergy*, and *interlocking directorates* and explain why these concepts are important for understanding the media.
10) Contrast the *democratic postulate* and the *propaganda model*.
11) Define the five filters of the propaganda model and explain how these filters limit the breadth of information found in the media.
12) Explain whether the media intentionally filter information for the purposes of propaganda.

Introduction

The term *media* is a plural form of the word *medium*, which has been defined as "one of the means or channels of general communication, information, or entertainment in society, as newspapers, radio, or television."[1] The media can be considered "the means of communication, as radio and television, newspapers, and magazines, that reach or influence people widely."[2]

The media are often referred to as the "mass media" as well as the "mainstream media" which are "media that are easily, inexpensively, and simultaneously accessible to large segments of a population."[3] These sources include newspapers, magazines, books, television, radio, film, recordings, the Internet, and so forth. Mass media are "critical carriers and definers of popular culture."[4] The *mainstream media* are those sources most commonly relied upon for information, including television stations such as ABC, NBC, CBS, CNN,

Fox, and similar channels, as well as widely read newspapers like the *New York Times*, *Washington Post*, *Wall Street Journal* and so forth.

There are, of course, alternative sources of media information out there, especially in these times of great technology and globalization. Such sources include radio stations, Internet sites, as well as alternative media organizations like Alternet, Democracy Now, Truthout, Common Dreams, and other outlets that utilize and celebrate advocacy journalism. *Advocacy journalism* intentionally and openly presents news and analysis from a non-objective viewpoint in order to achieve a favored outcome (such as victory by a political candidate or political party or greater attention being paid to some issue). Many websites and blogs are involved in what amounts to advocacy journalism. While *propaganda* involves the intentional spreading of false information for the purposes of helping one's own cause or hurting another, advocacy journalism is based on facts and is not intended to be false. Further, advocacy journalism is different than the mainstream media in that it is not intended to be *objective* or neutral (something seen as impossible by advocacy journalists).

This chapter introduces the most important concepts for understanding the media and how the media deal with issues of crime and criminal justice. This includes discussions of how the media are organized, the intimate relationships between media and big business, and goals of the media. The primary goal of this chapter is to introduce the most important concepts related to the media to set the stage for our examination of how the media cover crime and criminal justice.

Types of Media

There are at least three kinds of media, not including advertising (which is present in all three media types). First, there are the news media. Second, there are the entertainment media. Finally, there is infotainment. The primary goal of the *news media* is to provide information on major events, issues, problems, and trends. The primary goal of the *entertainment media* is to entertain—i.e., to give people something enjoyable to do that diverts them from more serious concerns. Finally, *infotainment* exists in-between the news and entertainment media. Infotainment amounts to a blurring of the lines between the news and entertainment.

Merriam-Webster's Dictionary defines infotainment as "a television program that presents information (as news) in a manner intended to be entertaining."[5] Of course, infotainment does not have to occur on television, it can exist in any media format. Thus, infotainment includes any media content presenting information in an entertaining manner. How the media cover crime and criminal justice in each of these types of media is the focus of this book.

Historically, people have thought of the news media as objective and realistic. Yet, this does not mean that the way crime and criminal justice are shown in the news is accurate. Most probably recognize that entertainment media are generally not aimed at being either realistic or objective but instead at entertaining people. For example, movies depicting crime and criminal justice processes are generally aimed at entertaining viewers rather than informing them of the realities of crime and criminal justice. Infotainment, which tends to blur the boundaries between news and entertainment media, may at times appear objective and even realistic when in fact it is almost always subjective and unrealistic in its portrayals.

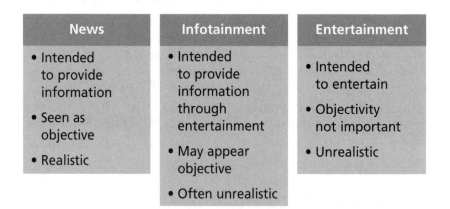

News	Infotainment	Entertainment
• Intended to provide information • Seen as objective • Realistic	• Intended to provide information through entertainment • May appear objective • Often unrealistic	• Intended to entertain • Objectivity not important • Unrealistic

Infotainment exists in-between news media and entertainment media along a continuum of types of media. Infotainment is increasingly popular when it comes to shows about crime and criminal justice.

In case you are wondering where those relatively new forms of media mentioned in the Preface to the book fit in, there are websites and blogs devoted to both news and entertainment. Social network sites (e.g., Facebook, MySpace) are used mostly for entertainment purposes, although they can also be used for organizing purposes to bring about social change. Go ahead and search for a cause you care about—chances are there are many pages on these sites devoted to it.

How the Media Are Organized

Three Rings of the Media

Media sources are organized within a hierarchy of controlling institutions. Long ago, Stephen Hess described the media as having an inner ring, a middle ring, and an outer ring.[6] The *inner ring of the media* includes the major television networks such as ABC, NBC, CBS, CNN and Fox News; major news magazines such as *Time*, *Newsweek*, and *U.S. News & World Report*; national newspapers such as *The New York Times*, the *Washington Post*, *USA Today*, and *The Wall Street Journal*; and the Associated Press wire service. The *middle ring of the media* and the *outer ring of the media* are more prevalent but have far less influence on the news than the institutions in the inner ring.

As noted in the Preface to the book, many Americans now rely heavily on websites, social network sites, blogs, and so forth for both news and entertainment. Many of these are from inner ring sources; yet many are not. With the advent of blog technology, literally anyone can voice their opinion on any issue of importance to them. Many bloggers have been quite successful through their own serious investigations that they regularly "scoop" the mainstream news in breaking stories prior to even inner ring sources; at other times their reports make it into the mainstream press. To the degree that people rely on such sources aside from inner ring sources of information, the inner ring becomes less powerful in society.

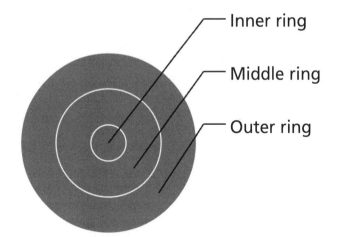

The inner ring sources of media are the most widely accessed media sources and have the largest influence on people.

Inner-ring sources are the main sources of information for Americans about many issues.[7] Crime, as a major issue for society, is usually news.[8] The Center for Media and Public Affairs, for example, finds that at any given time, roughly 30% of local news is devoted to crime and criminal justice.[9] According to Kenneth Dowler, crime is popular in all forms of media. He writes: "Western society is fascinated with crime and justice. From films, books, newspapers, magazines, television broadcasts, to everyday conversations, we are constantly engaging in crime 'talk.' "[10]

While crime and criminal justice are staples of local news, crime usually makes the national news only when a crime or series of crimes is thought to warrant national attention. For example, after the terrorist attacks of September 11, 2001, a large portion of the news was devoted to these mass murders; coverage of terrorism and to the newly announced "war on terrorism" subsequently dominated the news for months and even years.[11]

The media are the main source for news about crime and criminal justice policy for citizens. As noted by David Krajicek: "The press provides our window on public problems, on the government's strategies to solve them, and on how well those strategies succeed (or fail)."[12] When it comes to crime, since most Americans will not be victimized by serious crimes other than theft, they are far more likely to get their information from media sources than from personal experience. This is extremely important because media depictions of crime are often inaccurate, as will be shown throughout this book.

However, not all media sources have the same impact on us. The media sources in the inner ring have greater influence than other sources. According to John Harrigan: "The organization at the top of the media hierarchy decides what counts as news."[13] This is true because most journalists consult these sources for their own news.[14] Reporters of crime news commonly "copy" what other media reporters are doing. When reputable sources cover crime problems in the media, other reporters take their lead and follow with very similar stories. This is precisely how a "crime problem" often emerges in society in the first place.

The Associated Press (AP) is an important part of the inner-ring of the media. Virtually all of the 1,700 newspapers in the United States subscribe to the AP, the largest news organization in the world. The AP is a nonprofit cooperative that serves more than 5,000 television and U.S. radio stations and more than 8,500 media outlets throughout the world through AP online. The AP compiles thousands of stories each day, of which only a couple of dozen are sent to the local, regional, national, and international wires for inclusion in various media outlets.[15]

When a story is carried by the AP, it will appear all over the nation in newspapers, radio broadcasts, and television news. A crime that occurs in California may become newsworthy all over the nation because of the AP. Citizens across America are repeatedly shown high speed police chases in Los Angeles, for example, often broadcast live from cameras aboard "news" helicopters, regardless of the lack of relevance to people in other parts of the country.

Noam Chomsky provides an example of how the inner ring of the media control the news. He writes that

> the elite media, sometimes called the agenda-setting media because they are the ones with the big resources, they set the framework in which everyone else operates.... If you are watching the Associated Press, who grind out a constant flow of news, in the mid-afternoon it breaks and there is something that comes along every day that says "Notice to Editors: Tomorrow's *New York Times* is going to have the following stories on the front page." The point of that is, if you're an editor of a newspaper in Dayton, Ohio and you don't have the resources to figure out what the news is, or you don't want to think about it anyway, this tells you what the news is.[16]

Because newsworthy events are determined by media outlets that are owned by large corporations, the public's image of reality is at least partially defined by the wealthy and powerful. The issue of corporate ownership of the media is discussed below.

The Media and Business: Profit over Information?

The major news media are owned and thus controlled by major corporations: "By the late 1980s, eight corporations controlled eight of the inner-ring media and a host of middle- and outer-ring media, including 40 television stations, over 200 cable television systems, more than 60 radio stations, 59 magazines, and 41 book publishers."[17] Since the 1980s, ownership of the media has narrowed. In 1983, 50 corporations owned the media.

Ben Bagdikian chronicles the ever-growing stranglehold that major corporations have on news in the United States.[18] In 2004, "five huge corporations — Time Warner, Disney, Murdoch's News Corporation, Bertelsmann of Germany, and Viacom (formerly CBS) — own most of the newspapers, magazines, books, radio and TV stations, and movie studios of the United States." Instead of local media control, the mainstream press are owned and operated by a handful of major profit-seeking corporations who have "more communications power than was exercised by any despot or dictatorship in history."[19] Below are the major holdings of each of these media corporations:

- General Electric media-related holdings include television networks NBC and Telemundo, Universal Pictures, Focus Features, 26 television stations in the United States and cable networks MSNBC, Bravo and the Sci Fi Channel. GE also owns 80 percent of NBC Universal. 2008 revenues: $183 billion.
- The Walt Disney Company owns the ABC Television Network, cable networks including ESPN, the Disney Channel, SOAPnet, A&E and Lifetime, 277 radio stations, music and book publishing companies, production companies Touchstone, Miramax and Walt Disney Pictures, Pixar Animation Studios, the cellular service Disney Mobile, and theme parks around the world. 2008 revenues: $37.8 billion.
- News Corporation's media holdings include: the Fox Broadcasting Company, television and cable networks such as Fox, Fox Business Channel, National Geographic and FX, and print publications including the *Wall Street Journal*, the *New York Post*, *TVGuide*, the magazines *Barron's*, *SmartMoney* and *The Weekly Standard*, book publisher HarperCollins, film production companies 20th Century Fox, Fox Searchlight Pictures and Blue Sky Studios, numerous Web sites including MarketWatch.com, and non-media holdings including the National Rugby League. 2008 revenues: $33 billion.
- Time Warner is the largest media conglomerate in the world, with holdings including: CNN, the CW (a joint venture with CBS), HBO, Cinemax, Cartoon Network, TBS, TNT, America Online, MapQuest, Moviefone, Warner Bros. Pictures, Castle Rock and New Line Cinema, and more than 150 magazines including *Time*, *Sports Illustrated*, *Fortune*, *Marie Claire* and *People*. 2008 revenues: $29.8 billion.
- Viacom holdings include: MTV, Nickelodeon/Nick-at-Nite, VH1, BET, Comedy Central, Paramount Pictures, Paramount Home Entertainment, Atom Entertainment, and music game developer Harmonix. Viacom 18 is a joint venture with the Indian media company Global Broadcast news. 2008 revenues: $14.6 billion.
- CBS Corporation owns the CBS Television Network, CBS Television Distribution Group, the CW (a joint venture with Time Warner), Showtime, book publisher Simon & Schuster, 29 television stations, and CBS Radio, Inc, which has 140 stations. CBS is now the leading supplier of video to Google's new Video Marketplace. 2008 revenues: $14 billion.[20]

Noam Chomsky writes that the mainstream press consists of "major, very profitable, corporations." Since the media are "profit maximizing commercial organizations," efforts to seek profit may interfere with honest and objective journalism that can result in people being unaware of key facts necessary to make informed choices on matters of social policy.[21] Why does it matter when it comes to crime? Crime is often seen as a serious problem deemed worthy of significant media attention. Public policies are created to deal with, fight, solve, or prevent it. Citizens who see, hear, or read stories about crime and the policies created to address it may assume what they are seeing, hearing, or reading is accurate and objective. This is often untrue. That which is being depicted may be aimed at one simple goal—creating profit for the media corporation, whether true or not.

According to Robert McChesney, corporate owned media threaten the vital duties of journalists necessary for a healthy democracy, which include:

1) Acting as a watchdog of the powerful.
2) Separating truth from lies.
3) Presenting a wide variety of different opinions based on empirical information.

McChesney concludes that the mainstream press fails in this regard because of "the system of profit-driven journalism in largely noncompetitive markets that began to emerge over a century ago."[22]

It may be difficult to understand the important role that the media have historically played in American history. But the role is so important that the media have often been referred to as the *Fourth Estate* because they have been "uniquely capable by force of will, resources, and mission to uncover the misconduct, malfeasance, and hidden shame of the state."[23] Without the media acting as a watchdog of the powerful, the powerful can do and say things that American citizens will not be able to question or challenge due to being uninformed about the facts.

Media companies are owned by, as well as linked to, much bigger corporations. As a result, they are among the most powerful sector of the private economy. The corporate media sell a product and that product is audiences: "You have to sell a product to a market, and the market is, of course, advertisers (that is, other businesses). Whether it is television or newspapers, or whatever, they are selling audiences. Corporations sell audiences to other corporations. In the case of the elite media, it's big businesses."[24]

This is true for television stations as well as radio. The largest owner of radio stations in the United States is Clear Channel, which owns at least 1,200 radio stations. Most of its stations are operated via "remote control with the same prerecorded material" so that no matter where you live, you hear the same shows and songs.[25] This is problematic because local media would logically be more familiar with the needs of the local community and the demands of the people living there. Ben Bagdikian writes: "Given the United States' unique dependence on local civic decision making and its extraordinary multiplicity of local self-governing units and hundreds of media outlets, a rational system for a nation with such a vast diversity of people and places would be hundreds of individual local media owners …".[26] Instead, regardless of where you live, odds are you're listening to corporate owned media.

In 2005, Clear Channel radio entered into a five-year agreement with Fox News where Fox will provide news to Clear Channel radio stations. [27] This serves as an example of how media companies are linked to each other in powerful ways. Given the conservative slant of Fox News,[28] perhaps it is not surprising that some allege that Clear Channel and Cumulus, the two largest radio groups, "are committed to a daily flood of far-right propagandistic programming," a major source of news for about one in five Americans.[29] The issue of potential political biases on the radio, as well as in the mainstream media generally, will be addressed in Chapter 2.

Important Concepts of Corporate Influence

Several concepts are important to understanding corporate influence over the media.[30] First, *media consolidation* refers to when fewer and fewer corporations control information being relayed by the media. In 1983, there were 50 major media companies. By 1987, there were only 29. By 1990, there were only 23. By 1992, there were only 14. By 1997, only 10 companies controlled the media. By 2000, there were only six, and by 2004 just five, as noted earlier. These companies control the majority of media in the US.[31]

This book will illustrate the implications of media consolidation by corporations for media portrayals of crime and criminal justice. Other scholars have addressed the implications of corporate consolidated media for politics and democracy more generally, which will be discussed later in this chapter.

Second, *horizontal integration* refers to when a single corporation controls more and more of the media market in a given locale. Horizontal integration is a form of economic concentration where a company tries to acquire as much of an industry as possible. The ultimate form of horizontal integration is a monopoly.[32] Most media companies are not monopolies but instead are *oligopolies*.[33] According to Robert McChesney: "Major media markets—television networks, cable TV systems and channels, music, motion pictures, newspapers, book publishing, magazines, and retail sales—are almost all classic oligopolies with only a handful of significant players in each market."[34] Yet, these firms operate as monopolies, in that they aim to reduce outputs and increase prices in order to maximize profits.[35]

According to the Federal Trade Commission, it is not illegal to have a monopoly position in a market, but:

the antitrust laws make it unlawful to maintain or attempt to create a monopoly through tactics that either unreasonably exclude firms from the market or significantly impair their ability to compete. A single firm may commit a violation through its unilateral actions, or a violation may result if a group of firms work together to monopolize a market.[36]

In 1945, 80% of U.S. newspapers were independent, but by 1980, 80% were owned by corporate chains.[37] Today, virtually every newspaper is now published by a media *monopoly*. Specifically, "of all cities with a daily paper, 99 percent had only one newspaper management (in 1910 more than half of all newspaper cities had local daily competition, typically five or six papers)."[38] Chain newspapers owned by monopolies cover less serious news, have less vigor in the editorial departments, and hire less qualified journalists.[39] Further, the overriding goal of profit has led to newspapers cutting staff and reporting less news in favor of more routinized "fluff" and lifestyle stories.[40]

The implication of this for criminal justice reporting is important. For example, "newspapers today have *very little choice* in deciding whether to conduct criminal justice reporting or succumb to tabloid-style crime reporting. America's newspapers are in dire financial straits. The explosive availability of information from alternative sources, declining circulation, and diminishing advertising revenue have all contributed to extreme cost-cutting tactics undertaken by publishers. The result of cost-cutting tactics is a lesser paper— fewer reporters and less reporting."[41]

Papers also shun serious news because it is more expensive to cover than soft features, and soft features also tend to attract advertisers.[42] As it turns out, stories about crime are easy and inexpensive to cover. Perhaps this is one reason why they are so popular in the media. Advertising is important to the media, as will be demonstrated later in this chapter.

Third, *vertical integration* is when a single corporation owns companies that contribute to the production and distribution of a product or service in one sector of the economy. Vertical organization refers to owning both the content and means to distribute the content which lowers costs and risk while increasing profit.[43]

A good example of vertical integration is the merger of AOL and Time Warner in 1989. According to Ben Bagdikian: "Time Warner had by this time a large quantity of media products from magazines to movies (an undifferentiated commodity known on Wall Street as 'content') and AOL had the best pipeline through which to send this 'content' instantly to customers' computers."[44] Together, the companies could reach far more people with their products than they could independently.

When vertical and horizontal integration are considered together, we get the concept of synergy. *Synergy* is

> the vertical and horizontal integration of entertainment companies and the products they market. For example, when the same company that produces a performer's album also owns a venue (e.g., a radio station) in which to play and thus market the album, synergy is said to exist. It is enhanced when the company can also place the song in a popular television program it produces or makes it a theme song for a movie it has financed; multiple marketing outlets will reach different audiences and hopefully increase sales.[45]

One example of synergy is Pepsi, which owns Taco Bell and Pizza Hut. Not only are Pepsi products thus served in these restaurants but also any product that Pepsi wants to advertise (including musical artists it sponsors such as Michael Jackson and Madonna) will be featured in these restaurants. Because of synergy, when two separate entities are combined (like with AOL and Time Warner) the new entity is more powerful than merely the two previous entities added together.[46]

Fourth, *interlocking directorates* refer to when members of the Board of Directors from one company serve as Board members of other companies. In the case of the media, this is when Board members of media corporations also serve on Boards of other non-media corporations, raising the possibility of conflicts of interest. Members of media boards commonly sit on the boards of other Fortune 500 companies.[47] Some examples of interlocking directorates include Board members of ABC/Disney, who have sat on the Boards of City National Bank, FedEx, Staples, Edison International, Xerox, and Boeing; Board members of NBC/GE have served on the Boards of Anheuser-Busch, Avon, Chase Manhattan, Coca-Cola, Internet Security Systems, Knight-Ridder, Texaco, and the New York Stock Exchange; and Board members of CBS/Viacom have served on the boards of American Express, Chase Manhattan, Honeywell, Morgan Chase & Co, New York Stock Exchange, Prudential, and Rockwell International.[48]

It is not legal "to have directors who interlock directorates with competing firms, but most board members have such complex interrelations that the law is seldom applied."[49] It is probably not surprising, then, that a 2003 study found that the mainstream press had at least 45 interlocking directors as well as 141 joint business ventures.[50]

These interlocking arrangements serve media companies well. It allows and encourages them to "do business with commercial and investment bankers, obtaining lines of credit and loans, and receiving advice and service in selling stock and bond issues and in dealing with acquisition opportunities and takeover threats. Bank and other institutional investors are also large owners of media stock."[51]

These arrangements also serve the non-media companies well. For example, media companies linked to non-media companies are probably less likely to cover stories involving crimes committed by those companies or individuals employed by them. This may be one reason why corporate crime is not as visible to Americans as ordinary street crime.[52] This issue is revisited in Chapter 4.

Further, relationships between media companies and the government are strong; a large share of directors of media companies tend to be former government officials.[53] This ensures that media companies will be able to request and receive favors from government officials and agencies when it comes to matters of consolidation and regulation.

Understanding these four concepts allows one to see how major media corporations cooperate as much as they compete. *Media cooperation*—shared boards of directors, joint investments, property swaps, and so forth—is aimed at expanding the power of each corporation.[54] This cooperation, rather than true competition among various media outlets, results in "highly duplicative content" rather than different programs that might be demanded by American citizens given their wide variety of tastes, preferences, backgrounds, and experiences.[55] As noted earlier, crime is widespread in the media. That crime is so widespread in every media outlet is a good example of this duplicative content. That the dominant images of crime are also basically the same everywhere, is also evidence of this.

The Federal Trade Commission claims: "Free and open markets are the foundation of a vibrant economy. Aggressive competition among sellers in an open marketplace gives consumers—both individuals and businesses—the benefits of lower prices, higher quality products and services, more choices, and greater innovation.[56] Yet, "the media system is anything but competitive in the traditional economic sense of the term. Not only are all of the markets oligopolies, where almost all of the main players are owned by a handful of firms, the media giants also tend to work quite closely together."[57] The major media corporations also lobby together as part of the National Association of Broadcasters "to achieve the laws and regulations that increase their collective power over consumers."[58] This can be considered another form of interlocking activity.

Concerns about Corporate Owned Media

Two important outcomes of corporate ownership of media, consolidation of the media, horizontal and vertical integration, interlocking directorates and other links between media companies and major corporations are: 1) relatively similar content across media outlets devoid of context; and 2) a lack of critical coverage of important issues. This is problematic for several reasons. First, it means that the stories that appear as news will be roughly the same stories no matter where you live; there will be little variation even based on real differences across communities. Second, it means that stories will tend to be covered in the same superficial way; there will be little depth or context to the stories. Third, it means that many important issues will be ignored, which are typically issues that do not serve the interests of the corporations that own the media.

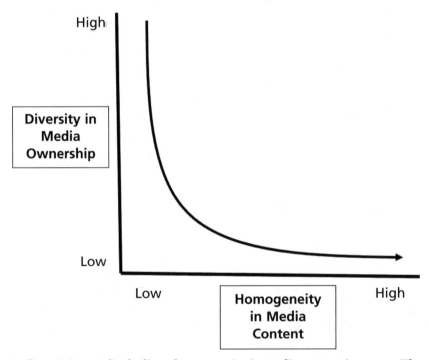

As diversity in media declines, homogeneity in media content increases. That is, as less and less corporations own and control the media, media content becomes increasingly the same across different media outlets.

Some claim that concentrated media power is a threat to democracy because it diminishes the influence of citizens in the political process and the choices we have of political candidates. For example, Ben Bagdikian argues:

It is not just national economics that is at stake.... Nor is it just the neglect of broadcast media giantism by the government agencies that by law are still required to operate 'in the public interest.' The public interest is to have the country's largest broadcasting system in the world provide diversity in news, opinion, and commentary that serves all Americans, right, left, and independent, as well as access to their local stations as well as true choices in national programs. What is at stake is American democracy itself. A country without all the significant news, points of view, and information its citizens need to be informed voters is risking the loss of democratic rights. Voters without genuine choices and without the information they need to choose what meets their own needs and wishes has produced something alarming: on Election Day our voters are forced to vote for what is the narrowest political choices among all industrial democracies of the world.[59]

Robert McChesney also asserts that the mainstream media are an antidemocratic force because they help maintain a system of government where most important decisions are "the province of the corporate sector" and they "are influenced by powerful special interests with little public awareness or input."[60] The culprit, according to McChesney, is *neoliberalism*, or policies such as deregulation of business that "maximize the role of markets and profit-making and minimize the role of nonmarket institutions" that are based on the belief that "society works best when business runs things and there is as little possibility of government 'interference' with business as possible."[61]

McChesney goes further, suggesting that media activity is most consistent with the "needs and concerns of a handful of enormous and powerful corporations" that are run by very wealthy people whose "interests are often distinct from those of the vast majority of humanity." McChesney asserts: "By any known theory of democracy, such a concentration of economic, cultural, and political power into so few hands—and mostly unaccountable hands at that—is absurd and unacceptable."[62] Yet, it is an empirical fact that today in the US, our media are owned and controlled by large corporations run for profit that are generally not accountable to citizens.

The Free Press is a "national, nonpartisan, nonprofit organization working to reform the media" that was started in 2002 by media scholar Robert McChesney along with others. It uses education, organization and advocacy to "promote diverse and independent media ownership, strong public media, quality journalism, and universal access to communications." Based on the belief that the publicly owned media have been corrupted by powerful, monied interests, Free Press aims to reform the media because doing so "is crucial not just for creating better news and entertainment, but to advancing every issue you care about. A vibrant, diverse and independent media is the cornerstone of a healthy democracy."[63]

According to the Free Press, media ownership matters because media owners determine:

- What news and information communities receive.
- What voices are heard—or silenced.
- Whether important issues get covered accurately—or covered at all.
- Who gets hired to report and produce the news.
- What music and which artists get airplay.
- How women and people of color are portrayed in the media.[64]

Free Press asserts that the major companies that own most of our media "are getting even bigger by taking over more and more of our local media outlets. But these massive conglomerates—like General Electric, Time Warner and News Corp.—only care about the bottom line, not serving the public interest. And allowing these few firms too much control over the flow of news and information is dangerous for our democracy." More specifically, consolidation of the media into fewer and fewer hands means:

- Fewer voices and viewpoints.
- Less diversity in ownership and programming.
- Less coverage of local issues that matter to communities.
- Less of the unbiased, independent, critical journalism we need to prevent abuses of power. [65]

🖱 **For more information about problems of corporate owned media, see the website for this book at: www.pscj.appstate.edu/media/corporate media.html**

For the purposes of this book, what is most relevant is that many viewers are unaware that the crime and criminal justice news they see on TV and in the newspapers is the version that large corporations choose to air. Would it be logical to expect these corporations to focus on their own acts of deviance and harmful behaviors? Further, would it be logical to expect corporate media to broadcast many stories about corporate crimes at all, given their close ties to and vested interests in the welfare of corporations? Robert McChesney answers no because "the corporate news media have a vested interest in the corporate system. The largest media firms are members in good standing in the corporate community and are closely linked to it through business relations, shared investors, interlocking directors, and common political values."[66] As will be discussed in this book, there is substantial evidence that the media tend to ignore corporate crimes. Perhaps this is why street crimes are more likely to be the focus of news than acts like corporate and white-collar crimes.

With the rare exception of cases such as Enron,[67] corporate crime is generally ignored by the mainstream press.[68] According to Sandra Evans and Richard Lundman, "newspapers protect corporate reputations by failing to provide frequent, prominent and criminally oriented coverage of common corporate crimes."[69] When an act committed by corporations is dangerous or harmful but not covered by corporate owned media, a logical conclusion is that the mainstream media have some vested interest in making sure such acts continue to fly under the radar.

This may explain why "the most commonly suppressed news items each year are stories involving corporations."[70] While the media fail to report on harmful and culpable acts of corporations, the corporations themselves spend hundreds of millions of dollars each year in advertisements, brochures, web sites and public events in order to put forth a more gentle image. Apparently, this works, as throughout the 1990s, roughly 70% of Americans had a favorable view of corporations, although this figure has declined recently in the wake of the numerous stories of corporate fraud.[71] Interestingly, a majority of Americans report thinking corporations make too much profit and hold too much power, yet Americans are evenly split on whether regulation of business is necessary or does more harm than good.[72]

For more information about the nature of corporations, see the website for this book at: ww.pscj.appstate.edu/media/corporations.html

---

Sometimes, the reason the mainstream media fail to cover acts of the powerful is because of joint business connections with them. As one example, the case of Henry Kissinger comes to mind. Christopher Hitchen's review of Kissinger's involvement in various "war crimes," "crimes against humanity," and other violations of international law, "including conspiracy to commit murder, kidnap, and torture," is perhaps the most complete telling of Kissinger's acts.[73] Kissinger helped orchestrate and carry out kidnappings, mass killings of innocent civilians, and assassinations of foreign leaders in various countries including Vietnam, Cambodia, Laos, Bangladesh, East Timor, Indochina, Cyprus, Greece, and Chile.

Some media companies (like AOL Time Warner) were unlikely to cover such acts in its national news magazines, television shows, and publishing houses because one of its book houses published both of Kissinger's memoirs and views of foreign policy.[74] Because of this, Kissinger remains a highly influential figure in American politics. Amazingly, reporter Bob Woodward reported that Kissinger was a regular visitor of President George W. Bush and Vice President Dick Cheney during the build-up to the Iraq war. He reportedly offered his advice about how to win the war and quell the counter-insurgency that arose in conditions characterized as civil war by top historians.[75]

Henry Kissinger served as Secretary of State and National Security Advisor in the United States government under Presidents Nixon and Ford. Some media outlets did not cover his wrongdoing because they represented him in business dealings. http://en.wikipedia.org/wiki/File:Henry_Kissinger.jpg.

Robert McChesney agrees that negative coverage of corporations is uncommon in the media, at least far less common than stories criticizing government. He suggests this "plays directly into the hands of those who wish to give more power and privileges of corporations" and also "undermines the ability of government to regulate in the public interest."[76]

McChesney poses an important challenge to readers:

Imagine if the president or director of the FBI ordered news media to desist from examining corporate power in the United States. That would be considered a grotesque violation of democratic freedoms and a direct challenge to the republic's viability ... Yet, when journalism—through professional practices—generates virtually the same outcome, it goes unmentioned and unrecognized in the political culture. It is a nonissue.[77]

In summary, U.S. corporations, through the inner ring of media outlets they own and control, define problems, identify crises, and thereby determine "what issues will be brought to the attention of political leaders" and U.S. citizens, while other issues and problems are ignored.[78] This is an amazing power held largely by the mainstream media.

You may wonder if any of this is intentional on the part of the media. That is, do media corporations intend to withhold vital information from citizens in order to serve limited financial interests and deprive our democracy, or is this simply an unintended outcome produced by media consolidation and profit-seeking?

Goals of the Media

If you were to ask the typical citizen what the media are for, he or she may say something like "to provide us with important information about important events." However, if you were to ask the same question of a media scholar, he or she may respond with "to serve the interests of those in power." Ben Bagdikian asserts that the "goals of media are complex; some are beneficial for citizens and others are profit-driven and result in social conditioning and control."[79]

Edward Herman and Noam Chomsky suggest there are two major interpretations of media coverage. The first is the "democratic postulate that the media are independent and committed to discovering and reporting the truth, and that they do not merely reflect the world as powerful groups wish it to be perceived."[81] The second is that they "serve to mobilize support for the special interests that dominate the state and private activity."[82]

With regard to the second postulate, Herman and Chomsky explain that:

> The mass media serve as a system for communicating messages and symbols to the general populace. It is their function to amuse, entertain, and inform, and to inculcate individuals with the values, beliefs, and codes of behavior that will integrate them into institutional structures of the larger society. In a world of concentrated wealth and major conflicts of class interest, to fulfill this role requires systematic propaganda.[83]

Recall that propaganda involves the intentional spreading of false information for the purposes of helping one's own cause or hurting another. Herman and Chomsky's theory of media propaganda asserts that "the media serve, and propagandize on behalf of, the powerful societal interests that control and finance them. The representatives of these interests have important agendas and

Thomas Jefferson (pictured) noted that "An enlightened citizenry is indispensable for the proper functioning of a republic." Similarly, James Madison wrote: "A popular Government without popular information or the means of acquiring it, is but a Prologue to a Farce or a Tragedy, or perhaps both." Robert McChesney calls the creation of an informed citizenry "the media's province."[80] Given that Americans are largely ignorant of many matters including world affairs, is it possible that the media are not doing their primary job of informing the public of key facts? http://upload.wikimedia.org/wikipedia/commons/b/bb/Rembrandt_Peale-Thomas_Jefferson.jpg.

principles that they want to advance, and they are well positioned to shape and constrain media policy."[84] Rather than providing the public with the information they need to intelligently participate in the political process, the propaganda model suggests the purpose of the media is to "inculcate and defend the economic, social, and political agenda of privileged groups that dominate the domestic society and the state." This occurs through the selection of topics to be covered and ignored, the framing of issues, the filtering of information, the relative emphasis placed on issues and the tone in which they are presented, and "by keeping debate within the bounds of acceptable premises."[85]

At times, it is relatively easy to distinguish propaganda from objective news. At other times, it comes from public relations (PR) firms and even government agencies that take great steps to disguise propaganda as news. This is problematic because most citizens watching the news are unable to distinguish between news and propaganda when it is so carefully disguised.

⌁ For more information about propaganda, including real-life examples of government propaganda, see the website for this book at: www.pscj.appstate.edu/media/propaganda.html

---

Propaganda Filters

Herman and Chomsky identify five filters important for understanding their propaganda model. The five filters include:

1) The size, concentrated ownership, owner wealth and profit orientation of the largest mass media firms.
2) Advertising as the primary source of income by the largest mass media firms.
3) The reliance of the media on information provided by government, business, and "experts" funded and approved by these primary sources and agents of power.
4) "Flak" as a means of disciplining the media.
5) "Anticommunism" as a national religion and control mechanism.[86]

Media Concentration and Profit Orientation

As for the first filter, Herman and Chomsky assert that the media are tiered (similar to the notion of rings, discussed earlier). The first-tier of the media (or the inner ring) has more "prestige, resources, and outreach" and "defines the news agenda and supplies much of the national and international news to the lower tiers of the media, and thus for the general public."[87] The first-tier includes major television stations, newspapers, magazines, and book publishers, which are "large, profit-seeking corporations, owner and controlled by quite wealthy people."[88]

Five first-tier media outlets own and control most of the media, including 90% of the television audience. These are the inner ring sources identified earlier. Second-tier outlets (the middle ring) are comprised of twenty-five smaller but still very powerful forces that are major players in one or two areas. The third-tier (the outer ring) consists of the rest of the media. The first-tier media outlets have very close relationships, including joint ventures in which they share ownership of a property with common shareholders. As noted earlier, this pressures them to cooperate more than it does to compete.[89] Clearly opposed to the democratic postulate, media companies "use their economic and political power to advance their interests and to dominate consumers."[90]

Media have grown larger and larger in part due to the "loosening of rules limiting media concentration, cross-ownership, and control by non-media companies." The rules have been loosened under pressure from lobbying groups such as the National Association of Broadcasters, of which all the first-tier media outlets are part. Further, restrictions have been abandoned "on radio-TV commercials, entertainment-mayhem programming, and 'fairness doctrine' threats, opening the door to the unrestrained commercial use of the airways."[91] The media system did not develop naturally into powerful conglomerates but instead resulted directly from "explicit government policies and in fact would not exist without those policies" including "government-granted and government-enforced monopoly broadcasting licenses, telecommunication franchises, and rights to content (a.k.a. copyright)."[92]

The argument from the top media scholars is that the media have become little more than profit-generating businesses. According to Edward Herman and Noam Chomsky, bottom-line considerations of profit have become more important along with increased corporate power over the media through mergers and centralization.[93] Herman and Chomsky point out that "the dominant media firms are quite large businesses; they are controlled by very wealthy people or by managers who are subject to sharp constraints by owners and other market-profit-oriented forces; and they are closely interlocked, and have important common interests, with other major corporations, banks, and government."[94] In this environment, "the pressures of stockholders, directors, and bankers to focus on the bottom line are powerful."[95]

Over the years, several media CEOs have been quoted as saying that what matters in their business is money. That is, media *is* business:

- "We have no obligation to make history. We have no obligation to make art. We have no obligation to make a statement. To make money is our only obligation." —Internal memo by Michael Eisner, 1981, CEO of Disney/ABC, quoted in *Media Mass Monopoly—Disney, Childhood and Corporate Power*
- "We are here to serve advertisers. That is our raison d'etre." —Michael Jordan, CEO of Westinghouse/CBS, 1997, in *Advertising Age*
- "We're not in the business of providing well-researched music. We're simply in the business of selling our customers' products." —Lowry Mays, Clear Channel CEO, 2003, in *The Problem of the Media*

If what really matters to the media is money, it is clear that coverage of crime helps generate profit. Simply stated, crime sells. This is likely one significant reason why crime is such a popular topic in the media. This issue will be revisited throughout the book.

Advertising

The second filter is advertising. With advertising, the free market does not yield a neutral system: "The *advertisers'* choices influence media prosperity and survival."[96] Journalism promotes the commercial values of owners and advertisers[97] and serving advertisers may very well be "the most important job" of the media.[98] The argument is that media are not only in the business of reflecting the world to viewers but are also in the business of selling a product.

Edward Herman and Noam Chomsky concur, claiming "the private media are corporations selling a product (readers and audiences) to other businesses

Adbusters **magazine created this corporate flag to reflect how fundamental corporations have become to American society. It also publishes "spoof ads" of major companies meant to raise awareness of strategies in advertising and the real consequences of products like fast food, fashion, and alcohol. http://www.adbusters.org/cultureshop/corporateFlag.**

(advertisers)."[99] In this context, the power of advertisers over television programming arises "from the simple fact that they buy and pay for the programs— they are the 'patrons' who provide the media subsidy. As such, the media compete for their patronage, developing specialized staff to solicit advertisers and necessarily having to explain how their programs serve advertisers' needs." The advertisers are thus " 'normative reference organizations,' whose requirements and demands the media must accommodate if they are to succeed."[100]

The evidence also suggests that advertisers choose carefully which programs they want to advertise with on the basis of their own principles. The programs are almost always culturally and politically conservative in nature: "Large corporate advertisers on television will rarely sponsor programs that engage in serious criticisms of corporate activities …".[101]

According to Herman and Chomsky the goal of advertisers is to try "to avoid programs with serious complexities and disturbing controversies that interfere with the 'buying mood.' They seek programs that will lightly entertain and thus fit in with the spirit of the primary purpose of program purchases—the dissemination of a selling message."[102] Advertisers often do not want to be associated with social or political topics that are seen as controversial: "Advertisers tend to prefer shows that reach their desired audience and do nothing to undermine their sales pitch."[103]

That companies want to avoid controversial programs and programs with more "liberal" themes may help us understand why the media portray crime and criminal justice the way they do. As will be shown later in the book, media coverage of crime and criminal justice tends to reinforce status quo approaches "fighting" or "waging war" against crime, which is inherently conservative in nature.

Ray Surette puts forth a slightly different perspective, arguing that entertainment is not really what is most important. Yet he also claims that neither is informing the public the primary purpose of the media: "The media must be understood as a collection of for-profit businesses. Each media business must make money to survive, and the primary purpose of media is not to entertain or inform an audience but to deliver an audience to an advertiser. From a media business perspective, advertising is the most important content."[104]

If this is true, consider the possibility that one reason crime is so prevalent on television is because stories about crime produce viewers; viewers mean higher ratings; higher ratings mean more consumers for advertisers; more consumers for advertising means more revenue for companies. Companies "wish to keep the audience tuned from one half-hour segment to the next and they prefer the 'buying mood' sustained as well." Even serious programming with high ratings may be questioned if it interrupts "the evening's flow of lightness and fantasy. In that sense, the whole evening is a single block of atmosphere—a selling atmosphere."[105] Television networks are on the same page as advertisers of products. Herman and Chomsky assert that television networks logically want "to maintain audience 'flow' levels, i.e., to keep people watching from program to program, in order to sustain advertising ratings and revenue."[106]

Corporations interested in selling products not only pressure networks to incorporate the messages of their products incorporated into the content of the show, but also now even meet with advertisers as they plan and develop shows.[107] This suggests the very real possibility that advertisers are helping create and design television shows in order to help sell their products.

Ben Bagdikian asserts that "editorial content of publications and broadcasting is dictated by the computer printouts on advertising agency desks, not the other way around. When there is a conflict between the printouts and an independent editor, the printouts win."[108] More than 80% of revenue generated by newspapers comes from advertisements, and half of revenue generated by magazines comes from ads.[109] Logically then, companies who advertise their products in the media can successfully make demands on media companies in terms of what types of content is reported to the public.[110]

Prior to the explosion of advertising in the media, newspapers were much more common and diverse in nature. Today, papers lacking advertisements are at a serious disadvantage since newspapers rely so heavily on advertising dollars to run their businesses. To compete with the major papers, the prices of smaller and independent papers "would tend to be higher, curtailing sales, and they would have less surplus to invest in improving the salability of the paper (features, attractive format, promotion, etc.)." Thus, an advertising-based system tends "to drive out of existence or into marginality the media companies and types that depend on revenue from sales alone. The reliance on advertising by newspapers results in a barrier that makes it impossible for smaller and independent newspapers to survive."[111]

Finally, it is important to note that research shows that advertising works. Consider this basic reality of business—business is in business for one purpose, to make money. Advertising is an expense, i.e., a loss of revenue. If advertising did not work, logic suggests that businesses would not spend money on it, since their goal is to make money rather than lose it. Research shows that even the product placements shown in music videos and movies lead to brisk sales of the products.[112]

Relying on Official Sources

The third filter refers to the intimate relationship between the media and the government. According to Edward Herman and Noam Chomsky, the symbiotic relationship comes out of economic necessity and reciprocity of interest:

> The media need a steady, reliable flow of the raw material of news. They have daily news demands and imperative news schedules that they must meet. They cannot have reporters and cameras at all places where important stories may break. Economics dictates that they concentrate their resources where significant news often occurs, where

important rumors and leaks abound, and where regular press conferences are held.[113]

Press conferences by official sources (i.e., government officials and prominent public figures) are the basis for legitimate news.[114] Thus those in positions of power have the ability to "set the news agenda by what they speak about and, just important, what they keep quiet about."[115] People in positions of power that often appear in stories about crime include law-makers, police officials, and attorneys.

How logical is it to expect government agents to speak critically of their actions or to even raise issues related to their performance? The answer is, obviously, not very. We can thus logically expect relying on public officials for information about crime and criminal justice to limit the breadth of the information that appears in the news. This is an important lesson to remember when examining media coverage of government activity, including police, courts, and corrections.

According to Ben Bagdikian, those citizens in positions of power are the ones most likely to be quoted and featured in the mainstream press. Yet, their pronouncements about social problems such as crime are only part of the truth. Meanwhile: "Citizen groups issuing serious contrary studies and proposals for mending gaps in the social fabric get only sporadic and minimal attention in the major media."[116] The result is that some of our most pressing problems are not addressed in the mainstream press, including many that actually are of great concern to American citizens.

Experts too tend to be drawn from the establishment which results in a "strong mainstream bias built into the news." This assures that those with different opinions from those in power will rarely appear in the media. As a result, the media to some appear as "stenographers to those in power."[117] The implications of relying on government officials such as law makers, police officers, and prosecutors as guests and experts for criminal justice practice are identified later in this book.

Given that those most likely to appear in the press are government officials, it may often appear to viewers that there is widespread agreement about the nature of a threat or problem, even when there is not. When two or more expert opinions conflict (rarely), "it is increasingly rare that reporters bother to determine who is telling the truth."[118] This obviously does not help viewers discern the facts relevant for policy debates pertaining to issues such as crime control and crime prevention.

The government and corporations also make many efforts to make things easy for news organizations. They:

- Provide the media with facilities in which to gather.

- Give journalists advance copies of speeches and forthcoming reports.
- Schedule press conferences at hours well-geared to news deadlines.
- Write press releases in usable language.
- Carefully organize press conferences and "photo opportunity" sessions.[119]

This gives powerful interests in the government and business world special access to newsmakers that normal citizens do not have. Since "large bureaucracies of the powerful *subsidize* the mass media," they "gain special access by their contribution to reducing the media's costs of acquiring the raw materials of, and producing, news. The large entities that provide this subsidy become 'routine' news sources and have privileged access to the gates. Non-routine sources must struggle for access, and may be ignored by the arbitrary decision of the gatekeepers."[120] This seems to limit the breadth of debate on important issues such as how best to reduce societal problems like crime, drug abuse, and terrorism. Consider this example: how likely is it that top law enforcement officials and even beat level cops will identify solutions to crime that exist outside of the policing world? This is seen as unfortunate by those who recognize that the solutions to crime problems often exist outside of policing.

Edward Herman and Noam Chomsky state that "powerful sources regularly take advantage of media routines and dependency to 'manage' the media, to manipulate them into following a special agenda and framework ... Part of this management process consists of inundating the media with stories, which serve sometimes to foist a particular line and frame on the media."[121] An example is drug control policy. Those who appear in stories about the drug war are the "drug warriors" and their supporters in politics and law enforcement.[122] One hardly ever sees experts on the "other side" of the debate promoting alternatives to the drug war such as legalization, decriminalization, much less the more effective harm reduction or public health approaches such as treatment and prevention.[123] Thus, the drug war goes on and on, in spite of overwhelming evidence of its failures as a public policy.[124]

Flak

The next filter is flak—"negative responses to a media statement or program" that come in the form of letters, phone calls, petitions, speeches, bills, "and other modes of complaint, threat, and punitive action."[125] Programs and positions that generate flak tend to be less likely to appear in the media. The powerful are much more able to generate flak, and "especially flak that is costly and threatening" and they use it to influence programs and positions in the media.[126] Herman and Chomsky argue that flak is one mechanism used by the powerful to stop programs from airing that might be negative in nature about the corporation in question or about corporate power more generally.

Citizens also can produce flak. Yet, we have far less resources including money, time, knowledge and organizational capability to effectively challenge media corporations with flak.

Anti-communism

The final filter is the ideology of anticommunism, logical in a capitalistic system, which serves as a political control mechanism that allegedly harms the political left and diminishes their ability to be heard.[127] Media coverage is incomplete, according to Ben Bagdikian, because the news is acquired by "governmental and private power centers" while "important contrary information" like that presented by people with different interests is shunned because it is considered too liberal or radical.[128] The notion of a *conservative bias* in the media may be hard to believe for many citizens who have been told repeatedly that the media are plagued by a *liberal bias*.[129]

The notion of a liberal bias in the media may be a myth that serves to disarm the press.[130] According to Seth Ackerman, this is similar to "working the ref" in a sports match in order to influence future calls (or no calls).[131] Such a phenomenon may explain why the mainstream media failed so miserably to ask the tough questions needed of our leaders when they announced that war with Iraq was necessary when in fact it was not. Basically, they were afraid of being labeled "liberal."[132]

A study by Media Matters for America of syndicated columnists published in nearly every daily paper in the United States found evidence of a conservative bias throughout most of America. They found that, "in paper after paper, state after state, and region after region, conservative syndicated columnists get more space than their progressive counterparts."[133] Specific findings included:

- Sixty percent of the nation's daily newspapers print more conservative syndicated columnists every week than progressive syndicated columnists. Only 20 percent run more progressives (i.e., liberals) than conservatives, while the remaining 20 percent are evenly balanced.
- In a given week, nationally syndicated progressive columnists are published in newspapers with a combined total circulation of 125 million. Conservative columnists, on the other hand, are published in newspapers with a combined total circulation of more than 152 million.
- The top 10 columnists as ranked by the number of papers in which they are carried include five conservatives, two centrists, and only three progressives.

- The top 10 columnists as ranked by the total circulation of the papers in which they are published also include five conservatives, two centrists, and only three progressives.
- In 38 states, the conservative voice is greater than the progressive voice—in other words, conservative columns reach more readers in total than progressive columns. In only 12 states is the progressive voice greater than the conservative voice.
- In three out of the four broad regions of the country—the West, the South, and the Midwest—conservative syndicated columnists reach more readers than progressive syndicated columnists. Only in the Northeast do progressives reach more readers, and only by a margin of 2 percent.
- In eight of the nine divisions into which the U.S. Census Bureau divides the country, conservative syndicated columnists reach more readers than progressive syndicated columnists in any given week. Only in the Middle Atlantic division do progressive columnists reach more readers each week.[134]

The fact that conservative columnists have so much more access to newspaper readers than do progressive or liberal columnists is meaningful because "newspapers are the preferred news medium of those most interested in the news." For example, a 2006 Pew Research Center study found that 66% of those who said they follow political news closely also reported regularly reading newspapers (this was the most out of any medium).

On talk radio, conservatives also dominate. For example, according to the Pew Center for Excellence in Journalism, conservative talk show host Rush Limbaugh had an average weekly audience of 14.25 million in 2008. Conservative Sean Hannity had 13.25 million weekly listeners. Conservatives Michael Savage and Laura Schlessinger had 8.25 million listeners each and conservative Glenn Beck had 6.75 million listeners. Conservative talked Neil Boortz had 4.25 million listeners. As for liberals, Ed Schultz had only 3 million listeners and Randi Rhodes had only 1 million listeners. Three other liberal talkers all enjoyed only 1.5 million listeners.[135]

In the current age where communism is not viewed as particularly threatening relative to other threats such as terrorism and "socialism" (which reared its head in the 2008 presidential election andwas thrown around as a criticism against health care reform efforts in 2009), other anti-ideologies are used in the media, meaning any belief system that is inconsistent with capitalism and business will receive far less positive coverage, and promoters of the ideology will have far less access than those that promote the dominant ideology of the mainstream media. For this reason, people with views too far outside the mainstream generally do not appear in the mainstream media. When they do, they are often identified simply as "protestor" or "communist" or some other similar term in spite of their actual job titles.[136]

Outcomes of the Five Filters

What are the net effects of these five filters for media content? According to Edward Herman and Noam Chomsky: "The five filters narrow the range of news that passes through the gates, and even more sharply limit what can become 'big news,' subject to sustained news campaign."[137] This does not mean there is not room for disagreement in the media or for less common or popular views to have their voices heard. The media permit and even encourage "spirited debate, criticism, and dissent, as long as these remain faithfully within the system of presuppositions and principles that constitute an elite consensus, a system so powerful as to be internalized largely without awareness."[138] That is, there is debate but only bounded debate. Herman and Chomsky would say that only certain people are even invited to the debate, and those who are engaged in the debate are nearly free to say what they want, meaning they do not often perceive pressure from above.

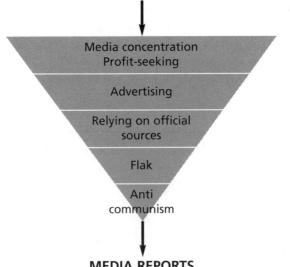

According to Herman and Chomsky's propaganda model, information passes through five filters in order to determine if it is suitable for broadcasting to the public via the media. Only a small amount of information is thus reported in the news media.

The pressure to conform to the acceptable bounds exists but it is not overt; rather, it comes in the form of market forces, internalized assumptions, and self-censorship.[139] This suggests that the barriers to fair and comprehensive news are structural factors, which include ownership, dependence on major funding sources such as advertisers, and "mutual interests and relationships between the media and those who make the news and have the power to define it and explain what it means."[140] Media outlets have "some limited autonomy," individuals have their own professional values which can influence media work, policies are not always uniformly or perfectly enforced, and "media policy itself may allow some measure of dissent and reporting that calls into question the accepted viewpoint." Yet, "such dissent and inconvenient facts are kept within bounds and at the margins."[141]

Ben Bagdikian cautions us that we should not see the mainstream media as some large, single entity. Yet he does conclude that the media "suffer from built-in biases that protect corporate power and consequently weaken the public's ability to understand forces that create the American scene. These biases favor the status quo ...".[142]

Although there is real news to be found in the media as well as the occasional investigative reports and documentaries, "the pop-cultural behemoths are mainly interested in entertainment, which produces large audiences."[143] The argument among media scholars is that entertainment diverts attention away from important issues, generates public apathy, and helps maintain the status quo. That is, our current focus on celebrities and relatively trivial stories keeps public attention off much more serious topics.

Stories about celebrities may be so common because they are inexpensive and do not antagonize people in power.[144] Investigative stories also cost more and require knowledgeable and competent journalists.[145]

It is important to acknowledge that there is still serious investigative journalism in the mainstream press. One example comes from ProPublica, "an independent, non-profit newsroom that produces investigative journalism in the public interest." Their work "focuses exclusively on truly important stories, stories with 'moral force'" which is achieved "by producing journalism that shines a light on exploitation of the weak by the strong and on the failures of those with power to vindicate the trust placed in them."[146] The organization won the 2010 Pulitzer Prize for Investigative Reporting. ProPublica is funded by foundation grant money rather than owned by a corporation and as such is the exception to the rule of what most reporting has become.

An important point for this book is that when one is looking for bias in the media, one must look not only at what is covered and how it is covered, but also in what is *not* covered and why. According to McChesney, matters of the

When celebrity Paris Hilton was arrested and sentenced to 45 days in jail for violating probation stemming from a previous DUI arrest, was this important news? Apparently, because she appeared for a full hour on CNN's Larry King Live to talk about what is was like for her in jail. http://www.celebuzz.com/top-10-celebrity-mugshots-g51201i32076041/.

working class are generally absent from the media.[147] Lane Crothers concurs, showing that issues of social class are largely absent from television; when they are shown, conditions of poverty rarely get connected to the political decisions that create poverty and economic hardship (e.g., downsizing, outsourcing). Further, the wealthy are generally depicted as having earned their wealth through hard work, perseverance, postponing gratification and other sources that are completely divorced from luck, family connections, bias, and so forth.[148]

Discussions of income inequality are also largely absent from serious media coverage. Income inequality "has tremendously negative implications for our politics, culture, and social fabric, yet it is barely noted in our journalism."[149] For example, some research shows a positive relationship between income inequality and crime, especially violent crimes like homicide, assault, robbery, and rape.[150] A review of 45 studies by Lynne Vieraitis described relationships between income inequality, poverty, and violent crimes: (1) inequality and homicide is typically positive, (2) poverty and homicide is typically positive, and (3) inequality and assault is typically positive.[151] A recent study of homicide trends in 83 US cities with populations of more than 100,000 people found that resource deprivation was associated with homicide. Thus, cities with more families living in poverty, greater income inequality, reductions in family income, as well as other factors such as single parents and population turnover, have higher rates of homicide.[152] We could logically reduce murder if we reduced income inequality; yet the issue is largely ignored in the press.

For more information about income inequality, see the website for this book at: www.pscj.appstate.edu/media/income.html

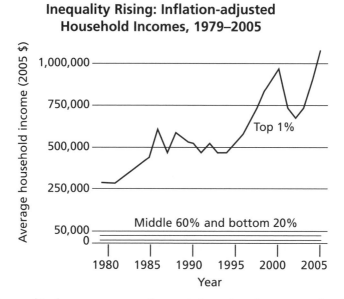

Income inequality has grown over the past three decades, yet stories about the significance of it for society are generally absent in the media. http://www.plotkin.com/blog-archives/bestinequalitygraph-figure1-version3.png.

Critical analysis of military spending is also generally lacking from the press. Even though the United States "spends a fortune on the military for no publicly debated or accepted reason ... it serves several important purposes for our economic elite, not the least of which is as a lucrative form of corporate welfare."[153] In spite of massive spending on military operations, the media largely ignore this issue. Yet, the costs of the proposed health care reforms debated in Congress in 2009 received an enormous amount of attention, even though at less than $90 billion per year it is a fraction of what we spend on military spending every year (about $700 billion). (See chart, next page.)

Another issue that lacks meaningful coverage is America's overreliance on incarceration and the effects this has on state and federal budgets: "The United States has 5 percent of the world's population and 25 percent of the world's prisoners" even though our crime rates are no higher than most European nations. One might think this would be controversial to many Americans especially since half of the nation's inmates are incarcerated for non violent and

U.S. Military Spending vs. The World in 2008
(in billions of U.S. dollars, with % of total global)

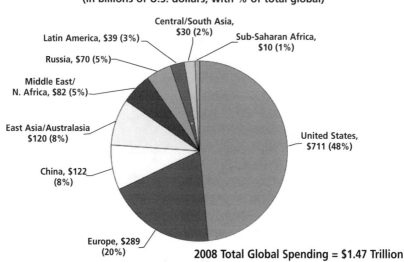

Central/South Asia, $30 (2%)

Latin America, $39 (3%)

Sub-Saharan Africa, $10 (1%)

Russia, $70 (5%)

Middle East/ N. Africa, $82 (5%)

East Asia/Australasia $120 (8%)

China, $122 (8%)

United States, $711 (48%)

Europe, $289 (20%)

2008 Total Global Spending = $1.47 Trillion

NOTES: Data from International Institute for Strategic Studies, *The Military Balance 2008*, and DOD. The total for the United States is the FY 2009 request and includes $170 billion for military operatons in Iraq and Afghanistan, as well as funding for DOE nuclear weapons activities. All other figures are projections based on 2006, the last year for which accurate data is available.

U.S. spending on military defense far out surpasses any other country and now makes up roughly half of all money spend on defense by all countries in the world. http://www.armscontrolcenter.org/policy/securityspending/articles/ fy09_dod_request_global/.

drug crimes, offenses that do far less damage each year than corporate and white-collar crimes (which rarely lead to incarceration). Yet, the media generally ignore this issue, too.

One reason why this issue may receive little media attention is the demographic characteristics of those locked up. Generally speaking, the nation's inmates are poor and either black or Latino.[154] These are people who are the least politically active and of the least interest "to the owners and advertisers of the commercial news media."[155] This issue is addressed in Chapter 7.

Summary

The term *media* refers to the main means of communication, information, and entertainment in society. The media are often referred to as the "mass media" as well as the "mainstream media," media that are easily, inexpensively, and simultaneously accessible to large segments of a population. There are at least three kinds of media, not including advertising. First, there are the news media. Second, there are the entertainment media. Finally, there is infotainment. The news media aim to provide information on major events, issues, problems, and trends. The entertainment media aim to entertain. Infotainment aims to provide information in an entertaining format.

Media sources are organized within a hierarchy of controlling institutions into an inner ring, a middle ring, and an outer ring. The inner ring of the media includes major television networks, news magazines, and national newspapers. The middle ring of the media and the outer ring of the media are more prevalent but have far less influence on the news than the institutions in the inner ring. Inner-ring sources are the main sources of information for Americans about many issues including crime.

The media are the main source for news about crime and criminal justice policy for citizens. However, not all media sources have the same impact on us. The media sources in the inner ring have greater influence than other sources.

The major news media are owned and thus controlled by major corporations. Six large corporations own most of the media in the United States. Corporate owned media threaten the vital duties of journalists necessary for a healthy democracy, which include: acting as a watchdog of the powerful; separating truth from lies; and presenting a wide variety of different opinions based on empirical information. Media companies are also linked to much bigger corporations. As a result, they are among the most powerful sector of the private economy.

Several concepts are important to understanding corporate influence over the media. First, media consolidation refers to when fewer and fewer corporations control information being relayed by the media. Second, horizontal integration refers to when a single corporation controls more and more of the media market in a given locale. Third, vertical integration is when a single corporation owns companies that contribute to the production and distribution of a product or service in one sector of the economy. Fourth, synergy is the vertical and horizontal integration of entertainment companies and the products they market, resulting in even greater power for the company. Fifth, interlocking directorates refer to when members of the Board of Directors from one company serve as Board members of other companies.

Understanding these concepts allows one to see how major media corporations cooperate as much as they compete. Cooperation is aimed at expanding the power of each corporation. Two important outcomes of corporate ownership of media, consolidation of the media, horizontal and vertical integration, interlocking directorates and other links between media companies and major corporations are relatively similar content across media outlets devoid of context and a lack of critical coverage of important issues.

There are two major interpretations of media coverage. The first is the democratic postulate that the media are independent and committed to discovering and reporting the truth. The second is that they mobilize support for the most powerful special interests in society.

Five filters in the propaganda model are: 1) The size, concentrated ownership, owner wealth and profit orientation of the largest mass media firms; 2) Advertising as the primary source of income by the largest mass media firms; 3) The reliance of the media on information provided by government, business, and "experts" funded and approved by these primary sources and agents of power; 4) "Flak" as a means of disciplining the media; and 5) "Anticommunism" as a national religion and control mechanism. These five filters narrow the range of news that passes through the gates and sharply limit what can become big news.

Discussion Questions

1) What are the *media*?
2) What are the *mass media* or *mainstream media*?
3) Differentiate between the three major kinds of media.
4) Which forms of media are more objective and realistic and which are less objective and realistic? Explain.
5) What are the *inner ring, middle ring*, and *outer ring* news sources?
6) Why does the inner ring media matter the most?
7) From where do people get their information about crime and criminal justice policy?
8) Who owns the most important media in the United States?
9) Define *media consolidation, horizontal integration, vertical integration, synergy*, and *interlocking directorates*. Explain why these concepts are important for understanding the media.
10) Contrast the *democratic postulate* and the *propaganda model*.
11) Define the five filters of the propaganda model and explain how these filters limit the breadth of information found in the media.
12) Do you think the media intentionally filter information for the purposes of propaganda? Explain.

Chapter 2

Introduction to the Media, Part II: What the Media Do and Do Not Do, and How They Do It

Learning Objectives

After reading this chapter, you will be able to:

1) Explain how the media impact what the public thinks about.
2) Explain how the media impact perceptions of social problems.
3) Identify the sources from where people get their information.
4) Explain whether the media are accurate in their depictions of important stories such as crime and politics.
5) Explain whether the media favor one political party over the other in their coverage of major issues.
6) Contrast the *objective model* of media coverage with the *subjective model* of media coverage.

7) Define *neutrality, balance,* and *reliability* and explain how these relate to media objectivity.

8) Explain why objective journalism is difficult, if not impossible, to accomplish and discuss the role of decisions of newsworthiness, priority, framing and marketability in news coverage.

9) Identify and define the major stages of construction of social problems in the media.

10) Define and contrast *frames* and *narratives* and identify and explain the most common frames and narratives used in media coverage of crime and criminal justice.

11) Define *socially constructed reality* and contrast it experienced reality with symbolic reality.

12) Define and provide examples of a *moral panic.*

13) Explain the media sources most relied upon by Americans for information.

Introduction

Most people believe the media are inaccurate in their depictions of important stories such as crime and politics. The media are generally the major source of information for people when it comes to social problems such as crime. This is because most people are not victimized by serious crimes, particularly acts of violence, and because the media are so ubiquitous.

There are two competing explanations of media coverage of problems such as crime. The first says that empirical realities of crime exist and can be captured objectively. According to this perspective, media coverage is generally *objective* in nature, accurately reflecting reality in its coverage. The second says knowledge about issues such as crime is *socially constructed* by people and thus cannot be objectively captured by the media. According to this perspective, objectivity is impossible and media coverage of social problems such as crime will be subjective in nature.

This chapter assesses whether the media are objective or subjective in an effort to answer the question, are the media depicting the whole truth, or only part(s) of the truth that serve limited interests? The chapter begins with a discussion of what the media do and do not do. The most important issue is whether the people, when exposed to media content, simply absorb it, believe it and change their worldview as a result.

What the Media Do and Do Not Do

Because people do not simply absorb ideological propaganda,[1] the media do not tell the public what to think, but they may tell the public what to think about.[2] That is, whatever is covered in the media is perceived to be important and worthy of viewer attention. Whether the attention is actually warranted on the basis of the nature and severity of the issue being covered is debatable.

Scholars have demonstrated that the media clearly play a major role in creating and maintaining perceptions of social problems.[3] According to Jill Edy and Patrick Meirick, "the more the media cover an issue, the more top-of-mind and salient that issue is for the public, and the thoughts that easily come to mind are the ones that people sample in decision making."[4] As will be shown later in this book, crime became seen as the most important problem to Americans in the 1990s, a time when rates of crime actually fell. This was when crime was more covered in the media than at any other time probably in U.S. history, suggesting media coverage of crime helped create public concern about crime even when society was generally become safer.

According to David Altheide the "news media contribute to public agendas, official and political rhetoric, and public perceptions of social problems as well as preferences for certain solutions … For many people, the mass media in general and the new media in particular are a 'window' on the world."[5] Further, the media "inform public opinion" and "contribute in no small way to setting social and political agendas."[6]

Without question, the news media, in their broadcasts and editorials, alert and even alarm the public and lawmakers about important events and issues.[7] Given that people are "passive consumers" of most forms of the media (such as television), it is not surprising that media coverage shapes a person's conception of reality: "people use knowledge they obtain from the media to construct a picture of the world, an image of reality on which they base their actions."[8] Much research shows that the media help construct images of deviance and criminality as well, as will become very clear in this book.[9]

In terms of crime, Gary Potter and Victor Kappeler assert: "Media coverage directs people's attention to specific crimes and helps to shape those crimes as social problems."[10] The main problem with media coverage of crime, as you will see in this book, is that it is dangerously inaccurate. The media also alter the perceptions people have of criminal justice activity and in ways that end up justifying continuation of the status quo approaches to "fighting" crime.[11]

You may be thinking, well don't consumers of media—citizens—really have control over what they decide to watch? Edward Herman and Noam Chomsky reason: "The public is not sovereign over the media—the owners and man-

When the news broadcasts an image like this of a convenience store robbery, what are the messages being sent to citizens about the nature of crime? http://www.silive.com/news/index.ssf/2008/05/cops_release_image_of_3_men_su. html.

agers, seeking ads, decide what is to be offered, and the public must choose among these. People watch and read in good part on the basis of what is readily available and intensively promoted."[12] Although it is true that the airwaves are public property, they are now owned and controlled by private interests.[13]

The belief that the media merely give the people what they want may be a myth.[14] For example, Robert McChesney asserts: "The corporate media culture is hardly the result of some abstract value-free media market that 'gives the people what they want.' Highly concentrated, it gives the dominant corporations market power to give their shareholders what they can make the most profit from."[15]

Public demand plays a role in what appears in the media, but to some degree public demand may result from what is and has been broadcast for so many years: "Had a similar commitment to exposés of government and corporate corruption been made, a public taste might well have developed for those stories … But that is not an option that the people are given."[16] The media gives us what we want but only the range of topics that can generate the greatest profits: "People are exposed to the media fare that the giants can profit from, they develop a taste for it, they consume it, and then the media giants claim they must make more of it to satisfy demand. What is demanded depends to a very large extent on what is produced rather than the other way around."[17]

Ben Bagdikian agrees, noting that viewers should not be blamed for what is on television and in the media. Instead, "what underlies messages of superficiality, materialism, blandness, and escapism is corporate demands on television programs." The television industry denies this, saying "that the networks are only giving people that they people demand. But it is not what the public says it wants: It is what the advertisers demand."[18]

When it comes to violence, "it has been part of American popular culture since well before the emergence of modern electronic entertainment. The shock value of violence has been demonstrated to be an effective means of drawing and keeping an audience. Violence … sells."[19] And it only sells because we like it.

Others assert that consumers share some blame for media content. For example, consider the argument of Lane Crothers, who explains that American culture reflects "the values of the nation from which it emerges."[20] Part of what Americans value is conflict and conflict resolution, crime and criminal justice being a good example of this. The frame most used in America to understand conflict and conflict resolution is individualistic in nature. Not coincidentally, the criminal law tends to define harmful acts committed by one individual against another as "crime" and especially as "serious crime," the police are involved overwhelmingly in arresting individuals who have harmed other individuals (as opposed to corporations who have harmed hundreds or even thousands of people), the vast majority of criminal convictions are of individuals who harmed other individuals, and so forth. So it should not be surprising that the majority of media coverage when it comes to discussing conflict, crime, and criminal justice is also individualistic in nature. This issue is revisited later in Chapter 4.

It should be pointed out that much of what appears in the media today is somewhat "automatic" in that whatever worked in the past is seen as likely to work in the future.[21] There is evidence that crimes that are easily explainable and that fit a known pattern are more likely to be covered.[22] Further, sex and violence are "tried and true" so we can expect to see them in the press for years to come.[23] Crime stories have become the "centerpiece of journalism, especially local TV news."[24] Stories about violence, sex, and vulgarity are the "tried-and-true mechanisms for commercial media" and part of the "lowest common denominator" programming that appeals to a wide body of people.[25] In fact, sex is often depicted as violent or linked to violent outcomes such as abuse and murder.[26] Lane Crothers also notes that women are commonly depicted in the media as objects.

Of course, the media are not the only source of information from which a person constructs his or her own reality. Four primary sources are used to construct reality, including personal experiences, significant others (peers, family, friends), other social groups and institutions (schools, churches, government agencies), and the mass media. Ray Surette holds that "knowledge from all of these sources is mixed together, and from this mix, each individual constructs the 'world.' "[27] Logically, the influence of the mass media likely increases as the influence of the other sources declines.[28]

Given that 90% of Americans will not be victimized by serious street crime[29] and that most people do not know anyone who chooses to talk about personal experience of criminal victimization, the media are a prime source of information about crime.[30] The media are also the primary source of information about criminal justice for most people.[31] This is problematic for one simple reason—media coverage of crime and criminal justice is inaccurate, as will be shown in this book.

Models of Media Behavior

The Objective Model

Some scholars and many citizens believe that the media objectively report the news.[32] The term *objective* means "expressing or dealing with facts or conditions as perceived without distortion by personal feelings, prejudices, or interpretations."[33] According to the *objective model* of media coverage, the media objectively report the news with no intent of bias or favoritism.

According to Peter White, objectivity in the news refers to at least three things –neutrality, balance, and reliability.[34] First, *neutrality* refers to keeping one's opinions out of the story. Jay Davis questions whether objectivity in the media is possible. His definition of objectivity pertains to neutrality—"keeping one's own beliefs, opinions or feelings separate from the story." Davis concludes: "This definition is more textbook than honest, however. Most journalists would agree that true impartiality is impossible. Even the most evenhanded reporter is subject to personal bias."[35] This is part of the reason some have claimed a liberal bias in the news, because most reporters tend to be Democrats, vote Democratic, and give money to the Democratic Party.[36] As noted in the last chapter, the notion of a liberal bias in the press may be a myth; the political affiliation of reporters is probably less important than those who own the media outlets.[37]

Statements in the media that merely describe the world as it exists are called *factual claims*. Statements that attempt to give meaning to the facts are called *interpretive claims*.[38] Interpretative claims allow subjectivity and potential biases to enter the media. An example of a factual claim would pertain to crime rate trend variation—e.g., "murder rates doubled in the city in the past five years." A subsequent interpretative claim might be "since murder rates have doubled in the city in the past five years, we need to start getting tough with youthful offenders to send the message that crime does not pay." The interpretive claim is based on the factual claim but is not necessarily true. Instead, it is one person's interpretation of the facts based on his or her viewpoint and underlying biases.

Second, *balance* means efforts to tell "both sides" of the story in an equal manner. Trying to cover "both sides" of a story can actually be a threat to objectivity. For example, Jay Davis asserts:

> Spend a week watching any of the network news reports and you are likely to conclude that all issues have only two sides and that middle-aged, white males have the only insight on them. From Sunday afternoon interview programs to ABC's Nightline, satisfying the U.S. media's standards of "objectivity" seems to require bringing opposing personalities together to debate issues of foreign and domestic policy. The ensuing dialogue, usually between Democrats and Republicans or some equivalent, suggests that all sides of the issue are covered.

In fact, presenting two opposing sides "tends to undermine creative discussion of the many shades of belief that actually represent opinion on complex issues. If all issues are presented in black-and-white, yes-and-no terms, if one is either pro-life or pro-choice, pro-intervention or anti-intervention, what happens to discussion of cases that fail to fit the neatly established dichotomy?" Not surprisingly, people with views inconsistent with the two polar extremes often put forth by the two major political parties are generally less prevalent in the media.

Similarly, Sharon Beder notes: "Ironically, journalistic objectivity discourages a search for evidence; the balancing of opinions often replaces journalistic investigation altogether."[39] Recall also that that investigative journalism is increasingly rare in the news because of the profit-orientation of the media.

Third, *reliability* refers to basing reporting on experts and empirical evidence. The practice of relying on government sources for information, identified in Chapter 1 as a potential source of bias in favor of the status quo, is ironically one way journalists attempt to be objective. Quoting authoritative sources such as politicians or other experts with sufficient knowledge to make informed comments allows journalists to distance themselves from their stories so that they do not appear as their own opinions.[40]

The objective model of the media assumes that empirical realities of crime exist and can be captured and shown via media objectively. In fact, crime does not exist in reality but instead is invented by human beings when they define certain behaviors as wrong, bad, deviant, or harmful.[41] This means objective coverage of crime is simply impossible, for crime does not objectively exist. To be clear, there is killing in nature (e.g., a lion kills a zebra), taking of property in nature (e.g., one squirrel steals a nut from another squirrel) and so forth, but these are not crimes until they are defined as illegal through the passage of criminal laws (and obviously zebras and squirrels do not pass criminal laws!). Thus, crime is invented by humans. Given that there are many forms of killing and property taking among humans that are not defined as murder or theft, this is evidence of the subjective nature of crime itself. Further, those who believe in the *subjective model* to be discussed later, believe that knowledge itself is *socially constructed*.

Yet, the way in which crime is covered in the media can be objective in nature. According to Naomi Rockler-Gladen, objectivity—defined as "descriptive, simple language that gets to the point and is not emotional"—can be accomplished with a particular writing style called the *inverted pyramid*. She explains that "this is a formulaic writing style where the most important facts (who, what, where, when, why, and how) are listed first, followed by facts that are of less and less importance."[42] Rockler-Gladen sees this style as appropriate for today's media consumers, who "often read or watch just a portion of a news story before hurrying off to do the next thing" in order to get the "jist of the story without reading or watching the whole thing."

Still, Rockler-Gladen agrees that objective journalism is difficult, if not impossible, due to several factors, including:

- *Decisions of newsworthiness*—deciding which stories to cover and which to ignore.
- *Decisions of priority*—deciding where to run a story (first, last, at all?).
- *Decisions of framing*—deciding how to tell a story, from which perspective.
- *Decisions of marketability*—deciding between conflicting demands of the public and advertisers.

These factors allow potential biases and subjectivity to impact the media. As shown in the previous chapter, when it comes to all outlets of the mainstream media, large corporations are the ones that decide which stories to cover and which to ignore (newsworthiness), how much or how little to prioritize a story (priority), how the story is told (framing), and in what ways the story will be marketed (marketability). Thus, even though editors and journalists may attempt to be objective, true objectivity is not possible. According to Rockler-Gladen: "Most working journalists are committed to the principle of objectivity. They make a strong effort to report news free of bias that is as useful as possible to the public. However, the public needs to be aware of the constraints that make true objectivity a difficult goal, and consume news critically."

Sharon Beder discusses some of these issues, as well as others. She suggests that media coverage is often subjective due to personal judgments "about what is a good story, who will be interviewed for it, what questions will be asked, which parts of those interviews will be printed or broadcast, what facts are relevant and how the story is written."[43] Martin Less and Norman Solomon agree, noting that "value judgments infuse everything in the news media ... Which of the infinite observations confronting the reporter will be ignored? Which of the facts noted will be included in the story? Which of the reported events will become the first paragraph? Which story will be prominently displayed on page 1 and which buried inside or discarded? ... Mass media not only report the news—they also literally make the news."[44]

Interestingly, an article in *Newsweek* magazine (owned by The Washington Post Company, which publishes the newspaper by the same name and is also in business in television broadcasting, cable television systems, electronic information services, and educational and career services), asked, "Is the mainstream press unbiased? No, but we aren't ideological. What we really thrive on is conflict."[45] By ideological, the writer means favoring one political party over another. It should go without saying that crime involves great conflict; thus, it is of great interest to the media.

According to the article:

> A recurring rap against the press is that it lacks objectivity. The criticism is fair, in the sense that it is almost impossible to be completely objective. Subjectivity always creeps into the choices made by reporters and editors on what to include or what to emphasize in a story. News people are all too human, and sometimes they are not even aware of their biases. But on the whole, the mainstream press does try, with imperfect results, to be fair.[46]

If the author is correct, this means that media objectivity is impossible due to the natural tendency of subjectivity.

Still, there is at least some truth to the objective model of media coverage. There must be some basic truth to claims that a social problem exists in order for it to even come to the attention of the media. Otherwise this would mean the media literally invent problems. There is little evidence that this occurs. That is, the media do not cover events that *never* happen (although they do tend to cover events that rarely happen).

If citizens successfully call attention to a problem, resulting in media attention, we can even say the media are being responsive to objective conditions as perceived by the general public. One example is when groups operating at the grass roots level are born in response to perceptions of social problems. According to scholars, social movements evolving at the grass roots occur in five stages: incipiency; coalescence; institutionalization; fragmentation; and demise.[47] *Incipiency* represents the beginning of a social movement. At this stage there is no strong leadership and no organized membership.[48] *Coalescence* refers to when "formal and informal organizations develop out of segments of the sympathetic public that have become the most aroused by perceived threats to the preservation or realization of their interests."[49] Media coverage of a problem can help lead to coalescence. *Institutionalization* occurs "when the government and other traditional institutions take official notice of a problem or movement and work out a series of standard coping mechanisms to manage it."[50] Once media coverage begins and becomes common, it is certain that institutionalization has occurred. *Fragmentation* occurs when the coalition that forced the emergence of the movement breaks apart or weakens due to the co-opting of the issue by the government. Finally, *demise* occurs when claims-makers lose interest in the issue.[51]

An example of the stages in a social movement can be seen with the illicit drug marijuana in the 1970s. In the 1970s, many states had decriminalized the use of marijuana. Jimmy Carter, who would go on to become the 39th President of the United States, favored legalization. Prominent conservatives such as William Buckley also favored ending prohibition of the drug. America may have been on the verge of legalization or decriminalization of marijuana. Yet, in the mid 1970s the "parents' movement against marijuana" began. According to PBS: "A nationwide movement emerged of conservative parents' groups lobbying for stricter regulation of marijuana and the prevention of drug use by teenagers. Some of these groups became quite powerful and, with the support of the [Drug Enforcement Administration] and the National Institute on Drug Abuse (NIDA), were instrumental in affecting public attitudes which led to the 1980s War on Drugs."[52] Major government-sponsored efforts aimed at reducing drug use began in the 1980s, including Drug Abuse Resistance Education (DARE) and Nancy Reagan's "Just Say No" Program.[53]

Ultimately, societal mores became more consistent with strict prohibition of drugs, and President George H.W. Bush re-declared the war on drugs in 1989. The war has waged on ever sense. The war on drugs is reexamined later in this chapter as part of an examination into moral panics and crime.

The Subjective Model

Most scholars see media coverage of problems such as crime in very subjective terms. The term *subjective* means "to or being experience or knowledge as conditioned by personal mental characteristics or states; peculiar to a particular individual; or modified or affected by personal views, experience, or background"[54] Much research demonstrates that media coverage of crime and similar problems is subjective in nature.

First Lady Nancy Reagan began her "Just Say No" campaign against illicit drugs in 1985 as part of President Ronald Reagan's war on drugs in the 1980s. http://en.wikipedia.org/wiki/File:NRJUSTSAYNORALLY.jpg.

At this point, it is probably important to again consider the realities of mainstream media established in Chapter 1:

- The major news media are owned and thus controlled by major corporations.
- Mainstream media outlets have been consolidated into fewer and fewer hands, each of which is part of the corporate system.
- Inner-ring or upper tier media outlets have grown larger and more influential through horizontal and vertical integration.
- Agenda setting media serve in numerous ways with other corporations including interlocking directorates.
- The media are mainly concerned with profit, particularly advertising dollars.
- The media rely heavily on information provided by government sources.
- The powerful have greater ability to produce "flak" in order to influence media coverage.
- Perspectives that threaten the status quo are least likely to appear in the media.

Given these realities, is it possible that the media objectively report on problems such as crime? Is it even logical to expect media coverage to be objective? Most would probably say no; instead, the media subjectively cover crime and even construct or create crime problems.

However, it is important to recall a point made in the Preface to the book as well as in Chapter 1 that many Americans now rely heavily on websites, social network sites, blogs, and so forth for both news and entertainment. These sources, especially outside of the inner ring of the media, are often non-objective;

in fact, they state this upfront as non-problematic since they are involved in advocacy journalism.

When it comes to how the mainstream media construct or create crime problems, scholars agree that social problems are socially constructed (or invented) from objective facts in five major steps. These scholars believe in the *social construction* of knowledge. According to these scholars, there is always a shred of truth with regard to the nature of a problem being depicted in the media, meaning the problem does exist in reality. Thus, the first stage in the social construction process is news reporting of a real (but limited) social problem. However, media coverage of the problem is inaccurate and/or widespread enough that it ends up blowing the problem out of proportion to the actual threat posed by the problem. The second stage in the social construction process occurs when the media blow the limited problem out of proportion to the threat it actually poses, creating the illusion of a larger problem than actually exists. The third stage of the social construction process is when the nature of problem is *typified* in media coverage, meaning it is represented in a typical fashion each time through a pre-established frame.

Frames are tools used by the media to more easily categorize stories about issues like crime. Ray Surette notes that "preexisting frames make the processing, labeling, and understanding of crimes easier for the person holding that frame's view of reality. If a crime can be quickly placed into a preestablished frame, it will be seen as another example of a particular type of crime needing a particular type of response."[55]

Five frames commonly seen in the media include the faulty criminal justice frame, the blocked opportunities frame, the social breakdown frame, the violent media frame, and the racist system frame.[56] The *faulty criminal justice frame* attributes crime to weak or soft criminal justice punishment, leading citizens to believe that we need to get tougher in order to reduce crime. The *blocked opportunities frame* attributes criminality to social conditions such as poverty and inequality in society, leading citizens to believe that the solution to crime includes providing better opportunities for the poor. The *social breakdown frame* attributes criminality to problems in families and communities, suggesting the solution to crime must entail rebuilding marriages and neighborhoods. Ironically, the *violent media frame* attributes criminality to violence in the media, suggesting that reforms to the media must take place in order to reduce the nature and amount of violence in the media. Finally, the *racist system frame* suggests that criminal justice itself is unfair in that it systematically targets people of color. Thus, reforms must be initiated to make criminal justice processing fairer.

Similarly, *narratives* are well-established portraits or images of criminals, victims, and criminal justice officials that are easily recognized in the media. Surette provides the following examples of common crime narratives: the *ideal offender* is an outsider, stranger, foreigner, intruder lacking "essential human qualities" that is beyond rehabilitation; the *ideal victim* is an innocent, naïve, trusting person who needs protection from the bad people in society; and the *ideal hero* is noble, strong and sacrifices of himself or herself in the fight against crime.[57]

More specifically, there is the *innately evil predatory criminal* (an individual who hurts others without any concern or regret due to some inborn condition such as mental illness); the *naïve innocent victim* (an individual who is harmed by crime through no fault of his or her own); and the *masculine, heroic crime-fighter* (an individual who "fights" crime every day for a living, such as a police officer). These narratives can be used "to quickly establish the characteristics of a criminal, a victim, or a crime-fighter and as supportive examples for larger crime and justice frames."[58]

As it turns out, the narratives of the evil criminal, the innocent victim, and the heroic crime fighter are among the most commonly used portraits and images used in the media in stories about crime and criminal justice. Each is a good example of how the media subjectively cover crime stories rather than presenting the objective realities. In reality, many if not most offenders are normal people reacting to extreme circumstances in their lives, conditions that produce evil actions. Further, many crime victims are neither truly innocent nor naïve; often they facilitate their own victimization (by engaging in risky or dangerous behaviors) or even willingly participate in it (as in the case of drug use and prostitution). In the case of criminal justice personnel, many would likely reject the label of hero; they are, like most people, employed in legitimate fields and simply dedicated to their jobs.

When you hear the term "crime" or "victim," what images come to mind? According to Brian Spitzberg and Michelle Cadiz, the term "crime victim" often evokes "a set of archetypal images: Innocence, violence, powerlessness, weaponry, and tragedy. The iconicity of these archetypes is in no small part a product of media typifications rather than the factual data of victimization." The argument of scholars, including Spitzberg and Cadiz, is that the media have the power "to penetrate people's everyday lives" through the images, stories, and programs they produce that "not only aid in defining what society deems relevant and true, but also in the sculpting of society itself. With techniques ranging from graphic pictures to vivid language, the media are able to reach vast audiences with any particular message or perspective."[59]

The fourth stage in the social construction process is called linkage, and it is related to the third stage. After problems are framed using popular narratives, they are ultimately linked to other social problems, typically related to powerless groups. For example, the notion of "crack babies" was created by media coverage of the crack cocaine "epidemic" in the late 1980s and early 1990s. Babies were filmed lying on hospital beds shaking and rolling about supposedly due to crack cocaine withdrawal symptoms.[60]

The fifth stage in the social construction process occurs when a policy is created (e.g., a new law), which is legitimated through the media. In the case of crack babies, laws were passed to arrest mothers as well as strip women of their parental rights if their babies were born with cocaine in their systems.[61]

One can hardly imagine a more compelling image to generate alarm than a vulnerable baby, in this case a supposed "crack baby." http://cocaine.org/crackbaby/crackbaby.jpg.

Understanding the social construction process allows us to see how sometimes the media can transform a relatively minor problem into a major one. In the case of crack cocaine, use of the drug was actually quite rare during the crack cocaine scare, yet intense media coverage resulted in a series of draconian laws as well as the creation of a new federal agency to lead the nation's drug war. These issues are examined later in the chapter.

Try to imagine a recent crime story, for example, one related to a threat of some kind of violent act or terrorism against some place in your community. How does this threat become newsworthy in your community and ultimately, to the whole nation? Crime problems are actually created and spread because of media coverage. For example, when a threat is received, local radio and television stations and newspapers will cover the story, leading to isolated local stories. As other, unrelated threats are received in other locations, the problem becomes more newsworthy and leads to increased, diverse coverage in the media. Add to this reality the fact that "contemporary media cover local crime through a national lens. In addition to raising selected local crimes to national prominence, local crimes is portrayed in the media as being beyond the ability and resources of local criminal justice."[62]

To the consumer of news, with the increased coverage, it appears that the problem is widespread, growing, or even happening everywhere. With each new threat, all previous threats are rehashed, leading the viewer with the perception that these threats are more common than they truly are and even that they are connected. Now, the public becomes concerned and legislative bodies begin to discuss what can be done about the problem, ultimately leading to some tough talk by politicians in the media and perhaps new laws.

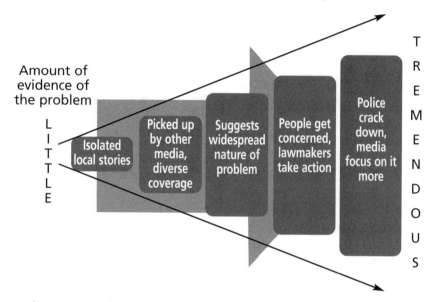

Media coverage of a problem can start out as local, isolated stories, and over time through increased and diverse coverage create and feed the perception that the problem is larger or more threatening than it actually is, which can lead to action by law-makers and police and increased fear in the public.

Any time politicians talk tough or pass new laws, there is more coverage of the problem, additional analysis, and justifications for the changes in law. To the viewer, even though the problem may not be much of a problem in reality, it appears that the problem has grown immensely, because there is much more evidence of the problem in all forms of media. So, in essence, the media are involved in constructing or creating crime problems; they are literally creating more evidence of the problem through their actions.

One's *socially constructed reality* is made up of *experienced reality* as well as *symbolic reality*. The former is made up of that which is directly experienced, such as victimization from crime, whereas the latter is that which is believed to be true but that has never been personally experienced. Most of us are never victims of serious violent crimes, thus our knowledge of them is most symbolic in nature. According to Ray Surette, a large part of one's symbolic reality with regard to a social problem such as crime comes from media coverage.[63] This is clearly the case with crime and terrorism, as well as much policing, courts, and corrections.

When different constructions of social problems conflict, it is the media that decide which constructions generally win. Those constructions that are dramatic, sponsored by powerful groups and consistent with the status quo are most likely to win.[64] This is consistent with the evidence presented in the last chapter concerning corporate ownership of the media.

Moral Panics

Changes to public policies typically occur after powerful interests construct or create social problems from objective social conditions.[65] When an objective social problem is blown out of proportion, the result can be a *moral panic*. Moral panics occur when:

> A condition, episode, person or group of persons emerges to become defined as a threat to societal values and interests; its nature is presented in a stylized and stereotypical fashion by the mass media; the moral barricades are manned by editors, bishops, politicians, and other right-thinking people; socially accredited experts pronounce their diagnoses and solutions.[66]

Because moral panics "typically involve an exaggeration of a social phenomenon, the public response also is often exaggerated and can create its own long lasting repercussions for society in terms of drastic changes in laws and social policy."[67]

⤶ For a classic example of a moral panic based on Halloween candy, see the website for this book at: ww.pscj.appstate.edu/media/moral panics.html

---

The United States has witnessed several moral panics when it comes to crime and similar problems. For example, a moral panic occurred with regard to crack cocaine and "crack babies" in the 1980s.[68] This does not mean that illegal drug use (and especially drug abuse) is not problematic. Moral panics over drugs can emerge from the general public if the objective threats posed by drug use and abuse are viewed as significant enough to warrant legitimate concerns.

The danger of moral panics is that they often lead to unnecessary changes in existing public policies or entirely new policies that are based on exaggerated threats. Misguided policies result from at least three factors: political opportunism; media profit maximization; and desire among criminal justice professionals to increase their spheres of influence.[69] Following this logic, politicians create concern about crime, drugs and similar issues in order to gain personally from such claims in the form of election and re-election; they achieve this largely by using the media as their own mouthpiece. After media coverage increases, so does public concern. Indeed, research shows that public concern about crime and drugs increases after threats have been hyped in the mass media.[70] Finally, criminal justice professionals and government institutions agree to fight the problem, not only because they see them as serious problems but also because it assures them continued resources, clients, and thus bureaucratic survival.

Concern over crime, drugs and similar issues typically occurs in a cycle whereby some government entity claims the existence of an undesirable condition and then legitimizes the concern, garnering public support through the media by using "constructors" who provide evidence of the problem. As noted earlier, claims-makers then "typify" the problem by characterizing its nature.[71] For example, illicit drugs are typified as "harmful" even when used responsibly and/or recreationally. They are characterized as "bad" regardless of the context in which they are being used. Any illicit drug use is wrong even if it is not abuse.[72] Finally, the problem is connected to other social problems in order to make it seem even worse. For example, illicit drugs including marijuana were recently linked to acts of terrorism in television commercials and print ads created by the government agencies, paid for by taxpayers.[73]

Several myths about drugs exemplify this typification. For example, the "dope fiend mythology" promulgated by the U.S. government in the early 1900s that pertained to users of heroin, cocaine, and other then legally available drugs contained these elements: "the drug addict is a violent criminal, the addict is a moral degenerate (e.g., a liar, thief, etc.), drug peddlers and addicts want to convert others into addicts, and the addict takes drugs because of an abnormal personality."[74]

Another example is the typification of the use of marijuana, as indicated in a pamphlet circulated by the Bureau of Narcotics in the 1930s:

> Prolonged use of Marihuana frequently develops a delirious rage which sometimes leads to high crimes, such as assault and murder. Hence Marihuana has been called the "killer drug." The habitual use of this narcotic poison always causes a marked deterioration and sometimes produces insanity ...
>
> While the Marihuana habit leads to physical wreckage and mental decay, its effects upon character and morality are even more devastating. The victim frequently undergoes such moral degeneracy that he will lie and steal without scruple.[75]

The propaganda circulated by the Bureau of Narcotics included the story of a "murder of a Florida family and their pet dog by a wayward son who had taken one toke of marijuana."[76]

Empirical evidence about the relative harmlessness of marijuana was ignored. Dozens of other similar stories were printed in papers across the country, including the *New York Times*. Such stories both instituted and maintained moral panics.

Here, marijuana is depicted as an evil God and called the "assassin of youth." http://www.druglibrary.org/schaffer/hemp/history/HYSTERIA-ASSASSIN-MOLOCH.JPG.

One possible reason why empirical evidence concerning marijuana was ignored in favor of dramatic (and nonsensical) characterizations and stories such as those above, is that several of the individuals involved in creating concern over marijuana use had ulterior motives for their actions. In 1930, the Bureau of Narcotics was formed within the U.S. Treasury Department. Harry Anslinger was appointed director by the Secretary of the Treasury, Andrew Mellon, who also happened to be Anslinger's uncle (by marriage) and owner of the Mellon Bank. Mellon Bank was one of the DuPont Corporation's banks. DuPont was a major timber & paper company. These players also had close links to William Randolph Hearst, another timber & paper mogul who published several large newspapers.

Hearst used his newspapers to crusade against marijuana and this benefitted its paper manufacturing division and Hearst's plans for widespread use of polyester, both of which were threatened by hemp. DuPont also had just developed nylon, which too was threatened by hemp. It has been alleged that the reason marijuana was criminalized was due not to its harmful nature but instead to efforts by these men to protect their economic interests.

Hearst and Anslinger also held racist attitudes toward Mexicans, Chinese, and African Americans.[77] For these reasons, they launched a campaign against the "killer weed" and "assassin of youth" (marijuana).[78] One result was the Marijuana Tax Act of 1937, which required a tax stamp to sell marijuana, established laborious procedures to prescribe the drug, and put forth very tough sentences for law violations (such as "life" for selling to a minor). The Bureau of Narcotics also wrote a sample bill banning pot that was eventually adopted by forty states.

Many scholars claim that wars on drugs as inanimate objects "tend to be concerned less with the drugs they purportedly target than with those who are perceived to be the primary users of the drugs."[79] For example:

- The war on opium in the late 1800s and early 1900s was focused on Chinese laborers who represented unwanted labor competition. Thus, laws passed in the late 19th Century, which forbade importation and manufacture of opium by Chinese, excluded the Chinese in America from participating fully in the labor market.[80]
- The war on marijuana in the 1930s was grounded in racism against Mexican immigrants, who were characterized as "drug-crazed criminals" taking jobs away from Americans during the Great Depression.[81]
- Crack cocaine use by the urban was used by political leaders in the 1980s to divert attention from serious social and economic problems.[82]

Each of these drug scares blamed all sorts of societal evils on "outsiders"[83]— poor minority groups—and crime and drug problems were typified as " 'underclass' problems resulting from insufficient social control."[84]

According to Phillip Jenkins, a moral panic benefits politicians.[85] It allows them to focus attention on relatively powerless groups rather than focusing on other, more serious threats. Brian Spitzberg and Michelle Cadiz assert that the media also "appear to be eager and complicit partners with police and political bodies in the construction of 'crime waves.' "[86] Stories about crime, including exaggerations, are newsworthy and interesting. They raise concern

The film "Reefer Madness" was made in 1936 and featured a group of high school students who used marijuana. Outcomes include a suicide, murder, rape, and hit and run accident. Although the film is now largely seen as a joke, it was not meant to be taken this way; instead it was intended as evidence of the danger of marijuana use. http://en.wikipedia.org/wiki/File:ReeferMadness Poster.jpg.

among readers and viewers and are profitable for the press.[87] Thus, the media hold much responsibility for generating moral panics.

In the 1980s, all sorts of societal problems were blamed on crack cocaine, largely because media portrayals of crack cocaine were highly inaccurate.[88] This doubtlessly served to create a moral panic. The scare began in late 1985, when the *New York Times* ran a cover story announcing the arrival of crack to the city. In 1986, *Time* and *Newsweek* magazines ran five cover stories each on crack cocaine, calling crack cocaine the largest issue of the year.[89] In the second half of 1986, NBC News featured 400 stories on the drug. In July 1986 alone, the three major networks ran 74 drug stories on their nightly newscasts.[90] Drug-related stories in the *New York Times* increased from 43 in the second half of 1985 to 92 and 220 in the first and second halves of 1986, respectively,[91] and thousands of stories about crack appeared in magazines and newspapers.[92]

After the *New York Times* coverage, CBS produced a two-hour show called "48 Hours on Crack Street," and NBC followed with "Cocaine Country." In April 1986, the National Institute on Drug Abuse (NIDA) released a report called "Cocaine: The Big Lie," and 13 public service announcements that aired between 1,500 and 2,500 times on 75 local networks. This was followed by 74 stories on crack cocaine on ABC, CBS, and NBC in July 1986 alone. In November 1986, approximately 1,000 stories appeared about crack in national magazines, where crack was called "the biggest story since Vietnam," a "plague," and a "national epidemic."[93]

Jenifer Cobbina analyzed 124 newspaper articles in the *New York Times,* the *Chicago Tribune*, the *Washington Post*, and the *Los Angeles Times* from 1985–1987 and 2001–2003 to determine if race and social class of crack cocaine and methamphetamine users and traffickers impacted how the media depicted these two drugs. She found that "media reports on crack cocaine frequently referenced African Americans and depicted the drug in conjunction with violent crime. However, articles on methamphetamine were more likely to reference poor Whites and associate this drug as a public health problem."[94]

Nearly half (45%) of stories about crack focused on the association of crack-and-violence. Only 10% of stories about methamphetamine associated the drug with violence. Cobbina writes: "Unlike coverage on crack, media reports on meth did not demonize the drug. Thus, compared to crack users, meth abusers were less likely to be viewed as threatening to the public. As a result, the notion of Whites as non-criminals remains unchallenged."[95] Nearly half (25%) of the stories about meth framed the drug as a public health and environmental issue rather than one of violent crime.

The study by Cobbina also found that stories about crack

> were two times more likely than meth articles to express the need for harsher crime control policies. Journalists' reported several calls for "get tough" policies, such as the war on drugs, mandatory prison terms, and three strike laws, in response to the alleged crack epidemic in the mid-1980s.... Reporters rely quite heavily on public officials to obtain media reports ... Thus, it is easy to understand how the media's reliance on government officials for information about crime provides political governments the opportunity to advance their own partisan interests through the use of propaganda.[96]

As media coverage of drugs increased, people were paying attention. Not surprisingly, citizens were more likely to recognize drugs as the "most important problem" in response to the notable attention in the national news. Drug coverage in the media was more extensive in the 1980s than at other times. For example, the CBS program "48 Hours on Crack Street" obtained the highest rating of any news show of this type in the 1980s.[97] Public concern over drug use peaked in the 1980s, evolving into a full-fledged moral panic.

Once the media and public were all stirred up, laws were passed aimed at toughening sentences for crack cocaine. For example, the Anti-Drug Abuse Act of 1986 created a 100:1 disparity for crack and powder cocaine (5 grams of crack would mandate a 5 year prison sentence, versus 500 grams of powder cocaine). The U.S. Sentencing Commission recommended to Congress that this disparity be eliminated, yet Congress rejected the recommendation (which was the first time Congress ever rejected the Commission). Additionally, the Anti-Drug Abuse Act of 1988 lengthened sentences for drug offenses and created the Office of National Drug Control Policy (ONDCP).

The intense media coverage of crack cocaine is problematic because it was inaccurate and dishonest. News coverage did not reflect reality, as crack cocaine use was actually quite rare during this period.[98] Additionally, cocaine use was in fact declining at this time. According to NIDA, most peaks in illicit drug use occurred between 1979 and 1982, except for cocaine which peaked between 1982 and 1985.[99] Media coverage of cocaine use increased in the late 1980s even after drug use had already begun to decline. For example, new users of cocaine numbered 1.2 million in 1980, grew to 1.5 million by 1983, and fell to 994,000 by 1986. Although in 1987, the number grew to 1 million, each subsequent year saw declines in the numbers of new users of cocaine so that by 1990, there were 587,000 new users.[100]

New users of crack cocaine did rise for seven consecutive years between 1980 and 1986, from 65,000 to 271,000 new users. The number then fell in 1987 to 262,000 but then rose again until 1989, when the number was 377,000 new users.[101] Although the number of crack users thus rose from 1980 to 1989 (so too did the size of the U.S. population), never did even as many as 500,000 people use crack cocaine at any given time in the entire country. Further, only 377,000 of 246.5 million people in the U.S. were current users of crack in 1989 (this is 0.15%) of the population!

This coverage of drugs in the media typified social problems as stemming from the psychopharmacological properties of drugs such as crack cocaine (e.g., when a user becomes violent because of the effects of the drug on the brain), when in reality most of the associated violence stemmed from volatile crack cocaine markets.[102] Most of the violence associated with the illicit drug trade was *systemic* (e.g., drug dealers killed rival drug dealers) and *economic compulsive* (e.g., people robbed others to get money to buy drugs). News stories were also generally inaccurate and/or misleading in the way they characterized addiction to crack cocaine as "instantaneous," as if everyone who tried crack would become addicted immediately.[103] More recent media conceptions of dangerous drugs include violence associated with methamphetamine, including gangs, drug dealers, dangers associated with meth labs, and use of the drug and domestic violence.[104] The fact remains that most of the violence associated with drugs today is due to their illicit nature, as in the case of widespread violence in Mexico and the United States associated with the prohibition of marijuana.

The crack war was thus based on fallacies and the media reported those fallacies as truth. The crack crisis also served to construct an atmosphere conducive to getting tough on crime and maintaining status quo (drug war) approaches to fighting drugs. As the data show, the public was not concerned about drugs until after the media coverage captured their attention. President Ronald Reagan's re-declaration of war against drugs in August 1986 created an "orgy" of media coverage of crack cocaine, and public opinion about the seriousness of the "drug problem" changed as a result.[105] In mid-August 1986, drugs became the most important problem facing the nation in public opinion polls.[106] Compare this to June 2004 when only 1% of Americans said that drugs are the most important problem facing the country.[107]

Erich Goode and Nachman Ben-Yehuda summarize public concern over drugs, as reported in public opinion poll results:

> Periodically, the Gallup poll asks a sample of Americans the question, "What do you think is the most important problem facing this country today?" Drug abuse declined among the most important problems named by the public in Gallup polls between the early 1970s (February 1973, 20 percent) and the late 1970s (February, May, and October 1979, no mention at all), a period, ironically ... when drug use among the American public was at an all-time high.... Between 1979 and 1984, drug use and abuse did not appear at all in the Gallup polls among the most often mentioned problems facing the country, indicating a relatively and consistently low level of concern about the issue. This changed in the mid 1980s. In January, May, and October of 1985, the proportion of those polled mentioning drug abuse as the nation's number one problem fluctuated from 2 to 6 to 3 percent. In July 1986, this figure increased to 8 percent, which placed it fourth among major American social problems. In a set of parallel polls, conducted by the New York Times and CBS News in April 1986, only 2 percent named drug abuse as the nation's number one problem; by August, the figure had increased to 13 percent.... The figure contin-

ued to grow through nearly the remainder of the 1980s until, in September 1989, a whopping 64 percent of the respondents in the New York Times/CBS News poll said that drug abuse represented the most important problem facing the country; this response is one of the most intense preoccupations by the American public on any issue in polling history.[108]

Why did people suddenly become so concerned about illicit drugs? It was clearly not due to increased drug use, as illicit drug use peaked in 1979 and declined throughout the 1980s. Scholars suggest that since media coverage of drugs increased in the 1980s, it is likely that media coverage of drugs is to blame for increased concern about drugs. Recall from the last chapter that although the media do not tell people what to think, they do tell people what to think about.

Not surprisingly, this chronology bolsters opinions about the constructed nature of the drug problem. Scholars suggest that drug control policies growing out of problems like the crack wars of the 1980s (including the toughening of sentences for crack cocaine versus powder cocaine in 1986 and even the creation of ONDCP in 1988), generally do not arise out of the objective nature of drug use per se, but instead tend to develop out of moral panics created and promoted by actors in the political realm. With crack cocaine, concerns did not arise out of the public health domain, but instead were prompted by politicians who decided to seize on an easy issue to promote drugs as the cause of so many social problems.[109]

Whatever your personal view on media coverage of social problems—that it is objective or subjective in nature, the fact remains that media coverage of any problem, including crime, is inaccurate. The main reason is because media coverage of a problem like crime cannot possibly capture all the important realities about it. This means public perception of crime will not reflect reality.

🖰 For other examples of moral panics centered on crime, see the website for this book at: ww.pscj.appstate.edu/media/moralpanics.html

---

Does It Matter? Are People Exposed to the Media?

Selective media coverage of issues of crime and criminal justice might be less problematic if viewers did not expose themselves to it. Yet, according to Ben Bagdikian, the mainstream media are "nearly escapable."[110] In fact, it is not uncommon for television stations to be broadcasting news on televisions at

All Crimes

Crimes known
to the police

Crimes reported
in the news

Public
perception of
crime

Media coverage of problems such as crime is necessarily inaccurate because they cannot possibly capture the complete reality of crime. What becomes known to the public is not at all representative of the true reality of crime.

doctors' offices, restaurants, gyms, and so forth. This means people are exposed to the media even passively on a regular basis.

At the same time, many forms of the news media are losing money as well as consumers. According to *The State of the News Media* by the Pew Project for Excellence in Journalism, newspapers are struggling, local news is struggling, cable news flourishes (especially during election cycles), reliance on the Internet for news is increasing, declining revenue is the main problem in the media (and this has been worsened by the recent economic recession).[111] Further, newspaper revenue has declined significantly and circulation is down.[112] Research also shows that the more people rely on computers (i.e., the Internet) for the news, the less they read newspapers. Further, this negatively impacts the degree of "connectedness" that people have to each other as well as their local communities.[113]

Among network television news, NBC averaged the most viewers per night, followed by ABC and CBS. Among cable news outlets, the Fox News Network led CNN and MSNBC. Among Internet news sources, most Americans got their news from Yahoo News, followed by MSNBC, CNN, AOL News and the *New York Times*. Local television news was still the major source of news in 2008 although it lost a lot of its audience. In 2008, only 52% of Americans were regular viewers of the local news. This is important because crime makes up about 30% of the local news, as shown in Chapter 1. In terms of magazines, *Time* led *Newsweek* and *U.S. News and World Report* in circulation but each lost significant customers in 2008.

A study by the Pew Research Center for the People and the Press shows that 54% regularly watch local news, 34% watch cable TV news, 28% watch nightly network news and 23% watch morning network news. About 40% read a newspaper and 36% listen to news on the radio. Finally, about 21% get news from the Internet regularly (three or more times per week). The average amount of time spent per day watching TV news was 53 minutes, followed by 43 minutes listening to radio news, 40 minutes reading the newspaper, and 32 minutes reading news online.[114]

So, most Americans do not follow the news closely. Yet, the nature of crime news is that it does not have to be followed closely, particularly at the national level. As will be illustrated later, crime news is prevalent at all levels of news coverage, even the local level. It should not be surprising, then, that the media are the people's main source of information about crime.[115] Kenneth Tunnell cites a National Crime Survey that found that 96% of Americans reported they relied on the media for information about crime.[116] Chuck Fields and Robert Jerin cite research showing that most Gallup poll respondents report believing that the media are accurate in their depictions of crime.[117]

Television is a more significant source of news for most than newspapers.[118] The average American spends more than three hours per day—about nine times as long as playing sports, exercising and all other leisure-time physical activities combined—watching TV.[119] In fact, the average American has his or her TV on for almost 7 hours per day! The average American child watches television between three and four hours per day.[120] Over the course of the whole year, the average child spends more time watching TV than he or she does in school, and most parents have no rules about how much TV their children can watch or even what they watch! Further, two to seventeen year olds spend more than four hours per day "in front of electronic screens (televisions, computers, and video games)."[121] People are less exposed to other sources of news information, such as newspapers, because television is more easily consumed; it can be taken in passively and does not require the ability to read in order to watch.[122]

According to the Gallup Polling Organization, who polls Americans on a variety of topics: "Americans are more likely now than at any point in the previous 15 years to say that news organizations' stories and reports are inaccurate. Additionally, about half of Americans perceive that there is a bias towards one political party or the other in the way news organizations report the news, and by a two-to-one margin, those who feel there is a bias say it favors the Democrats." Given that the mainstream media are owned by large corporations — who tend to be conservative by definition (and that newspaper editorials and talk radio are dominated by conservatives) — this is an interesting finding!

According to the Pew Project for Excellence in Journalism: "The public retained a deep skepticism about what they see, hear and read in the media. No major news outlet—broadcast or cable, print or online—stood out as particularly credible. There was no indication that Americans altered their fundamental judgment that the news media are politically biased, that stories are often inaccurate and that journalists do not care about the people they report on."[123]

There is a partisan divide with regard to news consumption. Both "liberals" and conservatives" see problems with certain media outlets (although they see problems in different outlets): "There continued to be a greater trust in the paper or TV station that people actually use than the generic 'media.' This suggests that the credibility issues with the media are, at least in part, frustration with outlets that people are choosing not to use. They are irritated with the press generally, but have choices they prefer."

In July 2007, 44% of Americans said they thought the media protects democracy versus 36% who said it hurts democracy. Compare this with July 1985 when the numbers were 54% and 23%, respectively. Further, in July 2007, only 39% of people said they think the media gets the facts straight versus 53% who said stories are often inaccurate. The comparative numbers for July 1985 were 55% and 34%, respectively. So, there is an increased awareness among Americans about the role that the media play in its democracy.

In terms of both believability and respectability for newspapers, the *Wall Street Journal* ranked the highest, followed by "your local newspaper." In last place is the *National Enquirer*. For news networks, CNN was ranked the highest for believability, just ahead of CBS' *60 Minutes*, local TV news and NPR. Fox News ranked just behind NBC and ABC but just ahead of the *NewsHour* (PBS) and CBS News, followed in last by the BBC. These numbers varied widely by self-identified political party affiliation (e.g., liberals believe MSNBC while conservatives believe Fox).

The Pew Research Center for the People and the Press adds that: "Public displeasure with the national news media is clear, but this sentiment has not eroded the credibility of major news organizations. While public evaluations of most news organizations' credibility are lower than they were in the mid-1980s, the basic believability ratings have not changed since the Center's last survey in 1996."[124]

The words people choose to describe the national media reflect their discontent. 'Biased' and 'sensational' were used nearly as often as 'good' and 'informative' when survey participants were asked to come up with one word to describe their impression of the national news media. On balance, negative words outnumbered positive ones 52% to 30%." Further: "Displeasure with the national news media in general does not translate, however, into lower believability ratings for specific news organizations. On average, majorities say they can believe most, but not all of what national news organizations say. A fair share of Americans are real doubters, however."

Gallup Polls consistently show that a majority of Americans believe that crime has increased on a national scale over the past year and that at least 40% of Americans in any year believe crime has increased in their own neighborhoods. According to the Gallup Organization, when speaking of its 2003 poll: "The poll was conducted as the news media were covering a series of sniper shootings in the Washington, D.C. area, which could affect the public's perceptions about the crime rate." Even though respondents were no more likely to report being worried about being a crime victim and were no more likely to report taking precautions to prevent their own victimization, this poll shows the power of the media when it comes to informing public opinion. As noted earlier, when the media cover crime more, it leads to the perception that crime is increasing, even when it is not.

Since images of crime tend to depict certain groups of society more than others as bad, deviant, and immoral, they reinforce stereotypes created by U.S. criminal law. In Chapter 3 you'll see that the law is made disproportionately by older, wealthier, white males. Further, the people who vote for law-makers tend to be older, wealthier than the average person, and white, and most people do not vote regularly. Finally, successful political campaigns require an enormous amount of money. This money tends to come from older, wealthier whites, in the form of personal campaign contributions, Political Action Committee (PAC) donations, and lobbying. These facts raise the serious possibility that the criminal law will tend to define those harmful acts as crimes that are committed by people most unlike law-makers. These people—young, poor, minority males—are most likely to end up being processed through agencies of criminal justice, ending up incarcerated.[125] To the degree media coverage of crime and criminal justice tends to show these people more than others, it reinforces the belief that poor, young, minority males are more criminal than the rest of us.

Summary

The media do not tell the public what to think, but they may tell the public what to think about. Those topics and issues that are covered in the media are often perceived to be important and worthy of viewer attention. The media clearly play a major role in creating and maintaining perceptions of social problems. By broadcasting stories, the media alert and even alarm the public and lawmakers about important events and issues.

Yet, the media are not the only source of information from which a person constructs his or her own reality. Four primary sources are used, including personal experiences, significant others (peers, family, friends), other social groups and institutions (schools, churches, government agencies), and the mass media. The influence of the mass media likely increases as the influence of the other sources declines. When it comes to crime and criminal justice, the media are a prime source of information, largely because most people have limited experience with criminal victimization or agencies of criminal justice.

There are two competing explanations of media coverage of problems such as crime, the objective model and the subjective model. The first holds that the media objectively report the news with no intent of bias or favoritism, and that the media try to remain neutral, balanced, and reliable. Objective journalism is difficult, if not impossible, due to several factors, including: decisions of newsworthiness, priority, framing, and marketability.

The latter holds that the media play a major role in socially constructing knowledge. This process occurs in five major steps. The first stage in the social construction process is news reporting of a real (but limited) social problem. The second stage in the social construction process occurs when the media blow the limited problem out of proportion to the threat it actually poses, creating the illusion of a larger problem than actually exists. The third stage of the social construction process is when the nature of the problem is typified in media coverage, meaning it is represented in a typical fashion each time through a pre-established frame. Here, common frames and narratives are used to make stories easier to tell. The fourth stage in the social construction process is called linkage where problems are linked to other social problems typically related to powerless groups. The fifth stage in the social construction process occurs when a policy is created (e.g., a new law), which is legitimated through the media. Understanding the social construction process allows us to see how sometimes the media can transform a relatively minor problem into a major one.

Socially constructed reality is made up of experienced reality as well as symbolic reality. The former is made up of that which is directly experienced, such as victimization from crime, whereas the latter is that which is believed to be true but that has never been personally experienced. Most of us are never victims of serious violent crimes, thus our knowledge of them is mostly symbolic in nature. A large part of one's symbolic reality with regard to a social problem such as crime comes from media coverage.

Changes to public policies typically occur after powerful interests construct or create social problems from objective social conditions. When an objective social problem is blown out of proportion, the result can be a moral panic. Moral panics are common in the U.S. and often revolve around social problems such as drugs and crime.

Television is a more significant source of news for most than newspapers. The average American spends more than three hours per day watching TV and the average American has his or her TV on for almost 7 hours per day. People are less exposed to other sources of news information, such as newspapers, because television is more easily consumed; it can be taken in passively and does not require the ability to read in order to watch.

Discussion Questions

1) Do the media tell the public what to think or what to think about? Explain.
2) How do the media impact social problems?
3) From what other sources besides the media do people get information? Is the media the most important source of information about crime and criminal justice? Explain.
4) Are the media accurate in their depictions of important stories such as crime and politics? Explain.
5) Do the media favor one political party over the other in their coverage of major issues? Explain.
6) Contrast the *objective model* of media coverage with the *subjective model* of media coverage.
7) Define *neutrality*, *balance*, and *reliability* and explain how these relate to objectivity.
8) What makes objective journalism difficult, if not impossible, to accomplish. Discuss the role of decisions of *newsworthiness*, *priority*, *framing* and *marketability* in news coverage.
9) What are the major stages of construction of social problems in the media?
10) Define and contrast *frames* and *narratives*. What are the most common frames and narratives used in media coverage of crime and criminal justice?
11) Define *socially constructed reality* and contrast it with *experienced reality* and *symbolic reality*. Provide examples of each.
12) What is a *moral panic*? Provide examples.
13) What media sources are most relied upon by Americans for information? How much time do Americans spend with each source of information?

Chapter 3

Media Coverage of Law-making and Crime, Part I: Focus on the Random, the Serious, and the Violent

Learning Objectives

After reading this chapter, you will be able to:

1) Explain to what degree corporations donate to political campaigns.
2) Explain how the criminal law might be biased in favor of some interests over others.

3) Discuss who makes the law, who votes for it, who donates money to it, and explain why this matters.
4) Explain to what degree law-making activities are covered in the media and when new laws are likely to be covered and when are they not likely to be covered.
5) Outline major problems with the USA PATRIOT Act.
6) Explain why the media failed to provide critical coverage of the USA PA-TRIOT Act.
7) Identify major misconceptions of crime held by many citizens.
8) Explain how the media are responsible for these misconceptions of crime.
9) Explain which types of crime generate the most media coverage.
10) Explain why *serious crimes* generate the most media coverage.
11) Identify what types of homicides are most likely to be covered in the media.
12) Explain why serial killing is so popular in the media.
13) Explain why random crime is so popular in the media.
14) Characterize media coverage of social problems such as school violence and sexual assault and stalking.

Introduction

Most of the research into media coverage of crime and criminal justice pertains to how the media cover crime. Findings consistently show that the mainstream media tend to cover street crime much more frequently than acts of white-collar and corporate crime, even though the latter are much more damaging to society. Further, research into media coverage tends to be focused on the most violent, random, bizarre, and sensational types of street crimes, even though these are the least common types of crimes. And of course, entertainment media are heavily focused on crime and violence— from movies to music to video games. What has received far less attention from scholars is how the media cover (and ignore) the process of law-making. This chapter examines how the media cover law-making and some forms of crime. Findings are related to important concepts introduced in Chapters 1 and 2.

Media and the Law

The way the media exercise their power begins with law-making. Corporations, including those that own the media, are among the three major sources of money for political campaigns, along with wealthy individuals and political action committees (PACs). According to the Center for Responsive Politics, the communications and electronics lobby gave $3.2 billion to political candidates and parties between 1998 and 2009, 59% to Democrats and 41% to Republicans. This includes $263 million given by TV/Movies/Music companies, 70% of which went to Democrats. Perhaps it is not surprising that, when Republicans controlled Congress earlier in the century, a much larger portion of funds went to the Republican Party. The communications and electronics lobby, representing major media corporations, is one of the top 15 industries donating to federal political parties and candidates in any given year.[1]

Access to the Law

Most legal scholars agree that the wealthy have much more access to the law than the common citizen. This is because the wealthy are more likely to be among the law-making bodies of society, more likely to vote for them, and more likely to give money to them through donations and lobbying efforts.

Justitia, the lady justice, is depicted on courthouses and other government buildings across the country. Her blindfold is often interpreted to mean the government is blind to race, gender, social class and other extra-legal factors so that everyone is treated equally in the eyes of the law. In fact, there is much evidence that the law is tilted in favor of some interests above others, largely because of who has the greatest access to the law. http://www.publicpropertyuk.com/wp-content/uploads/2010/08/lady-justice1.jpg.

First, when compared to the general population, lawmakers look very different from the average American. They are older and much more likely to be male, white, and wealthy. For example, in 2010, the base pay of Senators and Representatives in Congress was $174,000. Congressional leaders receive $193,400 per year, whereas the Speaker of the House receives $223,500. This is more than four times the average pay of Congress' constituents. Base salary is only what legislators get paid; it does not include their net worth nor the numerous benefits and perks they receive.[2] Further, the average Senator in 2008 was worth nearly $15 million, whereas the average member of the House was worth about $5 million.[3]

Many claim that these millionaire lawmakers have potential conflicts of interest given their financial interests in various corporations.[4] It's at least important to recognize that law-makers are tied to the same corporations that own the media as well as other corporations that share similar views.

Lawmakers at the state level also tend to be wealthier than their constituents. Although their pay tends to actually be quite modest relative to that of federal lawmakers, state legislators are employed on a part-time basis, and they tend to already be wealthy due to their full-time careers, in industries such as law, business, banking, and so forth.[5]

Second, most people do not regularly vote. Of those that do, voters are also not representative of the general population. Voters tend to be older, white, and wealthier. For example, the highest level of voter registration and reported voting is for people who earn more than $150,000 per year, while the lowest is for people who earn less than $15,000 per year.[6]

Third, most people do not give money to political parties of candidates. Yet, there is a lot of money involved in the political system, and money helps determine the outcomes of most elections. The average House candidate raised more than $660,000 in 2006, and the average Senate candidate raised more than $3.3 million. Where does this money come from? It comes from major corporations, wealthy individuals, and *Political Action Committees* (PACs) in the form of campaign donations. PACs are groups organized to raise and spend money on political campaigns. PACs typically represent corporate, labor, and ideological interests, and are allowed to give $2,300 to any candidate per election, $5,000 to any other PAC, $10,000 to any state or local party committee, and $28,500 annually to any national party. Individuals can also donate the same amounts per election.[7]

Recall from Chapter 1 that the major media corporations lobby together as part of the National Association of Broadcasters (NAB), which is evidence of the cooperative rather than competitive nature of media companies. In 2008, the NAB gave $1,017,784 in campaign contributions to federal officials and parties. This ranked 7th in TV/Movies/Music media companies, following Comcast, Time Warner (CNN News), National Amusements, National Cable & Telecommunications Association, Disney (ABC News), and the News Corporation (Fox News), and ranked ahead of General Electric (NBC), Sony, and Clear Channel.[8]

The top ten industries donating to American politics through lobbying include pharmaceuticals, insurance, computers, business associations, electric utilities, education, real estate, hospitals, oil and gas, and entertainment media (TV, movies, music).[9] What is important is that these industries give money to both political parties; the significance is that whichever party wins will have received sizeable sums of money from these industries. Meanwhile, far less than 1% of the population donates $200 or more to a political candidate or party in any given year. Thus, the typical citizen is left with the realization that his or her vote, letter, phone call, fax, e-mail, personal visit, and vote carries relatively little weight in a political process driven by money.

Given these realities, we could logically expect the institution of the law to be founded on similar interests as the institutions of the media and that the law would likely serve the interests of the corporations that own the media. Further, we could logically expect the mainstream media to have little interest in exposing potential problems with the law that may benefit those interests. None of this is meant to sound conspiratorial; there is little to no evidence that lawmakers and media corporations agree ahead of time to ignore behaviors by corporations or to serve their limited interests.

Passage of Laws

Coverage of law-making activities is common in the media, particularly the activities of local, state, and federal legislative activities. When new laws are passed, mainstream media commonly report their passage, effective dates, as well as implementation. Typically, passage of new laws (especially local ordinance and state laws) is noted in newspaper stories, reminding us of the importance of newspapers as well as locally aware newspapers (as opposed to chain newspapers owned by large corporations that are less interested in and capable of covering local stories). That laws are codified and then summarized in the media is extremely important to inform citizens of what the law says, because ignorance of the law is no excuse in cases where it is violated.

The passage of criminal law is highly significant for all criminal justice activity, for without the law, there would be no need to arrest, convict, and punish people for breaking the law. A behavior becomes a crime only when it is labeled a crime through the passage of a *law*. The law consists of rules for behavior that carry consequences when violated. When lawmakers at the state and federal level view behaviors as wrong, immoral, unethical, or harmful, there is a significant possibility that the behaviors will be legislated as crimes. Thus, crimes are created when elected representatives decide to codify, or write down, behaviors as wrong, immoral, unethical, or harmful.

Crimes are created by the U.S. Congress at the federal level, by legislatures at the state level, and by courts at every level of government when they interpret the law and set precedents through case law.[10] The Congress at the federal level and all state legislatures have the power to define behaviors as crimes. For example, at both levels of government, it is against the law to force or coerce someone into unwanted sexual activity; this is called rape or sexual assault.

Courts interpret the meaning of the written law and, in so doing, actually clarify what the written law means. In the case of sexual assault, courts will confront issues pertaining to defining terms such as "coercion" or "force." Courts help make law by setting precedents that all other courts in the same jurisdiction will be required to follow.

The media generally devote coverage to court activities such as rulings on matters of law. This is especially true in highly publicized cases that are tracked from the initial crime all the way to each and every court ruling pertaining to it. Perhaps not surprisingly, rulings by the U.S. Supreme Court receive the most attention in the press. Cases with large implications, like *Bush v Gore* (2000)—which ultimately decided the 2000 Presidential election—receive enormous attention in the media. Not reported in the mainstream press in the *Bush* case were allegations made by middle and outer ring (second and third-tier) journalists that members of the U.S. Supreme Court had potential conflicts of interests that may have swayed their votes toward the Bush argument in the case.[11]

Interestingly, in spite of the intense coverage of the *Bush v Gore* case, it did not lead to increased understanding of Supreme Court behavior.[12] Perhaps this is because the media generally portray the Supreme Court as "inherently apolitical," or not influenced heavily by policies. Scholars assert this is the "myth of legality." Research does show that when media reports depict the Court as political, citizens react more negatively.[13]

Lack of Depth/Context: The Case of the USA PATRIOT Act

Given that there are thousands of laws passed across the United States every year, it is not surprising that the media do not devote stories to all or even most of these laws. Yet, surprisingly, the media often fail to report in any depth

There was intense coverage of the 2000 presidential election between Texas Governor George W. Bush and Tennessee Senator Al Gore, including the ultimate 5–4 decision stopping all recounts and effectively awarding George W. Bush the presidency. Theodore Olson, pictured, would successfully argue the case for Bush and then go on to serve as Solicitor General of the United States. http://upload.wikimedia.org/wikipedia/commons/9/99/Theodore_Olsen_-_2010_-_David_Shankbone.jpg.

and with little context on the passage of very important laws. For example, consider media coverage of the USA PATRIOT Act (an acronym for "Uniting and Strengthening America by Providing Appropriate Tools Required to Intercept and Obstruct Terrorism"), which was passed and signed into law within two months of the terrorist attacks of September 11, 2001. This law was meant to be a temporary law (to sunset at the end of 2005) and was intended to prevent another devastating attack on U.S. soil, which U.S. officials asserted was imminent.[14] Although many parts of the law were non-problematic and indeed necessary to protect the country, other parts of the law posed serious threats to civil liberties and were probably not necessary to protect the nation from terrorism.

For example, the law allows government police agencies to access medical, financial, library, educational, and other personal records of any people as long "a significant purpose" is for "the gathering of foreign intelligence" and to forbid librarians and business owners & employees from informing people that their records have been requested or seized. Government agents can tap any and all phones of citizens and monitor their Internet use, tracking every phone call made and received and every web site visited. Under orders from the Justice Department, police can also enter people's homes and seize their property without even informing them a search has taken place (through "sneak and peek warrants"). Law enforcement agencies are empowered to spy on religious and political organizations and individuals without any evidence of criminal activity. Americans can be labeled "domestic terrorists" if they engage in "[criminal] acts dangerous to human life" in a way that "influences the policy of a government by intimidation or coercion" or "intimidates or coerces a civilian population."

One of the most troubling provisions of the law is how it modified the use of Foreign Intelligence Surveillance Act (FISA) warrants. The FISA Court is a top-secret court created in 1978 by Congress for "the purpose" of regulating foreign intelligence gathering activities. Amended by the USA PATRIOT Act, the Court now can grant secret warrants for investigation of normal criminal matters, as long as "a significant purpose" is for intelligence gathering. Senator Orrin Hatch (R-UT), offered the following clarification, as part of the Congressional Record (2002): "It was our intent when we included the plain language of Section 218 of the USA PATRIOT Act and when we voted for the Act as a whole to change FISA to allow a foreign intelligence surveillance warrant to be obtained when 'a significant' purpose of the surveillance was to gather foreign intelligence, even when the primary purpose of the surveillance was the gathering of criminal evidence." The change in language from "the purpose" to "a significant purpose" is important, because it allows the Justice Department to investigate normal American citizens for nonterrorist criminal matters using secret warrants granted by the top secret FISA Court, thereby eroding the Fourth Amendment's protection of unreasonable search and seizure. Since such warrants are secret, they may not be challenged or appealed by suspects.

In fact, a July 2004 report by the U.S. Justice Department—*Report from the Field: The USA PATRIOT Act at Work*—admits that normal American citizens have been investigated, arrested, convicted, and punished for engaging in ordinary, non terrorist related crimes (such as child pornography, domestic violence, sexual assault, and an array of computer-related crimes). What is troublesome about these cases is that the USA PATRIOT Act was not stated as a law that would be used this way (its stated purpose was "To deter and punish terrorist acts in the United States and around the world, to enhance law enforcement investigatory tools, and for other purposes"), and the law is thus being used to make an end run around the U.S. Constitution to solve normal, non-terrorist criminal cases.

🖐 For more about how the USA PATRIOT Act erodes Constitutional rights, see the website for this book at: www.pscj.appstate.edu/media/usa patriotact.html

---

One might think that such an erosion of American's civil liberties as contained in the Bill of Rights to the U.S. Constitution would receive significant media attention. Yet, this was not the case. Lisa Abdolian and Harold Takooshian assert:

> Many commentators, including members of the media itself, say the press has failed to do its job as the guardian of democracy. Very few news reports filled in the basic blanks—the who, what, where, when, and why—about U.S. policy, the USA PATRIOT Act, and the government's insistence on the need for secrecy and more power. Very few news reports discussed the dangers involved in pushing aside civil liberties during a national crisis. In fact, most stories about the country's response were positive.... the USA PATRIOT Act was hailed as a unified nation's quick response to the terrorist strike. Some of the more troubling aspects of the legislation received little or no scrutiny by the media until months after it became law.[15]

The authors assert that, in the wake of the horrific attacks, it would have been "unthinkable" for the media to critically analyze and report on the 342 page bill. Thus: "Most mainstream media simply reported that the legislation had passed." For example, stories about the bill's passage made it to the front page of mainstream newspapers. Yet, there was "little debate" about its provisions "during a time when even a member of Congress would provoke cries of heresy by questioning the President's request for additional powers to catch the evil-doers." Further, the major television networks "barely mentioned the new law. When the legislation was signed by the President, most stories in major newspapers focused on the positive aspects of the bill. In fact, shortly after its passage, some members of the press questioned whether the legislation went far enough to protect Americans." This was true even for supposedly left-leaning (i.e., liberal) outlets such as National Public Radio (NPR). A review of media coverage of the law by Fairness in Accuracy and Reporting (FAIR) in November 2001 found that there was literally no debate in the press on the nightly network newscasts.[16]

Reporters rarely asked critical questions about the law. When they did, they were told things like this by White House spokesman Ari Fleischer: "The press is asking a lot of questions that I suspect the American people would prefer not to be asked, or answered."[17] Perhaps the lack of critical coverage is not surprising given comments such as these from Attorney General John Ashcroft: " ... to those who scare peace-loving people with phantoms of lost liberty, my message is this: Your tactics only aid terrorists for they erode our national unity and diminish our resolve. They give ammunition to America' s enemies and pause to America' s friends. They encourage people of good will to remain silent in the face of evil."

Further, Ashcroft went on a national tour promoting the benefits of the law to law enforcement and military audiences. According to Peter Hart and Rachel Coen, he also actually asked the media for their help to accurately portray the law as something not new, not different and not "some vast incursion into the freedoms of the American people." Yet, as shown in a July 2003 report by the American Civil Liberties Union—"Patriot Propaganda: The Justice Department's Campaign to Mislead The Public About the Patriot Act"—Justice Department officials consistently made false statements about the law in the media.[18]

The mainstream press did not strongly challenge government officials about the law, in part because of their symbiotic relationship. As shown in Chapter 1, government officials rely on the media to get the word out about their favored policies and proposed laws, and the media rely on government officials for information and stories. As shown in Chapter 2, relying on government officials is thought by media personnel to make stories more objective because it makes them more reliable. Yet, recall that this is one of the five filters offered by Edward Herman and Noam Chomsky, something that limits the breadth of coverage on given topics. In the case of the USA PATRIOT Act, relying on government officials for information limited the breadth of discourse on the law. The lack of attention paid to the negative aspects of the USA PATRIOT Act may also be a good example of the anti-communist filter of the media put forth by Herman and Chomsky given that critics of the law were characterized by government officials as unpatriotic and even anti-American (even though they were actually trying to defend the civil liberties upon which America was supposedly founded).[19]

Even media outlets justified their lack of criticism, sometimes in the boldest of ways. For example, an op-ed in the *Washington Times* noted: "The media should be falling in line. The danger is great enough for us to cut back now on civil liberties. It's all a question of balance. I have been a civil libertarian and will be again in a couple of years. The terrorists will win when they kill us, and we will win when we kill them."[20] Of course, the *Washington Times* is owned by Rupert Murdoch, who also owns Fox News (which has been identified by research as a highly conservative news network).

Analyses of media coverage of the law suggest critical media coverage of the law did not occur until various organizations and institutions (e.g., the American Library Association) began to complain about and organize against the law.[21]

Eventually, critical coverage began but not for more than a year after the passage of the USA PATRIOT Act. For example, one story on NPR from November 2002 dealt with computers being confiscated by the Federal Bureau of Investigation in a Patterson, New Jersey, library. According to Lisa Abdolian and Harold Takooshian: "The story was straightforward with several highlighted opinions about racial profiling. The most telling aspect was the librarian's response to the FBI's visit: 'They had partitioned a hard drive, and you can do that and ... track things more easily, but we undid that. I mean we have people who have the expertise who could say, 'Well, wait a second. What did they do to this hard drive?'"[22]

Other stories included:

- A *Miami Herald* story about how the law "remained shrouded in mystery."
- A *Newsday* series titled "Taking Liberties" about secrecy and immigrants being targeted by elements of the law.
- A story in the *New York Times* about secrecy in the Bush Administration.
- A column in the *Los Angeles Times* questioning the necessity of the law.
- A story in the *San Jose Mercury News* challenging the law on grounds that it "tarnishes American ideals."
- A story in *The Nation* magazine suggesting abuse of power by government agencies.[23]

After communities began taking a stand by passing resolutions condemning certain provisions of the law, conservative media giants hosted spokespersons for community groups concerns about the law, yet attacked them as unpatriotic and worse. For example, Fox's Bill O'Reilly told Cambridge City Council member Brian Murphy that the city's decision not to cooperate with the [law] was unpatriotic and dangerous. Murphy explained that citizens of Cambridge were concerned because "this was passed in the wake of the heinous attacks of September 11 ... and was done without a lot of debate, without a lot of discussion." O'Reilly's response was: "So it looks to me like you're hysterical in Cambridge, not an uncommon thing for that town ... and you may be seditious, that you may be undermining this government" O'Reilly added, "You're basically taking steps that could lead to anarchy if every municipality did the same thing. And you're leaving all Americans vulnerable to this.... you're protesting and you're undermining the government." Murphy responded: "We are absolutely patriotic. But our patriotism doesn't derive from a law that tries to cram the word "patriot" into its title so that it can wrap itself in the flag, but rather a patriotism ... that derives from the Constitution and the Bill of Rights and the civil liberties that have really made this country ... the greatest nation there is." O'Reilly answered, "You're protesting and you're undermining the government and you don't even know if anybody's rights are being violated."[24]

Another example was Fox's Sean Hannity, who took on Hope Marston, a member of the Eugene, Oregon City Council. Marston suggested the city passed a resolution against the law because "people ... are concerned about liberty and protecting our Bill of Rights," and Hannity then described the resolution as "meaningless." He continued: "Hope, you know, you may have forgotten, but America got attacked on September 11th. You may have forgotten all of this. There are people plotting and planning and scheming right now in America ... And you're creating hysteria where there need not be hysteria."[25]

In fact, not only have citizens learned that the law has been used in normal criminal matters, we also know that the FBI has requested records from libraries and businesses thousands of times, that peace groups have been infiltrated, that people have been spied on based on their religion, and even the Justice Department has documented violations of civil liberties and civil rights under the USA PATRIOT Act.[26] Thus, more than 400 government bodies representing towns and counties as well as 8 state legislatures have passed resolutions condemning the USA PATRIOT Act. Nevertheless, the law has not been rescinded. Further, the provisions that were due to sunset at the end of 2005 have now been made permanent law.[27] Most Americans are unaware of these realities, likely because the media have failed to devote significant attention to them.

When the Justice Department planned for a "PATRIOT Act II"—the Domestic Security Enhancement Act of 2003—there was little media coverage of it either. According to a report by FAIR, the following media outlets mentioned the proposed law:

- A segment on Fox's "The Big Story With John Gibson."
- A story in the *Washington Post* on the front page followed by a news brief and an editorial.
- Articles in *New York Times* and *Los Angeles Times* on inside pages, as well as the *Chicago Tribune* and New York's *Newsday.*
- A brief news item in the *Seattle Times* and editorials in the *San Francisco Chronicle* and *Rocky Mountain News.*[28]

The law would have created a DNA database of "suspected terrorists," allow the U.S. government to "expatriate" American citizens "if, with the intent to relinquish his nationality, he becomes a member of, or provides material support to, a group that the United Stated has designated as a 'terrorist organization'" among other things. Yet, according to FAIR: "The story was apparently ignored by ABC, CBS and NBC's nightly newscasts and newsmagazine shows." This may be evidence of the anti-communist filter used by the media to weed out seemingly unimportant stories (in their eyes) from inclusion in the news. Still, it should be pointed out that even the limited media coverage of the proposed law may have been enough to prevent it from being enacted.

Given that the media are the primary source of information for Americans on matters related to the law and crime,[29] the lack of media coverage of such important laws raises troubling concerns. Most notably, if the news media fail to ask critical questions of government on such laws—much less even report on them—how will Americans become aware of them and then learn the truth about them? Recall the argument of Chapter 1 that a healthy democracy requires information. The mainstream press is the primary source of such information. Thus, an absence of media coverage of such laws can be seen as a threat to democracy itself.

Media and Crime

To begin, it is important to understand that crime news is a subset of "disorder news" and is typically cast as a threat to the social order.[30] Knowing this may help us understand how crime is typically portrayed in the media, as a phenomenon that comes from the bottom of society—the poor, the minority, the evil and the "crazy."

According to Steven Chermak, five criteria help determine whether a crime is newsworthy: 1) the nature of the offense; 2) demographic factors of the victim and offender; 3) the uniqueness of the event; 4) event salience; and 5) various characteristics of media agency.[31] According to Chermak, violence is more newsworthy than crimes committed against property, crimes against white and vulnerable victims like children are more newsworthy (especially if committed by people of color), novel incidents are often more newsworthy, and crimes that occur locally are more newsworthy. These are other issues will be discussed in this chapter.

Although images of crime are widespread in the media, the perceptions of crime held by Americans tend to be inaccurate. In fact, misconceptions of crime start at childhood, and the media play a major role in creating them.[32] According to Robert Bohm and Jeffery Walker, "the most important source of common conceptions and myths of crime and criminal justice is the media."[33]

Misconceptions of Crime

Matthew Robinson and Daniel Murphy show that citizens tend to hold three significant misconceptions of crime. First, people tend to assume that criminals are different from noncriminals (when in fact everyone is a criminal). Second, when people think of crime, they tend to think of violent crime (even though the vast majority of crime is property crime). Third, people are most afraid of street crime (even though the most dangerous crime is committed by elites).

With regard to the first point, even from the earliest self-report studies conducted—where potential offenders are asked about their involvement in criminality—studies have shown that virtually everyone is a criminal.[34] Tom O'Connor notes: "The results of most self-report studies are shocking. They typically indicate, that for any population (even a law-abiding one), about 90 percent of the people in the sample have committed a crime for which the punishment is more than a year in prison."[35]

Some people start committing crimes earlier than others (i.e., in early childhood), most start later (i.e., in adolescence). Some commit more serious crimes than others, most commit less serious crimes. Some persist in crime over their entire lives, most mature out of crime.[36] So, there are differences in the nature and extent of offenses committed by criminals; yet, it is clear that we are all criminals. This suggests, as long ago posited by Emile Durkheim, that crime is normal. In the words of Durkheim:

> Crime is present not only in the majority of societies of one particular species but in all societies of all types. There is no society that is not confronted with the problem of criminality. Its form changes; the acts thus characterized are not the same everywhere; but, everywhere and always, there have been men who have behaved in such a way as to draw upon themselves penal repression.[37]

Not only is street crime normal in the United States, we've long known that corporate crime is normal. For example, Edwin Sutherland's classic study of seventy of the largest corporations in the United States found that every one of them had violated the law at least once, with the average number of known violations being fourteen. Further, 98 percent of the corporations were recidivists, or repeat offenders, and 60 percent had been convicted of criminal offenses in courts.[38] Amazingly, corporate crime is even more widespread today than back in Sutherland's day.[39]

Even though criminality is normal in the U.S., media coverage of crime leads to the perception that it is abnormal and that it comes from people who are different than us—from certain racial, and class groups as well as the mentally ill. This issue is examined in this chapter as well as in Chapter 4.

With regard to the second point about the nature of crime, research demonstrates that when Americans think of crime, they tend to think of violent crime.

In fact, the great bulk of crime in any given year is committed against property, and the most common form of property crime in the United States is simple theft. For example, the Federal Bureau of Investigation (FBI) reports that in 2008 there were 6.6 million thefts known to the police, which represented 59% percent of all crimes known to the police in that year. Property crimes (theft, burglary, and motor vehicle theft) make up almost 90% of all crimes known to the police in any given year. If one added in robbery, a violent crime aimed at gaining property, the percentage of crimes committed against property rises above 90% of all crimes.[40]

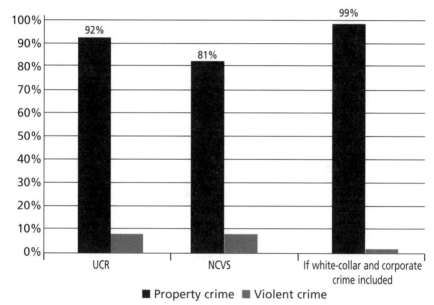

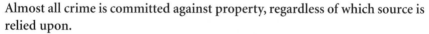

Almost all crime is committed against property, regardless of which source is relied upon.

These crime data are from the Uniform Crime Reports (UCR), a source which only includes crimes known to the police. Yet, data from the National Crime Victimization Survey (NCVS)—data that include victimizations *not* reported to the police—depict a similar picture. For example, 2005 NCVS data show that 77 percent of all criminal victimizations were committed against property.[41] When robbery and purse snatchings are included, property crimes made up 80.6 percent of all victimizations in 2005.[42]

Neither the UCR nor the NCVS contain significant data on white-collar and corporate crime. When one adds property loss due to corporations' illegal and deviant behaviors, more than 99 percent of all crime is likely property crime. One major reason why Americans think of violent crime instead of property crime is that the media focus on it so widely. This issue is addressed later in the chapter.

Regarding the third point, Americans are under the impression that the greatest threat to their personal safety and property comes from below—the poor. This is a myth.[43] In reality, the greatest threats to the health and welfare of American citizens come from above—the wealthy.[44] This is another way of saying that *street crimes* (those crimes disproportionately committed by the poor and middle class) are actually not as dangerous as *corporate and white-collar crimes* which together encompass elite deviance.[45] *Elite deviance* includes not only criminal acts but also unethical acts, civil and regulatory violations, and other harmful acts committed intentionally (i.e., on purpose), recklessly (i.e., without regard for life or property), negligently (i.e., by failing to do something required of you), or knowingly (i.e., with the knowledge that an outcome is likely to occur). Elite deviance includes *white-collar crime,*[46] *corporate crime,*[47] *corporate violence,*[48] *occupational crime,*[49] *governmental deviance,*[50] *crimes of the state,*[51] *crimes of privilege,*[52] *profit without honor,*[53] and those *crimes by any other name*[54] committed by our *trusted criminals.*[55]

Since there are no national data source on white-collar and corporate crime, we must rely on estimates by government agencies and research scholars to establish the harms caused by white-collar and corporate crime. When including the annual costs of health care fraud ($80 billion), insurance fraud ($80 billion), computer fraud ($67 billion), securities and commodities fraud ($40 billion), telemarketing fraud ($40 billion), automotive repair fraud ($22 billion), check fraud ($10 billion), and defective products ($700 billion including indirect costs such as lost productivity), the costs of elite deviance top $1 trillion per year![56] As for street crime, direct costs include about $20 billion annually; when indirect costs such as lost productivity are added, the costs exceed $100 billion. Whatever the true amount caused by elite deviance, white-collar and corporate crime is far more damaging than street crime.

Not surprisingly, Americans fear street crime far more than they do acts of white-collar and corporate crime. This is entirely predictable given the way the media cover crime.[57] This chapter and Chapter 4 will show how the media focus on street crime and ignore white-collar and corporate crime. The results, according to Dan Gardner, are dangerous—we focus on those behaviors that pose smaller risks to us than the ones we ignore.[58] This puts us at greater risk of victimization by those things we ignore.

Donna Bishop offers three major facts about media coverage of crime. First, more than 25% of media coverage of crime is about murder, even though "murders constitute less than one percent of all crimes known to the police." Second, "the incidence of particular types of violence is exaggerated." Even

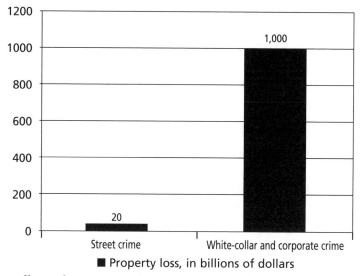

Property loss, in billions of dollars

White-collar and corporate crime cost far more than street crime every year.

though most violent crime is committed by someone against someone they know, "stranger crime is much more likely to be covered." Third, media coverage of crime is racially distorted: "Most violent crime is intraracial, but violent offenses involving black male assailants and white victims are much more likely to receive saturation news coverage."[59] These and other issues are discussed below and in Chapter 4.

Serious and Violent Crime

Of all types of crime, "serious crime" generates more media coverage.[60] The term "serious" is synonymous with street crime but it also has a specific meaning. In the 1920s, the International Association of Chiefs of Police (IACP) formed a committee to create a uniform system for recording police statistics. Crimes were originally evaluated on the basis of the following criteria:

- Harmfulness.
- Frequency of occurrence.
- Pervasiveness in all geographic areas of the country.
- Likelihood of being reported to the police.

After a preliminary compilation in 1929 of a list of crimes that met these criteria, the committee completed their plan for developing the Uniform Crime Reports (now compiled each year by the Federal Bureau of Investigation). Statistics on these crimes were collected beginning in the 1930s.

As noted within each year's UCR publication: "Seven offenses were chosen to serve as an Index for gauging the overall volume and rate of crime."[61] These offenses, known as *Part I Index Offenses*, included the violent crimes of murder and nonnegligent manslaughter, forcible rape, robbery, and aggravated assault and the property crimes of burglary, theft, and motor vehicle theft. In 1979, arson was added to the UCR list, for a total of eight "serious" crimes.

These serious street crimes tend to bring forth images of poor people, the very people most focused on by the media when it comes to criminality. Consider the aftermath of Hurricane Katrina, in 2005, for example. Most media focused on the crimes committed by a very small segment of people, creating the impression that the entire city of New Orleans was suffering from lawlessness, looting, murder, rape, and other mayhem.[62] What received far less media coverage by most mainstream media outlets was the degree of culpability of elites in this disaster.[63] Among other things, powerful people were responsible for the disappearance of the wetlands just offshore that would have weakened the hurricane prior to its landfall, as well as for cuts in funding for the New Orleans Corps of Engineers that prevented work on major hurricane protection and flooding projects, and for shipping National Guardsmen and supplies normally used in rescue efforts to Iraq to fight a war!

Why would the media focus so much on crimes committed by suffering people in the aftermath of a natural disaster (as well as those who flocked there to pray on them), while simultaneously ignoring the culpable behaviors of those elites who made decisions that exacerbated the damage done by the storm? Consider again lessons learned in the first two chapters of this book: First, mainstream press are owned by large corporations; Second, media corporations are strongly vested in the corporate system and have numerous close ties with elites in both the corporate and government worlds; Third, the media tend to filter out stories that seriously threaten the status quo, including stories that trouble the executives that own the press as well as serious, critical stories that will interfere with the buying mood; Fourth, entertainment draws larger audiences than serious journalism; Fifth, street violence is, for many, entertaining. Finally, it is logical that bringing up issues of culpability of the Bush Administration for its limited natural disaster preparations and cutbacks to hurricane preparation funding may result in a reaffirmation of a "liberal bias" in the news media.

Given the definition of a serious offense, you might expect that the street crimes of murder, rape, robbery, assault and so forth would be the ones that cause the greatest harm (either physical or financial), occur with great frequency, are pervasive throughout the country, and are likely to be reported to the police. In discussing the eight types of serious crime in each annual UCR report, it is claimed that "These are serious crimes by nature and/or volume."[64]

That is, these crimes supposedly cause the most harm, occur with the greatest frequency, and are the most widespread. However, this is not the case. Corporate and white-collar crime actually occur with greater frequency, are more widespread, and do more harm than serious street crimes. As will be shown in this chapter, the media tend to instead focus their attention on street crime, especially serious street crime and particularly violent street crime.

Recall a lesson from earlier in the book that the media thrives on conflict. Violent crime obviously fits the bill. Jim Ruiz and D.F. Treadwell add: "One of the unwritten rules of the news media is that good news is not news."[65] Violent crime victimization is bad news, thus it is deemed newsworthy by virtually every news agency. Chris Greer adds that crimes that can be easily made to fit into antipodal sides—the cold-blooded, evil offender versus the innocent victim are more likely to be considered newsworthy.[66] These are the dominant narratives of media coverage of crime, as noted in the last chapter. Violent crime can also fit this description well. Finally, others point out that the potential to titillate is important.[67] For whatever reason, violent crimes are seen as titillating to the public.

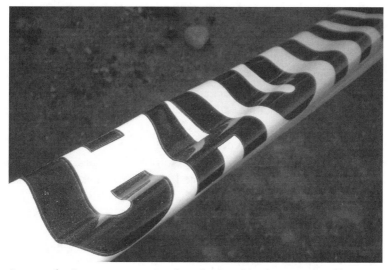

The image of crime scene tape is often depicted in the news media, especially when it comes to serious and violent street crimes. http://en.wikipedia.org/wiki/File:Caution_Tape.jpg.

The media are more interested in those "serious" crimes that involve dramatic, sentimental, whimsical and unusual elements, and that involve famous peo-

ple. Robert Bohm and Jeffery Walker suggest that this is especially true with regard to coverage of crime in entertainment media.[68] Yet, research also clearly
demonstrates that crime news is focused on the most violent types of crime,[69]
at least those that occur at the street level.[70] Of particular interest to the media
are the rarest and "most egregious examples" of crime.

As should be abundantly clear by now, media portrayals of crime are "se-
lectively determine[d]" by media outlets.[71] Generally, decisions are made to
feature the most sensational, significant, and emotional aspects of crime that
lead to higher rates of public viewing due to their universally appealing nature.[72] Sensational stories, live stories, and stories that involve guns are more
likely to appear in U.S. markets.[73] For example, the media cover the most sensational and unusual parricide cases (i.e., killings of parents).[74]

As David Krajicek said about his own work as a crime reporter, crime reports
focus on the miserable, the deviant, the strange, and the "particularly cruel."[75]
The common saying, "if it bleeds, it leads," accurately characterizes the philosophy of the media in the United States. Roslyn Muraskin and Shelly Domash agree, writing: "The cliché phrase, 'if it bleeds, it leads' is unfortunately
the case with the American media; the search for heinous, outrageous and even
sexy crimes, no matter how rare the incident … is sure to boost ratings."[76] Some
have referred to the nightly news as "Armageddon—Live at 6 (p.m.)!"[77]

Television news generally shows violence at a rate much higher than its incidence in society would seem to justify.[78] As noted by David Krajicek: "Murder and sexual offenses are the marquee offenses … and certain cases, generally
based upon nubility or celebrity, are anointed for extravagant coverage."[79] And
so-called *mega cases* (which typically pertain to celebrities) generate the most
media attention.[80] Such cases will be discussed later in this chapter.

Consider how prevalent violence is depicted on the nightly news: "The Center for Media and Public Affairs found that crime has been the most prominently
featured topic on the evening news since 1993, with 7,448 stories, or about 1
in 7 evening news stories."[81] And 1 in 20 stories since 1993 has been about
murder.[82] A study of single crime stories featured on ABC World News Tonight,
CBS Evening News, and NBC Nightly News by the Center for Media and Public Affairs found that murder led all stories by far, followed by gun control, the
death penalty, and terrorism.[83]

A review of studies of media coverage and crime found that for every two
stories of property crimes, there were eight stories of violent crimes. Newspapers in the mid-1980s covered the violent crimes of murder, rape, robbery,
and assault four times more than they did the property crimes of theft, burglary, and motor vehicle theft, even though property crimes make up at least
90% of street crimes in any given year.[84]

By focusing on certain types of crimes over others, the media are involved in "constructing" the typical view of crime, even when they are only reporting "extreme, dramatic cases: the public is more likely to think they are representative because of the emphasis by the media."[85] This is consistent not with the objective model discussed in Chapter 2 but instead with the subjective model. Gary Potter and Victor Kappeler explain: "Media coverage directs people's attention to specific crimes and helps to shape those crimes as social problems." This means Americans are much more concerned with violent crimes such as murder, even though they are much more likely to be victimized by property crimes such as theft and burglary (and especially acts of white-collar and corporate crime that receive virtually no coverage).[86]

While all forms of news are interested in crime—what Kenneth Tunnell refers to as the "commodification of crime"[87]—not all stations cover crime the same. For example, a five-week content analysis of crime stories reported on television news, including three nightly newscasts from a national network, a big city television station, and a small town channel found that coverage of crime varied widely on the three channels.[88] Specifically, the big city station showed more crime stories than the national station and the local station. Further, while the national newscast focused mostly on violence (55%), it also had significant coverage of acts of white-collar and corporate crime (23%). The big city station were more focused on violence (65%) and less focused on white-collar and corporate crime (10%). As for the local stations, it was focused far more on drug offenses (33%), while violence accounted for only 30% of the crime stories. There were no stories about white-collar and corporate crime.

Homicide

Homicide, being violent and perceived as the most serious crime of all, is usually news. One study showed that 26% of news stories were focused on murder, even though murder regularly accounts for only a tiny fraction of 1% of all crimes known to the police.[89] Although murder may be the most heinous of all crimes, this disproportionate focus does not seem justified by its prevalence in the United States. When compared to other countries, the U.S. rate of murder is average.

At the same time, even though about half of the crimes that are reported to the police are nonviolent, they made up only 4% of the stories in the same study. Additionally, it is the most heinous and bizarre of all murders that tend to be most widely discussed in the media.[90]

Another study of newspaper coverage of homicide in Houston, Texas found that those homicides that were the least common (i.e., female victims, young

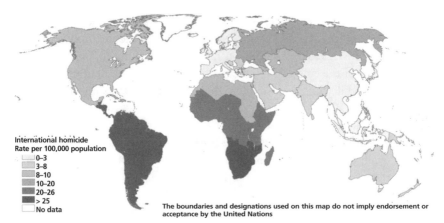

International homicide
Rate per 100,000 population
0–3
3–8
8–10
10–20
20–26
> 25
No data

The boundaries and designations used on this map do not imply endorsement or acceptance by the United Nations

The rate of murder in the United States is average when compared to other countries, and is roughly one-tenth what it is in countries with the highest rates. http://www.unodc.org/images/data-and-analysis/homicide_rate_map.pdf.

victims, multiple victim incidents) were the most likely to be covered. Homicides that were the most common were the least covered (i.e., male victims, minority victims, single victim incidents).[91] This is consistent with the claim of Jessica Pollak and Charis Kubrin that "news reporting follows the law of opposites—the characteristics of crime, criminals, and victims represented in the media are in most respects the polar opposite of the pattern suggested by official crime statistics."[92] It is also evidence that the media are interested in the unusual, whatever it is.

The majority of the 249 homicide incidents investigated by the Houston Police Department involved minority male offenders and victims, only 21% of the homicides involved female victims, and only 10% involved female suspects. The average age of the victim was 32 years old. Only 19% of the cases involved victims under the age of 21 and only 8% involved victims over ages 40 or older. Minority offenders (African-American and Asian) made up 47% of homicides. Further, most of the homicides were characterized by a single victim and offender. And 22% involved a stranger perpetrator and 19% were related to robberies. Only 14% of the murders involved a minority offender and a non-minority victim.

Of all the murders, 82% received some coverage in the paper. Murders involving minority suspects, that resulted from robberies, and that involved unusual weapons were more likely to be covered. Murders with female victims and White/Latino victims were also more likely to be covered. And murders involving minority offenders were more likely to be covered and also had more words devoted to them.

Another study of homicides covered in the *Chicago Tribune* and *Sun-Times* found that the most important predictor of juvenile crime coverage was the age of the offender and victim. Specifically, murders with (alleged) younger offenders as well as younger victims were more likely to be covered. Homicides allegedly committed by Whites and females and with female victims were more likely to receive newspaper coverage.[93]

Jesenia Pizarro, Steven Chermak, and Jeffrey Gruenewald studied 572 homicides between 1997 and 2004 in Newark, New Jersey. They found that even though a similar amount of adult and juvenile suspect homicides were covered by the media, juvenile homicides received more media attention than those involving adults. Further, certain types of homicides were likely to be covered in the media (e.g., homicides with younger offenders; more victims; and murders of parents, siblings, and children).[94] It is likely that media cover the types of crimes with which a majority of their consumers can best identify.

Media coverage of homicides also did not match the reality of murder in Newark. Specifically:

> domestic incidents involving juveniles, multiple victim murders, robberies, and those involving victims who were not involved in illegal or deviant activities are more likely to receive media attention even though the reality of homicides in Newark differs. Newark homicides are typically single victim incidents that occur as a result of interpersonal disputes between people who know each other, and have some kind of involvement in deviant or illegal activities. This is problematic because if the media emphasize uncommon crimes, or unique elements of crime events, then the public may be left with a distorted picture of the crime problem where they live and elsewhere.[95]

A study of a 7-part series of homicides in the *Los Angeles Times* found that only 13% of the homicides in the city were covered by the paper. Most of the coverage was of the initial crime (78%) followed by stories that featured an arrest (17%). Stories about courtroom procedures and correctional punishments that followed were extremely rare.[96]

Murders of women, as well as the young (under age 15 years) and old (over 65 years) were most commonly covered. Murders of whites were far more likely to be covered than murders of blacks and Hispanics, inter-ethnic murders were more likely to be covered than intra-ethnic murders, and murders of the more educated were more likely to be feature than murders of the less educated.

Murders in wealthy neighborhoods received more coverage, as did murders by strangers. Importantly, newspaper coverage did not accurately depict murders in the city, which were disproportionately committed by young minority males against young minority males in poor neighborhoods. Susan Sorensen and colleagues note: "If different kinds of homicides were covered in the news media in the proportion in which they occur, the general public might have an accurate sense of the scope and nature of the homicide that occurs in their communities ... cases covered by the media are chosen for their deviance from the statistical norm."[97]

Given the information provide in Chapters 1 and 2, it may be logical to assume that covering crime inaccurately (and even distorting perceptions of crime) is profitable. Programs that inaccurately portray crime and criminal justice "attract a large viewing audience, which, in turn, sells advertising and generates profit."[98] For whatever reasons, inaccurate reporting about crime works. According to Robert Bohm and Jeffrey Walker, "the principal reason why the ... media perpetuates ... myths is that they attract a large viewing audience, which in turn, sells advertising and generates profit."[99]

It also should be acknowledged that myths of crime and criminal justice also "are used to justify larger budgets, more personnel, and higher pay" as well as to expand the "private crime-control industry."[100] This suggests there is little incentive in the media or criminal justice agencies to accurately depict criminal justice.

Serial Killers

Perhaps more than any other type of crime, serial killing receives a special place in the hierarchy of crimes covered by the media. According to J.C. Oleson, the public has

> a seemingly insatiable appetite for crime ... At any given moment, there is usually a movie about cops and killers playing at the local metroplex theater. Our airwaves are congested with primetime television programs about homicide detectives, sex offender units, and crime scene investigators. We clamor for taut psychological thrillers and we watch gory slasher films ... It is true of books as well as movies. Amid the poetry and literature, our bookstores have devoted shelves (and sometimes whole sections) to true crime publications ... Accordingly, notorious offenders like Jesse James, Al Capone, and Charles Manson have been elevated into the pantheon of villains: individuals who enjoy hero-like adoration but who represent the shadowy aspect of the hero archetype ... At the pinnacle of this infatuation with crime towers the serial killer.[101]

This is true; out of all types of crime, there have been more stories told, books written, and movies made about serial killers. Ironically, serial killers are the least common type of killer and are responsible for only a tiny portion of all murder in any given year.

The "Most Wanted" sketch of the "Unabomber," Ted Kaczynski, who in spite of killing only 3 people over the period over almost 20 years, appeared on the national news numerous times. http://en.wikipedia.org/wiki/File:Una bomber-sketch.png.

Serial killers who received major news press go back at least as far as Jack the Ripper. Since that time, the media have created major myths of serial killers.[102] Among the major myths of serial killers are these:

- Serial killers are all dysfunctional loners.
- Serial killers are all white males.
- Serial killers are only motivated by sex.
- All serial murderers travel and operate interstate.
- Serial killers cannot stop killing.
- All serial killers are insane or evil geniuses.
- Serial killers want to get caught.

In fact, many serial killers are highly functional; whites are not overrepresented among serial killers; there are several motivations for serial killings (like with other murders); many serial killers have committed their murders in their own towns or other single locations; serial killers have been identified that have stopped killing on their own; only a handful of serial killers have been found legally insane; and most serial killers do their best to avoid getting caught. Note how several of the myths of serial killers fit the dominant narratives of crime coverage (e.g., the evil offender who is somehow individually deficient and thus different from the average "non-criminal" person). This is probably one reason why serial killers receive so much media attention.

🖰 For examples of serial killers and the media coverage they genrated, see the website for this book at: www.pscj.appstate.edu/media/serialkillers.html

---

Interestingly, studies show that serial killers sometimes use the media to communicate with the police and larger society.[103] Consider the case of Dennis Rader, for example. Rader killed 10 people between 1974 and 1991 (his killings occurred in 1974, 1977, 1985–6, and 1991), but he was not captured until 2005. Based on the nature of his crimes, Rader was dubbed by the media "BTK" for "Blindfold, Torture, Kill." Rader sent letters boasting of his crimes to the police and to the media while he was actively killing, and his latest correspondence with the police in the 2000s where he complained about not getting enough attention in the press led to his arrest. At least two hour-long documentaries about his crimes have been broadcast on network and cable television. Rader is serving multiple life sentences in Kansas.

Terrorists also use the media, an issue that is addressed in the online chapter dealing with terrorism and counterterrorism.[104] Visit the web site for the book to read that chapter. To some degree, then, these criminals rely on the media to get their messages out, whatever they may be. The implication of this will be discussed in Chapter 5.

Random Crime

As noted earlier, the media are preoccupied with random crime, which partly explains the focus on serial killers as well as terrorism.[105] It also explains the focus on random crimes such as carjacking. A study of Louisiana newspapers found that they more often report on unusual carjackings (that produce injury to victims and offenders, especially those involving homicides) than on the typical carjacking as described in previous national, state, and city-specific carjacking research.[106] This is evidence that the media focus not only on random crimes like carjacking but also on the most unusual of the random crimes.

Not surprisingly, one type of crime that has received a tremendous amount of coverage in recent years is school violence. After the tragic mass murder of a dozen students and a teacher at Columbine High School in Littleton, Colorado, in 1999, the national news on each of the three major network news stations (ABC, NBC, CBS) devoted no less than half of each night's newscasts to this subject for approximately a month after the murders. But despite a common-sense impression to the contrary, in fact school violence was not increasing during this time period, but was rather decreasing!

The number of homicides at schools in the United States declined steadily in the 1990s. Lost in coverage about the mass murder at Columbine in 1999 was the fact that school violence had declined in the 1990s. Further, homicides at school were the lowest in 1999 than any other year in the 1990s. That is, kids were safer that year than any other year in the 1990s. Further, schools were much safer for children than most other places where children congregate.

In fact, the vast majority of children are murdered at home, typically by people they know, including their own parents! For example, in the 2006–07 school year, there were an estimated 55.5 million students enrolled in prekindergarten through grade 12 in the United States. Among youth ages 5–18 years, there were 35 school-associated violent deaths from July 1, 2006, through June 30, 2007. These numbers included 27 homicides and 8 suicides, meaning roughly one in 1.6 million kids died at school as a result of homicide or suicide. Meanwhile, there were 1,646 homicides and 1,408 suicides of school-age youth in 2005. According to the U.S. Department of Education: "In each year during the period 1992–93 to 2005–06, there were generally at least 50 times as many murders of youth away from school than at school and generally at least 140 times as many suicides of youth away from school than at school."[107]

Clearly, in the case of what is actually most threatening to our children, the media miss the boat. By not focusing on what is actually most dangerous to kids, the media help maintain an environment where policies that could address graver threats are not created. Media elites have decided those threats are not newsworthy and so public concern has not been created by the media.

All of this matters precisely because research shows that media coverage of school shootings leads to overestimation of risk of victimization.[108] Barry Glassner claims we fear the things we are most aware which happen to be the most unusual and atypical threats — things like school violence.[109] As explained by Jeffrey Victor: "One threat or another grabs attention on the evening news. There are child kidnappers and molesters, drug dealers who peddle to school children, teenage gang killers, teenage mass murderers in schools, and crack addicts. Moreover, an epidemic of single mothers and gay couples is said to threaten the fabric of society."[110] Ironically, these things are the least likely to happen to us or people we know.

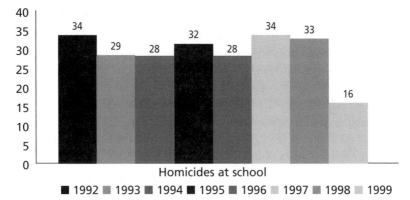

School violence actually declined throughout the 1990s, in spite of the Columbine High School attacks that killed 12 student victims and a teacher in April 1999. Data taken from "Indicators of School Crime and Safety: 2004." Figure 1.2. http://nces.ed.gov/pubs2005/crime_safe04/figures.asp.

Clearly, the frequency of school shootings relative to other types of shootings do not justify the coverage devoted to school shootings. For example, in the 1997–1998 school year (the year prior to Columbine), there were 6,146 deaths by firearms among 15- to 24-year-olds. Only 35 of those deaths occurred at school. Yet, crime coverage in 1998 featured 1,392 stories about crime on NBC, CBS, and ABC evening news. Meanwhile, leading causes of death of young people (such as accidents) are rarely reported on the news, and even most youth murders do not make the news.

The news also fails to provide any context for events such as school shootings. Consider that, according to Killingbeck, in 1997–1998, there were "44,351 public and private secondary schools and 91,661 public and private elementary schools for a total of 136,012 schools." Further, there "are on average 180 days of school per year when schools are in session for a total of 24.5 million school sessions." Thus, the 9 school shootings that occurred that year "represent .00003 percent of the approximately 24.5 million times school was in session for the day somewhere in America. As horrific and tragic as each of these events was, given the number of days individual schools in America are in session, on most days and in most places it is safe for a child to go to school."[111] This context was lost on Americans because it was not regularly provided in media coverage of school shootings.

Killingbeck suggests that, in order to provide context for such a tragedy as the mass murder at Columbine, the media should have explained: "(1) that school killings are not on the increase; (2) that such killings make up a small minority of all killings of and by juveniles; (3) that children are three times more likely to be killed by adults than by other juveniles; and (4) that there is no trend toward younger and younger juvenile killings." [112] That this context was not provided might explain bad outcomes resulting from school violence. For example, Donna Killingbeck suggests that media coverage of school shootings along with other elements of popular culture are associated with increasing levels of fear in citizens, as well as misguided anti-crime policy and "the development of an industry focused on school violence."[113]

In 1999, the Columbine High School shooting was the top crime story covered on evening news broadcasts with 319 stories. This was more than five times the total of any other incident. According to Killingbeck: "Students and faculty at Columbine High School, as well as reporters, referred to the shooters as members of the 'Trench Coat Mafia.'" In fact, this was merely a myth, one of many, generated by media coverage of the shooting. Dave Cullen's review of the mass murder that occurred at Columbine reveals the following myths:

- They were members of the "Trench Coat Mafia." In fact, most members of this group had already graduated and the killers were not affiliated with it.
- The killers were outcasts. In fact, the killers had many friends.
- They only targeted jocks, blacks, and Christians. In fact, the attack was meant to kill people randomly, using mostly bombs. The bombs failed to detonate, so they fired indiscriminately with guns.
- The killers made a hit list. In fact, they did have an enemies list, but the list included many people, including celebrities, and no one on the list was killed.
- They intentionally killed a girl because she said she believed in God. In fact, another girl had been asked this after she had been shot, and she managed to escape after the killers were distracted.
- The killers were motivated by rock musician Marilyn Manson. In fact, the killers liked Techno music not Marilyn Manson.
- They planned to hijack a plane and fly it into a building. In fact, this was a fantasy of one of the killers but both intended to die at the school on the day of the attacks.[114]

As in the case of media-generated myths of serial killers, note how the myths of the Columbine attacks are in line with the dominant narratives of crime coverage (i.e., these were abnormal, deeply troubled kids who can be easily distinguished from normal, "non-criminal" kids). As in the case of serial killers, the media packaged the Columbine mass murder using long-established, proven, and profitable narratives to sell the crime story, even though inaccurately.

Another study of school shootings between October 1997 and May 1999 by the Center for Media and Public Affairs found that the most deadly shooting (i.e., Columbine High School in Littleton, Colorado) received by far the most media coverage.[115] Further, media coverage of the eight shootings studied presented common myths or archetypes of these events, including that the shooters were obsessed with guns and violence, that they were loners or outcasts, they had violent or criminal pasts, they belonged to a gang, or they were mentally ill. Less common were depictions suggesting the shooters were normal or good kids (also uncommon were stories suggesting they were racists). The media most commonly depicted the shooters as coming from religious or churchgoing communities and families as well as safe and quiet areas.

In terms of blame for the shootings, media coverage most suggested that it belonged to violence in the media and in popular culture, guns in society, high school hierarchies, lack of parental involvement and mental illness. The most commonly suggested solutions in media coverage of these shootings were more gun control and better school security (both of which are actually largely ineffective when it comes to preventing school violence).[116]

It is interesting that the most common explanations for school shootings found in the media revolved around several factors such as violence in the media. Recall from Chapter 2 that the *violent media* frame is one of five popular frames identified by Ray Surette. Reporters as well as those interviewed for stories about school violence were aware of media effects on real-world violence, yet ironically this does not at all challenge the way the media cover violence.

How much news was devoted to the massacre at the campus of the Virginia Polytechnic Institute and University in April 2007? A 23-year-old student—Seung-Hui Cho—killed 32 people at in what is the deadliest attack ever with guns in U.S. history. He sent videos to NBC News showing himself with guns and trying to explain why he launched the attacks. Just as with the mass murder at Columbine High School in 1999, there was intense media coverage of this mass murder at Virginia Tech. The act was random, excessively violent, extremely rare, and committed by a man with a past record of mental health problems. This made it a perfect story for the national news.

According to one scholar: "Major media outlets—primarily CNN, ABC, NBC, CBS, and FOX—started their mad scramble to discover who Seung-Hui Cho, the shooter, was, and to snatch him from anonymity. In the process to understand who or what the perpetrator of this act of violence was, various governmental authorities and media outlets necessarily dug through his history and, most importantly, his mental health records, for these appeared to be the actions of a madman, at least as madness is institutionally defined in the contemporary United States."[117]

While this was the worst mass murder ever committed by a single person with firearms in the United States, far more deadly things happened even on that day. Yet, since they were not "violent," "random," "rare" or "bizarre" they did not receive any coverage. For example, on the average day in the United States, roughly 1,178 people die from tobacco, which kills 430,000 Americans every year. Another 821 die from poor diet and inactivity, which kills about 300,000 Americans every year. Another 110 die in car crashes, which kills 40,000 Americans every year. Another 55 die from defective products, which kill 20,000 every year. While there are clearly differences between an intentional mass murder of thirty-two people committed by a troubled student, the other forms of killing just mentioned are also committed with *culpability* — responsibility or moral blameworthiness. When the media ignores these acts, it creates a false impression in the viewer what is most likely to kill them.

🖰 For another example of random type of crime that genrated media coverage, see the website for this book at: www.pscj.appstate.edu/media/random.html

---

These kind of random but very uncommon acts of violence are precisely what the media are most interested in.[118] According to Joel Best, random violence is "a frightening term, one that evokes visions of patternless, purposeless chaos, of a society in collapse. It is also a term that ignores virtually everything criminologists know about crime."[119] Recall the frame introduced in Chapter 2 called the *social breakdown frame*. Random violence fits this frame well, in that random violence suggests the norms and culture of American life are under attack and must be defended. Any story that fits this frame will be presented to the public, typically in a dramatic and emotional way. Such coverage logically increases support of status quo approaches to crime reduction, which ironically do not address sources of societal deterioration whatsoever.

Most agree that America's leaders have been caught up in a moral panic about school violence and shootings. Recall that moral panics involve "an exaggeration of a social phenomenon, the public response also is often exaggerated and can create its own long lasting repercussions for society in terms of drastic changes in laws and social policy."[120] The repressive policies that have resulted from this moral panic have been largely ineffective at reducing school violence, have led to less privacy and freedom for students (as well as unnecessary expulsions for children who unknowingly brought items such as plastic knives in their lunch boxes, packed by their parents, to cut their peanut butter and jelly sandwiches and apples), are due largely to fear of school violence generated by widespread media coverage of school shootings.[121]

Sexual Assault and Stalking

Studies find that the mainstream press inaccurately covers sexual assault, meaning they create archetypes about the crime that do not represent the typical rape.[122] The most common archetype is of the young white girl who has been abducted, sexually assaulted, and/or killed by a stranger, such as Polly Klaas and Jon Benet Ramsey. These archetypal victims fit the narrative of the innocent victim who has been harmed by the evil, predatory criminal. Yet, most victims of sexual assault and other acts of violence are harmed by family members or other people they know.[123] Yet, the fact remains unknown to most, in part due to how the media cover the crime. For example, in newspapers, more coverage is given to the least likely assault scenarios (e.g., strangers who attack white older women and young girls in the middle-class).[124]

Some studies of rape and sexual assault show that the media suggest the victims, usually over the age of 18 years, "invite" their attacks.[125] Studies show how the media depict younger victims, usually children, as "innocent" and preyed upon by monstrous or less than human individuals. Other studies show that in movies "rape is committed by sadistic, disturbed, lower class individuals who prey on children and the vulnerable."[126] When put in the context of crime and criminal justice in the media, these findings are not surprising.[127]

Kenneth Dowler asserts that media portrayals of sex crimes promote myths about sex crime and are "distorted and sensational." Dowler's study of local television newscasts shows that 10% of crime stories were sex-related, and those stories about sex crimes often focused on elements of fear. Further, "sex crime stories were more likely to be reported in the later stages of criminal justice, which included the court, sentencing, and disposition phase."[128] Most criminal justice stories focus on earlier stages of the process, particularly law enforcement, which will be discussed later in the book.

When it comes to child molesters, it may be surprising to learn that more than half of child molesters are never even mentioned in the news media. Those offenders most likely to be mentioned include those charged with more serious crimes and multiple counts, those who allegedly committed additional violence or had multiple victims, and those who were imprisoned for long periods. Not surprising is that the media tend to exaggerate "stranger danger" while underreporting intra-familial cases.[129]

One of the major concerns recently expounded upon by police in the media relates to sex offenders. Emily Horowitz suggests that legislators know they will be blamed in the media for crimes committed by paroled sex offenders and that elected officials seen as "soft on perverts" will ultimately pay some political price. She attributes this reality to what she calls a moral panic about sex offenders in part because proposed and enacted laws and policies targeting sex offenders are based on "false fears, false assumptions, and hysteria."[130]

The study by Horowitz finds that the total number of news stories about "sexual predators" (as measured by that term being found in the headline, lead paragraph, or the body of the article) increased in newspapers from 107 in 1991 to 5,006 in 2006. Similarly, news stories with the term "sex offender" in the headline increased during the same time period from 536 to 15,558.

Interestingly, rates of sex crimes fell dramatically during this same time period, supporting the claim of a moral panic. Specifically, rates of sexual assault fell from 2.2 per 1,000 people to 0.5 per 1,000 people from 1991 to 2005.[131]

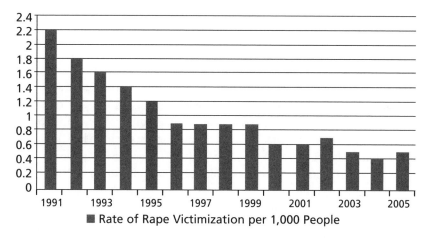

■ Rate of Rape Victimization per 1,000 People

The rate of rape victimization, as measured in the National Crime Victimization Survey (NCVS) declined significantly at the same time when reports of "sex offenders" and "sexual predators" increased significantly.

Further, according to Horowitz, rates of child sexual abuse decreased from 2.3 per 1,000 children in 1991 to 1.2 per 1,000 children in July 2003.

According to Horowitz:

> The increasing frequency of news stories and legislation relating to sex offenders, and the corresponding decrease in sex offenses, makes it clear that the national news media has increasingly focused on this topic for reasons other than an increase in incidents. News stories are thus not a response to more sex offenses, but rather to increasing public interest (because stories about sex offenders are interesting or titillating), and/or to increasing political or legislative attention. The relationship is cyclical, because political figures respond to the media interest in sex offenders with new and innovative legal responses, and at the same time, the media responds to legal initiatives with further media coverage.

One of the major misconceptions held by many is that sex offenders have high rates of recidivism, and thus policies such as *civil incapacitation* and *sex offender registration* are justified by the continued threat of sex offenders. Yet, research generally shows that recidivism rates for sex offenders are quite low, varying from 3% to 13%.[132] Another misconception is that children are likely to be harmed by strangers when in fact most perpetrators of child sexual abuse are known to their victims; more than 90% of juvenile abusers knew their victims.[133]

As part of her study, Horowitz found that statements made by politicians and others advocating sex offender prevention policies were generally presented in media articles without much criticism. This likely owes itself to the fact that the media rely so heavily on government officials for information, as noted in Chapters 1 and 2. Further, who would speak in the media on behalf of sex offenders?

According to Brian Spitzberg and Michelle Cadiz, media coverage of the crime of stalking is also plagued by popular stereotypes, including that: 1) stalking is a particular problem of celebrity; 2) stalkers tend to be strangers; 3) stalking is a gendered crime; 4) stalkers tend to be mentally disturbed and dangerous; and 5) stalking is mutually exclusive of normal courtship.[134] The media tend to portray stalking as a violent threat posed by strangers though violence tends to mostly occur in only a fraction of stalking relationships. Further, the media tend to portray stalking as violent acts committed by "sick, psychopathic individuals" even though most stalking occurs in the context of an already existing relationship. Finally, stalking tends to be portrayed in the media as something aberrant, bizarre, or deviant even though it "is little more than an extreme version of existing norms and rituals of courtship."[135] Just as with other crimes analyzed in this chapter, coverage of stalking in the media fits the dominant narratives of offender and victim very well.

Summary

The way the media exercise their power begins with law-making. Corporations, including those that own the media, are among the three major sources of money for political campaigns, along with wealthy individuals and political action committees (PACs).

The wealthy have much more access to the law than the common citizen. This is because the wealthy are more likely to be among the law-making bodies of society, more likely to vote for them, and more likely to give money to them through donations and lobbying efforts.

The institution of the law is founded on similar interests as the institutions of the media and the law likely serves the interests of the corporations that own the media. Further, the mainstream media have little interest in exposing potential problems with the law that may benefit those interests.

Coverage of law-making activities is common in the media, particularly the activities of local, state, and federal legislative activities. When new laws are passed, mainstream media commonly report their passage, effective dates, as well as implementation. Typically, passage of new laws (especially local ordinance and state laws) is noted in newspaper stories, reminding us of the importance of newspapers as well as locally aware newspapers (as opposed to chain newspapers owned by large corporations that are less interested in and capable of covering local stories). However, the majority of laws are not reported on by the media because there are literally thousands of new laws passed every year.

The media also generally devote coverage to court activities such as rulings on matters of law, but usually only in highly publicized cases that are tracked from the initial crime all the way to each and every court ruling pertaining to it; rulings by the U.S. Supreme Court receive the most attention in the press.

Surprisingly, the media often fail to report in any depth and with little context on the passage of very important laws. One good example is of the USA PATRIOT Act, which received very little critical coverage after it was proposed and ultimately passed into law. The mainstream press did not challenge government officials, in part because of their symbiotic relationship: government officials rely on the media to get the word out about their favored policies and proposed laws, and the media rely on government officials for information and stories; and relying on government officials is thought by media personnel to make stories more objective because it makes them more reliable.

Media coverage of crime is largely responsible for major misconceptions of crime. First, people tend to assume that criminals are different from non-criminals (when in fact everyone is a criminal). Second, when people think of crime, they tend to think of violent crime (even though the vast majority of crime is property crime). Third, people are most afraid of street crime (even though the most dangerous crime is committed by elites). These misconceptions of crime are not surprising given the way the media cover crime.

Of all types of crime, "serious crime" generates more media coverage. The term "serious" is synonymous with street crime. In fact, those crimes labeled as most serious by the government actually do not happen the most or cause the most damage in society. Corporate and white-collar crime actually occur with greater frequency, are more widespread, and do more harm than serious street crimes. The media tend to instead focus their attention on street crime, especially serious street crime and particularly violent street crime.

The media are more interested in those "serious" crimes that involve dramatic, sentimental, whimsical and unusual elements, and that involve famous people. Research also clearly demonstrates that crime news is focused on the most violent types of crime, at least those that occur at the street level. Of particular interest to the media are the rarest and "most egregious examples" of crime. Homicide, being violent and perceived as the most serious crime of all, is usually news. Additionally, it is the most heinous and bizarre of all murders that tend to be most widely discussed in the media. Further, serial killing receives a special place in the hierarchy of crimes covered by the media. Out of all types of crime, there have been more stories told, books written, and movies made about serial killers even though serial killers are the least common type of killer and are responsible for only a tiny portion of all murder in any given year.

The media are also preoccupied with random crime. One type of crime that has received a tremendous amount of coverage in recent years is school violence. Media coverage of school violence was not justified by its incidence in society, nor were trends of school violence increasing in the 1990s when coverage peaked. Coverage of the Columbine massacre created several myths of the killings, each of which was false.

The media also inaccurately cover sexual assault. The most common archetype is of the young white girl who has been abducted, sexually assaulted, and/or killed by a stranger, such as Polly Klaas and Jon Benet Ramsey. These archetypal victims fit the narrative of the innocent victim who has been harmed by the evil, predatory criminal. Yet, most victims of sexual assault and other acts of violence are harmed by family members or other people they know. Media coverage of the crime of stalking is also plagued by popular, often untrue stereotypes.

Covering such crimes inaccurately and even distorting perceptions of crime is profitable. Programs that inaccurately portray crime and criminal justice attract large viewing audiences, sell advertising, and generate profit.

Discussion Questions

1) To what degree do corporations donate to political campaigns?
2) How might the criminal law be potentially biased in favor of some interests over others?
3) Discuss who makes the law, who votes for it, who donates money to it, and explain why this matters.
4) To what degree are law-making activities covered in the media? When are new laws likely to be covered and when are they not likely to be covered? Explain.
5) Outline major problems with the USA PATRIOT Act.
6) Explain why the media failed to provide critical coverage of the USA PATRIOT Act?
7) What are the major misconceptions of crime held by many citizens?
8) How are the media responsible for these misconceptions of crime?
9) What types of crime generate the most media coverage?

10) Why do *serious crimes* generate the most media coverage?
11) What types of homicides are most likely to be covered in the media?
12) Why is serial killing so popular in the media?
13) Why is random crime so popular in the media?
14) Was media coverage of school violence in the 1990s justified by its incidence in society? Explain.
15) Do the media accurately portray sexual assault and stalking? Explain using examples.

Chapter 4

Media Coverage of Law-making and Crime, Part II: Focus on the Black, the Young, and the "Crazy"

Learning Objectives

After reading this chapter, you will be able to:

1) Explain what is meant by the claim that "critical" news stories are often lacking in the news.
2) Explain how the news often lacks important context.
3) Explain how the lack of critical news and context fails to serve citizens.

4) Explain how the media inaccurately cover crime trends.
5) Explain how media coverage of crime leads to fear of crime.
6) Show how popular crime stories are in the news.
7) Define "trivial," "soft", or "lifestyle" stories using examples and explain why they are so popular in the media.
8) Demonstrate which groups of society are most featured in media accounts of crime and criminal justice.
9) Define a *racial hoax* using examples.
10) Explain why women less frequently come to the attention of the media and explain under which circumstances they are most likely to come to the attention of the media.
11) Differentiate between juvenile courts and adult courts.
12) Demonstrate when children are most likely to be featured in the press and discuss how they are most often depicted.
13) Identify the most common form of criminal motivation depicted in the media as well as the types of motivation that are least featured in the media.
14) Discuss how the mentally ill are depicted in the media.
15) Define the *cultivation thesis, substitution thesis*, and *resonance thesis* and explain which is supported by empirical evidence.
16) Define the *Chicken Little Phenomenon*.
17) Outline the negative outcomes associated with heavy exposure to television.
18) Explain how exposure to media leads to violence.
19) Demonstrate how corporate crimes are ignored by the media.

Introduction

The last chapter showed how media coverage of crime is inaccurate. It tends to focus mostly on random crimes, serious crimes, and especially violent crimes. As noted by Roslyn Muraskin and Shelly Domash: "Crime as it is portrayed on television shows itself to be more dangerous, more threatening, more violent, and certainly more random than in the real world."[1]

This chapter discusses additional findings related to media studies of crime. For example, media coverage of crime is acontextual, meaning that it fails to provide consumers with an accurate understanding of how uncommon criminal victimization is. The chapter also addresses the issue of how crime is framed in the media in terms of race, gender and age, as well as how criminal motivation is depicted in the media. Media coverage of white-collar and corporate crime is also addressed. Finally, the impact of media coverage of violence on consumers and society is examined. Findings are related to important concepts introduced in Chapters 1 and 2.

No Context Necessary

Stories about crime and criminal justice that are "critical" in nature are typically lacking in American news. The term "critical" refers to stories that question status quo approaches to understanding crime as well as trying to deal with it.

The term "context" refers to the environment or setting in which something occurs which gives it greater meaning. Consider media coverage of school violence, discussed in Chapter 3. Stories about school violence tend to ignore the context of school shootings, including that they are extremely rare and not much of a threat to young people relative to other threats. The result is that people do not know how uncommon it is; further, they perceive it to be a greater threat than it really is.

Instead of providing such context, media coverage "barrages with facts and official statements" and of course not always the most important facts. To assure that news selection does not appear ideologically driven, "reporters and editors grab a news hook to justify a news story. If something happens, it is news." Yet, larger issues that are crying out for news attention receive little to no coverage. Twenty-four-hour, around-the-clock news channels have likely fed this phenomenon.[2]

John Harrigan claims that the media are biased in favor of "visually dramatic or sensational events that will attract a wide viewing audience."[3] Such media depictions of crime problems are inherently inaccurate—they have to be. The alternative is to tell the truth, which is virtually guaranteed to be more mundane and therefore will not attract as many viewers. Imagine how many Americans have been caused sleepless nights and great worry over anonymous and very vague terrorist threats when the government has claimed it does not know how, where, when, or if, America might be attacked, but that "intelligence" indicates that "recent chatter" among terrorist suspects "has increased."

Stories about crime and criminal justice do not provide much real information about problems of crime and criminal justice. David Krajicek claims that media coverage of crime almost never attempts to answer the most important question of all: "So what?" Instead, the majority of crime coverage can be depicted as "drive-by journalism—a ton of anecdote and graphic detail about individual cases ... but not an ounce of leavening context to help frame and explain crime."[4] Mortimer Zuckerman writes: "Television, in particular, is so focused on pictures and so limited by time that in the normal run of reporting it cannot begin to provide the context that gives meaning and perspective."[5]

Think of news reporters you have seen on the news, standing live at the scene of a crime that happened hours ago. The fact that there is nothing going on there now is apparently irrelevant. Because the reporter is there live, the illusion of importance is maintained. As noted by Lawrence Grossman: "The crime scene, marked off in yellow police tape, doesn't move; no matter when the reporter arrives there's always a picture to shoot, preferably live. No need to spend off-camera time digging, researching, or even thinking. Just get to the crime scene, get the wind blowing through your hair, and the rest will take care of itself."[6]

Reporters often appear live at scenes where crimes have occurred, long after anything has happened and even though nothing is happening at the time. http://upload. wikimedia.org/wikipedia/common/0/0d/ Reporter.jpg.

Lack of context in the news does not serve Americans well because it misinforms them. It is beneficial for politicians who want to put forth brief and simplistic stances on crime and criminal justice, most commonly depicted as the 10- or 15-second "sound bites" heard in any election year.[7] In terms of criminal justice policy, the media simply "cover" what politicians pledge and promise about getting tough on crime because the media are caught up in the same moral panic about crime, because they have become so caught up in the chase that they have forgotten to expose the public to intelligent crime reporting, and because crime news is inexpensive and attracts viewers.[8] Recall from Chapters 1 and 2 that the media rely heavily on government officials for much of the information they present.

Russ Immarigeon suggests that large-scale structural factors are responsible for such narratives. He writes that "media conglomeration and other corporate shifts within the publishing industry aided, and benefited from, increasingly sensationalistic tabloid coverage of 'true crime,' which over the long term boosted media profitability." Additionally, "shifts in reporting styles, often associated with narrowing corporate control of seemingly disparate media outlets, contributed to fast-track selling rather than in-depth coverage of crime—especially violent crime—issues."[9] The causes of media inaccuracy are revisited in Chapter 9.

The Same Crime Over and Over

One important realization about how the media cover crime is that the media tend to cover the same crime repeatedly as it processes through the criminal justice network. With any recent development in a case, the details of the original crime are rehashed, fostering an impression that the crime occurred more than once. When the case goes to trial or is plea bargained, when a sentence is passed down, and so on, the viewer learns these details from the media once more. The effect is a general feeling that there is much more crime out there than there really is. Of course, the media sometimes focus on crimes as they progress all the way through the police, courts, and corrections. This can be justified based on viewer interest.

Another common event in the media is connecting a recent crime to another from the past even when they are not at all connected. This too leaves the news consumer with the perception that there is more crime in society than actually exists. This is part of failing to provide context by the media. To the extent that media coverage of crime is repetitive and pervasive, it is more likely that it will affect people's attitudes about crime.[10]

Crime Appears More Widespread Than It Is

According to Roslyn Muraskin and Shelly Domash, media coverage of crime gives us the impression "that crime is rampant due to the reporting of so many stories" about crime.[11] Robert McChesney agrees, writing that the "plethora of crime stories has led heavy TV watchers to think crime is far worse in their communities than it actually is."[12] Part of this owes itself to the fact that the media often fail to provide the important context about the nature and extent of crime.

In fact, unless you were born before 1973, you are safer today from street crime than at any time in recent U.S. history. Interestingly, Gallup polls taken every year show that public concern about crime is not a function of fluctuations in actual crime rates. The percentage of people who indicated crime and violence as the nation's number one problem increased dramatically in the early 1990s, and concern over crime peaked in 1994. What explains this?

During the early to mid 1990s, concern rose about violent crime in response to several crimes that were given tremendous coverage. Some of these included the videotaped beating of Rodney King by police officers in 1991, as well as the subsequent acquittal of the officers in the case in 1992 and the rioting which occurred afterward, and the kidnapping and killing of young Polly Klaas from her parent's home by a stranger in 1993.

Even though street crime rates now are very low compared with other times in U.S. history, and relatively average compared to other countries, Americans are afraid. Americans report feeling less safe walking in their own neighborhoods after dark than citizens of other countries characterized by higher crime rates.[13] To some degree, the terrorist attacks of 9/11 changed this, as American became more afraid of terrorism than violent crime.[14] Yet, as concern over terrorism wanes (and the nation's economy improves), concern over violent crime will likely return.

Why are Americans so concerned about street crime even though property crime has decreased consistently since the 1970s and violent crime since the 1990s? Is it that we see so much of it in the news and in television shows, movies and other media formats? Some of the increases in fear may be due to the politicization of crime and resulting media coverage.

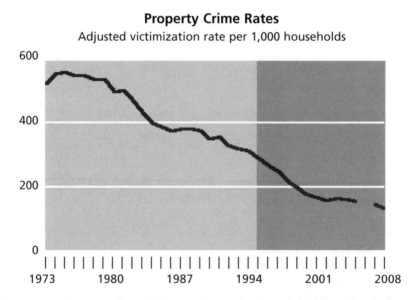

Property Crime Rates

Adjusted victimization rate per 1,000 households

Property crime rates have fallen consistently since the 1970s. The dark portion of the chart reflects a change in methodology of the victimization survey on which these data are based, and the missing data from 2006 shows a break in survey collection. http://bjs.ojp.usdoj.gov/content/glance/house2.cfm.

Even when crime is going down, stories about declines in crime are like "a dinghy bobbing in a rolling sea" of stories about individual, thoughtless, and salacious crime reports.[15] Individual stories erroneously suggest that crime is increasing even when it is not.[16] This is one example of how media activity reinforces myths about crime: people believe that crime is increasing even when it is not.[17] The media achieve this by providing "a steady diet of the growing and omnipotent danger of interpersonal crime."[18]

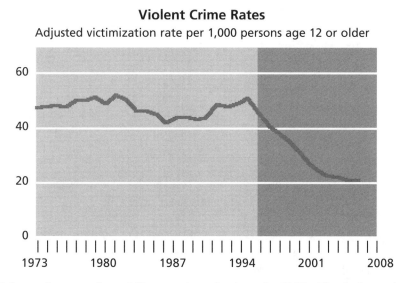

Violent Crime Rates

Adjusted victimization rate per 1,000 persons age 12 or older

Violent crime rates have fallen consistently since the 1990s. The dark portion of the chart reflects a change in methodology of the victimization survey on which these data are based, and the missing data from 2006 shows a break in survey collection. http://bjs.ojp.usdoj.gov/content/glance/viort.cfm.

For example, in the mid-1990s, when violent crime was decreasing to its lowest levels in twenty years, crime coverage on television and in the newspapers increased in one city by more than 400%.[19] In 1993, the three major news networks ran 1,632 crime stories on their evening newscasts, up from 785 in 1992 and 571 in 1991. This occurred even though victimization rates of the NCVS and crime rates of the UCR were down during this time.[20] Not surprisingly, 88% of Americans in 1994 thought crime was at an all-time high.[21] Additionally, between 1992 and 1993, major network evening news coverage of homicide tripled even as homicide rates remained unchanged, and from 1993 to 1996, major network news increased coverage of homicide 721%.[22]

According to Donna Killingbeck, even though homicide rates decreased since 1993, one out of every seven news stories covered the topic and crime coverage generally tripled since 1993.[23]

Studies of violent crime rates and drug use rates compared with media coverage of violent crime and drug crimes on television and in the newspapers show clearly that amount of coverage is not directly related to actual trends of violence or drug use. Instead, coverage tends to increase for reasons unrelated to actual trends of crime and drug use. And public concern peaks about crime and drug use along with media coverage, rather than actual crime or drug use trends.[24]

Approximately 30% of local television news relates to crime, as does more than one-tenth of national news and about one-quarter of newspaper space.[25] In many markets, stories about crime comprise about 25–35% of the news.[26] Some studies find that crime stories make up as much as 61% of newscasts, and one found that "13% of all newscasts began with three crime stories in a row, back to back to back."[27] In fact, you've probably seen a local newscast that follows the typical format of local news across the United States—crime, crime, bad story, crime, trivial story, crime, bad story, weather, sports, feel good, trivial story.

The term "trivial" refers to so-called "soft" or "lifestyle" news pertaining to celebrity lifestyles, gossip and similar stories. Between 1977 and 1997, coverage of "hard" news declined from 67% to 41%, whereas news about celebrities tripled from 2% to 7%! Additionally, "soft" news doubled from 13% to about 25%. "Network news times was increasingly devoted to celebrity news, and the 'morning news' shows emphasized more commercial and product advertising to promote the conglomerates that owned them."[28]

The format of the local news noted above is highly routinized across the nation. Recall that, to some degree, what becomes news is now automatic—what worked in the past will work again now as well as in the future. This suggests that there may be less conscious thought devoted to the content of the news by news agency executives than most assume.

Crime is a popular news item for at least two reasons. First, it is connected to fear which is a "staple of the entertainment format." Second, it is easy to cover and thus "fits well with scheduling and personnel constraints of local television."[29] News about crime is "institutionalized as a good way to 'hook' an audience and 'hold' them throughout the newscast."[30] One main reason crime is given so much media coverage is because of organizational factors such as the fact that the media are for-profit entities. These issues were discussed in Chapters 1 and 2 and will be revisited in Chapter 9. As noted repeatedly, crime sells.

The main problem with this over reporting is that news stories about crime are not rational and tempered. They are not in-depth, critical, informative accounts. Instead, they amount to numerous "raw dispatches about the crime of the moment, the frightening—and often false—trend of the week, the prurient murder of the month, the sensational trial of the year."[31] The purpose of such coverage it to "hook and hold" viewers for purposes of achieving higher ratings, as noted earlier.

Fascinating research on the media and crime is found in *Scooped!*, written by a former crime reporter, David Krajicek. The subtitle of this inside look at media coverage of crime reflects its author's informed opinion: *Media Miss Real Story on Crime While Chasing Sex, Sleaze, and Celebrities*. Krajicek's main claim about the media is this: "Take a predisposition toward simplicity and anecdote, add unsophisticated reporting, a degenerating peer culture, an over-worked news staff, the rapture of sex and celebrities, and—poof!—you've got today's crime journalism."[32]

Disgusted with this type of crime reporting, Krajicek quit his job as a reporter. Why? In his words, he explains:

> While we [reporters] were sitting in vans counting arrests, we missed the most important story on the crime beat: the collapse of the U.S. criminal justice system as an effective means of fighting crime, maintaining order, ensuring public safety, and meting out equitable justice.... I came to conclude that the media had been scooped by myopia, sleazy story distractions, and an unhealthy devotion to the official police agenda.[33]

Krajicek argues that the media misrepresent reality, much the same as what Jeffery Reiman points out about the image of crime in U.S. society. Reiman describes the American conception of crime as a problem of the poor as distorted, much like a reflection in a carnival mirror.[34] In Krajicek's words: "Today, reading a newspaper or watching a news telecast can be like looking at the country's reflection in a fun-house mirror. The society we see presented in the news is a warped place, often morbid and alarming."

Further, according to Krajicek, it should be no surprise to you that for a lot of people, "the term crime evokes an image of a young African American male who is armed with a handgun and commits a robbery, rape, or murder. In the minds of many Americans, crime is synonymous with black crime."

The Color of Crime

The media generally are most focused on acts of racial minorities,[35] especially blacks.[36] Further, racial minorities are generally portrayed in a negative light.[37] According to Lane Crothers, whites are shown in the media as "the best-educated, most effective, most law-abiding members of society. They are seen to fill most positions of authority in the political, economic, and social systems ..." whereas when it comes to blacks they have, for centuries, been depicted as "out-of-control, sexually aggressive predator(s)" and explicitly as criminals (especially black men).[38]

Katheryn Russell-Brown explains that Americans "are being exposed to images, stories, and representations that enhance the myth of Black criminality. This myth is spread in print and visual media—for example, through newspapers, magazines, television shows, commercials, the news, and music videos."[39] According to her exhaustive reviews of the evidence: "The media's representation of young Black men as criminal perpetrators is so uniform that most people treat them as imagined bogeymen. Studies indicate that Whites, Latinos, Asian Americas, American Indians, and even African Americans believe they are most likely to be victimized by Black men."[40] This should not be surprising given that we all are exposed to the same media images of crime.

Consider this infamous quote from civil rights leader and reverend Jesse Jackson. In 1996 he said: "There is nothing more painful to me ... than to walk down the street and hear footsteps and start thinking about robbery, then look around and see somebody white and feel relieved." That even Jackson thinks "black" when he thinks crime says a lot about the power of media-generated images of crime.

According to Donna Bishop:

> It is in the interest of the media to highlight violent crime, especially violence committed by young black males, because this is the kind of crime than the public fears most. This is not to suggest that the media intentionally try to generate fear or champion a punitive crime control agenda, but they exploit fear and inadvertently promote that agenda in the interest of profit. Dramatic accounts of the most feared crimes sell newspapers and magazines. They attract viewers to television news and other crime-related programming, and generate advertising revenues. Violent crime is cheap and easy to report (it does not require in-depth investigative reporting) and it has wide audience appeal.[41]

Bishop's argument is consistent with the main themes identified in Chapters 1 and 2 pertaining to the influence that profit-seeking has on corporate controlled media.

These dominant images of black criminals and people of color in a negative light not only impact perceptions of crime. Research also demonstrates that negative portrayals of minorities are associated with lower self-esteem as well as less societal integration among members of those groups depicted in the media.[42]

Racial hoaxes obviously do not help. *Racial hoaxes* occur when someone invents a crime and says they were assaulted by a person of another race, or an actual victim blames their victimization on a person of another race.[43] Well-known racial hoaxes include the following cases:

- Charles Stuart—In 1989, shot his pregnant wife and himself while in a car in a Boston neighborhood and then blamed the crime on a fictional black man.
- Susan Smith—In 1994, drove her children, still strapped into their car seats, into a lake, and then claimed to have been carjacked by a fictional black man who drove away with her kids.
- Ashley Todd—In 2008, carved a backwards "B" into her face, and then made up a false story about being robbed and attacked by a fictional black man.

Susan Smith alleged that this man forced her out of her car at a red light and drove away in her car with her two children. In reality, Smith drove her car with the two children strapped in their car seats into a lake and watched them drown, then made up the whole story about the carjacking. This case was a classic "racial hoax." http://pics.live journal.com/girlbitesdog/pic/0003b4ab.

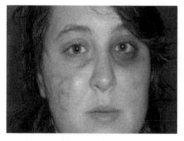

Ashley Todd said she was robbed by a tall black man, who after noticing a "John McCain" bumper sticker on her car then assaulted her by carving a "B" on her face, allegedly in support of "Barack Obama" for president. Todd made up the story and carved the backwards "B" in her own face while looking in the mirror. This is another "racial hoax." http://www.huffingtonpost.com/2008/10/24/mccain-supporter-who-clai_n_137484.html.

According to Katheryn Russell-Brown, "the majority of the hoaxes involve someone white falsely claiming they were harmed by someone black. In terms of gender, about a third of the cases involve women." Further, "primarily it is the African-American male. And I describe it as the *criminalblackman* ... one ... run-on word because they are the key targets of the hoaxes. And not surprisingly because across race, most people fear young, African-American males."[44] It should also be pointed out that racial hoaxes are not always committed by Whites against Blacks. For example, the 1987 case of 15-year-old Tawana Brawley comes to mind. After being found in a dumpster in New York state, supposedly covered in feces and with racial insults written on her body, she claimed that a group of white men (including police officers) had assaulted her and raped her. This case received an enormous amount of media attention, and yet, as it turns out, the attack was a hoax. More recently, the case of an alleged rape of a black woman by a group of white Duke Lacrosse players also turned out to be a hoax.

Coverage of homicides in the media tends to be more intense when the crime is interracial in nature.[45] Further, when crimes by blacks are covered they are at times covered in ways that lead to fear of blacks and the black community in general.[46]

One study found that when offenders are not identified by race in the news, most viewers assume that the offenders are black and that police are white. This is especially true for heavy news viewers.[47] This may serve as evidence that when people think of crime, they tend to think of black crime, since this is so prevalent on television and in other media forms.

Interestingly, being exposed to black suspects on the news increases the odds that people will come to see criminality itself as a function of dispositional factors such as personality traits.[48] This means viewers see blacks as responsible for their criminality rather than being promoted to act by structural impediments. Those who are heavy watchers of the news featuring blacks as suspects are more likely to view the world as dangerous.[49] Perhaps it is not surprising then that exposure to black suspects leads to increased support for punitive crime control policies such as capital punishment and three-strikes legislation. Travis Dixon attributes this to the fact that blacks have been "so associated with criminality on news programs."

Those who hold black stereotypes are less likely to perceive blacks as facing structural limitations: "as news viewing increases, the perception that Blacks face structural limitations decreases."[50] Those who hold black stereotypes are also more likely to see offenders as culpable, especially when the stories feature black offenders.[51] This is evidence of the media's impact on criminal justice policy; the media help create myths of black dangerousness, which ultimately results in an expansion of criminal punishment against blacks.

Meanwhile, whites are overrepresented as victims and police officers.[52] This fits well with the popular conception of whites as innocent.

Why do black crimes get so much attention in the press? Because those "crimes that receive the most attention—from the media, from politicians, and from criminal justice policy makers—are 'street crimes' such as murder, robbery, and rape."[53] Robert McChesney's review of the research leads to the same conclusion that media coverage has "overemphasized African Americans as criminals and whites as victims" and "has had the perverse effect of encouraging popular support for draconian measures to stem the bogus 'crime wave.'"[54]

Interestingly, media coverage of serial murderers has created the widespread perception that all serial killers are rarely black, even though this is not the case.[55] In fact, although whites make up a majority of serial killers, they also make up a majority of members of society. Blacks commit about the share of serial killing you would expect given their portion of society.[56]

Not surprisingly, studies show that both demographic characteristics of those watching the news and those portrayed as offenders and victims have meaningful impacts on attitudes toward minorities in society. For example, in some cases, white women are more likely to see black males as guilty when they are shown as suspects of rape on television while white males are more likely to respond sympathetically to white male suspects on television.[57]

Female Violence and Victimization

Women are less likely to come to the attention of criminal justice agencies. This is largely due to the fact that women commit so much less crime than men. Yet. when women do get caught up in the criminal justice process, the courts are generally less punitive toward them. As one important example, women commit more than 10% of all murders in any given year, yet they make up less than 2% of all people on death row and 1% of all executions. This might amount to bias against men, who are responsible for a much larger portion of street crime and violence in general than women. But this may be due to what Joanne Belknap calls the *chivalry or paternalism hypothesis* which ends up protecting women from tougher punishments.[58]

Generally speaking, women are less likely to be victimized by crime, less likely to commit it, less likely to be arrested, less likely to be convicted, less likely to be sentenced to prison or jail, and generally are sentenced to less time than men. Because of this, there is good reason to expect that violence committed by women will not appear much in the media. In fact, female behavior typically comes to the attention of the media when it conflicts with the norms of society with regard to appropriate behavior by women.[59] Thus, it is not surprising that female violence is attractive to the media.

This is consistent with what Belknap calls the *evil woman hypothesis*, which posits that women will be treated more harshly for similar crimes than men, at least in some cases. Etta Morgan-Sharp suggests that the criminal justice network is tougher on women when they "do not adhere to prescribed gender roles."[60] This suggests that women may be reacted to more harshly by courts when they do things that are not generally expected of them.[61]

Eileen Wuornos killed seven men while hitchhiking as a prostitute in Florida in 1989 and 1990. Despite claiming she killed the men because they raped or attempted to rape her, Wuornos was convicted of murder, sentenced to death, and ultimately executed in 2002. Books, films, an opera, and even a mainstream Hollywood movie were made about Wuornos' life and crimes. http://prisonphotography.files.wordpress.com/2009/12/aileen_wuornos1.jpg.

The "evil woman hypothesis" might also be applicable to girls, for we certainly do not expect them to behave violently. According to Dawn Cecil: "Mean girls are depicted everywhere these days. While the news media started sensationalizing these girls in the 1990s, this type of behavior has been ingrained in popular culture for many years. One particular type of aggression most linked to females as opposed to males is *relational aggression*—lying, gossiping, spreading rumors, ostracizing, and so forth. According to Cecil: "While the media show both boys and girls using relational aggression, it is far more common to associate this type of behavior with females."[62] Specifically, relational aggression is portrayed as the sole province of white, middle-to-upper-class girls.[63] Minority girls, in contrast, are depicted as physically violent and masculine.[64]

One thing is certain, given the rarity of female violent behavior. That it is at times prominently featured in the media serves as further evidence of the media's fascination with the unusual. The magazine—W—recently included several photos of young women as part of a fashion shoot featuring models posing as juvenile delinquents. The layout seems to make light not only of criminality, but also of the horrible things that go on in prisons and jails (including forced homosexual sex).

Women are also featured as victims in the press. In many cases, women are depicted as responsible for their own victimization.[65] One study of newspaper coverage of women murder victims found that the paper used both direct and indirect methods of blaming the victim for her death. Direct tactics include describing the victim using negative language, noting that past instances were not reported, and characterizing past relationships as contributing to her murder. Indirect tactics include describing the perpetrator using sympathetic language, emphasizing problems suffered by the perpetrator, describing mental or physical problems of the victim, and characterizing domestic violence as a problem of two people in a relationship rather than one.[66] Another study, focused on the framing of domestic violence as a social problem, showed how better news coverage could lead to an increased likelihood that domestic violence would be seen as a social problems warranting public intervention.[67]

Child Offenders and Victims

Several social scientists, including some well-known criminologists, predicted a wave of violence committed by "juvenile super predators" in the 1990s that received widespread attention in the mainstream press. For example, Professor John Dilulio and colleagues wrote:

> Based on all that we have witnessed, researched and heard from people who are close to the action … here is what we believe: America is now home to thickening ranks of juvenile "super-predators"—radically impulsive, brutally remorseless youngsters, including ever more pre-teenage boys, who murder, assault, rape, rob, burglarize, deal deadly drugs, join gun-toting gangs and create serious communal disorders."

Similarly, one of the leading homicide experts in the nation, Professor James Fox, suggested that juveniles in the 1990s had "more dangerous drugs in their bodies, more deadly weapons in their hands, and a seemingly more casual attitude about violence.[68]

The wave of crime predicted by these criminologists, which received widespread media attention, never came. Yet, juvenile justice practice still shifted from a philosophy of treatment and rehabilitation toward one centered around tough punishment.

An analysis of media coverage of the nature and extent of juvenile delinquency by Donna Bishop found that since the 1960s, "a radical shift has taken place in American juvenile justice policy. Instead of focusing on protection and treatment, legislators and public officials have increasingly advocated punishment of young offenders to deter them from reoffending. They have implemented many strategies that threaten the nature, and ultimately, perhaps even the existence of the juvenile court."[69]

🖱 For more information about the juvenile court and how its philosophy has shifted over time, see the website for this book at: www. pscj.appstate.edu/media/juvenile.html

---

Attitudes about adolescents have also changed due in part to what Donna Bishop calls an "explosion of newspaper, magazine, and television coverage of youth violence." She suggests that "both television and the print media give excessive coverage to violent youth crime (especially when the offender is a minority), even when rates are declining."[70] Here are some examples of cover stories in popular magazines in the 1990s:

- "Children Without Pity" — *Time*, October 26, 1992
- "Teen Violence: Wild in the Streets" — *Newsweek*, August 2, 1993
- "Big Shots: An Inside Look at the Deadly Love Affair Between America's Kids and Their Guns" — *Time*, August 2, 1993
- "Heartbreaking Crimes: Kids Without a Conscience" — *People*, June 23, 1997
- "The Monsters Next Door" — *Time*, May 3, 1999.[71]

Such coverage simplifies the issue and creates fear, which tends to drive punitive responses.[72]

According to some studies, victims and offenders younger than 14 years of age are most likely to be reported in newspapers. Whites and males in this age group are also most likely to be reported.[73]

Studies examining how the media cover kids generally show that the media generally do not pay much attention to children except for when it is bad news.

For example, a study of nearly 10,000 network media stories by the Center for Media and Public Affairs (CMPA) found that only 4% of network television stories dealt with kids while local news stories on kids made up only 8% of all stories. The stories tended to focus on negative aspects of adolescence and juvenile behavior. Specifically, the most popular stories on local news were on crime and delinquency committed by young people. Network news focused more on stories related to education but even on network news the third and fourth most popular stories dealt with juvenile crime. CMPA writes: "Since local news covers events and activities in a small geographic area, it is more likely to target particular crimes and accidents involving local youths, whereas national news concentrates on broad trends and the big picture."[74]

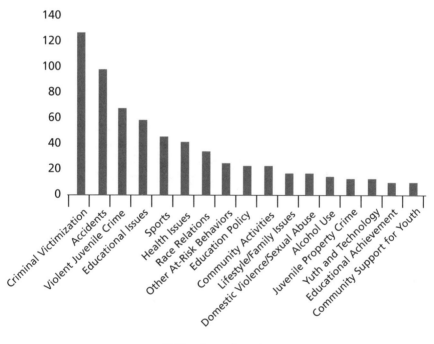

■ Number of stories

A study of local news items by the Center for Media and Public Affairs found that stories about crime, criminal victimization and other bad outcomes such as accidents were the most common stories.

A study by Danilo Yanich of more than 7,500 stories on more than 550 television broadcasts included about 1,700 crime-related stories. Yanich concluded that crime accounted for one-quarter of all stories and broadcast time; about one-third of the stories focused on juveniles as suspects and/or victims; stories about adult crime and juvenile delinquency were both generally handled early in the broadcast including often being the first story and often grouped together with other crime stories; and about two-thirds of stories featured a criminal justice official (consistent with the filter introduced in Chapter 1 of relying on official sources). Further, juveniles were more likely than adults to be depicted as victims; stories about juveniles were more likely to be focused on murder even though this crime is quite rare relative to the typical offense committed by juveniles.[75] This creates myths about what the typical juvenile crime looks like.

Other scholars have analyzed myths of juvenile gangs.[76] A study by Finn-Aage Esbensen and Karin Tusinski of gang-related articles appearing in the nation's "big three" newsweeklies (*Newsweek, Time, and U.S. News and World Report*) between 1980 and mid-2006 found evidence of "stereotypical depiction of gangs and gang members that promote misperceptions about youth gangs, their members, and their group characteristics." Specifically, coverage of gangs in these magazines suggested that they are male, ethnic and racial minorities, and emanating from the inner-city or urban areas. Gangs are depicted as organized and consisting of "well-defined roles for members (often associated with the notion of organized drug distribution and sales), with satellite sets across the country, and well-established leaders." Gangs are also portrayed as heavily armed and "involved in a wide array of illegal, especially violent, crimes. One problem with this picture is that it does not describe the typical gang or gang member because it over represents not only males and minorities, but also violence and the degree of organization within gangs."[77]

As noted earlier, the media cover what sells. Thus, it can logically be assumed that creating myths about gangs by focusing on the most violent and organized gangs attracts viewers and therefore helps the media achieve its goal of selling advertising to consumers.

As for children as victims, they tend to receive more attention in the media than older victims.[78] This is interesting since both are usually seen by criminologists and victims' rights advocates as "vulnerable populations." When it comes to children, however, they are seen as the most vulnerable and the least capable of defending themselves. They are also perceived as having limitless potential and thus most worthy of protection. Finally, stories of children victims are captivating of audiences, a major goal of the mainstream media.

It probably goes without saying that children as victims are perhaps the most "innocent" of all crime victims. Thus, stories about children crime victims fit the dominant narrative of the "innocent" victim in the mainstream press. Fitting individual crime stories into this widely used narrative is quite easy to advance.

Some suggest that media outlets have been instrumental in finding kidnapped children. The "Americas Missing Broadcast Emergency Response Alert system" (or AMBER) was designed to be used by local and state governments to stop serious child kidnappings that were already in progress by alerting citizen to be on the lookout for a missing victim and his or her kidnapper(s). Yet, Timothy Griffin and Monica Miller assert that the AMBER Alert system does not work and is little more than "crime control theater." They suggest it is "a socially constructed 'solution' to a socially constructed problem, enabling public officials to symbolically address an essentially intractable threat."[79] Whether this is true is unknown, yet it is certain that AMBER alerts do attract consumer attention and thus do serve the media's goals of higher ratings.

Focus on Individual Motives

Depictions of criminal motivation in the media tend to be individualistic, which means they leave citizens with the impression that what motivates criminality is individual-level factors such as jealously, emotional instability, mental illness, greed, and so forth.[80] According to Robert Bohm and Jeffery Walker, crime is seen in the United States largely as an individual phenomenon, meaning it arises due to individual-level causes, "the result of a personal defect—especially of poor, young males between the ages of 15 and 24.... there is no social or structural solution to the problem of crime."[81]

Ray Surette concurs, writing: "With its individually rooted causes, crime is constructed as an autonomous plague on society, its genesis not associated with other historical, social, or structural conditions."[82] These are criminals of their own will, "certainly not of society's will. Such criminals can, therefore, be guiltlessly battled and eliminated."[83]

According to Kenneth Dowler, "crime reporting is criticized for ignoring the relationship between crime and broader social conditions. While news reports associate criminal violence with youth, maleness, and minority group membership, the news media ignore how labor markets, employment opportunities, poverty ... relate to crime...." Dowler explains:

> Ultimately, the tendency to portray crime as perpetrated mainly by pathological individuals precludes alternative explanations ... Consequently, crime portrayals are almost based exclusively on individual characteristics rather than on social conditions, and the causes of crime are

perceived to be rooted in individual failings rather than social explanations. Deviant behavior is viewed as an individual choice, while social, economic, or structural explanations are ignored or deemed irrelevant.[84]

The typical characterization of the individually responsible offender is consistent both with the dominant narrative of the innately evil criminal in the media as well as the cultural belief in American society of free will, which underlies all criminal justice practice. Stated simply, if criminals did not have free will and moral responsibility for their behavior, what sense would it make to arrest, convict and punish them? This characterization of the individually responsible offender is thus logically related to punitive responses to crime (at least for some people).

Ironically, criminological scholars help reinforce the perception that crime emanates from individual-level factors by focusing their attention so squarely on acts of "serious" street crime (which is typically committed by one person against another). Not only does this mean that most of the research fails to address white-collar and corporate crime, it also impacts what criminologists hold to be key "truths" of crime.

✍ For more information about how the discipline of criminology focuses on street crime and why this matters, see the website for this book at: www.pscj.appstate.edu/media/criminology.html

---

Perhaps criminologists focus their attention on street crime—which deeply impacts what they conclude about crime in general—in part due to media coverage of crime. We criminologists are regularly exposed to images of crime in the media, and we too were raised with them. It's thus logical to assume that our views of crime are and have always been directly impacted by the images we've seen in the media.

Even though the media tend to cast motivations for crime as emanating from within individuals, more Americans suggest that "attacking the social and economic problems that lead to crime through better education and job training" comes closer to their own views about what should be effective at reducing crime than "improving law enforcement with more prisons, police, and judges" (65% versus 31%, respectively).[85] Higher portions of certain groups are more likely to say "attacking the social and economic problems that lead to crime through better education and job training," including non-whites (especially blacks), younger people (especially under the age of 30), people with college degrees (especially those with post graduate degrees), those living in urban areas, and Democrats (especially liberals). This is consistent with the blocked opportunities frame suggested by Ray Surette. Recall from Chapter 2 that Surette offered five frames commonly seen in the media, including the faulty criminal justice frame, the *blocked opportunities* frame, the social breakdown frame, the violent media frame, and the racist system frame.[86] The blocked opportunities frame attributes criminality to social conditions such as poverty and inequality in society, leading citizens to believe that the solution to crime includes providing better opportunities for the poor. Interestingly, in spite of the common depiction in the media, crime emanating from individual circumstances, most Americans seem to see crime in a broader sense as connected to social and economic conditions. Why this is so is unknown.

For decades criminologists have asserted that an allegiance to the American Dream is criminogenic.[87] For example, according to *strain theorists* such as Robert Merton, while everyone is raised to pursue the same goals associated with achieving the American Dream (e.g., wealth, success), the legitimate/legal means to achieve these goals are not equally available to all.[88] Merton and other strain theorists suggest that the means to achieve the goals associated with the American Dream are structured by social class, meaning that the poor are less able to achieve success legally and thus sometimes "innovate" or create new means (including illegal means such as selling drugs) in order to achieve their goals.[89] That is, "blocked opportunities" produce crime, something Americans seem quite aware of.

Although citizens seem to be aware of the possibility that the American Dream promotes criminality through strain and anomie, the mainstream media are generally uninterested in questioning the unquestionable beneficence of the American Dream. To do so would contravene the corporate media's goal of promoting consumerism through advertising. Recall that the mainstream media are part of and have bought into the capitalistic, corporate system that itself relies on selling goods and services for its very survival.

Interestingly, scholars including *anomie theorists* such as Steven Messner and Richard Rosenfeld have suggested that the American Dream itself is criminogenic. Specifically, overemphasizing the goals associated with the American Dream and under emphasizing the appropriate means to achieve those goals (e.g., school, work) results in an "anything goes" mentality among citizens where what matters most is whether you gain wealth and success rather than whether you achieve it legally or illegally.[90] Further, the dominance of the economy in U.S. society over other non-economic institutions such as the family and schools assures higher crime rates because efforts to strengthen the economy erode the ability of non-economic institutions to instill appropriate and important values in children.[91] If these arguments are correct, it is not just blocked opportunities that explain criminality, it is pursuing opportunities in the first place. It is safe to say that media coverage of crime simply does not raise this as a possibility.

According to Kenneth Dowler, even when economic or other motives for criminality are identified in the media, they are "based in generalities, not specifics; in other words, specific crimes are ascribed to general motives. For example, the beating death of a teen is attributed to 'gang violence'; an incident in which a young man is beaten and dragged from a car is attributed to 'road rage.' The majority of stories in which motives are given are based in clichés, with which the audience can readily identify."[92] These tend to be consistent with the major themes and narratives identified in Chapter 2. To flush out the specific motives for crime in America would require careful, critical, contextual investigative reporting, something that is generally lacking in the media.

One important outcome of the media's focus on individual motivations for criminality is greater pressure for crime control solutions to the crime problem. For example, Ray Surette explains that given that the "repeated message in the media is that crime is largely perpetrated by predatory individuals who are basically different from the rest of us; that criminality is predominantly the result of individual problems; and that crimes are acts freely committed by individuals who have a wide range of alternate choices" crime control responses such as arrest, conviction, and punishment are entirely logical.[93]

Mentally Ill Offenders

According to Jennifer Bullock and Bruce Arrigo, the media also play a large role in creating the illusion that mentally ill individuals are responsible for a large share of violence in society. They write:

> The stereotype of the dangerous mentally ill person is pervasive in American society. Some of the most popular entertainment media feature this stereotype. Movies such as *The Silence of the Lambs*, *Psycho*, and *Slingblade* depict frightening images of fictitious 'mental patients' committing violent acts, and do a great deal to reinforce the notion that the mentally ill are dangerous.[94]

Recall that one of the dominant themes or narratives in the media of the mentally ill is of the sinister and psychotic murderer who looks abnormal and who victimizes innocent people.[95] Of course, real-life cases also play a role in reinforcing the belief that mentally ill people are dangerous. The following cases received enormous attention from the media:

- John Hinckley—in 1981, attempted to assassinate President Ronald Reagan but was found not guilty by reason of insanity and was committed to mental institution.
- Ted Kaczynski—from 1978 to 1995, the Unabomber killed 3 people and injured many others with his mail bombs, suffered from schizophrenia but did not plead guilty by reason of insanity. He was arrested and sentenced to life imprisonment in a supermaximum prison in Colorado.
- Russell Weston—in 1998, killed two police officers at the U.S. Capitol while suffering from schizophrenia. He was held not competent to stand trial and committed to a mental institution.
- Colin Ferguson—in 1993 murdered 6 people on a train in New York City. His original defense claimed he was temporarily insane, but Ferguson fired them and represented himself. He was convicted and sentenced to hundreds of years in prison.
- Andrea Yates—in 2001 drowned her 5 children in her bathtub in Houston, Texas, after suffering from postpartum depression with psychosis. She was found guilty but subsequently her conviction was overturned and she was committed to a mental institution.
- Lashaun Harris—in 2005 threw her 3 children into the San Francisco Bay where they drowned. She suffered from schizophrenia and was found not guilty by reason of insanity and committed to a mental institution.
- Seung-Hui Cho—in 2007 killed 32 people at the Virginia Polytechnic Institute and State University (Virginia Tech) and then killed himself. He suffered from anxiety and depression and had been under mental health therapy.

In media depictions of crime, people are surrounded by such images of violence committed by "deranged" individuals:

> Both television and newspapers routinely report such stories as a man who shot his boss, a woman who left her newborn baby to die, or a child who disappeared on the way home from school. Attributing societal violence to the mentally ill provides the community with an explanation they can understand, as well as a source of blame for the violence.[96]

That such images have some basis in reality reminds us that the media do not invent problems out of the thin air; instead, media coverage subjectively covers such cases in ways that fail to provide sufficient context necessary to fully understand the true nature of the problem.[97] The media thus construct the problem of violent mentally ill people from real cases, as suggested in Chapter 2.

The point is, however, that mentally ill people are not more violent than people without mental illnesses. Mental illnesses are most likely to result in violence when the following conditions prevail:

- The person is suffering from paranoia and is experiencing delusions.
- The person is not being formally treated.
- The person is self-medicating (i.e., using or abusing drugs).[98]

Because of this, the brain disorder, schizophrenia, is thought to be associated with an increased incidence of violent behavior, although there is disagreement among scholars about the strength of this relationship. These facts are not known by most, in part due to how the media portray crime in American society.

Media and Fear of Crime: The Chicken Little Phenomenon

Many criminologists have asserted that exposure to media images of crime will promote fear in viewers, which should not be surprising given the tendency of media to cover violence, murder, school shootings, and so forth. This is based at least in part on what is known as the cultivation thesis. According to Ronald Weitzer and Charis Kubrin, the *cultivation thesis*

> portrays the media world as very different from the real world, with the implication that heavy consumption of media messages distorts audience beliefs about the world and influences cognitive and emotional states ... In this view, the greater one's exposure to the media, the more likely it is that one's perceptions of the real world will match what is most frequently depicted in the media. Further, the media world, especially television, differs greatly from the real world of crime and may cultivate a perception that the world is a scary place. Repeated exposure to media coverage of crime may thus generate fear and insecurity among viewers ... [99]

According to Robin Nabi and Karyn Riddle, the cultivation thesis asserts that viewers of television "are more likely to perceive the world in ways that mirror reality as presented on TV rather than more objective measures of social reality."[100] Further, people who are heavy viewers of television have themes stored in their brains that are "more accessible in memory and thus more influential in making judgments ..."[101]

According to the *substitution thesis*, "heavy exposure to media portrayals of crime has particularly strong effects on those with no direct experience of crime; for these individuals, media images of crime become a surrogate for real-world experience." As a result, people who are least likely to be victimized (e.g., the wealthy, elderly, women, etc.) should be more impacted by crime messages in the media.[102]

Finally, the *resonance thesis* suggests "that when media images are consistent with lived experience (e.g., criminal victimization, residing in a high-crime community), media and experience mutually reinforce citizens' fear." Because many high-crime communities are inhabited by a large number of Blacks and because Blacks have higher victimization rates of crime, the resonance thesis predicts a stronger media-fear relationship among Blacks. "That is, exposure to crime news in the media, coupled with greater personal vulnerability or experience of neighborhood crime, should produce a heightened fear of crime among Blacks."[103]

In their study, Weitzer and Kubrin found that those who say they rely most on local television for their news as their most important news source were more fearful of crime, even after controlling for numerous variables. Interestingly, Blacks were more likely than Whites to report relying on local television for their news, and they were also more fearful of crime.

According to Weitzer and Kubrin:

> Blacks are influenced both by local television news and by real-world conditions—namely, property crime victimization and perceived risk of street drugs to themselves and family members. That Blacks are concerned about street drugs is understandable in a city like Washington, DC, where street-level drug markets are concentrated in poor Black neighborhoods. For Blacks, the combined effect of local television news and the above crime factors provides support for the resonance thesis.[104]

Further, those living in communities with high crime rates and who rely on local television for news were very fearful of crime, while those who lived in communities with low levels of crime were not fearful even when relying on local television news. Weitzer and Kubrin explain:

> When the sample is disaggregated by neighborhood violent crime level, residents of communities with high violent crime rates are especially likely to be affected, in their fear of crime, by local television newscasts. By contrast, local television news exposure does not increase fear for residents of low violent-crime communities. The finding that local news effects are stronger for residents of high violent crime areas … lends further support to the resonance thesis.[105]

The vast majority of studies on media and violence show that the effects are real and meaningful[106] although some scholars characterize them as weak.[107] One claim about media coverage of crime that has been confirmed recently is that it is related to level of fear of crime, in support of the cultivation thesis.[108] In particular, so-called crime-time news leads to increased fear among its viewers.[109] Further, sensational crimes tend to generate fear of crime.[110]

Why do people who are exposed media become afraid of crime? The *Chicken Little Phenomenon* explains that when news broadcasts cover violence, without providing any context, it leaves viewers with no real sense of their relative risks of violent crime victimization. All viewers, regardless of where they live or who they are, come to believe that their risk of victimization is significant, and therefore become afraid. Media coverage of crime stories creates the sense that the sky is falling!

David Krajicek calls the result a "tattooing of the national psyche."[111] The National Criminal Justice Commission demonstrates how the media have created the illusion that all Americans have a realistic chance of being murdered by strangers, even though murder is the rarest of all crimes and is most likely committed by people known to the victims.[112] As one example, in the mid 1990s, *USA Today* published a headline that claimed: "Random Killings Hit a High." The subtitle claimed "All have 'realistic chance' of being victim, says FBI."[113] This was absolutely false. In fact, the chance that any U.S. resident over the age of 11 years will be murdered was only 1 in 14,286 in 1996.[114] This risk has substantially declined since then, for not only has the U.S. population increased to just over 300 million people, the number of murders has declined significantly since the 1990s.

Generally, the more viewers are exposed to television, the more likely they are to see the world as a "mean and scary place" and the more likely they are distrust others, feel insecure and vulnerable, and view crime as a serious problem.[115] This is also consistent with the cultivation thesis. David Altheide concurs, saying that television leaves people seeing the world as " 'scary,' dangerous, and fearful."[116]

Kenneth Dowler surveyed more than 1,000 people and found that people averaged approximately 15 hours of television viewing per week. Further, 42% said they are regular viewers of crime shows while 20% said that newspapers are their main source of crime news.[117] Dowler found that those people who regularly viewed crime dramas were more likely to fear crime. Other variables were also related to fear of crime, including gender, education, income, age, perceived neighborhood problems and police effectiveness. Those most afraid of crime were more likely to favor punitive responses to crime. Other variables related to punitive attitudes included income, marital status, race, and education.

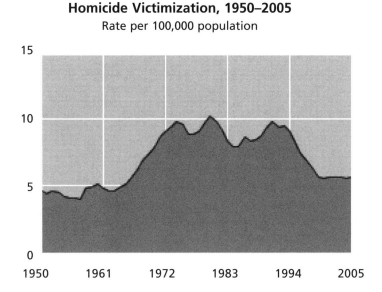

Homicide Victimization, 1950–2005
Rate per 100,000 population

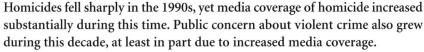

Homicides fell sharply in the 1990s, yet media coverage of homicide increased substantially during this time. Public concern about violent crime also grew during this decade, at least in part due to increased media coverage.

Heavy TV exposure leads to an increased fear of crime, an overestimation of the likelihood of becoming a victim of violence, beliefs that one's neighborhood is unsafe, assumptions that crime rates are increasing, and increased support for punitive anticrime measures.[118] Another result of TV viewing is that it can "dull the critical-thinking ability" of Americans and lead to apathy, thereby making simplistic solutions to complex problems more appealing and making Americans less interested in important issues.[119]

The impact of media on fear depends on numerous factors, including neighborhood composition. One study showed, for example, that exposure to the media was associated with higher levels of fear for those living in communities with large numbers of black residents.[120] This is consistent with the resonance thesis.

An analysis of crime news and fear of crime by Ted Chiricos and colleagues found that frequency of exposure to television news and radio news was related to fear of crime.[121] Yet, reading newspapers was not found to be related to fear of crime, even though most newspaper crime coverage is violent or sensational in nature.[122] This likely owes itself to the fact that newspapers lack the emotional elements seen on TV.

Viewers of television news—which overestimates the incidence of violent crime and underestimates the incidence of property crime—are also more likely to overestimate the level of violent crime and underestimate the level of property crime in their communities. [123]

Exposure to crime-related tabloid headlines and repeated exposure to violence-related stories are also associated with higher levels of worry about becoming a victim of violence.[124] Other outcomes of being confronted with numerous scenes of crime and violence include: (1) having more favorable evaluations of people with similar religious and political beliefs and more unfavorable evaluations of those who differ on these dimensions, (2) being more punitive toward moral transgressors and more benevolent to heroic individuals, (3) being more physically aggressive toward others with dissimilar political orientations, and (4) striving more vigorously to meet cultural standards of value.[125]

According to some analyses, however, the effects of television viewing depend on who is doing the viewing.[126] In some research, television viewing and fear of crime are related only in certain segments of the population (e.g., older Caucasian females), consistent with the substitution thesis. This finding may be attributed to the fact that the most likely depicted crime victims on television are middle-aged or older Caucasian women.[127]

Thus, for some, "the media have the ability, indirectly at least, to manipulate the fear of crime."[128] Sarah Eschholtz summarizes the research by claiming that

> for newspaper consumption the character of the message is important: local, random, and sensational stories evoke the most fear, whereas, distant, specific, and less sensational stories may have a calming effect on individuals. For television, the quantity of television viewed in general, violent programming in particular, and certain audience characteristics are generally associated with higher levels of fear.[129]

Few go as far as to suggest that the media intentionally create fear in viewers. But the fear that is created reinforces mythology about crime and criminal justice,[130] causing citizens to avoid, and police to apprehend, people who are perceived as posing the greatest threats to our well-being.[131] These people tend to be darker in skin color and lacking in wealth as compared to the average American, as shown earlier in this chapter. Michael Moore, in his Oscar winning documentary film, *Bowling for Columbine*, implies that media coverage of crime leads Americans to become afraid and spend more time at home, watching television where they are thus exposed to more commercial messages from the corporations that own the media and who pay to advertise to their products. This is certainly consistent with the argument of media scholars introduced in Chapter 1.

Given all this coverage of crime in the United States, for many citizens "the United States must seem to be a hopelessly savage place that stands teetering on the lip of the Apocalypse."[132] Gallup polls conducted throughout the 1980s and 1990s showed that even as crime declined, people were more likely to call it the number one problem facing the nation. Additionally, the percentage of people who feared walking alone at night, was highly variable over the years despite relatively consistent declines in crime since the early 1970s. In March 1994, the Times Mirror Center for the People and the Press reported a poll showing that 50% of the respondents feared they would be victims of crime. Another 30% said that crime was the nation's number one problem. Compare this with Gallup polls showing that a large number of citizens thought in 1994 that crime was the most important problem facing the country. Perhaps it is not surprising to learn that coverage of crime on the three major networks peaked a year earlier, in 1993.

Violence Begets Violence?

Studies of the impact of media on violence are crystal clear in their findings and implications for society. The National Institute on Media and the Family reports the following statistics and findings about media and violence:

- By the time a child is eighteen years old, he or she will witness on television (with average viewing time) 200,000 acts of violence including 40,000 murders.
- Children, ages 8 to 18, spend more time (44.5 hours per week–6½ hours daily) in front of computer, television, and game screens than any other activity in their lives except sleeping.
- Since the 1950s, more than 1,000 studies have been done on the effects of violence in television and movies. The majority of these studies conclude that children who watch significant amounts of television and movie violence are more likely to exhibit aggressive behavior, attitudes and values.
- The American Medical Association, American Academy of Pediatrics, American Psychological Association, American Academy of Family Physicians, and American Academy of Child & Adolescent Psychiatry all agree that violence in the media influences the behavior of children, especially younger children who are more impressionable, less able to distinguish between fantasy and reality, less able to discern motives for violence, and more likely to learn by observing and imitating.
- Children who watch more TV and play more video games are not only exposed to more media violence, but are more likely to act more aggres-

sively with peers, to assume the worst in their interactions with peers, to become less sensitive to violence and those who suffer from violence, to seek out additional violence in entertainment, to see the world as violent and mean, and to see violence as an acceptable way of solving problems.[133]

The American Academy of Pediatrics claims the main messages children learn from television violence are: 1) violence is an acceptable way to deal with problems; and 2) violence does no real harm (since people on television reappear even after being hurt or killed, or simply vanish from the scene).[134] This encourages violence in children who see it. Similarly, the American Academy of Child & Adolescent Psychiatry (AACAP) states that "80 percent of the programs that children watch contain violence. There is widespread agreement that children who are allowed to see violence on television show more aggressive behavior than those who don't."[135]

According to Michelle Brown, crimes widely popularized by the media have often been blamed, ironically, on various forms of media. One mechanism through which this occurs is when the media generate so-called *copycat crimes*.[136] For example, Lee Boyd Malvo (one of the Washington, DC "snipers") was reportedly obsessed with the film *The Matrix*. A ring of car thieves allegedly patterned their crimes after the video game *Grand Theft Auto*. Robert Harris and Jon Venables, who murdered a toddler, were said to have re-enacted scenes from *Child's Play 3* in their murder. The mass murders at Columbine High School were blamed on the rock band Marilyn Manson. And various films have produced violent confrontations between rival gangs over the years, including *Get Rich or Die Tryin'*; *New Jack City*; and *Boyz N' The Hood*.[137]

David Altheide discusses the significance of media focus on violent crime for the average citizen:

> Serious personal criminal attacks happen rarely, but they are regarded as typical and quite common by American citizens because virtually all mass media reports about crime focus on the most spectacular, dramatic, and violent. With the images of blood, guns, psychopaths, and suffering in front of them and inside their heads, it is quite difficult to offer programmatic criticisms of our current approach to crime and accompanying issues such as prisons and other modes of dispute resolution, including restitution and negotiations. As long as crime and mayhem are forthcoming, only a recycling of affirmations tied to previous popular culture.[138]

Externalities of violent programming in the media include more violence in society, larger criminal justice apparatuses to deal with it, and less freedom for all.[139] An example of more violence in society comes from one study of television viewing and homicide arrests, which found that increased television penetration 15 years earlier actually predicted greater arrest rates for homicide later. This is presumably because viewers learn that violence is acceptable in some circumstances by watching violent content on television.[140]

On top of this, since violent crime is equated with crime in the media, viewers are more likely to support "'tough on crime legislation,' including mandatory sentencing, 'three strikes and you're out,' and capital punishment."[141] This is yet another way that media perpetuates violence, in this case, through society's criminal justice practices.[142]

David Krajicek explains the specific links between media coverage of crime and such repressive criminal justice practices. He says the media provide crime-anxious Americans with excited accounts of horrible crimes; present tenuous evidence that the crimes, however anomalous, could happen to each of us; seek out the accountable individuals (judges and probation officers); devise snappy slogans to package the problem neatly; and serve up images of scowling politicians thumping their lecterns about the latest legislation that surely would stop such atrocities: "We're finally getting tough on crime. We're no longer coddling criminals. We're making America's streets safe again."[143] Whether crime news is based on fact and is representative of the truth is irrelevant—"the politicians wanted expedient answers, not information"—"efficacy means nothing; image is everything."[144]

Some scholars also claim there may be a relationship between screen violence and homicide in some specific cases.[145] When it comes to television and films, they include some of the most grotesquely violent images in our society. This will be discussed more in Chapter 8.

Ignore Corporate and White-collar Crime

With all this talk and review of research about crime, where does white-collar and corporate crime fit in? Recall the argument from Chapter 2 that the media play a large role in helping determine what becomes perceived as a problem. According to Ray Surette, "by emphasizing or ignoring topics, [the media] may influence the list of issues that are important to the public." [146] As noted earlier, corporate crimes are virtually ignored by the media; thus most people, even criminology and criminal justice students, do not perceive such acts as threatening to their own personal safety.[147]

It is important to remember that when looking for bias in the media, one must look not only at what is covered and how it is covered, but also in what is *not* covered and why. Since mainstream media tend to ignore white-collar and corporate crime, this is a serious bias in mainstream media[148] Ignoring corporate and white-collar crime is troubling precisely because the harms associated with such acts clearly dwarf those resulting from all street crimes combined in any given year.

According to the experts, corporate crime not only causes more financial losses each year than street crime, but also injures and kills more people annually than street crime.[149] Americans do not know this, however, largely due to media coverage of violence. According to David Friedrichs:

> Perceptions of violence and fear are often shaped by the media. Conventional forms of violence are pervasively featured in film, television, newspapers, and most other media ... The public has been socialized to think of violent crime principally in terms of either individual offenders or a small group of offenders (e.g., a gang); violent crimes are disproportionately associated with deranged or manifestly evil offenders, and are most readily thought of in terms of murder, rape, or felonious assault. Overall, it has been easier to portray the crimes of individual psychopaths than those of corporations, and such crime makes for much more colorful copy than corporate crime. When the media expose unsafe, harmful, and destructive activities of corporations, they risk, as well, losing advertising revenue from such corporations; this is only one of the more obvious reasons why the media focus on conventional violence.[150]

If Friedrichs is correct, the media have a vested interest in *not* covering corporate crime.

John McMullan provides the following account of what he referred to as a corporate crime:

> At 5:20 a.m. on 9 May 1992, an explosion ripped through a coal mine in Plymouth, Nova Scotia, killing 26 miners, 11 of whom remain buried there to this day. According to the report of the Westray Mine Public Inquiry, sparks from the cutting head of a continuous mining machine ignited methane gas, creating a fire and explosion that then stirred up coal particles, creating a coal-dust explosion.

According to McMullan, there was "ample evidence of criminal conduct involving manslaughter for failing to keep coal dust in the mine in check and negligence in operating an unsafe mine: inadequate equipment, poorly trained employees, no proper methane-control or stone-dusting plans, and tampering with the mine's design without proper approval."

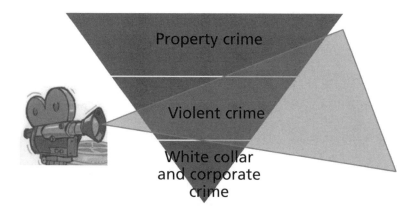

Most of the media focus on only a small fraction of crime. There is more focus on street crime than acts of elites such as corporate crime. Coverage of street crime is generally limited to certain types of crime, particularly violent and random crimes. Thus, only a fraction of crime is depicted in the media. Even a smaller amount of corporate and white-collar crime is discussed in the media.

The largest share of coverage of this crime in the media was "the discursive formation of legal disaster" (31%). Here, stories focused on the regulatory process, criminal justice proceedings, and so forth. These stories were "technical, formal, formulaic, and coded in play-by-play 'he said … she said' statements that narrate the legal logics" of both sides of the case. This reality is probably due to the effort to be "balanced" and thus appear to be objective, as explained in Chapter 2. According to McMullan, the legal framework "works to suppress the violent effects of the explosion, to exceptionalize its meaning, to re-frame human suffering as legal tragedy, and to distance the corporation from the consequences of the event."

The next most common share of coverage was the "human tragedy" formation (17%). Here, stories suggested that the incident was a natural accident. Such work is inherently dangerous and such accidents are unavoidable. This allows victim stories to be told as part of the *innocent victim* narrative.

While actual causes were rarely identified by the news, it was more common that the causes were identified as individual rather than organizational. This is entirely consistent with how street crime is covered in the news, as noted earlier. Further, attributions of blame and responsibility were rarely made in news coverage. In the majority of such workplace incidents they are referred to as "accidents," even in cases where corporations knowingly and repeatedly fail to correct safety violations that risk life and property. Given what has already been established in this book about the close relationship between the media and other corporations, it is probably not surprising that the media are not very eager to assign blame to corporations even when they commit dangerous and costly acts.

The recent cases of a mine explosion in West Virginia and the explosion aboard a BP oil rig in the Gulf of Mexico received a lot of media coverage, especially the latter because it led to the largest ever oil spill in the history of the United States. While some media reports focused on actions (including crimes) that may have produced the oil spill, most of the coverage has focused on the effects of the oil spill on the environment and how the oil spill could be stopped. Most Americans don't even know that these two events also killed 40 people; this is likely due to the fact that the issue has not been widely addressed in the mainstream media.

With the rare exception of cases such as Bernie Madoff, white-collar crime is also generally ignored by the press. Crimes such as fraud

> are treated by the mass media as extensions of "infotainment," such as individual and corporate celebrities in trouble; "normal" people turning to fraud because of drugs, gambling or sex; readily visualizable and often short fraud events (like "identity fraud" or "card skimming") connected to "organized crime" or "terrorism;" or long-term concealment of fraud that shows the "Establishment" to be incompetent or business people/politicians to be hypocrites.[151]

This type of coverage is consistent with the dominant motivations of crime shown in the media, which tend to be individualistic in nature. When white-collar type offenders are depicted in the media, they are shown as individuals who are shrewd, ruthless, or evil. Just as with street crime, motivation is shown in the media as stemming from some individual source such as greed.[152]

It is important to note that enforcement of white-collar crime depends to a small degree on media coverage of it.[153] Thus, we can expect white-collar crime laws to *not* be significantly enforced as long as the media continue to ignore them. The same can be said of organized crime.[154]

After the Enron scandal in the early 21st Century, politicians, all the way up to President George W. Bush, were featured prominently in the media characterizing white-collar and corporate offenders as bad apples.[155] What is rarely considered is the possibility that much white-collar and corporate criminality results not from bad apples but instead a bad barrel (i.e., there are systemic or structural causes of such crimes). Corporate owned media, however, are reluctant to seriously consider this possibility because they are so vested in it. It is also easier and cheaper to characterize white-collar and corporate offenders as bad people, and it better fits the way crime in general is portrayed in the press.

Neglect of this topic stems from the risk of libel suits; interrelationships between the media and business; the pro-business orientation of the media; and difficulties associated with investigating white-collar crime.[156] The media focus almost exclusively on street crimes, so that three classes of people are depicted—the upper class, the middle class, and the "criminal class."[157]

Bernard Madoff recently pleaded guilty to various forms of fraud that cost investors nearly $65 billion in losses, the largest ever white-collar crime in the United States. He was sentenced to 150 years in prison. http://en.wikipedia.org/wiki/File:BernardMadoff.jpg.

In the wake of the corporate scandals that sent our stock market crashing, led to hundreds of billions of dollars in losses to investors, and resulted in tens of thousands of Americans losing their jobs and retirement savings, the media did provide significant coverage of corporate crime in America. We learned of the fraud and embezzlement of Enron, Arthur Anderson, WorldCom, Tyco, and dozens of other corporations. Unfortunately, once new laws were passed that supposedly "cracked down" on "bad apples," our attention was diverted away from such crimes toward a coming war with Iraq. And now, as if corporate crime is a thing of the past, the media rarely even mention it.

According to Robert McChesney

> The intense coverage of the widespread corporate malfeasance in 2002–2003 was very unusual. Careful analysis of the coverage provided evidence of how unusual; after all, the fraud that led to the collapse of major corporations like Enron and WorldCom had been going on for years with the knowledge of some pretty powerful people, yet it had never come to our attention until it was too late.[158]

Ben Bagdikian points out that the "unprecedented magnitude of corporate fraud, theft, and collusion was not by fly-by-night sleazy operations but by some of the country's largest corporations" aided by conspirators in the auditing and banking industry.[159] Perhaps this explains the lack of serious investigation into what caused the fraud in the first place. Recall that mainstream media are owned by large corporations and have close connections with other large corporations.

A study of how mainstream television networks covered the corporate crime scandals of 2001–2002 found that coverage of the crimes peaked in early 2002.[160] From January to July 2001, there were 489 stories on ABC, NBC, and CBS about business, yet only 52 were about the scandals (11%). From January to July 2002 there were 613 stories about business and 471 centered on the scandals (77%). This is significant because the Enron scandal broke in the news at the end of November 2001; at the end of July 2002, WorldCom filed the largest bankruptcy in U.S. business history. During this period, "the networks broadcast almost as many stories on corporate scandals as they did on business stories for the same period a year before." Further, 77% of the stories dealing with business were centered on the corporate scandals.

✒️ For more information about media coverage of these corporate crimes, see the website for this book at: www.pscj.appstate.edu/media/ corporatecrime.html

---

Ironically, some media companies committed the very same behaviors that got companies like Enron and WorldCom in trouble. Time Warner (owner of CNN), for example, who had joint business ventures with WorldCom and Qwest, allegedly distorted its books and inflated its revenues. Viacom (former owner of CBS) also had links to Enron. According to McChesney: "Media firms historically have been understandably reluctant to cover their own misdeeds in their news media, and they could hardly be enthusiastic about a no-holds-barred journalism that would uncover the entire corporate crime story."[161] Logically, Time Warner and Viacom had pretty serious reasons for not providing in-depth analyses of the corporate fraud that rocked the country.

As for politicians, they "stand a far greater chance of becoming the object of news media scrutiny if they are rumored to have ten outstanding parking tickets or to have skipped out on a bar bill [or to have been involved with a young intern who is now missing] than if they quietly use their power to funnel billions of public dollars to powerful special interests."[162] Turn on the TV news today and odds are you'll see an example of the former kind of story. Recently, for example, there has been intense media coverage of Former Senator John Edwards' affair and subsequent fathering of a child with his mistress.

All of this is problematic precisely because the media serve as the major source of information about crime for most people.[163] Crime stories funnel out to media viewers, but they are in no way accurate of what most crime really is; nor is public perception of crime.

Summary

Stories about crime and criminal justice that are "critical" in nature are typically lacking in American news. Stories about crime and criminal justice also tend to be lacking in any meaningful context. The media are biased in favor of visually dramatic and sensational events that attract wide viewing audiences. Such media depictions of crime problems are inherently inaccurate.

Lack of context in the news does not serve Americans well because it misinforms them. It is beneficial for politicians who want to put forth brief and simplistic stances on crime and criminal justice, most commonly depicted as the 10- or 15-second "sound bites" heard in any election year. In terms of criminal justice policy, the media simply "cover" what politicians pledge and promise about getting tough on crime because the media are caught up in the same moral panic about crime.

Media coverage of crime gives us the impression that crime is rampant. In fact, street crime has fallen for decades, property crime since the 1970s and violent crime since the 1990s. Even when crime is going down, stories about declines in crime are rare.

Approximately 30% of local television news relates to crime, as does more than one-tenth of national news and about one-quarter of newspaper space. In many markets, stories about crime comprise about 25–35% of the news. Some studies find that crime stories make up as much as 61% of newscasts, and one found that 13% of all newscasts began with three crime stories in a row, back to back to back.

The media generally are most focused on acts of racial minorities, especially blacks. Further, racial minorities are generally negatively portrayed. These dominant images of black criminals and people of color in a negative light not only impact perceptions of crime. Research also demonstrates that negative portrayals of minorities are associated with lower self-esteem as well as less societal integration among members of those groups depicted in the media.

Racial hoaxes occur when someone invents a crime and says they were assaulted by a person of another race, or an actual victim blames their victimization on a person of another race. The majority of the hoaxes involve someone white falsely claiming they were harmed by someone black, primarily an African American male. Meanwhile, whites are overrepresented as victims and police officers. This fits well with the popular conception of whites as innocent.

Women are less likely to come to the attention of criminal justice agencies. This is largely due to the fact that women commit so much less crime than men. When women do get caught up in the criminal justice process, the courts are generally less punitive toward them. Female behavior typically comes to the attention of the media when it conflicts with the norms of society with regard to appropriate behavior by women. Thus, it is not surprising that female violence is attractive to the media. Women are also featured as victims in the press. In many cases, women are depicted as responsible for their own victimization.

Studies examining how the media cover kids generally show that the media generally do not pay much attention to children except for when it is bad news. Media stories tend to focus on negative aspects of adolescence and juvenile behavior. Specifically, the most popular stories on local news are on crime and delinquency committed by young people.

Child victims tend to receive more attention in the media than older victims. Children are seen as the most vulnerable and the least capable of defending themselves. They are also perceived as having limitless potential and thus most worthy of protection. Finally, stories of children victims are captivating of audiences, a major goal of the mainstream media. Children as victims are perhaps the most "innocent" of all crime victims. Thus, stories about children crime victims fit the dominant narrative of the "innocent" victim in the mainstream press. Fitting individual crime stories into this widely used narrative is quite easy.

Depictions of criminal motivation in the media tend to be individualistic, which means they leave citizens with the impression that what motivates criminality is individual-level factors such as jealousy, emotional instability, mental illness, greed, and so forth. The typical characterization of the individually responsible offender is consistent both with the dominant narrative of the innately evil criminal in the media as well as the cultural belief in American society of free will, which underlies all criminal justice practice. One important outcome of the media's focus on individual motivations for criminality is greater pressure for crime control solutions to the crime problem.

The media also play a large role in creating the illusion that mentally ill individuals are responsible for a large share of violence in society. One of the dominant themes or narratives in the media of the mentally ill is of the sinister and psychotic murderer who looks abnormal and who victimizes innocent people. However, mentally ill people are not more violent than people without mental illnesses. Mental illnesses are most likely to result in violence when the following conditions prevail: The person is suffering from paranoia and is experiencing delusions; is not being formally treated; and is self-medicating (i.e., using or abusing drugs). These facts are not known by most, in part due to how the media portray crime in American society.

Many criminologists have asserted that exposure to media images of crime will promote fear in viewers, which should not be surprising given the tendency of media to cover violence, murder, school shootings, and so forth. The *cultivation thesis* suggests that exposure to media cultivates a perception that the world is a scary place. Repeated exposure to media coverage of crime may thus generate fear and insecurity among viewers. The *substitution thesis* holds that exposure to media portrayals of crime has its strongest effects on those with no direct experience of crime. The *resonance thesis* suggests that exposure to media portrayals of crime has its strongest effects on those with direct experience of crime.

The *Chicken Little Phenomenon* refers to when broadcasts cover violence, without providing any context, leaving viewers with no real sense of their relative risks of violent crime victimization. All viewers, regardless of where they live or who they are, come to believe that their risk of victimization is significant, and therefore become afraid.

Heavy TV exposure leads to an increased fear of crime, an overestimation of the likelihood of becoming a victim of violence, beliefs that one's neighborhood is unsafe, assumptions that crime rates are increasing, and increased support for punitive anticrime measures. Exposure to violence in the media can also lead to more violence in society. The American Academy of Pediatrics claims the main messages children learn from television violence are: violence is an acceptable way to deal with problems; and violence does no real harm (since people on television reappear even after being hurt or killed, or simply vanish from the scene).

Corporate crimes are virtually ignored by the media; thus most people, even criminology and criminal justice students, do not perceive such acts as threatening to their own personal safety. Ignoring corporate and white-collar crime is troubling precisely because the harms associated with such acts clearly dwarf those resulting from all street crimes combined in any given year; corporate crime not only causes more financial losses each year than street crime, but also injures and kills more people annually than street crime. Americans do not know this, however, largely due to media coverage of violence.

Even when white-collar type offenders are depicted in the media, they are shown as individuals who are shrewd, ruthless, or evil. Just as with street crime, motivation is shown in the media as stemming from some individual source such as greed. Relatively little focus is provided on the contexts in which corporations operate and the structures that promote the greedy behavior in the first place.

Discussion Questions

1) In the chapter, it was argued that stories about crime and criminal justice that are "critical" in nature are typically lacking in American news. What is meant by the term "critical?"

2) It was also argued that stories about crime and criminal justice also tend to be lacking in any meaningful context. What is meant by the term "context?"

3) How does the lack of critical reporting and context fail to serve citizens?

4) Does media coverage of crime tend to lead to the belief that there is more crime in society than really exists? Explain.

5) How does media coverage of crime lead to fear of crime? Explain using examples.

6) How much of the stories found in the news media are devoted to crime?

7) What are "trivial," "soft," or "lifestyle" stories? And why are they so popular in the media?

8) Which groups of society are most featured in media accounts of crime and criminal justice? How do these groups tend to be portrayed? Why?

9) What is a *racial hoax*? Provide examples.

10) Why do women less frequently come to the attention of the media? Under which circumstances are they most likely to come to the attention of the media? Why?

11) What are the main differences between juvenile courts and adult courts? Why have these differences eroded over time?

12) When are children most likely to be featured in the press? How are they most likely to be depicted in the media?

13) What is the most common form of criminal motivation depicted in the media? Which types of motivation are least featured in the media? What really motivates most crime?

14) How are the mentally ill depicted in the media? Does media coverage provide an accurate depiction of mental illness?

15) Define the *cultivation thesis, substitution thesis,* and *resonance thesis*. Which is supported by empirical evidence? Explain.

16) Define the *Chicken Little Phenomenon*.

17) Heavy exposure to television has been linked to various negative outcomes. Identify and discuss these outcomes.

18) How does exposure to media lead to violence? Explain and provide examples.

19) Are corporate and white-collar crimes ignored by the media? And why does this matter?

Chapter 5

Media Coverage of Policing: The Effective Law Enforcer, the Bad Cop, and Crime Prevention

Learning Objectives

After reading this chapter, you will be able to:

1) Discuss whether media coverage of the U.S. criminal justice network is accurate.

2) Explain why the police receive so much more media coverage than the courts and corrections and discuss the impact this has on public perceptions of criminal justice.

3) Describe how the media accurately and inaccurately depict the police.

4) Explain how media focus on local policing and local crime helps reinforce the notion that street crime is more harmful and a greater threat to citizens.

5) Identify and define the five major roles of police officers in the United States and how police spend most of their time.

6) Explain which roles of police are most featured in the media and why.

7) Explain how the media reinforce the perception that the police are actually effective at reducing crime.

8) Explain whether policing actually impacts the crime rate in a meaningful way.

9) Explain how media coverage of policing suggests that they are not constrained by the criminal law.

10) Define the *perp walk* and explain how this is a threat to the presumption of innocence and due process.

11) Discuss whether most coverage of police is positive or negative in nature.

12) Identify and define seven popular images of police in the media today.

13) Demonstrate the ways police are often depicted negatively in the media.

14) Differentiate between the *bad apple frame* and the *rotten barrel frame* and show which is most common in the media.

15) Describe the effects of *zero tolerance policing*.

16) Define *police profiling* and explain whether this practice is justified.

17) Show how policing may be biased against some groups.

18) Discuss whether *police brutality* is common and explain why it is of interest to the media.

19) Explain how the media can do great good in terms of helping reduce harms in society.

20) Explain whether popular crime prevention programs like "McGruff the Crime Dog" and "Crimestoppers" have been effective.

Introduction

What do images of police from the news, as well as television and movies suggest to you about American policing? As it turns out, the most prevalent images of police found in news accounts as well as other forms of media are misleading.[1] For example, while police serve valuable functions to the American people, including crime victims, police spend very little time fighting crime.[2]

Yet, the dominant image of the police officer in the United States is of the law enforcer. Like with myths about crime, the news media and entertainment media are largely responsible for myths about policing. This chapter examines how the media cover policing.

According to David Perlmutter, inaccurate coverage of the police in the media leads to myths about policing in the real world as well as unrealistic expectations of citizens.[3] Among the inaccuracies documented by Perlmutter include: media images of police show them as far more active than they really are (when in reality most policing is quite routine and boring); media images of police show them constantly fighting crime (when in reality most policing involves providing social services and engaging in administrative tasks); and media images of police show them engaged in violence (when in reality fights by police with suspects and use of force are quite rare).[4]

The news media also often portray the police as heroic, professional crime fighters.[5] Although this has some basis in reality, the majority of what police do has little to do with crime. These and other issues are discussed in this chapter.

Front-end Loaded

Before beginning the analysis of policing specifically, it is important to note from the outset that media coverage inaccurately portrays the U.S. criminal justice network as a whole. Nancy Marion explains that the early steps in the criminal justice process (law enforcement, investigation and arrest) are emphasized whereas the other steps are almost invisible.[6] It appears that most criminal justice images are "front-end loaded" meaning there is far more focus on policing than courts and corrections.[7] This is one of the most important lessons of media coverage of criminal justice—it is disproportionately focused on the police, which itself can create misconceptions of the realities of criminal justice in America.

For more information about the criminal justice process and how it works, see the website for this book at: www.pscj.appstate.edu/media/ cjprocess.html

---

At least three arguments can be made to justify the increased focus on police relative to courts and corrections. First, police are the entry point of what is commonly referred to as the "criminal justice system." Without police making arrests, courts and corrections would have no "clients." That is, if police did not make arrests, there would be no one to try, convict, and punish. Second, police do a lot more than just fight crime. Thus, the numerous services

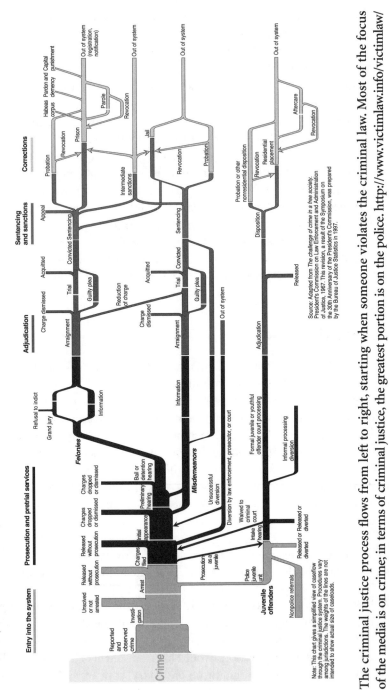

What is the sequence of events in the criminal justice system?

The criminal justice process flows from left to right, starting when someone violates the criminal law. Most of the focus of the media is on crime; in terms of criminal justice, the greatest portion is on the police. http://www.victimlaw.info/victimlaw/resources/include/BJScjsflowco.pdf.

they provide to their communities may justify increased media coverage. Third, and very interesting, is that police also receive the largest share of resources in criminal justice. For example, in 2006, Americans spent about $99 billion for policing, compared with $69 billion for corrections and only $46 billion for courts.[8] Thus, 46% of justice dollars are spent on police, followed by 33% on corrections and only 21% on courts. That we spend more on police may indicate may indicate our priorities as a nation, which would logically be reflected in media coverage of criminal justice.

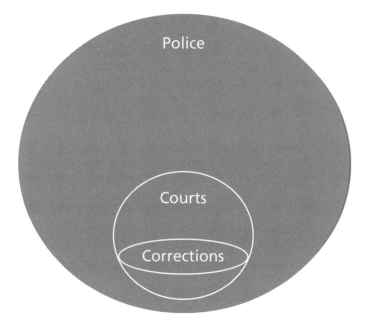

Because of the greater focus on police than courts and corrections, Americans likely get a skewed view about the relative size and importance of each branch of criminal justice. There is far more coverage of police in the media than of courts and corrections.

The fact that the media focus more on police than courts and corrections may create the perception among media consumers that the police are more important than the other branches of criminal justice. To say the least, this is debatable. To those who most value public safety and crime control, devoting a greater share of resources and media attention to police may be warranted. Yet, to those who value due process and "innocent until proven guilty," they may be troubled by the implications for justice.

Disproportionate Focus on Local Cops and Local Crime

As of 2007, there were 14,676 police agencies in the United States and 699,850 full-time sworn police officers. About 71% of the police agencies were local police departments, and another 17% were county sheriff departments. Thus, 88% of police agencies are responsible for policing what can be thought of as local governments, or cities and counties. Of the police officers, about 53% were employed by cities while about 21% were employed by counties. Thus, 74% of police officers in the United States work for local cities and counties; the typical police agency and the typical officer in the United States are at the local level of government.[9]

From these data, we can conclude that police activities are very much a local phenomenon. Further, it is also true that most law enforcement officers work for small departments who serve small geographical areas.[10] The media, as it turns out, are generally accurate in their disproportionate focus on local agencies and officers because they tend to be most focused on the jobs of local police. Most news stories about police focus on local police agencies and officers.

Amazingly, even though white-collar and corporate crimes cost us far more in terms of financial losses and physical harms (e.g., injuries and deaths), the vast majority of police agencies and officers (local departments and officers) are not focused on it. Prior to the terrorist attacks of September 11, 2001, roughly 5% of all officers in the United States were focused on white-collar and corporate crimes.[11] This number has declined since then as agencies such as the Federal Bureau of Investigation (FBI) and officers have shifted their attention to terrorism and counter-terrorism investigations.[12]

Coverage of police activity in the media primarily focuses on street crime, particularly violent offenses. Of course, only a select number of crimes and police activities are presented in the media. These news story images need not be, and often are not, accurate representations of the prevalence of crime or the effectiveness of police intervention.[13] One study of 63 large U.S. cities found that media coverage affects police employment levels, likely because crime-related stories are prominently featured in newspapers.[14]

Media focus on local policing and local crime logically helps reinforce the notion that street crime is more harmful and a greater threat to citizens, even though this is not the case. Recall a lesson from Chapter 4 that the media generally ignore white-collar and corporate crime due mostly to reasons related to its close connections to corporate power as well as its profit-seeking orientation.

Overemphasize the Law Enforcement Role

Police officers in the United States serve five basic roles:

- *Enforcing laws*: This includes investigating reported crimes, collecting and protecting evidence from crime scenes, apprehending suspects, and assisting the prosecution in obtaining convictions.
- *Preserving the peace*: This includes intervening in noncriminal conduct in public places (such as at concerts, sporting events, and on the roads) that could escalate into criminal activity if left unchecked.
- *Preventing crime*: This includes activities designed to stop crime before it occurs, such as education campaigns, preventive patrols, and community policing.
- *Providing services*: This includes performing functions normally served by other social service agencies, such as counseling, referring citizens for social services, assisting people with various needs, and keeping traffic moving.
- *Upholding rights*: This includes respecting all persons' rights regardless of race, ethnicity, class, gender, and other factors, and respecting individual Constitutional protections.[15]

These roles are generally derived from a statement by the *Law Enforcement Code of Conduct* passed by the International Association of Chiefs of Police, which reads: "The fundamental duties of a police officer include serving the community, safeguarding lives and property, protecting the innocent, keeping the peace and ensuring the rights of all to liberty, equality and justice."

Of these five roles, the *typical police officer* spends most of his or her time each day *not* fighting crime.[16] Estimates suggest that police spend only about 5% to 15% of their time dealing with criminal matters.[17] So how do police spend their time? The majority of a police officer's time is spent on administrative tasks and providing services to the public.[18] Services provided by police include checking buildings for security violations, regulating traffic, investigating accidents, providing information to citizens, crowd control, finding lost children, providing first aid, handling animal calls, mediating disputes, and negotiating settlements between citizens.[19] As noted by Peter Manning: "Of the police functions or activities most central to accumulated police obligations, none is more salient than supplying the range of public services required in complex, pluralistic, urban societies."[20] So, although "law enforcer" or "crime fighter" is the stereotypical image of the police officer—largely because of media coverage of crime—the typical city patrol officer or county sheriff in the United States spends the smallest amount of his or her day dealing with crime.

At the state and federal levels, the picture is very similar. State officers are most frequently assigned to responding to calls for service (crime and non-crime related), followed by investigative duties, administrative, technical, and training duties, and court-related duties. At the federal level, most officers have primary responsibility for investigations and enforcement, followed by corrections-related duties, police services, court operations, and security and protection.[21]

In spite of the realities of policing, the typical image of the police officer in the media is of the law enforcer. As explained by David Barlow and Melissa Hickman Barlow: "The most common perception about the police is that their role is to fight crime and protect citizens from harm.... It is a myth, however, that these activities constitute the fundamental role of the police in the United States."[22] This myth is reinforced with media coverage of police.

According to Barlow and Barlow:

> Stories about the crime-fighting activities of the police are abundant in newspapers and on the evening news in scenes of police officers taking dangerous suspects into custody or leading them into the court-room. Both news and entertainment media perpetuate the view of police as crime fighters, and they do so with help from police agencies. News media are usually only interested in police stories when they involve notable criminal activity because this is the aspect of policing deemed most newsworthy. Similarly, fictional crime dramas on television and in the movies typically depict police in a crime-fighting role.[23]

In fact, the great bulk of policing is relatively boring. The typical police officer spends a large portion of each day simply waiting around for calls for service. When these calls come, they rarely involve criminal activity, particularly *hot calls* where a suspect can actually be captured but instead *cold calls* where the offender has already fled the scene.[24]

Some more critical scholars have pointed out that the great bulk of police activity is aimed at protecting the existing social order or the status quo, which includes resolving conflicts, intervening with authority in various situations, and keeping open the lines of capitalistic commerce. For example, historians have pointed out that law enforcement agencies have been routinely used to maintain current power arrangements. Examples include slave patrols, disruption of labor organizing and demonstrations, strike busting, interfering with civil rights, and so forth.[25] Not surprisingly, given the facts identified in Chapters 1 and 2 about who owns the media and how they determine what is newsworthy and what is not, most Americans are unaware of these functions served by the police. Even more current examples of these activities (e.g., countering protests at the World Trade Organization meetings) are commonly depicted in ways that make peaceful protestors seem dangerous or naïve and unrealistic about the role of the economy in our lives.

Police Are Effective at Reducing Crime

Not only do the media tend to focus on the law enforcement role, they also reinforce the perception that the police are actually effective at reducing crime. This occurs for various reasons. First, police often appear in newspapers, both in crime stories and as experts for stories about crime and crime prevention. Recall that the media rely on government insiders including police for information about crime and criminal justice. Second, police use external relations to influence how they are portrayed in the media.[26] In crime stories, police tend to be portrayed as effective in responding to criminal incidents. Perhaps this is why exposure to local television news increases citizens' views of the police.[27] Two scholars claim that: "Nearly every police department, district attorney's office, or attorney general's office regularly produces press releases that praise the professionalism and thoroughness of the investigation, assert the certainty of the defendant's guilt, and proclaim the need for harsh punishment. These releases are produced by experts in media relations, and are consumed and republished, more or less verbatim, as stories by newspapers."[28] This practice has become more common as the ability of newspapers to conduct serious investigations has declined with shrinking resources.

Yet, in reality, policing has little impact on crime. This is partly due to the fact that they spend so little time actually fighting crime, as noted earlier. It also is partly due to the fact that policing does not address the known correlates of crime. For example, Carl Klockars writes:

> All of the major factors influencing how much crime there is or is not are factors over which police have no control whatsoever. Police can do nothing about the age, sex, racial, or ethnic distribution of the population. They cannot control economic conditions; poverty; inequality; occupational opportunity; moral, religious, family, or secular education; or dramatic social, cultural, or political change. These are the "big ticket" items in determining the amount and distribution of crime. Compared to them what police do or do not do matters very little.[29]

It should not be surprising then, that adding more police to the nation's streets tends not to have a large effect on the crime rate.[30] Nor does better arming police or cracking down on relatively minor offenses or signs of disorder reduce crime.[31] According to Lawrence Sherman:

> The available evidence supports two major conclusions about policing for crime prevention. One is that the effects of police on crime are complex, and often surprising. The other is that the more focused the police strategy, the more likely it is to prevent crime. The first conclusion follows from the findings that arrests can sometimes increase crime, that traffic enforcement may reduce robbery and gun crime, that the optimal deterrent effect of a police patrol may be produced by 15 minutes of presence in a hot spot, and that prevention effects generally fade over time without modification and renewal of police practices. The second conclusion follows from the likely failure to achieve crime prevention merely by adding more police or shortening response time across the board.[32]

Notice how these conclusions are inconsistent with what citizens generally think about policing. Recall that since the media tend to depict crime as a threat to the existing social order (i.e., the *social breakdown frame*), the logical implication is that we need the police to maintain the social order. In fact, the social order relies as much if not more on parents, schools, religious institutions and other social control institutions in society; i.e., informal social control is more effective than formal social control.[33]

As for *community policing*, so strongly promoted by politicians including President Bill Clinton, Sherman concludes that without a clear focus on crime risk factors, community policing shows no effect on crime. However, "directed patrols, proactive arrests and problem-solving at high-crime 'hot spots' has shown substantial evidence of crime prevention. Police can prevent robbery, disorder, gun violence, drunk driving and domestic violence, but only by using certain methods under certain conditions."[34]

It is true that *problem-oriented policing* can be effective. According to Herman Goldstein, problem-oriented policing is

> an approach to policing in which discrete pieces of police business (each consisting of a cluster of similar incidents, whether crime or acts of disorder, that the police are expected to handle) are subject to microscopic examination (drawing on the especially honed skills of crime analysts and the accumulated experience of operating field personnel) in hopes that what is freshly learned about each problem will lead to discovering a new and more effective strategy for dealing with it.[35]

President Bill Clinton boasted in the 1990s that crime rates fell in the nation's cities because he had put 100,000 new "community police officers" on the street. In fact, community policing is still not widely understood, much less practiced, in the United States. http://www.theonion.com/content/node/29811.

Problem-oriented policing places a high value on new responses that aim to prevent crime, that are not dependent on criminal justice and that "engage other public agencies, the community and the private sector when their involvement has the potential for significantly contributing to the reduction of the problem." Finally, problem-oriented policing "carries a commitment to implementing the new strategy, rigorously evaluating its effectiveness, and, subsequently, reporting the results in ways that will benefit other police agencies and that will ultimately contribute to building a body of knowledge that supports the further professionalization of the police."[36] Unfortunately, given the likelihood of success, images of problem-oriented policing are very uncommon in the media. Instead, the media focus heavily on law enforcement, which amounts to waiting for a crime to occur and then reacting by making an arrest. One would be hard-pressed to imagine a less effective approach to reducing crime than allowing citizens to become victims of crime and then trying to respond.

Reinforce Crime Control

Media images of police rarely show them constrained by the criminal law, when in reality their actions are constrained by the law in very important ways.

Although media images of crime may suggest that they can (and should) do whatever it takes to solve crimes in order to protect the public, officers in the real world are required to follow due process protections established in law and enforced by the courts. As explained by Robin Andersen, media depictions of police make the point that "if the police suspect them of something, they must therefore be guilty of a crime. Constitutional assumptions about due process and civil liberties, such as protections against unwarranted search and seizure and the presumption of innocence, are antithetical to the crime-tabloid formula, which does not conceal its approval of the abuse of police power."[37]

Stated simply, media images of policing reinforce crime control values. As noted by Ray Surette: "In the end, crime control is applauded, due process is disparaged. Individual causes of crime, assumed guilt of suspects, and an 'us' versus 'them' portrait dominates ...".[38] Thus, Surette concludes that the *faulty system frame* is popular in police media depictions. Recall from Chapter 2 that this frame attributes crime to weak or soft criminal justice punishment, leading citizens to believe that we need to get tougher in order to reduce crime. Robert Bohm and Jeffrey Walker concur, writing that illegal police tactics are sanctioned in the media as is the message that police should not be constrained by constitutional protections.[39]

There has always been tension between those who believe in due process and those who believe in crime control. These terms represent two fictional models of justice put forth by Herbert Packer.[40] Although neither of the two models actually exists or ever can in reality, Packer attempted to describe two polar extremes—one model most concerned with preserving individual liberties and the other with maintaining order in the community and fighting crime.

The due process model is aimed at ensuring that individual liberties are protected at all costs, even if guilty people sometimes go free. In other words, the due process model values individual freedom, and the way to protect individual freedom is to uphold Constitutional protections. It places a high value on the adversarial nature of justice, whereby a prosecutor and defense attorney battle it out in court to find the truth and make sure that justice is achieved. Reliability is the most important value of the due process model, for it is imperative that the right person be convicted of the crime of which he or she is accused. Packer's metaphor for this model was an "obstacle course" because, in order to ensure that no innocent persons were wrongfully convicted, the prosecution would have to overcome numerous obstacles in order to convict anyone.

On the other extreme, the crime control model is aimed at protecting the community by lowering crime rates, even if, on occasion, innocent persons are mistakenly convicted. The crime control model also values individual freedom but suggests that the way to protect individual freedom is to protect people from criminals. It places a high value on informal processes such as plea bargaining (when a prosecutor and defense attorney agree out of court to an appropriate sentence for an accused criminal) to expedite criminal justice operations. In this model, very few criminal trials are held, because they are expensive and unnecessary for establishing legal guilt (because the police rarely arrest innocent people). Efficiency is the most important value of the crime control model, for it is imperative that the criminal justice network operates as quickly as possible in order to keep up with the large numbers of criminal cases that enter it each day. Packer's metaphor for this model was an "assembly line" because individual defendants would be quickly processed through the criminal justice network.

Media coverage of police as well as of crime more generally, reinforces support for crime control approaches. Without any doubt, American criminal justice has become more similar to the crime control model as a result.

Interestingly, many scholars have now demonstrated that the nation's crime control efforts do not significantly reduce crime.[43] For example, America's unprecedented explosion of imprisonment in the 1970s, 1980s, and 1990s was responsible for only roughly 25% of the reductions in violent crime experienced in the United States. The vast majority of crime reductions were due to other factors, including an aging population and better economy.[44] And our policy of mass incarceration has significant costs. These issues will be discussed in Chapter 7.

The "Perp Walk"

The so-called *perp walk* is a threat to presumption of innocence and the due process model. According to Jim Ruiz and D.F. Treadwell, the perp walk is widespread in police practice. This is when a suspect is " 'walked' in front of the press so that he can be photographed or filmed. The perp walk both publicizes the police's crime-fighting efforts and provides the press with a dramatic illustration to accompany stories about the arrest." [41] Sometimes there is no actual walk but instead a suspect is just allowed to be photographed while being transported in a police car.

The perp walk helps maintain the notion that the police are "rugged crusaders whose job is glamorous, tough, and often fraught with danger. With the perpetrator's (or 'perp's') apprehension, the 'crime-fighter' demonstrates his or her effectiveness and worth. The general public has largely accepted this corrosive crime-fighting image of police officers."[42]

Seemingly lost on most people are the issues of due process and the presumption of innocence that underlies it. What are the implications for justice of widely showing a suspect's face and name at the point of arrest? One might reasonably conclude that the perp walk threatens due process and also reinforces the notion that when the police arrest someone they typically get the right person (or else he or she must have done something wrong).

When suspects are brought before the press in the so-called "perp walk" it likely leads to the widespread perception that they are guilty. http://risingtide northamerica.org/wordpress/wp-content/uploads/2007/03/p1010217.JPG.

Good Cop, Bad Cop

Most coverage of policing is positive in nature. As noted earlier, police use the media to assure that they are depicted in positive ways in the press. The very image of the "crime fighter" police officer in the media also resonates well with citizens. Further, the media rely on police officials for information, giving media institutions reason to portray the police in a positive light. Yet, recall that the media are most interested in covering what sells. As noted in Chapters 1 and 2, negativity and conflict sells; thus, there is reason to expect the media to be interested in the bad aspects of policing as well.

Ray Surette puts forth seven popular images of police in the media today, including:

- *Rogue cops*—These are stories of individual police officers who work mostly on their own to fight crime through any means necessary. Such officers are shown overcoming bureaucratic obstacles as well as due process concerns that typically restrain police work.
- *Corrupt cops*—These are stories of individual police officers who have gone bad often due to pressures placed on them by superiors or politicians. Such officers are shown doing illegal and unethical things.
- *Honest cops*—These are stories of individual police officers whose honesty and hard-working attitude are shown to be rare within the realm of

policing. Such officers are shown as exceptions to an otherwise corrupt system of policing.

- *Buddy cops*—These are stories of police officers working as a pair. Such officers typically are forced to work together in spite of personality differences and are often of different races.
- *Action comedy cops*—These are stories of police officers involved in high-flying adventure and hair-raising stunts. Such officers are shown having fun in dangerous ways where few people actually get hurt.
- *Female cops*—These are stories of individual women police officers. Such officers are shown as overcoming popular stereotypes of women.
- *Aging cops*—These are stories of individual police officers, who because of their age, are seen by many as past their prime and who are frustrated with the way things are done by younger officers.[45]

Police are thus shown in the media as both good and bad.[46] The good images include stories of the effective "G-man" (government man) in entertainment media in films and series such as *Dragnet, The Untouchables, Dirty Harry* and so forth. In these depictions, the police are serious, aggressive, and effective. They appear as soldiers in a war against crime where offenders are the enemy. The most effective anticrime policies are thus "warlike rather than socially restorative and reconstructive."[47] There will be more on this in Chapter 8 when images of police in the entertainment and infotainment media are examined.

🖱 For more information about "restorative justice," see the website for this book at: www.pscj.appstate.edu/media/restorative.html

---

The bad images of police include stories in the news about police profiling, brutality, corruption, as well as popular media images of the "lampooned police" found in films and series such as *Police Academy, Naked Gun, Reno 911* and so forth. In these depictions, the police are silly, loony, and ineffective.[48] Again, this issue is visited in Chapter 8.

Perhaps not surprisingly, given the media's attraction to negativity and conflict, negative portrayals of the police are common in the media. Three specific issues stand out—police profiling, police brutality, and corruption. Keep in mind when reading these negative portrayals that when these issues are depicted, they are often framed within a *bad apple* frame rather than a *rotten barrel* frame.[49] This means that they are shown to arise from bad officers—individual bad apples—rather than structural problems in policing (or a *rotten barrel*). This is probably not surprising given the media's ultimate focus on individuals as well as the fact that it has "bought into" the system of policing due to its close links to government agencies and efforts.

Police Profiling

Law enforcement efforts can interfere with one responsibility of police: to safeguard citizens' Constitutional protections. The Law Enforcement Code of Conduct introduced earlier in this chapter clearly states:

> A police officer shall perform all duties impartially, without favor or affection or ill will and without regard to status, sex, race, religion, political belief or aspiration. All citizens will be treated equally with courtesy, consideration and dignity.
>
> Officers will never allow personal feelings, animosities or friendships to influence official conduct. Laws will be enforced appropriately and courteously and, in carrying out their responsibilities, officers will strive to obtain maximum cooperation from the public. They will conduct themselves in appearance and deportment in such a manner as to inspire confidence and respect for the position of public trust they hold.

Evidence has mounted that in major American cities "zero tolerance" policing has led to abuses against minorities and the poor.[50] Yet, zero tolerance approaches remain popular among media images of the police officer.

Zero tolerance policing is based on the assumption that if the police crack down on relatively minor problems, they will be able to prevent even serious criminality. Examples include nuisance abatement, harassment of loiterers, street sweeps of the homeless, arresting or rounding up the mentally ill, as well as removing signs of physical disorder from the community (e.g., graffiti, trash, boarded up buildings).

American police focus on particular types of people because of their own personal experience or that of their institution and profession, which suggests that certain people are more likely than others to violate the law. Those people who seem to receive the greatest focus by the police are minorities and the poor, through a process referred to as racial profiling. *Racial profiling* occurs when police use extra-legal factors like race as signs of risk.[51] The results can be dramatic.[52]

The media likely play a role in profiling. Recall the notion of the *criminal-blackman* from Chapter 4. Since the media focus disproportionately on black crime, it is logical that police officers also are affected by these images. To whatever degree police officers see the image of a black man when they envision crime, it is likely they will engage in racial profiling.

African Americans, particularly young men, are most likely to be pulled over by the police, in part due to racial profiling by the police. http://en.wikipedia.org/wiki/File:Police_car_with_emergency_lights_on.jpg.

The phenomenon "Driving While Black" reflects the fact that blacks are disproportionately stopped for traffic violations compared to whites.[53] Studies from more than a dozen states now have documented racial profiling, although not all studies find evidence of profiling, suggesting it occurs in some places but perhaps not others.[54] Given the fact that in many places police are looking for certain people more than others, as well as that police are disproportionately located in certain neighborhoods more than others, it is not surprising that certain people are more likely to have run-ins with police, be stopped, detained, and questioned by police, and be arrested and have force used against them. Data from the Bureau of Justice Statistics show that those most likely to have face-to-face contacts with police include young people, males, and whites, although blacks are overrepresented among police contacts. Further, the most common reason for contact with police is a traffic stop (typically due to speeding).[55]

Those most likely to be arrested are males (three times more likely than female drivers to be arrested) and blacks (twice as likely as white drivers to be arrested). Hispanics are most likely to receive tickets, whereas black drivers are about twice as likely to be arrested and whites are more likely to be receive a warning. The same data show that males, blacks and Hispanics suffer from the highest rates of serious police actions following a stop. For example, male drivers are more likely than female drivers to be ticketed and/or arrested, and blacks and Hispanics are more likely than whites to have force used against them. Blacks are three to four times more likely as whites following a stop to have force used against them, and Hispanics are roughly twice as likely as whites following a stop to have force used against them. Although blacks make up only about 1 out of every 10 contacts with police, they make up roughly 1 out of every 4 contacts where force was used. This is suggestive of either differential suspect behavior by police or a greater willingness by police to use force against blacks. Finally, upon being stopped by the police, African Americans and Hispanics are roughly twice as likely to have their have their cars or persons searched, and they are less likely to report feeling that the stop was legitimate. Given that the chance of arrest is not much greater for African Americans than whites searched by police, these statistics are suggestive of racial profiling.[56]

As for the typical arrestee in the United States, he is a young, urban, poor, African American male. According to Jeffrey Reiman: "This is the Typical Criminal feared by most law-abiding Americans. Poor, young, urban, [disproportionately] African American males make up the core of the enemy forces in the war against crime."[57] Victor Kappeler and his colleagues concur, noting: "The vast majority of people arrested and processed through the criminal justice system are poor, unemployed, and undereducated."[58]

The fact that police typically arrest urban street criminals should not be surprising. Arrest rates from the Uniform Crime Reports consistently are four to five times higher for blacks over age 18 than for whites over 18 and two to three times higher for blacks under age 18 than for whites under 18. Blacks make up roughly one-third of arrests in any given year even though they account for only 12% of the U.S. population.[59]

Studies also show that minorities in the United States are more likely to have force used against them by the police.[60] Data from the Bureau of Justice Statistics show that those most likely to experience force are young, black males. In any given year, Blacks are roughly 3 to 4 times more likely than whites to have force used against them than whites, and Hispanics are roughly twice as likely as whites to have force used against them. Blacks are also most likely to be shot and killed by the police, followed by Hispanics and then whites.[61]

These outcomes typically attract the attention of the media, which police argue is a detriment to them and their profession. Unfortunately, these realities have persisted for some time, although media attention has likely helped reduce these problems in society, in part by helping change societal morals as well as the law.

Recall lessons learned in Chapters 1 and 2 of the book. The media are owned by large, for-profit companies; bad news sells; the media thrive on conflict. These are possible reasons why the media focus on issues such as police profiling. This likely also explains media focus on police brutality.

Police Brutality

Another issue in policing that often comes of the attention of the media is police brutality.[62] Research shows that knowledge of police brutality is largely constructed by the media.[63] Luckily for both citizens and the police, use of police force is relatively rare. Force is used in only about 1% of all citizen encounters, and when considering all calls for police service, police use of force is even rarer. According to the International Chiefs of Police, the rate of police force is only 0.04%, meaning police do *not* use force 99.96% of the time.[64] Compare this with popular images of police brutality in the media and an inescapable conclusion is that the media create the misconception that police brutality is more common than it is.

Further, a large majority of instances of the use of force is deemed justified. A national study of police use of force by Tony Pate and Lorie Fridell found what one might expect about police use of force: less serious types of force are used more frequently than more serious types. Their study also found that citizen complaints for excessive force were rarely filed. Nationally, the rate for city police departments was 11.3 complaints per 100,000 people.[65]

Rodney King's beating by Los Angeles police officers received widespread media coverage. After the officers were acquitted of the charges against King, riots erupted in Los Angeles, leading to even more media coverage. http://en.wiki pedia.org/wiki/File: Rk910303.jpg.

We cannot know for certain the prevalence of *excessive* use of force by police but a good bet is that it is far less common than perceived by Americans. We do know, however, that it is minority men who are most likely to be subjected to it.[66] The 1999 and 2000 shootings by New York City police of Amadou Diallo and Malcolm Ferguson, two unarmed African American men, show that even questionable police shootings still persist. These two men were shot only two blocks away from each other by the New York City Police Department's Street Narcotics Enforcement Unit. Given that both men were unarmed, the police were accused of using excessive force. Although the four officers in the first case, who shot a combined 41 rounds at the fleeing Diallo, were acquitted of criminal charges because they shot Diallo as he reached for his wallet (which the officers thought was a gun), many Americans were not satisfied with the verdicts, and a march on New York City and Washington, D.C. was organized in protest of these shootings.

The case of Abner Louima, a Haitian immigrant, shocked even those who had a negative view of police to begin with. In the summer of 1997, Louima was attacked by four police officers. Two officers used the baton of one of the officers to sodomize Louima and then shoved the baton into his mouth, knocking out several of his teeth, as if they hated him personally. These officers were fired and convicted on criminal charges, although some of the convictions were later overturned. In October 2008, Latino American Michael Mineo was arrested by three police officers in New York City and allegedly sodomized. The officers have been charged with crimes in this case, as well.

In October 2005, Robert Davis, a 64-year-old retired elementary school teacher, was beaten by three New Orleans police officers and two federal officers. He was charged with disorderly conduct, being intoxicated in public and assaulting an officer. Although officers claimed he was drunk at the time of the arrest, Mr. Davis said he was sober and had not consumed any alcohol for many years. Davis claimed he was going to the store to buy a pack of cigarettes when police began to harass him; subsequently they beat him so badly he lay on the ground in a pool of his own blood. Film producer Rich Mathews, who was in New Orleans filming the aftermath of Hurricane Katrina and who happened to be on the scene of the Davis incident, was pushed into a police car by a police officer who shouted, "I've been here for six weeks trying to keep [expletive] ... alive ... [expletive] go home." Several of the officers in the case were fired and charged with crimes.[67]

These types of incidents have received widespread media attention; perhaps because they so clearly violate the core principles of the Law Enforcement Code of Conduct. For example, the Code states: "With no compromise for crime and relentless prosecution of criminals, I will enforce the law courteously and appropriately without fear or favor, malice or ill will, never employing unnecessary force or violence and never accepting gratuities."

A recent story by ProPublica, the independent media organization introduced in Chapter 1, focused on police brutality in New Orleans after Hurricane Katrina. Its report alleges that police officers shot and killed one man, then burned his body to destroy evidence, and beat other men as well. Additional reporting on the case is featured on the Public Broadcasting System's (PBS) *Frontline* television show.

Limits have been placed on police use of force to protect citizens and police officers alike. Ideally, use of force by the police is determined by the behaviors of citizens with whom police come into contact. Police use of force can range from verbal commands to deadly force whereby a citizen is actually killed; the more resistant a citizen is to the police, the more force can be legally used against him or her. The necessary degree of force to be used against a citizen is determined in the officer's own judgment (i.e., his or her discretion), based on the behaviors of the citizen.

Given the propensity of the media to cover and focus on police brutality, it is logical that Americans tend to assume it occurs more frequently than it actually does. One study found that heavy consumers of network news were more likely than others to believe that police misconduct occurred frequently, especially for minority viewers.[68] Also, minorities who frequently watched network news were more likely to believe that Whites were treated better by the police.

Several factors impact views of the police.[69] Among the many factors relevant for citizen views of the police include personal experiences with the police, demographic factors including race, as well as media exposure.[70] According to Steven Chermak, Edmund McGarrell, and Jeff Gruenewald, even though police departments can effectively produce positive images of police in every day crime coverage on the news, "these efforts may be undermined by crisis events involving the police.... Police corruption, excessive use of force, and the inability to solve certain crimes are sometimes covered extensively in the news media over short periods of time."[71] This is problematic because such "crisis events" dramatically impact public perceptions of the police.

The TASER

One aspect of policing that has fairly recently come to the attention of the mainstream press is the use of TASERS by police officers to temporarily disable suspects and unruly citizens. TASER is an acronym for Thomas A. Swift Electric Rifle ... According to TASER International:

> The TASER uses a replaceable cartridge containing compressed nitrogen to deploy two small probes that are attached to the weapon by insulated conductive wires with a maximum length of 35 feet (10.6

meters). The weapon transmits electrical pulses along the wires and into the body affecting the sensory and motor functions of the peripheral nervous system. The energy can penetrate up to two cumulative inches of clothing, or one inch per probe.[72]

According to Justin Ready, Michael White, and Christopher Fisher, even though the technology can cause serious discomfort, this is not its intent. Instead, it is intended to be "a method of incapacitating the suspect using an electrical charge that overrides the central nervous system, resulting in the temporary loss of neuromuscular control. The short-term incapacitation of the subject provides the officer a brief window of time in which to gain compliance, control the individual, or apply handcuffs."[73]

Unfortunately, for whatever reason, the news media have focused on incidents in which police officers used TASERs against children, the elderly, and even public figures. This is problematic not because such stories are unimportant but rather because they are highly unusual. It should not be surprising that the media focus on unusual applications of the TASER; Chapter 3 demonstrated that the media also focus on the most unusual forms of crime.

Given that the media can be a "powerful force in shaping opinions about the appropriateness of police practices and technology," it is important to understand the realities of TASER use by police officers in the United States. A 2004 Amnesty International report identified more than 70 deaths that may have been caused by officer use of the TASER.[74]

Andrew Meyer, a journalism student at the University of Florida asked a long-winded question of Senator John Kerry, and had the TASER used against him for refusing to comply with the police even after they had wrestled him to the ground. He infamously yelled, "Don't TASE me bro'!" http://en.wikipedia. org/wiki/File:Police_issue_X26_TASER-white.jpg.

According to Ready and colleagues, articles about TASERs in the *New York Times* increased from 24 in 2002 to 44 in 2003, to 179 articles in 2004, then declined to 106 in 2005. This could lead readers to assume that use of the TASER by police is increasing, yet this may be a myth. Ready et al analyzed six possible myths about the TASER, including:

- *Myth 1.* TASER incidents involving vulnerable populations (i.e. minors, senior citizens and intoxicated individuals) receive more attention in the news media.
- *Myth 2.* Incidents in the news media usually involve suspects who are passively resisting.
- *Myth 3.* Mentally ill suspects are more likely to resist when police use the TASER.
- *Myth 4.* The news media show more ineffective TASER deployments than police data.
- *Myth 5.* The news media show more officer dissatisfaction than police records.
- *Myth 6.* The news media exaggerate the incidence of death resulting from the TASER.

The content analysis by Ready and colleagues of articles found that 16% of national news reports and 13% of regional news reports were of TASER incidents against minors and senior citizens, respectively, and reports of TASER incidents against intoxicated suspects made up 19% of national news reports and 29% of regional reports. Further, stories about people being verbally or passively resistant made up only 15% of news reports involve TASER incidents. Also, mental illness was not found to be "a significant predictor of suspect resistance after the TASER is deployed."

The authors note "partial support for the existence of media-generated myths with regard to TASER effectiveness. The national news reports show less suspect resistance ... after the TASER deployment than the police records ... while the regional news reports indicate greater suspect resistance. The authors "also note partial support for a media myth regarding officer dissatisfaction with the weapon," for national news reports showed a higher level of officer dissatisfaction with the TASER ... than police records while the regional news reports showed lower levels of police dissatisfaction.

Perhaps most notably, the authors found "a media-related myth regarding the potentially lethal effects of the TASER. There is only one reported NYPD case of a death occurring after TASER deployment (less than 1 percent of NYPD cases), but [32%] percent of national media reports and [69%] of regional news reports describe cases involving suspect death." According to the authors: "Clearly, there is an over-representation of death cases in the news media, but the authors question whether this can be attributed solely to a media-created myth regarding the TASER, or if the finding is part of the larger shift in reporting to focus on violence (i.e. if it bleeds it leads)." As shown in Chapter 3, the media are focused on violence, especially when it involves death. Lethal force by the police, especially against an unarmed suspect, is newsworthy. After all, such cases are violent, controversial, involve armed police officers and "innocent" civilians, and a large degree of the facts surrounding the cases come from the police.

The authors conclude:

> In sum, the evidence supporting the existence of media-generated myths about the TASER is not overly compelling, with the exception of cases involving death. The consistency of findings across data sources does not support allegations of an ideological bias in media reporting of TASER incidents. It does not appear that individual cases presented by the news media are deliberately sensationalized. However, the findings may reflect an institutional bias in which news providers are partial to sources that consistently provide news material—police agencies that offer reporters a steady stream of newsworthy information. This is interesting to consider within the context of the declining practice of investigative journalism in newsrooms across the USA, where there may be less time for reporters to interview subjects of TASER deployments and eyewitnesses who observe such incidents.

As explained in Chapters 1 and 2, the press relies overwhelmingly on official accounts of various phenomena. In the case of the TASER, relying on the police for information may create misconceptions about the lethality of the weapon.

Ready and colleagues explain how media coverage of police behavior can actually change the way the police behave:

> In response to intense media scrutiny of crime control efforts, police agencies sometimes modify or reconsider their practices, thus creating a reflexive feedback loop ... For example, in Memphis, TN in 1988 the media scrutinized police actions in a case where a mentally ill suspect was shot and killed. In response to mounting pressure, the police department created a Crisis Intervention Team (CIT), comprised of officers who received 40 hours of mandatory training on responding appropriately to the mentally ill. More recently, in November 2006, heavy media coverage followed the shooting of Sean Bell by New York City police officers. The NYPD reacted by commissioning the RAND Corporation to conduct a comprehensive evaluation of their use of force policies and procedures.[75]

The close connection between the police and the press can thus be seen as a good thing if it helps prevent events such as unnecessary shootings.

Logically, media coverage of police, including use of the TASER, can impact citizen perceptions of the police. According to Peter Manning "the police self is shaped by mass media" and this explains why police make serious efforts to control the way they are depicted in the media.[76] Steven Chermak concurs, saying "police departments actively construct public images of themselves so that news presentation benefits the organization rather than harms it."[77] Michael Hallett goes even further, raising the possibility that infotainment shows such as COPS are public relations efforts.[78] This issue is discussed more in Chapter 8.

Corruption

Another issue in policing that is often newsworthy is police corruption. Criminologists do not know how extensive and prevalent police corruption in the United States is because problems such as citizen mistreatment and falsification of records and evidence have never been subjected to a national study.[79] However, there are numerous well-known examples, particularly within larger American cities, of alarming corruption in American police departments. For example, the Mollen Commission in New York found evidence of police involvement in theft, drug trafficking, drug use, falsification of police reports, lying in court, and police brutality.[80] Shockingly, the most common form of corruption in New York was not police brutality; rather, it was for falsifying police records and testimony at criminal trials, a practice known as *testilying*, whereby officers often made up testimony in order to ensure criminal convictions. They would invent stories to justify their illegal and unethical police techniques, which violated suspects' Constitutional rights.

Other large police departments have witnessed major corruption scandals, as well. In Washington, D.C., partly as a result of a massive hiring of unqualified officers, some of whom even had criminal records, more than 200 police officers since 1989 have been arrested and charged with crimes, including 79 officers in 1993.[81] Departments that were faced with losing millions of dollars in federal funding if they did not hire more officers are the same ones that ended up hiring some very bad people. In Philadelphia, officers confessed in 1995 to planting evidence, personally profiting from the illegal drug trade, and making false arrests. This led to the reexamination of 2,000 criminal cases that may have led to wrongful conviction because of bad policing. Additionally, nearly 200 police officers in New Orleans were disciplined for their questionable activities, and 4 were charged with murder related to their involvement in drug offenses. The Christopher Commission in Los Angeles found "a significant number of LAPD officers who repeatedly misuse[d] force and persistently ignore[d] the written policies and guidelines of the Department regarding force."[82] Given the negative (and sometimes violent) nature of these incidents, each subject to widespread media attention.

One of the most widely reported on examples of corruption is the Rampart Area Corruption Incident from Los Angeles. This involved police officers being involved in a bank robbery, false imprisonment and beating of a handcuffed arrestee at a police substation, and the theft of 3 kilograms of cocaine from a police evidence room.

⤺ For more information about the Rampart Area Corruption Incident, see the website for this book at: www.pscj.appstate.edu/media/ rampart.html

---

Other allegations of corruption pertained to the planting of cocaine in the automobiles of unsuspecting Mexican immigrant laborers in Dallas, Texas and the framing of dozens of African Americans in Tulia, Texas for drug crimes they did not commit. In Dallas, Police Chief Terrell Bolton admitted that "bricks of cocaine" seized as evidence actually turned out to be ground sheetrock. Two undercover police officers and a paid informant who received $200,000 for his tips reported that drugs had been sold or shown to them, which led to dozens of arrests. Prosecutors dismissed 86 drug cases and released dozens of defendants (all of them Mexican immigrants or legal Hispanic residents). In Tulia, 43 residents of the small town were arrested for alleged drug offenses (40 of them were African Americans, accounting for 10% of the entire town's African American population). The only evidence against them was the testimony of one undercover officer, Tom Coleman, who worked alone, had no audio tapes, video surveillance, or eyewitnesses. Essentially, these people were framed and have all subsequently been released.[83]

Both of the latter events were examined by the media, especially outer ring (third-tier) outlets. The earlier events received even more attention from inner ring (first-tier) media outlets, probably because the events themselves were so unusual and outlandish and thus newsworthy.

Drug law enforcement may present the most significant opportunity for police bribery.[84] According to the Drug Policy Alliance:

> A 1998 report by the General Accounting Office notes that on-duty police officers involved in drug-related corruption engage in serious criminal activities such as (1) conducting unconstitutional searches and seizures; (2) stealing money and/or drugs from drug dealers; (3) selling stolen drugs; (4) protecting drug operations; (5) providing false testimony; and (6) submitting false crime reports. Approxi-

mately half of all police officers convicted as a result of FBI-led corruption cases between 1993 and 1997 were convicted for drug-related offenses and nationwide over 100 cases of drug-related corruption are prosecuted each year. Every one of the federal law enforcement agencies with significant drug enforcement responsibilities has seen an agent implicated.[85]

For whatever reason, drug-related corruption is not widely depicted in the media, except in the case of popular movies such as *Training Day* and some forms of music (e.g., "F ... the Police!" by NWA). Historically, citizens and even policy-makers have been reluctant to seriously challenge or even question the "drug war," in part for fear of being labeled "soft on crime" or "soft on drugs."

Recall lessons learned from earlier in the book. The mainstream media have long-established, close contacts with government officials, and rely on these people for information about their stories. This means the media will rarely even hear about problems with policies such as drug prohibition. This is consistent with the *relying on public officials for information filter* introduced in Chapter 1. Further, the mainstream media are likely to weed out information thought to be too much of a challenge to status quo approaches to fighting crime and other perceived social problems. This is consistent with the *anti-communism filter* introduced in Chapter 1.

How the Media Hinder Crime Control and Crime Prevention

The bulk of this book illustrates what is wrong with the media in the United States. Specifically, we have reviewed an enormous amount of research that demonstrates how the media tend to hinder crime control and crime prevention efforts. For example, the media:

- tend to promote fear of criminality (at least in some segments of the population).
- misrepresent the nature of criminality (e.g., by focusing on violent street crime) thereby creating misconceptions of who is dangerous and who is likely to be harmed.
- create misconceptions about the nature of policing.
- reinforce conservative, crime control mechanisms that largely fail to reduce crime and simultaneously erode civil liberties protections

When the media promote fear of criminality, this may lead some to take necessary steps to protect themselves from crime. Yet, given that one's risk of criminal victimization is typically much lower than suggested by the media, such steps would largely be unnecessary. Further, since media coverage of crime creates misconceptions about the types of crimes that will likely impact us, we end up taking precautions against the types of crimes least likely to affect us while ignoring those that are most likely to hurt us. The misconceptions about police, courts and corrections that result from inaccurate media coverage end up increasing support for "get tough on crime" criminal justice policies. Here the costs are financial in nature (e.g., wasted money), as well as social in nature (e.g., disproportionately catching, convicting, and punishing the poor and people of color). Since these largely fail to significant reduce street crime this is evidence that the media help maintain ineffective crime reduction policies.

In spite of all this "bad news," there is also some significant "good news" about the media and crime control & prevention. In fact, the media can do great good in terms of helping reduce harms in society.

How the Media Help Crime Control and Crime Prevention

The Public Health Example

We can look at public health examples to speculate about how the media may assist with effective crime control and crime prevention. For example, studies show that successful media campaigns have greatly reduced smoking and alcohol use among the U.S. population.[86] This is interesting given that studies of the media generally fail to demonstrate similar effects when it comes to illicit drug use such as marijuana which has been relatively constant since the late 1980s.

When it comes to the dangers of using tobacco, which have been more widely featured in media campaigns than alcohol (which tend to focus on drunk driving more specifically), the media have been instrumental in helping to spread the news about potential risks of smoking tobacco. For example, according to the Centers for Disease Control and Prevention (CDC), tobacco smoking is a leading cause of cancer. Specifically, the CDC reports that tobacco use is the leading cause of preventable death in the United States, making cigarettes the most commonly recognized defective product in the United States. Cigarettes are considered defective products by many because they kill and cause illness when used properly.

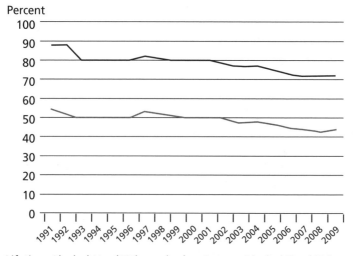

— Lifetime Alcohol Use (12th graders)— Current Alcohol Use (12th graders)

Data from Monitoring the Future show that lifetime and past-month alcohol use for young people has fallen as the dangers of drinking have been more widely publicized in the media, although binge drinking and heavy drinking have increased slightly among young people since the 1990s.

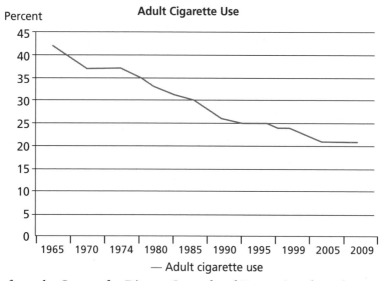

Data from the Centers for Disease Control and Prevention show that smoking rates for adults have fallen as the dangers of smoking have been more widely publicized in the media. http://www.cdc.gov/tobacco/ data_statistics/ tables/trends/cig_smoking/index.htm.

According to the CDC, smoking "harms nearly every organ of the body; causing many diseases and reducing the health of smokers in general."[88] As the leading cause of preventable death in the United States, cigarette smoking kills roughly 438,000 people every year in America (about 1 in 5 deaths).[89] Smoking will kill approximately 25 million Americans who are currently alive, including about 5 million children.[90] Smoking is thus more deadly than human immunodeficiency virus (HIV), motor vehicle injuries, suicides, murders and all deaths caused by alcohol and all illegal drugs combined![91] Further, smokers will die, on average, 14 years earlier than nonsmokers.[92]

The largest portion of smoking deaths are the result of lung cancer (124,000 deaths), heart disease (108,000 deaths), and emphysema, bronchitis, and chronic airways obstruction (90,000 deaths)[93] The CDC claims that "the risk of dying from lung cancer is more than 22 times higher among men who smoke cigarettes and about 12 times higher among women who smoke cigarettes compared with never smokers."[94] Further, smoking "results in a twofold to threefold increased risk of dying from coronary heart disease"[95] as well as a "tenfold increased risk of dying from chronic obstructive lung disease."[96]

For more information about the health risks of tobacco, see the website for this book at: www.pscj.appstate.edu/media/tobacco.html

---

As the messages about the dangers of tobacco use have been successfully broadcast through the media, tobacco use in the United States has fallen. For example, in 2008, only 21% of Americans smoked cigarettes, down from 42% in 1964. Thus, in just over four decades, smoking has fallen by half in the United States. Today, smoking is highest among the poor, the less educated, and is slightly more likely among African Americans than Caucasians. Further, smoking is most common among young people, like those in high school.[97] Interestingly, studies show that these groups spend less time engaged with the news media, thereby reducing the likelihood that information about the harmful nature of smoking in the media will impact behavior. These groups have also been successfully targeted by tobacco companies for decades. As one example, the cartoon character, Joe Camel, was one of the most successfully used media icons in the 20th Century. Depicted as smooth, tough, independent, strong, and lucky with the ladies, the character appealed to young people and encouraged them to smoke.

Studies of tobacco activities and internal documents of tobacco companies show that major tobacco corporations purposely misled the public and Congress for more than 40 years with regard to the dangers of smoking cigarettes; that they intentionally marketed to children and adolescents through cartoon characters such as "Joe Camel" as well as through product advertisements in magazines, movies, and popular hang-outs; that they increased the addictiveness of their products through adding nicotine and chemicals that heightened the effects of nicotine; that they attacked and attempted to discredit anti-smoking advocates and whistle-blowers; that they lied under oath to Congress when asked about the addictiveness of their products; that they financially coerced companies making smoking-cessation products; and even intentionally funded and produced faulty science through their own Tobacco Institute to cloud the significant issues.[98] Studies of tobacco advertising also showed they have their greatest impacts on kids.[99] While all this was going on, hundreds of thousands of Americans died every year from using the defective products manufactured and sold by tobacco companies.

The CEOs of the major tobacco companies appeared before Congress in 1994 and declared that tobacco was not addictive. For example, the CEO of RJR Tobacco stated: "cigarettes and nicotine clearly do not meet the classic definition of addiction." The CEO of Phillip Morris stated: "I believe nicotine is not addictive." The CEO of U.S. Tobacco replied: "I don't believe that nicotine or our products are addictive." The CEO of Lorillard Tobacco stated: "I believe that nicotine is not addictive." The CEO of Liggett said: "I believe that nicotine is not addictive." The CEO of Brown and Williamson Tobacco replied: "I believe that nicotine is not addictive." Finally, the CEO of American Tobacco stated: "And I, too, believe that nicotine is not addictive."[100]

In the late 1990s, major tobacco companies entered into a financial agreement with the states to pay hundreds of billions of dollars in compensatory damages to states over decades. The money was to be used for various purposes, including preventing youth smoking; in reality, some of the money has been used by states for various costs completely unrelated to smoking as they struggled with large deficits. However, some of the money has also been used on media programs that have been shown to reduce smoking, especially among young people.

Recall from Chapter 1 of the book that the democratic postulate is that "the media are independent and committed to discovering and reporting the truth" and that they serve the enormously important function in society of providing the information needed upon which to inform the public in part so that the powerful do not get away with lying, pursuing unwise policies, and so forth.[101] To the degree that this postulate is true—to the degree that the media actually serve this function—the media can do great good for citizens. The example of tobacco prevention above illustrates this very well.

Whereas media scholars tend to fall into one of two camps—those that believe in the democratic postulate, and those that believe in the propaganda model where the media "serve to mobilize support for the special interests that dominate the state and private activity"[102]—the truth probably lies somewhere in the middle. That is, while there is a great deal of evidence that media activity is generally in line with the interests of the corporations that own and control them, as well as with corporate interests generally, the people working in the media also care about democracy and often got into journalism and the media business in order to do serious journalism to benefit the people. Thus, the media often do function "as an important site for the production and dissemination of 'truth.'"

John McMullan lays out the case for a more complex model of media activity:

> Mediated knowledge, whereby lived experience is transmitted to news narrative, is usually accomplished via routine electronic or print-based media systems and depends on a number of distinct but interrelated factors that are extrinsic to an event's seriousness: geopolitical interests, market needs, advertising policies, organizational budgets, access to and control of information sources, cultural priorities and newsworthiness, and dominant discourses that enable, guide, and sustain news coverage. On the one side are investments, markets, conglomerates, and monopolies; on the other side are lobby groups, political agendas, and the power to censure.... Moreover, news making is also guided by intrinsic factors: editorial politics, story screening, the rhythms of the newsroom, the subculture of journalism, and cognitive conceptions of "audience interest" are all designed to shape the discursive content of the sayable. [103]

According to McMullan, neither the democratic postulate nor the propaganda model is entirely accurate. Instead, media content is determined in a complex system requiring the consideration of a wide variety of factors, including the demands and requests of the companies that own the media; on the businesses that advertise in the media; on perceived demands of the public; on perceived newsworthiness; on budgetary constraints; on agencies and individuals willing and unwilling to provide information; and on other local, regional, national and international political considerations. If the media were only concerned with providing information to the public, rather than entertainment and for-profit activities, we could expect them to do a great deal of good in society.

Effective Crime Prevention

Effective crime prevention programs and messages could also be put into place following the lead of the public health approach, assuming of course that there are capable agencies in criminal justice to create and promote credible, evidence-based crime prevention programs. Yet, this is unlikely so long as crime is seen as an individual failure rather than a public health problem.

Some effective crime prevention programs utilize media content and/or are prominently featured in the media. According to the International Center for the Prevention of Crime (ICPC): "Media exposure to crime and crime-related events can be an effective crime prevention strategy, and useful tool for sensitizing and educating the public on underestimated or overlooked social problems."[104]

ICPC discusses public education campaigns as an example, "whereby the media can play an active role in mobilizing support and advancing nationwide and international commitment to crime prevention, while distributing information to a vast audience at a fast pace." Among those thought to have enjoyed some degree of success include "campaigns on human trafficking, victim's support, mobilization for women's safety and child sexual abuse.... In the 1990s, increasing media coverage on human trafficking resulted in the expansion of resources, awareness and support towards the sexual slavery of women and girls."

As for local crime, ICPC asserts that "disseminating public information on self-protection and safety strategies against crime" can be effective since people rely so heavily on media for information about crime. As an example, "campaigns on prevention against residential burglary and information on the risks of using illegal drugs and alcohol, exemplify the means by which the media can have an important role in crime prevention."

Yet, generally speaking, there is little evidence of effectiveness when it comes to crime prevention programs. Analyses of popular crime prevention programs range from studies of "McGruff the Crime Dog"[105] to "Crimestoppers."[106] Both of these programs have been in place for many years and each is advertised in various media outlets including television. The effectiveness of such programs has not been demonstrated but it is likely that they have some (at least limited) impact on the willingness of citizens to engage in crime prevention activities on their own, as well as to cooperate with criminal justice agencies in reporting crime and helping locate reported offenders.

Some aspects of situational crime prevention rely on the media for their effectiveness. *Situational crime prevention* is aimed at eliminating opportunities for crime by managing, designing or manipulating the environment "in as systematic and permanent way as possible ... so as to increase the effort and risks of crime and reduce the rewards as perceived by a wide range of offenders"[107] Situational crime prevention is practiced by crime prevention units within a handful of central governments as well as scores of local municipalities.

There are now 25 different approaches to reduce crime. The five major categories of situational crime prevention include increasing the efforts for crime, increasing the risks of crime; reducing the rewards of crime; reducing provocations for crime; and removing excuses for crime. Within each of these categories, there are five specific approaches aimed at preventing crime.

McGruff the Crime Dog is a popular character throughout the United States. He has his own website, books, even at least one musical CD, teaching children about various aspects of crime prevention. http://behavioradvisor.ipower.com/ McGruff.jpg.

For example, increasing the effort of crime includes target hardening (e.g., locks and alarms), access control (e.g., requiring identification for entry), exit screens (e.g., reception desks), offender deflection (e.g., street closures), and tool control (e.g., disabling stolen electronic devices). These efforts make it harder for offenders to successfully commit their crimes. Increasing the risks of crime includes guardian extension (e.g., neighborhood watch), natural surveillance (e.g., open spaces), anonymity reduction (e.g., identification tags), place managers (e.g., more employees at work), and formal surveillance (e.g., security guards). These efforts increase the odds that offenders will be caught. Reducing the rewards for crime includes target concealment (e.g., making it harder for people to find you or your property), target removal (e.g., removable car radios), property identification (e.g., marking property), market disruption (e.g., monitoring stores), and denying benefits (e.g., cleaning up graffiti to eliminate satisfaction from those who spray paint walls). These efforts make criminality less rewarding. Reducing provocation for crime includes frustration reduction (e.g., training employees to be polite), dispute avoidance (e.g., reducing crowding in small spaces), reduced emotional arousal (e.g., controlling violent content in the media), peer pressure neutralization (e.g., anti-crime ads), and imitation discouragement (e.g., hiding behavior). These efforts lessen the conditions that often generate crime in the first place. Finally, removing excuses for crime includes rule setting (e.g., harassment codes), instructions posting (e.g., signs), consciousness alerts (e.g., speed indicator signs on the side of roads), compliance assistance (e.g., trash bins in public places), and controlling drugs and alcohol at events. These efforts are thought to make it harder for offenders to justify their criminality.[108]

Summary

Media coverage inaccurately portrays the U.S. criminal justice network as a whole. The early steps in the criminal justice process (law enforcement, investigation and arrest) are emphasized whereas the other steps are almost invisible. At least three arguments can be made to justify the increased focus on police relative to courts and corrections. First, police are the entry point of what is commonly referred to as the "criminal justice system." Without police making arrests, courts and corrections would have no "clients." Second, police do a lot more than just fight crime. Third, the police also receive the largest share of resources in criminal justice. The fact that the media focus more on police than courts and corrections may create the perception among media consumers that the police are more important than the other branches of criminal justice.

The typical police agency and the typical officer in the United States are at the local level of government; police activities are very much a local phenomenon. Further, it is also true that most law enforcement officers work for small departments who serve small geographical areas. The media are generally accurate in their disproportionate focus on local agencies and officers because they tend to be most focused on the jobs of local police.

Even though white-collar and corporate crimes cost us far more in terms of financial losses and physical harms (e.g., injuries and deaths), the vast majority of police agencies and officers (local departments and officers) are not focused on it. Coverage of police activity in the media primarily focuses on street crime, particularly violent offenses. Yet, only a select number of crimes and police activities are presented in the media. These news story images need not be, and often are not, accurate representations of the prevalence of crime or the effectiveness of police intervention. Logically, media focus on local policing and local crime helps reinforce the notion that street crime is more harmful and a greater threat to citizens, even though this is not the case.

Police officers in the United States serve five basic roles: enforcing laws; preserving the peace; preventing crime; providing services; and upholding rights. Of these five roles, the typical police officer spends most of his or her time each day *not* fighting crime. The majority of a police officer's time is spent on administrative tasks and providing services to the public.

Yet, the typical image of the police officer in the media is of the law enforcer or crime fighter. In fact, the great bulk of policing is relatively boring. The typical police officer spends a large portion of each day simply waiting around for calls for service. When these calls come, they rarely involve criminal activity, particularly hot calls where a suspect can actually be captured but instead cold calls where the offender has already fled the scene.

Not only do the media tend to focus on the law enforcement role, they also reinforce the perception that the police are actually effective at reducing crime. In reality, policing has little impact on crime. This is partly due to the fact that they spend so little time actually fighting crime. It also is partly due to the fact that policing does not address the known correlates of crime.

Media images of police rarely show them constrained by the criminal law, when in reality their actions are constrained by the law in very important ways. Although media images of crime may suggest that they can (and should) do whatever it takes to solve crimes in order to protect the public, officers in the real world are required to follow due process protections established in law and enforced by the courts. Stated simply, media images of policing reinforce crime control values.

Most coverage of policing is positive in nature although there is also media focus on negative aspects of policing. Seven popular images of police in the media today include rogue cops, corrupt cops, honest cops, buddy cops, action comedy cops, female cops, and aging cops. The bad images of police include stories in the news about police profiling, brutality, corruption, as well as popular media images of the "lampooned police."

When these issues are depicted, they are often framed within a bad apple frame rather than a rotten barrel frame. This means that they are shown to arise from bad officers—individual bad apples—rather than structural problems in policing.

Evidence has mounted that in major American cities "zero tolerance" policing has led to abuses against minorities and the poor. Yet, zero tolerance approaches remain popular among media images of the police officer.

American police focus on particular types of people because of their own personal experience or that of their institution and profession, which suggests that certain people are more likely than others to violate the law. Those people who seem to receive the greatest focus by the police are minorities and the poor, through a process referred to as racial profiling.

The phenomenon "Driving While Black" reflects the fact that blacks are disproportionately stopped for traffic violations compared to whites. Studies from more than a dozen states now have documented racial profiling, although not all studies find evidence of profiling, suggesting it occurs in some places but perhaps not others.

One aspect of policing that has fairly recently come to the attention of the mainstream press is the use of TASERS by police officers to temporarily disable suspects and unruly citizens. TASER is an acronym for Thomas A. Swift Electric Rifle. The news media have focused on incidents in which police officers used TASERs against children, the elderly, and even public figures. This is problematic not because such stories are unimportant but rather because they are highly unusual.

The media can do great good in terms of helping reduce harms in society. Public health examples suggest the media may assist with effective crime control and crime prevention.

Discussion Questions

1) Is media coverage of the U.S. criminal justice network accurate? Explain.
2) Why do the police receive so much more media coverage than the courts and corrections?
3) What impact does the media focus more on police have on public perceptions of criminal justice?
4) Describe how the media accurately and inaccurately depict the police.
5) How does media focus on local policing and local crime help reinforce the notion that street crime is more harmful and a greater threat to citizens.
6) What are the five major roles of police officers in the United States? Which roles do police spend most of their time.
7) Which roles of police are most featured in the media? Why?
8) How do the media reinforce the perception that the police are actually effective at reducing crime?
9) Does policing actually impact the crime rate in a meaningful way? Explain.
10) How does media coverage of policing suggest that they are not constrained by the criminal law?
11) What is the *perp walk*? How is this a threat to the presumption of innocence and due process?
12) Is most coverage of police positive or negative in nature? Explain with examples.
13) Identify and define seven popular images of police in the media today.
14) In what ways are police depicted negatively in the media?

15) Differentiate between the *bad apple frame* and the *rotten barrel frame*. Which is most common in the media?
16) Describe the effects of *zero tolerance policing*?
17) What is *police profiling*? In your opinion, is this practice justified?
18) In what ways is policing biased against some groups? Explain using examples.
19) Is *police brutality* common? Is it of interest to the media? Why?
20) Using examples, explain how the media can do great good in terms of helping reduce harms in society.
21) Have popular crime prevention programs like "McGruff the Crime Dog" and "Crimestoppers" been effective?

Chapter 6

Media Coverage of Courts and Judicial Processes: Trials, Publicity and Sentencing

Learning Objectives

After reading this chapter, you will be able to:

1) Identify and define the main functions of the courts.
2) Explain which types of activities of courts are often reported in the media and which go unreported.
3) Define the *dual court system*.
4) Define the term *jurisdiction*.
5) Discuss what level of court receives the most media attention and explain why.

6) Explain why there is far more coverage of courtroom activity involving the poor and people of color.

7) Define the *adversarial* process of courts and explain whether this is how courts really operate.

8) Define the *courtroom workgroup* and explain how this concept helps us understand the realities of courtroom activity.

9) Define the major roles of the prosecutor, defense attorney, and judge.

10) Describe the "imbalance of power" in the courts and explain why this is important.

11) Demonstrate how the media create the impression that defense attorneys are more powerful than prosecutors even though this is generally not the case.

12) Explain the significance for justice of *plea bargaining*.

13) Identify the major problems with plea bargaining.

14) Explain why the media do not focus on plea bargaining and other pretrial practices.

15) Explain why the media focus so much on only a few, high profile trials.

16) Identify and define the three common frames used in coverage of media trials.

17) Identify and discuss the main issues with cameras in the courtroom and pretrial publicity.

18) Explain whether criminal sentencing by the courts is commonly depicted in the media.

19) Outline the evidence that sentencing is biased in the United States against some groups of people.

Introduction

What do images of courts from the news, as well as television and movies suggest to you about American courts? As it turns out, the most prevalent images of courts found in news accounts and in other media are misleading. For example, while courts serve valuable functions to the American people, including adjudicating accused criminals, the vast majority of people accused of even serious felonies such as murder, rape, robbery, aggravated assault, theft, motor vehicle theft, burglary, and arson rarely receive criminal trials. Yet, the dominant image of the courts in the United States is of the criminal trial. This is one myth of courts that has largely been created by the media.

As explained by Ray Surette: "For many in today's world, mass media images are their primary source of knowledge about law, lawyers, and the legal system."[1] This is problematic because media coverage of the courts results in an inaccurate and distorted picture of judicial processes. As one example, Surette writes: "Directly and indirectly, the media paint a distorted image of the courts. When portrayed indirectly as in the law enforcement focused media, the courts are often alluded to as soft on crime, easy on criminals, due process-laden institutions that repeatedly release the obviously guilty and dangerous.... When shown directly, court officers are often more engaged in fighting crime than in practicing law."[2]

Like with policing, there is a sizable body of literature on media and the courts, although there has not been as much research into courts as there has into police.[3] The research into media coverage of courts illustrates that there are many myths associated with what courts do and how they do it. Further, there is much not known about courts, in part because of media coverage. These issues are discussed in this chapter.

Ignore Most of What Courts Do

If one got all his or her information about courts from the media, one would think that the only thing the courts do is hold trials. This is far from reality because courts do so much more. Yes, when citizens are arrested by police, they become clients for the courts. According to Larry Gaines and his colleagues:

> Simply stated, a court is a place where arguments are settled. The argument may be between the federal government and a corporation accused of violating environmental regulations, between business partners, between a criminal and the state, or any other number of parties. The court provides an environment in which the basis of the argument can be settled through the application of the law.[4]

One important function in deciding arguments is determining the legal guilt of the accused—that is, to determine if a person is guilty beyond a reasonable doubt of committing a crime.[5] The National Criminal Justice Commission writes of the courts: "Their responsibility is to be fair to all citizens charged with a crime and to impose a just punishment on those found guilty."[6]

Yet, courts do much more than determine guilt or innocence. They also determine whether someone receives bail prior to trial or sits in preventive detention awaiting disposition of their case. Courts conduct preliminary hearings and grand juries to determine if there is enough evidence to warrant a criminal trial. Courts determine the appropriate sentences for those convicted of crimes. Courts also hear and make rulings on appeals of law.

When it comes to appeals, cases in state Supreme Courts are more likely to be featured in the media when they focus on Constitutional issues (as opposed to statutory issues) and when they deal with death penalty cases. Other organizational factors related to the local media also influence whether cases received coverage.[7]

⌂ For more information about what the courts do behind closed doors, see the website for this book at: www.pscj.appstate.edu/media/courts.html

---

The vast majority of the activities of courts go unreported in the media. As a result, most people do not understand how the court system works or what it does. Media scholars claim that coverage of courtroom activity is driven in part by financial considerations about what the audience wants to see and what will produce market returns.[8] In other words, only some court functions sell.

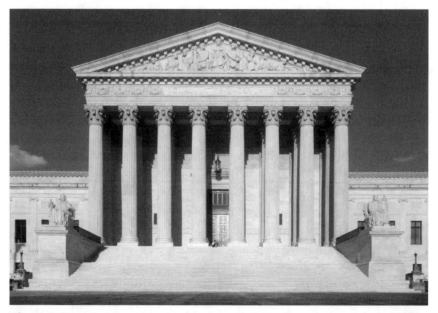

The U.S. Supreme Court in Washington, D.C., is the one court that perhaps best symbolizes "justice" to citizens. Yet, the Court hears the lowest amount of cases of all American courts, and only accepts about 1% of the cases that are appealed to it. http://en.wikipedia.org/wiki/File:USSupremeCourtWest Facade.JPG.

Trials, which often center on violent crime and feature conflict, are obviously appealing to the media.

One issue that Americans seem largely unaware of is that the courts interpret the law to tell us what it means. By interpreting the law, courts give meaning to many behaviors that are unclear. Examples include obscenity, bad parenting, corporal punishment, torture, and warranted & unwarranted government intrusions into our lives: "Judicial proceedings function, therefore, not only as mechanisms for resolving individual disputers but also as mechanisms for legitimizing the broader society's laws, policies, government agencies, and social structure."[9]

A recent example that has been vigorously debated is the issue of gay marriage. Many around the country have argued that the institution of marriage ought to be expanded to include gay couples; others have argued that marriage is between "one man and one woman." Many states specifically define marriage between a man and a woman, whereas others do not. In these states, courts must decide the meaning of marriage. In states where marriage is defined as one man and one woman, the courts may be called on to determine if the law violates the civil rights of gay couples who want to marry.

There are some (who have been heard loudly and seen commonly in the media) who have labeled judges that extended the right of marriage to homosexual couples as "activist judges." This claim is based on the belief that these judges are applying their own values to the law rather than applying the law as it is written. This notion of an "activist judge" ignores the basic reality of the law—it is often broadly and vaguely written. Being a judge requires that one interpret the meaning of the law, based not only on what is written but also how other judges have ruled on an issue. When state laws fail to define marriage specifically enough, this leaves room for judges to interpret the meaning of marriage.

Clearly, when a judge does not follow the law, he or she can be considered an activist judge. Yet, when the law is not clearly defined or understood, judges are the people we must rely on to tell us what it means.

Once a court rules on an issue, it becomes a *precedent* that is to be followed by other courts and judges. The concept of *stare decisis*—let the decision stand—requires that judges follow precedents. Yet, when precedents are viewed in the light of a law that evolves along with societal standards, occasionally precedents are overturned by the courts and a new precedent takes over. This can be labeled activism, as well, whether it is done by liberal or conservative judges.

The Court recently overturned two precedents in the case *Citizens United v. Federal Elections Commission* (2010, 08-205). In the case, decided in a five to four decision, the Court held that laws restricting electronic speech by corporations and unions in the final month before a primary election and two months before a general election was a violation of the First Amendment to the U.S. Constitution. The precedents were overturned not because society's standards or values had changed but instead because five Justices simply thought the precedents were poorly reasoned or decided. This is supported by the fact that the petitioners in the case did not even make the argument decided by the Court; instead, they were invited back by these five Justices to make the argument that these five Justices ultimately agreed with![10]

⌨ For more information about this important case, see the website for this book at: www.pscj.appstate.edu/media/citizensunited.html

---

Focus on State Courts and Street Crime

Because of the separation of powers clause of the U.S. Constitution, the United States has a *dual court system*; that is, federal and state governments each have their own distinct court systems, and the two systems operate independently of each other. There are more than 200 different court systems in the states, Washington D.C., and Puerto Rico, including more than 70 statewide trial courts systems with general jurisdiction and more than 130 courts of appeal.[11]

State and federal courts can be differentiated by their *jurisdiction*—that is, where they have "the authority or power to hear a case."[12] Where a case is heard depends on what type of law is violated. Crimes against states are typically handled in state courts, whereas crimes against the federal government are held in federal courts. Cases can also be heard in both courts without violating suspects' Fifth Amendment rights to freedom from double jeopardy because if both federal and state laws are violated, both courts can and often do hold trials.

The majority of media coverage of courts is on state level courts. This is likely because most crimes are violations of state laws; thus, state courts handle far more cases that federal courts. The types of crimes handled by federal and state courts are also often very different. For example, in 2004, state courts convicted about 1.1 million adults of felonies. The most common convictions were for drug offenses (34% of all convictions) and property crimes (29% of all convictions). Only 18% of convictions in state courts were for violent crimes, including only 8,400 murder and nonnegligent convictions (less than 1% of the total convictions in state courts).[13] In the same year in federal courts, less than 75,000 people were convicted of felonies. The most common convictions were for drug offenses (34% of all convictions) and property offenses (17% of all convictions). Less than 5% of all convictions in federal courts were for violent crimes.[14]

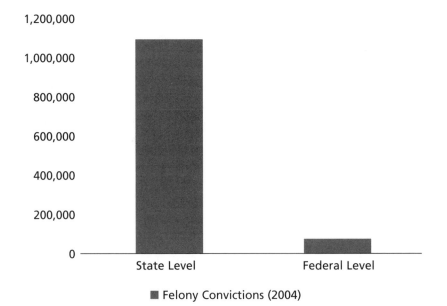

Felony Convictions (2004)

The great bulk of convictions for "serious crime" or felonies occur in state courts.

Thus, the majority of people convicted of felonies in each court were not convicted of violent crimes. Compare this with media coverage of crime shown in Chapters 3 and 4, which is disproportionately focused on violent crime, especially random violent crime committed by strangers.

Perhaps you are surprised that at this stage of the criminal justice process, most cases are not violent in nature. Given the coverage of violence by the media, Americans likely believe the courts help reduce violent crime; this is probably true, but the effect is likely much smaller than most would expect.

Further, given the harms caused by acts like corporate and white-collar crime, you may be even more surprised to learn that at the state and federal level of courts, these types of crimes make up a small portion of all cases. For example, less than 2% of all convictions in federal courts and less than 5% of all convictions in state courts were for the crime of fraud. Since these crimes are rarely in the courts, they are rarely covered in the media. This logically helps keep citizens focused on street crime.

Almost all of the convictions noted above come through plea bargains rather than jury trials. At the state level in 2004, 95% of convictions were achieved through plea bargains.[15] Further, at the federal level in 2004, 96% of convictions were achieved through plea bargains.[16] Even when cases do result in trial, obviously, the vast majority of cases receive no coverage from the media.[17]

Those rare cases that are covered tend to be atypical. As a result, false conceptions of what is "ordinary" are gained from these extraordinary cases. For example, the O.J. Simpson murder trial of 1995 wrongly showed Americans that the criminal justice network works too slowly and is more focused on defendants' rights than on victims' rights. For wealthy clients in highly publicized cases, the process of justice will be slow and deliberate. Yet, most court clients are poor and do not receive a trial; instead, they are convicted through the informal process of plea bargaining. These issues are discussed later in the chapter.

Disproportionate Focus on the Poor and People of Color

Generally speaking, there is far more media coverage of courtroom activity involving the poor and people of color. This is logical given that the poor and people of color and disproportionately likely to be courtroom clients, even if it does reinforce the myth that these people are more dangerous. Characteristics of state and federal court defendants demonstrate who our criminal justice network most often catches (or pursues). At the state level in 2004, 82% of convicted felons were men, 38% of defendants were black (versus 59% white and 2% other), 67% were under the age of 40 years. State court statistics from the largest counties thus show that the typical defendant is a young, minority male.[18]

In federal courts in 2003, most convicted for felonies were men (87%), white (71%, versus 25% blacks), and in their 20s or 30s (70%, versus 25% over the age of 40 and 5% 20 years and younger). Further, 48% did not graduate from high school (versus 30% that were high school graduates, 17% with some college, and 6% who graduated from college).[19] Thus, in federal courts, the typical conviction is of a young, uneducated white male, although blacks are overrepresented among felony convictions.

Court defendants are also disproportionately *indigent*, meaning they cannot afford an attorney. They make up more than 80% of people charged with felonies in the United States.[20] According to the Bureau of Justice Statistics, in any given year, roughly 80-85% of felony defendants in state courts and approximately 65-70% of federal defendants are publicly financed defense attorneys.[21] From these data, it can be confidently concluded that the typical client in American courts is poor. Although there have been numerous cases of wealthy people standing trial for very serious crimes, the fact that most media attention is on poor street criminals reinforces the myth of who is dangerous (the poor) and who is not (the rich).

Wealthy brothers Eric and Lyle Menendez went on trial for the murder of their parents in 1989. After a first ended in a mistrial (which was broadcast live on CourtTV), the second trial (where cameras were not allowed in the courtroom) led to convictions and life sentences for the brothers. http://en.wikipedia.org/wiki/File:Menendez_brothers_-_mug_shot.jpg.

When wealthy individuals are charged with heinous crimes, such as in the O.J. Simpson murder case, the media are usually interested in covering the story. The preliminary hearing and criminal trial of Simpson were widely watched in the United States. Media outlets provided nearly 24 hour coverage of these events, including live coverage of a "low speed chase" involving the police following Simpson in his white SUV. When Simpson was arrested, his image appeared on *Newsweek* magazine. *Time* magazine ran the same image in June 1994 but darkened the image to make Simpson appear darker and thus more "menacing." This fits well with how the media treat race and crime, as shown in Chapter 4.

Mischaracterize the Nature of Courtroom Procedures

The ideal of American justice is an "adversarial" process whereby prosecutors and defense attorneys fight for the truth and justice in a contest at trial. Further, to ensure justice, the court is supposed to be impartial. Ideally, this means that neutral actors are involved in objectively determining the relevant facts of each case in order to ensure that the guilty are convicted and the innocent are not. However, three realities illustrate that this adversarial, impartial process is largely a myth.

First, minorities and women are underrepresented in American courtroom workgroups.[22] African Americans are underrepresented as attorneys and judges.[23] For example, according to the Death Penalty Information Center, approximately 98% of district attorneys in states with the death penalty are white.[24] Thus, much as legislators who make the law are not representative of Americans in terms of demographics, those who work to convict or acquit suspected criminals also are not representative of Americans.

Second, there is a serious imbalance in the *courtroom workgroup*, which is made up of the main actors in this process within the criminal courts—the prosecutor, the defense attorney, and the judge.[25] Ideally, each member of the courtroom workgroup plays its own roles and has its own goals. In reality, each member's main job is not to rock the boat in the daily operations of American courts, which are described by David Neubauer as follows:

> Every day, the same group of courthouse regulars assembles in the same courtroom, sits or stands in the same places, and performs the same tasks as the day before. The types of defendants and the nature of the crimes they are accused of committing also remain constant. Only the names of the victim, witnesses, and defendants are different.[26]

In the ideal, the *prosecutor*, as a representative of the court, fights for the "people" in an effort to "get justice" for the crime victim and the community. His or her main job is to decide whether or not to press charges on the basis of the amount of quality evidence available to obtain a conviction. If the prosecution decides to press criminal charges, the next decision is to decide which charges to press. The prosecutor is supposedly a zealous pursuer of crime control in the interests of the community and the police.

The *defense attorney* ideally represents the "defendant" and has the main duty of being an advocate for the defendant. This is the main actor in the criminal justice process who is responsible for ensuring that Constitutional protections of the accused are upheld and protected. Defense attorneys are the actors in the court process responsible for upholding the due process function of the court, protecting "individuals from the unfair advantages that the government—with its immense resources—automatically enjoys in legal battles."[27]

Since most defendants in America's courts are indigent, they tend to be defended by *public defenders*. The typical defendant is not a wealthy person out to beat the system: "The average defendant in a criminal proceeding is indigent and not capable of hiring the 'best attorney money can buy." Instead, he or she is assigned a courthouse regular, who is usually paid a very low salary, works in a depressing environment, and has very few support services available.[28] Think of images of courtroom personnel you've seen in the media; odds are this reality is rarely seen.

The *judge*, as leader of the courtroom workgroup, ideally has the overriding goal of ensuring that proper legal procedures are followed as a case is processed through the courts. Judges decide if arrests are based on probable cause, inform charged suspects of their rights, determine if bail will be granted to defendants, rule on motions filed by the prosecution and the defense, officiate trials to make sure they are fair, and impose sentences on the legally guilty. Ideally, judges embody justice and ensure due process, but in reality, judges spend most of their time in the administrative role, which would include such activities as preparing budgets, scheduling cases, supervising employees, and maintaining court records. This image is also unknown to most.

Because of the number of cases they must handle, and because of the amount of time courthouse employees spend together, the group may generally share the overriding goal of disposing of cases as quickly as possible more often than they may fight for justice. As more and more citizens have "run-ins with the law"—that is, as more police are put on the street and as American police make more arrests—the courts suffer the consequences. Today, the courts are forced to handle too many cases. As a result, many cases are simply dismissed before they are even considered. Samuel Walker writes: "The justice system can only handle so much business. It does not 'collapse' like a building. It keeps on going, but only through adjustments that are often undesirable."[29]

Citizens think of a courtroom as an adversarial process where prosecutors and defense attorneys fight over the truth. In fact, nearly all felony cases are settled outside the courtroom when prosecutors and defense attorneys reach an agreement on a sentence without trial through the plea bargaining process. http://en.wikipedia.org/wiki/File:Historic_Courtroom.JPG.

This reality is largely unknown to citizens. Due in large part to media focus on the criminal trial, as well as entertainment shows focused on high stakes courtroom drama, people wrongly assume that prosecutors and defense attorneys battle it out in open court, under the watchful eyes of neutral judges. In fact, the reality of the courts is that each member of the court shares the same basic goal—to dispose of cases.

The court is thus more about cooperation than conflict. As noted by Samuel Walker, "the reality is that an administrative system is in effect, with a high degree of consensus and cooperation."[30] Most cases are handled informally in hallways and offices rather than in courtrooms, as in a crime control model rather than a due process model. Instead of criminal trials in which prosecutors and defense attorneys clash in an effort to determine the truth and do justice for all concerned parties, prosecutors, defense attorneys, and sometimes judges "shop" for "supermarket" justice through plea bargaining.[31]

The intimate nature of the daily operations of American courts makes the courtroom workgroup a "community" because the members develop shared understandings of how cases should normally be handled.[32] This means that even though prosecutors and defense attorneys are supposed to be adversaries, they rarely act this way.

It is clear that prosecutors have much more power in the criminal justice process than judges or defense attorneys.[33] *Power* is the ability to influence actions of others. Since the decision about whether an accused person will be brought to court rests solely with the prosecutor, he or she has an enormous amount of discretion and is clearly the most powerful member of the court. Stated plainly, if the prosecutor decides not to prosecute a case, the defense attorney and judge will in essence have no say in the outcome of that case. It is the discretion of the prosecutor to act or not to act that gives him or her so much power.[34]

This is especially true when large numbers of cases are sent from the police to courts. As American courts have become bogged down with more cases, judges have lost significant power, because they are even more reliant on prosecutors to determine which cases merit charges, trials, and justice. [35]

Because of this imbalance of power in the court, justice (i.e., due process) is severely threatened. Ideally, if Americans value justice, due process, "innocent until proven guilty," constitutional protections, and equality before the law, it seems that defense attorneys would have more power and a greater share of resources to ensure that their clients are processed fairly through the criminal justice network. Because most criminal defense attorneys work for the government (e.g., as public defenders), they have heavy caseloads, limited resources to investigate the facts of a case, and little or no financial incentive to take a case to trial. This may result in unequal justice for the rich and the poor.

Interestingly, Americans are also probably unaware that the prosecutor has the most power in the courtroom. This owes itself partly to media depictions of injustices such as guilty people wrongly going free due to their celebrity defense attorneys (as if every defendant receives the advantage of a "dream team" of attorneys). One such depiction is a book by Nancy Grace, a former prosecutor who rails against the evils of 24 hour news coverage of crime on her own television show. Ironically, Grace's show—*Nancy Grace*—focuses exclusively on high profile criminal cases (or ordinary violent crimes that become high profile cases in part because she covers them).[36] Recently, Grace was sued by the parents of a young woman who appeared on the show after the woman killed herself with a shotgun. The woman was on the show to discuss the disappearance of her young son. Grace had peppered her with tough questions about her son's disappearance; presumably Grace suspected the woman of hurting her own son. Prior to hosting her own show, Grace was a prosecutor in Atlanta, Georgia working on serious violent crimes.

Since prosecutors' offices are so much more powerful than the typically defense attorney, the information they release to the news is often printed verbatim as news—one-sided though it may be—with no facts whatsoever offered by the defense attorney. According to two former defense attorneys: "In every courtroom across the United States, prosecutors are urging jurors to believe that 'This case is simple,' while lawyers for the accused inevitably respond that 'No case is ever simple and no life is ever simple.' But only the former fits, above the fold, in today's newspaper."[37] Since defense attorneys generally have less resources than prosecutors, they are usually at a disadvantage when it comes to getting their side of the story told in the media.

The Great Myth of the Criminal Trial

The great bulk of courtroom activity occurs behind closed doors, in private and without the participation of witnesses or victims and without the presentation of real evidence. The reality of courts in the United States today is plea bargaining whereby the accused pleads guilty in exchange for lesser charges and/or a lesser sentence.

While people saw trials in their entirety on *Court TV* (now called *TruTV*) and in part on shows such as *Dateline NBC*, the reality is that trials are not the norm. People think that trials are the rule when, in fact, they are the "exceptional case."[38] The media thus "emphasize the rare-in-reality adversarial criminal trial" which leads the viewer to believe that the typical court case in the United States is "a high-stakes, complicated, arcane contest practiced by expert professionals and beyond the understanding of everyday citizens," even though the reality is the assembly-line justice of plea bargaining.[39] In other words, people think we are following a due process model of criminal justice when in fact we are more firmly entrenched in a crime control model.

Virtually all (95%) of felony cases in the United States in any given year are disposed of via plea bargaining. Criminal trials are a formalized means of determining the legal guilt of your fellow citizens. *Plea bargaining* is an informal process whereby defendants plead guilty to lesser charges in exchange for not taking up the court's valuable time or spending the state's money on trials. Clients give up their constitutional rights to cross-examine witnesses, to present a defense, to not incriminate themselves, to testify on their own behalf, and to appeal their convictions, all in exchange for a dismissal or reduction in charges, and/or a lesser sentence.[40] Larry Gaines and colleagues write that this type of assembly-line justice, consistent with a crime control model, "implies injustice. The term suggests that defendants are being hurried through the process, losing the safeguards built into our criminal justice system in the blur."[41]

Plea bargaining is a process driven by large numbers of caseloads, understaffed courts, an imbalance between the prosecution and defense, and the renewed emphasis on using law enforcement to solve drug use and public order offenses. There are so few trials in part because there are simply too many cases to have trials and not enough personnel or money to handle them all, and most of criminal spending and employees are devoted to police and corrections.

% Funding (2006)

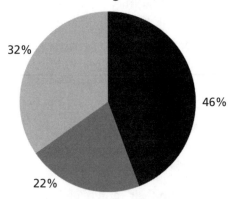

■ Police ■ Courts ■ Corrections

Source: In 2006, 46% of criminal justice funding went to police, followed by 32% for corrections, but only 22% for courts. One outcome of this imbalance of spending is an inability to hold trials for people accused of even serious crimes. http://ojp.usdoj.gov/bjs/glance/tables/exptyptab.htm.

Not surprisingly, plea bargaining results in a bias against poor clients, who are typically minorities, as well as the uneducated, who may not even know what is being done to them in the criminal justice process.[42] Stephen Bright, director of Atlanta's Southern Center for Human Rights, says it this way: "If you're the average poor person, you are going to be herded through the criminal justice system about like an animal is herded through the stockyards."[43]

Some may argue that no one would enter a guilty plea for a crime he or she did not commit, but a person living in conditions of poverty who is charged with a minor crime and refuses to plead guilty will only guarantee himself or herself a longer stay in jail awaiting a hearing — often longer than the likely sentence to be imposed upon conviction through a guilty plea.[44] Even in serious crimes, people who do not understand criminal procedure in the courts may also simply plead guilty on the advice of their own attorneys. If a public defender is representing the case, chances are the defendant will not have much of a chance to win at trial even if he or she is actually innocent, because: "In many jurisdictions, public defenders and state appointed attorneys are grossly underpaid, poorly trained, or simply lack the resources and time to prepare for a case — a pattern documented in cases ranging from the most minor to the most consequential, capital crimes."[45]

When a defendant enters a guilty plea, he or she is asked numerous questions by the judge in order to ensure that the defendant understands that he or she is giving up many constitutional rights and that the guilty plea was not coerced. *Coercion* is not clearly defined for the defendant in this process. Pleas might be understood as coerced if one considers the quality of defense provided by public defenders. Oftentimes, defendants plead guilty because of the threat of losing at trial and receiving a much more severe sentence. John Langbein claims that "the plea bargaining system operates by threat."[46] In the face of threats by the prosecution, defense attorneys essentially may tell their clients: "So you want your constitutional right to jury trial? By all means, be our guest. But beware. If you claim this right and are convicted, we will punish you twice, once for the offense, and once again for having displayed the temerity to exercise your constitutional right to jury trial." In other words, the goal of the public defender is to coerce his or her clients into surrendering their rights by threatening them with the possibility of greater sanctions.

The work environment of public defenders, who are responsible for defending the indigent (those who cannot afford their own attorneys), is typically depressing. Public defenders have large caseloads and limited resources relative to the prosecution, they work long hours, and they receive low pay. The indigent defendant must know that the likelihood of winning is remote. The result should not be surprising:

Some public defenders seem to have little interest in using every possible strategy to defend their clients. On numerous occasions, legal
errors are made by prosecutors and judges to which the public defender raises no objection. In addition, appeals are sometimes not
initiated by public defenders even when chances of successful appeal
seem to be good.[47]

Why would a public defender, who is ideally responsible for upholding the
Constitutional right to due process of law for the most vulnerable of all citizens—poor defendants faced with the incredible power of the government—
take part in plea bargaining? Jeffery Reiman answers: "Because the public defender works in day-to-day contact with the prosecutor and the judge, the
pressures on him or her to negotiate a plea as quickly as possible, instead of
rocking the boat by threatening to go to trial, are even greater than those that
work on court-assigned counsel."[48] In other words, the defense attorney is
usually on the same side as the prosecutor, and shares the same overriding
goal of disposing of cases. This means the reality of criminal courts is an administrative, cooperative model rather than an adversarial model like we all
assume.

One of the major problems with plea bargaining is that factual guilt is not determined in plea bargaining as it would be at a criminal trial. Guilt is assumed
rather than established. John Langbein calls plea bargaining "condemnation without adjudication"—that is, sentencing without an establishment of guilt.[49] Little investigation of the case against the defendant is conducted. Witnesses and victims
are not present to see or approve of justice being meted out to the guilty. The
question addressed by plea bargaining is not whether the defendant is actually guilty
of the charges but, rather, what to do with the defendant who is assumed to be
guilty. And one more thing—when guilty people plea bargain, they receive relatively lighter sentences than those convicted at trial for all crimes. This means
people convicted at trial for murder, rape, robbery, aggravated assault, burglary,
drug possession and drug trafficking get longer sentences than people convicted
through plea bargains. And victims of crime have no say in the matter.

For all of these reasons, nearly everyone seems to be against plea bargaining. It is surprising, then, that it happens so often:

Conservatives believe it is a major loophole through which criminals
beat the system and avoid punishment. Liberals, meanwhile, believe
that it is a source of grave injustices: prosecutors deliberately "overcharge";
defense attorneys make deals rather than fight for their clients; defendants are coerced into waiving their right to a trial; some defendants get much better deals than others.[50]

When we shine a light on the outcome of justice in the United States, we see that the reality of plea bargaining is not consistent with the American ideal of the criminal trial, which is mentioned in the Declaration of Independence, three amendments to the U.S. Constitution, and scores of Supreme Court cases. Obviously, Americans are unaware of this reality, for it is likely that if they knew, they would probably demand change.

Unfortunately, media coverage of courts creates the illusion that trials are the norm. Clearly this is not the case. There are likely several reasons why the media tend to ignore the reality of the criminal courts. First, it is private, so it is largely unknown to even the media. Second, it would not be attractive to viewers, readers and listeners to learn about the boring story of plea bargaining; there is no drama (at least no public drama in open court since plea agreements are typically reached in private). Thus it is inconsistent with the profit-seeking motive of the media. Third, trials represent conflict between competing sides and are thus much more attractive to viewers than pretrial practices such as plea bargaining.

High Profile Trials

Part of the reason people think of trials when they think of courts, is due to the widespread coverage of high profile trials in the press. High profile trials[51] and so called "notorious trials"[52] have received a lot of attention from the news and entertainment media. Paula Hannaford-Agor explains:

> The term "notorious trial" brings to mind images of celebrity parties or witnesses (and sometimes celebrity lawyers and even judges), heinous crimes, unusual legal issues or factual situations, and unrelenting media coverage in the press, on television and radio, and even online. But notorious trials come in many shapes and sizes. Most often we think of criminal trials, but civil cases such as the Vioxx product liability trials, the Wal-Mart employment discrimination case, and even complex shareholder suits in business fraud cases qualify as notorious. The term connotes national notoriety, but local or regional notoriety is also quite common, especially in political corruption cases or cases involving significant local or regional employers.

According to Richard Fox and his colleagues, media coverage of such high profile cases creates a circus-like atmosphere that results in major misconceptions of court realities.[53] Ray Surette notes that the first well-known trial in America was the 1859 trial of anarchist John Brown, which resulted in significant telegraph and newspaper coverage.[54] Other widely covered trials include the 1893

Lizzie Borden trial for the murder of her parents with an ax, the 1935 trial of Bruno Hauptmann for the kidnapping of and murder of Charles Lindbergh's infant son, and of course the 1995 O.J. Simpson double murder trial (which was broadcast on television in its entirety). Surette offers additional examples of different media trial themes, including those of the *abuse of power* theme (Nuremberg Trials of 1946, Rodney King beating trial in 1994, Clinton Impeachment proceedings of 1999); the *sinful rich* theme (Sam Sheppard murder trial in 1954, William Kennedy Smith rape trial in 1991, O.J. Simpson murder trial in 1995); the *evil stranger* theme (Julius and Ethel Rosenberg espionage trial in 1951, Bruno Hauptmann kidnapping and murder trial in 1935, Timothy McVeigh terrorism and murder trial in 1997); and the *psychotic killers* theme (Charles Manson murder trial in 1970, Jeffrey Dahmer murder trial in 1992, Scott Peterson murder trial in 2004).

According to Hannaford-Agor, such trials are quite rare. She claims that only about a dozen trials out of 150,000 every year receive any sustained national media coverage. Still, because notorious trials "are so closely watched, how courts manage them has a disproportionate impact on public trust and confidence in the justice system."

According to John Gibeaut, the "rich and famous get star treatment, creating the appearance of a two-tiered court system."[55] In fact, this is quite true. Criminologists and criminal justice scholars have long written about the *wedding cake model* of criminal trials.

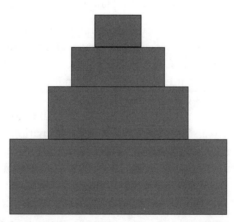

The metaphor of the "wedding cake" applies to criminal trials in the United States. The top layer, the least common and thus the smallest, is meant to depict those rare high profile trials that usually involve celebrities and/or heinous crimes. The bottom layer, the largest and thus most common, is meant to represent the far more common every day, routine cases such as misdemeanors.

According to Mary McKenzie:

> The relatively small first layer is made up of the celebrated cases in-
> volving the famous, wealthy, or powerful, or the not-so-powerful who
> victimize a famous person. Also included in this category are unknown
> criminals whose cases become celebrated … People in the first layer of
> the wedding cake receive a great deal of public attention, and their cases
> usually involve the full panoply of criminal justice procedures, includ-
> ing the famous defense attorneys, jury trials, and elaborate appeals.[56]

The second and third layers are comprised of "serious felonies encountered
daily in urban jurisdictions, such as robberies, burglaries, rapes, and homicides."
Second-layer cases are more serious, and/or are committed by more notorious offenders. They also tend to be committed by strangers, whereas crimes committed by people who know each other may be seen more as a "private matter"
and then perhaps less serious in nature. Third-layer cases are comprised largely
of crimes committed against property such as theft. Fourth-layer cases comprise the majority of cases. These are mostly minor offenses such as misdemeanors and public order offenses that are handled via plea bargains in an
assembly-line version of justice.[57]

Randall Shelden adds: "The first layer consists of the small number of 'celebrated cases.' The O.J. Simpson case comes to mind most immediately, along
with Susan Smith (convicted of killing her two sons), the Oklahoma bombing
case, the Menendez trial, the Rodney King case, and most recently the Scott
Peterson case, among others." According to Shelden, there are two major types
of cases within first-tier cases:

> (1) the rich and the famous (or someone who's intended victim was fa-
> mous, as in the John Hinckley case, where the victim was the President
> of the United States, Ronald Reagan), with O.J. Simpson being the most
> famous example in recent history. Also included would be various ex-
> amples of 'white collar' or 'corporate crime' such as the Savings and Loan
> Scandal and the Ford Pinto case; (2) those who are at the lowest end of
> the class system but whose case ends up as one of the landmark Supreme
> Court decisions, such as Dolree Mapp, Ernesto Miranda, and Danny
> Escobedo. These cases, although representing a minute proportion of all
> cases, tend to capture the public imagination and have an enormous
> impact on public perceptions of how the criminal justice system works.[58]

The problem, according to Shelden, is that citizens may "conclude that this
is how the system works, yet the exact opposite is far more typical, especially
when we consider that the majority of cases are handled in a rather routine

manner in virtually a matter of minutes and it is a rare case that ever goes before a jury."[59] In the case of the courts, the media do not accurately portray typical courtroom activity.

According to Ray Surette, three frames are currently used in coverage of media trials:

- *Abuse of power*—These are cases where powerful people, often politicians or even criminal justice personnel (e.g., police chiefs) have abused the power of their positions for personal gain.
- *Sinful rich*—These are cases where very wealthy people engage in acts that may seem unethical or immoral to others, including drug use, sexual deviance, and so forth.
- *Evil strangers*—These are cases where a person unknown to an innocent person (usually a child) does unspeakable harm through criminal activity motivated by perceived evils such as sexual pleasure.[60]

The messages of media trials, according to Surette, are: "the rich are immoral in their use of sex, drugs, and violence; ... people in power are evil, greedy, and should not be trusted and ... strangers and those with different lifestyles or values are inherently dangerous."[61] While there are obviously cases like these in reality, the great bulk of criminality is motivated by a much wider variety of conditions and situations that rarely are depicted in the media. What's interesting is that, even when it comes to crimes committed by the rich, the dominant construction of criminal motivation is focused on individual sources, just as in the case of street crime (see Chapter 4).

As we all know, high profile cases are generally covered long before they ever end up in trial. A study of 2004 network news found reporting about high-profile crimes—including the alleged molestation case of Michael Jackson, rape case of Kobe Bryant, murder case of Scott Peterson, and insider trading case of Martha Stewart—were different from reporting of other stories. The vast majority (84%) of the coverage of the former stories was carried on the morning network news, and these stories tended to offer only one viewpoint and contain anonymous (although transparent) sources. Clearly, these cases have proven an effective way of capturing citizen attention on issues of crime and justice for the media.[62]

Cameras in Court

Media coverage of real courtroom activity obviously requires that cameras be present in courtrooms. According to Wendy Pogorzelski and Thomas Brewer, the U.S. Supreme Court "has denied the electronic media a presumptive right to televise court proceedings, stopped short of finding an individual's right to a fair trial inherently infringed upon by the presence of a camera in court, and has maintained states' rights to experiment with televising court proceedings."[63] Thus, it is up to state law whether cameras are allowed in the courtroom to cover trials. Interestingly, the policy-making body of the federal courts—The Judicial Conference of the United States—opposes cameras in trial courts.

Pogorzelski and Brewer note:

> Cameras in court epitomize the interface between two significant institutions in our society: the media and the justice system. The media serve as the primary source of information and the criminal justice system as a primary source for legitimizing values and enforcing norms. To accomplish their respective objectives, these two institutions have developed an interdependent relationship. Both are in the business of creating meaning. The media transform events into news stories, thus attaching significance to selected acts and framing key issues and players in political, legal, and cultural events. The courts address matters that challenge the parameters of law, culture, and politics. By interpreting actions and policies within the context of previous judicial and legislative decisions, the courts affirm or reset these parameters and social life more generally. The media and the courts have a shared understanding of the other's role and responsibilities, but there is also a dynamic tension between them.[64]

The tension comes from the fact that criminal justice agents do not want their work to be influenced by outside observers who know little about criminal justice process. Further, the media want access to the courtroom in order to shine light on what goes on in America's courts, but without perhaps a full understanding of the potential consequences of broadcasting legal proceedings to the public.

It is obviously important that citizens have faith in their courts, as well as all legal institutions. The media can play a large role in assuring this outcome:

> When the populous feel confident that justice has been invoked they are often more willing to accept the outcome, even if they disagree. Thus "justice must satisfy the appearance of justice." The process of administering justice is also the process of establishing and enforcing norms and is fundamental to an orderly society. Therefore, the work of the justice system cannot happen in a vacuum and the courts rely on the media as one mechanism to publicize its responses to the social problem of crime and the pursuit of justice. Without such a vehicle of communication, the public's ability to evaluate the justice system is limited.[65]

Unfortunately, media accounts of court activities such as trials "are brief, time- and space-limited constructions that must make their points quickly ...".[66] As one example, a study of media coverage of courts in more than 200 newscasts of five different television stations found that most media coverage "consisted of reporter or anchorperson voice-overs and footage from outside the courtroom. When the media did use the video footage or particularly the audiotape from inside the courtroom, the coverage came in the form of sound bites."[67] Only 20% of the news coverage was of actual footage from inside the court.

These kinds of findings are likely due to the goals of the media, discussed in Chapters 1 and 2. Most courtroom activity—even trials—is not captivating or easy to sell. For this reason, courtroom procedures would rarely attract viewers, thereby not leading to high ratings, and media companies would have difficulty selling advertising in and around such programs.

Newspapers are obviously better able to provide more in-depth analysis of criminal trials and other issues in the courts, especially since they do not have to worry about also providing audio or media clips to accompany their stories (with the exception of online content). Unfortunately, aside from rare court rulings on matters of law or high profile trials, this type of analysis rarely occurs, largely because of shrinking resources available for newspapers.

Pre-trial Publicity

Another issue that has come to the attention of scholars is that of pretrial publicity.[68] This is an important issue because news about details of a crime influences the way jurors rate the importance of some kinds of evidence as well as the standards jurors may use to determine whether a defendant is guilty.[69]

In 1996, it was alleged in the media that security guard Richard Jewel may be the man who planted a bomb in Olympic Park at the Olympic games. In actuality, Jewel had nothing to do with the attack. http://chronicle.augusta.com/images/head lines/102996/jewel.jpg.

The potential danger of pre-trial publicity can be seen when considering the case of Richard Jewel, who was alleged to have been the person who planted a bomb in Olympic Park in Atlanta, Georgia during the 1996 Olympic games.

For 88 days prior to being cleared, Jewel was hounded at every stop, from his home, to the store, and so forth, as the leading suspect in the case. After being cleared, Jewell asserted that the FBI trampled on his rights "in its rush to show the world it could get its man." Further, he suggested that the news media "cared nothing about my feelings as a human being" as it covered his alleged involvement in the bombing.[70]

Jewell became a suspect because he discovered the package before it exploded while working as a security guard in the park. He was hounded for months by the media even though he had nothing to do with the attack. Ultimately, anti-abortion zealot Eric Robert Rudolph was convicted of the bombing after being captured by the police in rural, Western North Carolina. Rudolph was also convicted for the bombing of a family planning clinic in Birmingham, Alabama, as well as other bombings at an abortion clinic and a gay night club.

What are the civil liberties implications of putting the picture of a person arrested for a crime on television and the newspaper? At the very least, having one's image appear in the media means that one will likely be presumed guilty by many, including one's family, friends, and employer. This is a serious threat to the notion of "innocent until proven guilty" that supposedly underlies our criminal justice processes.

There are clear reasons why the media are interested in criminal cases before they go to trial. First, media outlets tend to cover crimes, especially high profile and random violent crimes such as the Olympic Park bombing. Thus when a suspect is named, it is logical to expect the media to continue to cover the story. Second, recall that the media are for-profit organizations. Since crime sells, the media will continue to send reporters to the scene—any scene—where they can cover elements of a crime. Recall that reporters are often sent to the scene of a crime even long after the crime; doing so apparently makes the report seem more important to media consumers.

Sentencing

Sentencing is the final phase of the courts and is often ignored by the media. A *sentence* is a penalty or sanction imposed on a person by a court upon conviction for a criminal offense.[71] For example, when a person is convicted of murder, he or she may be sentenced to the death penalty, life in prison, some other term of imprisonment, or, in rare cases, a long term of probation and/or house arrest.

An increasingly popular type of sentence available in American states is the *mandatory sentence*, which establishes a minimum sanction that must be served upon conviction for a criminal offense. Thus, everyone who is convicted of a

The case of alleged "Craigslist killer" Philip Markoff has received enormous media attention, including the alleged facts that he stored the victims' panties under the bed where he and his fiancée slept. When such facts are reported in the press, suspects appear to be being tried in the press, prior to the actual disposition of their case in the courts. http://www.romeobserver.com/articles/2010/08/19/news/doc4c695e0e20832706432470.txt.

crime that calls for a mandatory sentence will serve that amount of time.[72] Judges have no discretion in mandatory sentencing because, by definition, the sentence is mandatory. A specified imprisonment term must be given to the convicted offender by law. Samuel Walker concludes that mandatory sentences are responsible in part for the shift of power in the courts to prosecutors, as well as for "unduly harsh" punishments for some crimes.[73] Prosecutors are empowered by mandatory sentencing because they ultimately determine the sentence for those convicted of crimes, based on what crimes they decide to charge people with; if convicted, judges have no discretion to modify the sentence. As for unduly harsh sentences, these occur in the case of crime that have been legislated as serious even though they produce little or no harm to society.

The war on drugs is responsible for a large share of mandatory sentences. Consider, for example, 20-year-old Nicole Richardson of Mobile, Alabama, who was dating a drug dealer. When approached by an undercover officer about where to buy some drugs, Nicole said to talk to her boyfriend. Her sentence was 10 years in prison with no possibility of parole; her boyfriend, who cooperated with authorities, received a 5-year imprisonment sentence.[74] Sentencing judges, with no discretion in mandatory sentencing, are generally opposed to it, in part because of unfair outcomes such as Nicole's case.[75]

Good examples of mandatory sentences are the so-called *three-strikes laws* that have been passed by more than half the states in the United States. These laws usually require that upon conviction for a third felony, the offender will be sentenced to a period of imprisonment for the remainder of his or her natural life: "Neither the particular circumstances, nor the seriousness of the crimes charged, nor the duration of time that has elapsed between crimes is given consideration" in three-strikes laws. These laws also mandate that judges must "ignore mitigating factors in the background of offenders, as well as their ties to community, employment status, potential for rehabilitation, and obligations to children."[76]

🖰 For more information about the war on drugs and how it has failed to achieve its states goals, see the website for this book at: www.pscj.app state.edu/media/drugwar.html

---

Three-strikes laws grew out of a crime hysteria or moral panic caused by media hyping of a highly publicized violent crime against a young female child in California (i.e., Polly Klaas), and the idea grew out of the National Rifle Association. Many states, such as California, passed laws that were intended primarily for violent offenders but that failed to specify this intent. Many nonviolent offenders including drug offenders are being incarcerated under this law. Further, the law has been disproportionately against blacks.[77] Once again, Americans remain largely ignorant of these facts, largely because of the fact that the mainstream media fail to provide significant coverage of these realities. It is also true that many middle- and outer-ring (or second- and third-tier) media have critically analyzed the drug war as well as racial disparities produced in criminal justice processing. Yet, this is largely unknown to most because of the smaller reach of these media outlets.

In 2003, the Supreme Court upheld California's three-strikes sentencing law in the cases of *Ewing v. California*, 01-6978, and *Lockyer v. Andrade*, 01-1127, ruling 5-4 that long prison terms are constitutionally permissible even for minor offenders. The court upheld sentences of 25 years to life and 50 years to life for a thief who shoplifted clubs from a golf course and for a man who stole a handful of videotapes from Kmart, respectively. In the former case, Sandra Day O'Connor wrote:

> We do not sit as a "superlegislature" to second-guess these policy choices. It is enough that the State of California has a reasonable basis for believing that dramatically enhanced sentences for habitual felons

advances the goals of its criminal justice system in any substantial way ... [they] reflect[] a rational legislative judgment, entitled to deference, that offenders who have committed serious or violent felonies and who continue to commit felonies must be incapacitated.

The media rarely provide significant coverage of the sentencing phase of the courts. Exceptions occur in high profile cases, as noted earlier. There are also commonly follow-ups of crimes that received widespread media attention earlier in the criminal justice process (e.g., after the commission of a crime and a suspect has been arrested). It is also generally true that reforms to sentencing laws are only sometimes discussed in the press. This is most common when laws are passed that are named after crime victims; perhaps the best known example is "Megan's Law." Megan's Law "requires authorities to notify neighborhoods when a convicted sex offender moves in ... [and] was named after Megan Kanka, the New Jersey 7-year-old who was raped and murdered in 1994 by a previously convicted child molester who lived nearby."[78]

Bias in the Sentencing Process

For criminal justice processes to be just, they must be fair and "not be affected by extraneous factors, such as race, gender, or socioeconomic status."[79] Instead, sentences should be based on legal factors such as seriousness of offense and prior criminal record. According to Victor Kappeler and his colleagues:

> The empirical research done by criminal justice scholars has demonstrated with remarkable regularity that minority group members (particularly African Americans) and the poor get longer sentences and have less chance of gaining parole or probation, even when the seriousness of the crime and the criminal record of the defendants are held constant.[80]

A review of sentencing research by Samuel Walker and colleagues concludes that sentencing is characterized by *contextual discrimination* because they found evidence of bias in some court jurisdictions in different areas related to sentencing. They write:

> Judges in some jurisdictions continue to impose harsher sentences on racial minorities who murder or rape whites, and more lenient sentences on racial minorities whose victims are of their own racial or ethnic group. Judges in some jurisdictions continue to impose racially biased sentences in less serious cases; in these "borderline cases" racial

minorities get prison, whereas whites get probation. In jurisdictions with sentencing guidelines, judges depart from the presumptive sentence less often when the offender is African American or Hispanic than when the offender is white. Judges, in other words, continue to take race into account, either explicitly or implicitly, when determining the appropriate sentence.[81]

It is in borderline cases, then—the only cases in which discretion can come into play—where discretion does come into play. In other words, race and class biases affect sentencing when it is possible for them to do so. Such findings suggest that in at least some jurisdictions, when prosecutors and judges have discretion, they may be more likely to be biased against minorities than whites. Walker and colleagues also found evidence of sentencing biases in federal sentencing guideline cases as well as in drug cases.

The issue of bias in sentencing rarely comes to the attention of the media. For one thing, most cases disappear from the media's focus after the arrest stage. For another thing, examining racial disparities in sentencing and discovering their sources requires resources, something many media organizations are unwilling to invest in such stories. One organization that is willing to do such reporting is ProPublica, introduced in Chapter 1. Another is the Public Broadcasting System (PBS), whose show *Frontline* frequently addresses issues of crime and justice as they relate to race, ethnicity, social class, and so forth.

One issue that has received attention of the media is that of black killers convicted by all-white juries. While some black inmates have been executed by states after having been convicted by all-white juries, others have been set free when evidence came to light that potential black jurors were removed from the juries after prosecutors challenged them using *peremptory challenges* (which do not require them to state any reason or cause).[82]

When drug offenses are included in mandatory sentencing, such sentencing laws become a major source of criminal justice bias. For example, the 2007 National Survey of Drug Use and Health (NSDUH) shows that African Americans were only slightly more likely than whites to report to having used any illicit drug in the past month.[83] Yet, according to the Sourcebook of Criminal Justice Statistics, they made up more than one-third of arrests for drug abuse violations.[84] Other data show that the further one moves into the criminal justice process, the higher the proportion of blacks involved in drug offense criminal justice processing. For example, in any given year, blacks make up nearly half of all people convicted for drug offenses in state courts and as many as 75% of all people incarcerated for drug offenses in the U.S.. Throughout the United States, convicted drug offenders are disproportionately low-income minorities.

Federal sentencing against drug dealers demonstrates clear evidence of bias against people of color. Studies find that black and Latino drug offenders receive longer sentences than white drug offenders, even after controlling for relevant legal factors, and that white defendants receive more benefit from departures from federal sentencing guidelines.[85]

A particularly striking unfair pattern is the 100:1 ratio for sentences for crack cocaine and powder cocaine created by law in 1986, meaning that to receive a mandatory sentence of five years imprisonment, a person would need 100 times as much powder cocaine as crack (500 grams of powder versus 5 grams of crack). No one can say for sure if this discrepancy was racially motivated, but, in the late 1990s, African Americans accounted for 39% of crack cocaine users (and for only 13% of the general population) but 89% of those sentenced for federal crack crimes. As of 2007, only about 18% of crack cocaine users were black, while nearly 83% of defendants charged with crack cocaine crimes were black![86] The racial disparate impact of this law has received significant media attention, and the U.S. Sentencing Commission has repeatedly called for a repeal of the law. Congress finally took action to reduce but not eliminate these disparities in the "Fair Sentencing Act."

What is widely known is that media portrayal of crack use reinforced the stereotype or myth that it is an "African American drug."[87] Because harms associated with crack cocaine (e.g., "crack babies") were so broadly portrayed and discussed, not even a single African American member of Congress spoke out against the sentencing disparities between crack and powder cocaine at the time that the law was originally proposed and debated.[88] This is evidence of the moral panic that occurred with regard to crack cocaine in the 1980s, as discussed in Chapter 2.

Are Americans aware of these realities? No. This is predominantly because these issues have not been brought to their attention. The lack of media attention paid to disparities caused by drug law enforcement is surprising given that it is so controversial. Yet, in-depth, investigative analyses into issues such as these are costly. The media also rely on insiders for information about crime control policy; how many police officials will raise the issue of potential biases in their enforcement? Further, the media are generally pro status quo when it comes to "fighting crime." Thus, there are probably more reasons not to cover such issues than there are to cover them. Once again, middle- and outer-ring media (second- and third-tier media) have provided extensive coverage of the realities of the drug war and racially biased sentencing. Given the limited reach of these media organizations, most citizens are not informed about them.

Reinforce Crime Control

As is the case with media coverage of policing, media coverage of crimes in U.S. courts "tends to emphasize 'Crime Control' values" such as assuring "security from wrongdoers, just deserts, and punishment" while simultaneously devaluing due process concerns such as Constitutional protections of the accused. Only in celebrated cases do the media highlight due process values.[89] The possible result is lower respect of due process values among media consumers.

Research suggests that the media are focused on the interests of the state rather than the rights of the accused,[90] sending the message that "the courts and legal protections like the Bill of Rights are hampering law enforcement and helping criminals, terrorists, and other merchants of fear."[91] Given this, when politicians are labeled as being "liberal" or "soft on crime," they are essentially being associated with "outsiders, deviants or the 'other,'" which is "a common propaganda technique that neutralizes the opposition."[92]

Given that reporters rely on court insiders (especially prosecutors) for information, the result is that reporters will be encouraged to "cover some aspects of the news more than others."[93] It is a symbiotic relationship in which the reporters get information and court personnel ensure the type of coverage that is favorable to their daily activities.[94] Court sources "'feed'" court reporters, and thus the news is largely what the reporters have 'eaten.'"[95]
There are several reasons why crime control values will be emphasized over due process values. As noted earlier, the main reason is that members of the U.S. crime control bureaucracy (e.g., police, prosecutors) are more likely to interact with the media than advocates of due process. Reporters often rely on prosecutors' offices for their stories. Prosecutors may at times more helpful to reporters than defense attorneys in terms of clarifying facts and offering tips about stories. Because prosecutors are more concerned with crime control than with due process, logically their biases are reflected in any subsequent media coverage.[96] This is a reminder of one of the main filters of the media introduced in Chapter 1. Relying on official sources of information limits the breadth of stories in the media.

Another reason that media slant their coverage of criminal justice in a manner more consistent with a crime control model is that it is simply:

> easier to understand for reporters, their editors, and their audiences. Struggles between cops and robbers, good guys and bad guys, protectors and perpetrators are easy to write, to source, and to read or to view. Arcane rules and technicalities elude readers and viewers, many of whom have no idea what the rules are or what they mean.[97]

These kinds of stories are also consistent with the dominant themes and narratives of media coverage of crime, as introduced in Chapter 2.

Finally, since the most common people seen in the news are criminals and suspected criminals, viewers will likely develop values consistent with the crime control model of criminal justice. According to Ray Surette, "the courts are often alluded to as soft on crime, easy on criminals, due process-laden institutions that repeatedly release the obviously guilty and dangerous."[98] After criminals and suspects, the next most likely group to be seen on the news is crime victims and their families.[99]

Summary

Courts determine guilt or innocence but also engage in many other functions including determining whether someone receives bail or sits in preventive detention awaiting disposition of their case. Courts conducting preliminary hearings and grand juries to determine if there is enough evidence to warrant a criminal trial. Courts determine the appropriate sentences for those convicted of crimes. Courts also hear and make rulings on appeals of law. Much of this court activity goes unreported in the media. As a result, most people do not understand how the court system works or what it does.

Because of the separation of powers clause of the U.S. Constitution, the United States has a dual court system; that is, federal and state governments each have their own distinct court systems, and the two systems operate independently of each other. There are more than 200 different court systems in the states, Washington D.C., and Puerto Rico, including more than 70 statewide trial courts systems with general jurisdiction and more than 130 courts of appeal. State and federal courts can be differentiated by their jurisdiction — that is, where they have the authority or power to hear a case. Where a case is heard depends on what type of law is violated. Crimes against states are typically handled in state courts, whereas crimes against the federal government are held in federal courts. The majority of media coverage of courts is on state level courts. This is likely because most crimes are violations of state laws; thus, state courts handle far more cases that federal courts.

Generally speaking, there is far more coverage of courtroom activity involving the poor and people of color. This is logical given that the poor and people of color are disproportionately likely to be courtroom clients.

The ideal of American justice is an "adversarial" process whereby prosecutors and defense attorneys fight for the truth and justice in a contest at trial. Further, to ensure justice, the court is supposed to be impartial. Ideally, this means that neutral actors are involved in objectively determining the relevant facts of each case in order to ensure that the guilty are convicted and the innocent are not. However, this adversarial, impartial process is largely a myth.

The courtroom workgroup is mostly about cooperation rather than conflict. Trials are rare; instead, plea bargaining is the norm. Thus, battles between prosecutors and defense attorneys in front of a neutral judge infrequently occur.

This reality is largely unknown to citizens. Due in large part to media focus on the criminal trial, as well as entertainment shows focused on high stakes courtroom drama, people wrongly assume that prosecutors and defense attorneys battle it out in open court, under the watchful eyes of neutral judges. In fact, the reality of the courts is that each member of the court shares the same basic goal—to dispose of cases.

It is clear that prosecutors have much more power in the criminal justice process than judges or defense attorneys. Power is the ability to influence actions of others. Since the decision about whether an accused person will be brought to court rests solely with the prosecutor, he or she has an enormous amount of discretion and is clearly the most powerful member of the court. Stated plainly, if the prosecutor decides not to prosecute a case, the defense attorney and judge will in essence have no say in the outcome of that case. It is the discretion of the prosecutor to act or not to act that gives him or her so much power.

Because of this imbalance of power in the court, justice (i.e., due process) is severely threatened. Ideally, if Americans value justice, due process, "innocent until proven guilty," constitutional protections, and equality before the law, it seems that defense attorneys would have more power and a greater share of resources to ensure that their clients are processed fairly through the criminal justice network. Americans are also probably unaware that the prosecutor has the most power in the courtroom. This owes itself partly to media depictions of injustices such as guilty people wrongly going free due to their celebrity defense attorneys (as if every defendant receives the advantage of a "dream team" of attorneys).

The great bulk of courtroom activity occurs behind closed doors, in private and without the participation of witnesses or victims and without the presentation of real evidence. The reality of courts in the United States today is plea bargaining whereby the accused pleads guilty in exchange for lesser charges and/or a lesser sentence.

When we shine a light on the outcome of justice in the United States, we see that the reality of plea bargaining is not consistent with the American ideal of the criminal trial, which is mentioned in the Declaration of Independence, three amendments to the U.S. Constitution, and scores of Supreme Court cases. Obviously, Americans are unaware of this reality, for it is likely that if they knew, they would demand change. Unfortunately, media coverage of courts creates the illusion that trials are the norm. Clearly this is not the case.

Part of the reason people think of trials when they think of courts, is due to the widespread coverage of high profile trials in the press. High-profile trials and so called "notorious trials" receive a lot of attention from the news and entertainment media. Three frames are currently used in coverage of media trials, including abuse of power, the sinful rich, and evil strangers.

Cameras in the courtroom and pretrial publicity are important issues because they can impact public opinion about courtroom activity and influence the way jurors rate the importance of some kinds of evidence as well as the standards jurors may use to determine whether a defendant is guilty. There are serious civil liberties issues associated with cameras in the courtroom as well as media coverage of alleged crimes prior to trial.

Sentencing is the final phase of the courts and is often ignored by the media. Injustices associated with three strikes laws and the war on drugs are largely unknown to Americans because they are not regularly examined by mainstream media organizations.

The lack of media attention paid to disparities caused by drug law enforcement is surprising given that it is so controversial. Yet, in-depth, investigative analyses into issues such as these are costly. The media also rely on insiders for information about crime control policy; how many police officials will raise the issue of potential biases in their enforcement? Further, the media are generally pro status quo when it comes to "fighting crime." Thus, there are probably more reasons not to cover such issues than there are to cover them.

As is the case with media coverage of policing, media coverage of crimes in U.S. courts tends to emphasize crime control values. Only in celebrated cases do the media highlight due process values. The possible result is lower respect of due process values among media consumers.

Discussion Questions

1) What are the main functions of the courts?
2) Which types of activities of courts are often reported in the media and which go unreported? Why?
3) What is the *dual court system*?
4) Define the term *jurisdiction*.
5) What level of court receives the most media attention? Why?
6) Why do you think there is far more coverage of courtroom activity involving the poor and people of color?

7) The ideal of American justice is an "adversarial" process whereby prosecutors and defense attorneys fight for the truth and justice in a contest at trial. Is this how courts really operate? Explain.

8) What are some of the major problems with courts identified in the chapter?

9) What is the *courtroom workgroup* and how does this concept help us understand the realities of courtroom activity?

10) What are the main roles of the prosecutor, defense attorney, and judge?

11) Describe the "imbalance of power" in the courts and explain why this is important.

12) How do the media create the impression that defense attorneys are more powerful than prosecutors even though this is generally not the case?

13) What percentage of cases are plea bargained as opposed to tried in courts? Why does this matter?

14) What are the major problems with *plea bargaining*?

15) Why do you think the media do not focus on plea bargaining and other pre-trial practices?

16) Why do the media focus so much on only a few, high profile trials? Does this create misconceptions about the realities of the courts? Explain.

17) What are the three common frames used in coverage of media trials?

18) What are the main issues with cameras in the courtroom and pretrial publicity?

19) Is criminal sentencing by the courts commonly depicted in the media?

20) Outline the evidence that sentencing is biased in the United States against some groups of people.

Chapter 7

Media Coverage of Corrections: Life in Prison and Problems of Punishment

Learning Objectives

After reading this chapter, you will be able to:

1) Explain why corrections is the least covered aspect of criminal justice by the media.
2) Identify the circumstances that lead prisons to be covered in the news.
3) Summarize the Willie Horton case and explain why this case is significant for criminal justice.
4) Explain how politicians "use" the mainstream media to get their messages out to the public.

5) Identify the most common criminal punishment used in the United States and explain whether this form of punishment is commonly featured in the media.
6) Explain why the media are more focused on serious punishments such as imprisonment and the death penalty and less interested in probation.
7) Identify and define the major goals of punishment in the United States and explain whether these goals have been achieved.
8) Define *deterrence*. Explain whether people are usually deterred by the thought of major punishment.
9) Explain whether getting "tough on crime" works to reduce crime.
10) Discuss the significance of the fact that the United States leads the world in incarceration.
11) Outline all the costs of imprisonment.
12) Identify and define the major *pains of imprisonment*.
13) Identify the portion of people locked up in America suffers from mental illnesses and discuss whether this is known by Americans.
14) Discuss to what degree the media raise the issue of biases in American criminal justice and corrections.
15) Discuss to what degree death sentences and executions get covered by the media.

Introduction

What do images of punishment and corrections from the news, as well as television and movies suggest to you about American punishment? As it turns out, the most prevalent images of corrections found in news accounts as well as television and movies are misleading. For example, while the vast majority of people who are punished in the United States receive relatively mild sanctions such as probation (where they live and fulfill the conditions of their sentences in the community), media images of corrections suggest that the typical punishment used in the United States is imprisonment. This is true even though prisons rarely make the news.

Beyond this, the news media and entertainment media are largely responsible for myths even about prisons. This may be due to the tendency of the media to focus on isolated events within corrections. For example, Gary Kalman explains: "Escapes, crowding, violence, costs—more often than not when prisons make headlines in newspapers or on the evening news, the coverage is focused on an isolated event. The broader challenges facing correctional departments and other aspects of the justice system seldom get mentioned."[1] This is problematic because media coverage of corrections results in an inaccurate and distorted picture of American punishment. These issues are discussed in this chapter.

The Least Visible Component of Criminal Justice

Corrections is probably the least covered aspect of criminal justice by the media. Aside from documentaries and occasional stories of the nation's prisons, most Americans have no idea about the realities of American prisons, such as the enormous pains of imprisonment suffered each day by inmates. Corrections is not only the last stage of criminal justice but also the "last thought" of most Americans: "Society has always been more interested in catching criminals and holding media trials than in what happens to convicted offenders in our correctional institutions."[2]

Historically, corrections has been less visible to Americans whereas police "are seen in public daily" and the courts "are prominently displayed in our cities and can be easily visited."[3] Further, people tend to have direct experience with police officers and often with court personnel such as lawyers, but most people do not have direct experience with correctional facilities. This is not to say that no one has experiences with corrections, but experiences with serious criminal punishments such as prison and jail are concentrated among the poor.

Prisons are also little covered in the news.[4] According to Aaron Doyle and Richard Ericson: "Prisons are the most closed institutions in the justice system and receive less media attention than earlier stages of the criminal process."[5] This led these scholars to call imprisonment the "veiling of punishment." Another apt metaphor for our prison system is "out of sight, out of mind."

In one study, Steven Chermak found that about 17% of all criminal justice stories in newspapers and on television dealt with corrections. Stories about policing made up 52% of all stories, and stories about courts made up 30% of all stories. So, corrections is underrepresented in news stories about criminal justice. Further, most of the corrections stories dealt with cases as they progressed through the different stages of criminal justice rather than dealing directly with correctional facilities. As noted in Chapter 6, these are typically high profile cases that are followed by the media all the way to the point of correctional punishment. The most common news stories detailed the discovery of crimes, the arresting of suspects, and the appearance of the accused in court.[6]

Corrections is covered less because punishment is deemed less newsworthy than other aspects of criminal justice and less interesting to the public.[7] Further: "There is no corrections newsbeat that matches the police and court beats in journalism, so corrections stories are time consuming to produce because a preexisting journalism-corrections link does not exist."[8] This is understandable; gaining access to inmates and correctional facilities is much more burdensome than accessing police and court personnel and procedures.

Two scholars explain the significance of ignoring the nation's correctional populations:

> There are more than 2.2 million people in jails and prisons across the United States. They include people recently arrested for the first time and people wondering when, if ever, they will see an attorney. They include people serving nine-year prison terms and ninety-nine year prison terms, people with mental illness and mental retardation, people abused as children at home and abused as adults in prison. They include people languishing on death row and people nearing execution by lethal injection. None of those people can own a computer, and none have access to the Internet.
>
> ... People entangled in the criminal justice system cannot share their real experiences with the citizenry without a gatekeeper, and the citizenry cannot absorb those experiences. This is a problem not because people in jails and prisons have some legal right to unimpeded access to the Internet, but because society's increasing reliance on ordinary people to contribute to news coverage means that the perspectives of those in jails and prisons are featured even less by new media than by the traditional newspaper.[9]

Like with crime, news coverage of corrections focuses on the extraordinary rather than the ordinary, events such as riots, escapes, executions, and so forth.[10] Further, stories tend to be very negative in nature.[11] Three types of negative stories dominate news coverage of corrections: 1) stories about the failure of corrections to protect the public; 2) stories about amenities of prisoners; and 3) stories of corruption and misconduct.[12] These cases are likely popular because they are negative in nature, involve conflict, are controversial, and can be used to generate profits for the mainstream press.

Probably the most well-known example of correctional failure to protect the public is the case of Willie Horton. Democratic presidential hopeful Michael Dukakis was attacked in a television ad by future Republican president George H.W. Bush (the first) in 1988. As governor of Massachusetts, Dukakis had supported early release programs from prison as a means to reduce prison overcrowding and as a low-risk way to reintegrate offenders into the community through meaningful employment. An inmate from Massachusetts named Willie Horton, on his ninth furlough from prison, committed a brutal rape and assault. This incident led Bush to attack Dukakis as "soft on crime"; Bush assured citizens that if he was elected president, he would continue to expand criminal justice powers to fight crime. Even though the "Horton case was atypical and exaggerated," it worked: Bush was successfully elected president of the United States.[13]

Alida Merlo and Peter Benekos claim that the Willie Horton incident taught all politicians some important lessons about winning and losing:

- Don't be portrayed as being "soft on crime."
- Portray your opponent as "soft on crime."
- Simplify the crime issue.
- Reinforce messages with emotional context.

The mainstream media, with time constraints and budgetary needs, can be used by politicians to get these messages out to the public. This is precisely what happened in the Willie Horton case. Given the close connections between the media and law-makers, it is relatively easy to promote one's ideas about crime control, especially if they are consistent with the status quo approaches already being used.

Misrepresent the Nature of Punishment

When you think of punishment, what do you see? Prisons? The death penalty? These are currently considered valid sentencing options for judges who are responsible for meting out punishments in the United States (death is available in 35 states, the federal government, and the U.S. military, but is not practiced in 15 states and the District of Columbia). However, prison and death are two punishments that are relatively infrequently administered (compared to probation). Yet, sanctions such as incarceration are among the most covered in the mainstream media, especially in entertainment media (see Chapter 8).

The more common sanctions such as probation are given far less attention by the media. *Probation*, the least restrictive of punishments, is the most commonly used criminal sanction in the United States. According to the U.S. Department of Justice, probation is the court-ordered community supervision of convicted offenders by a probation agency, requiring the adherence to specific rules of conduct while living in the community.[14] Probation is not intended for serious, repetitive, violent criminals. Generally, it is not intended for people convicted on multiple charges, for people who were arrested while on probation or parole, for repeat offenders, for drug addicts, or for violent offenders.[15] In fact, the offense most likely to lead to a sentence of straight probation or a split sentence between incarceration and probation has in recent history been simple drug possession, while the least likely is murder, followed by

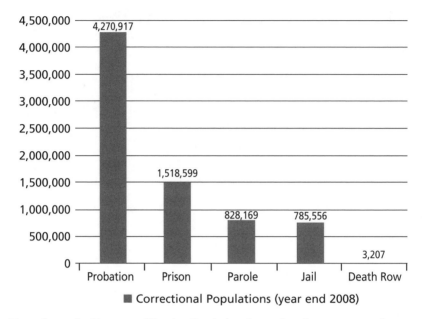

Correctional Populations (year end 2008)

Data from the Bureau of Justice Statistics show that far more people are on probation than under any other form of criminal sanction in the U.S.. While the U.S. leads the world in the number of people incarcerated as well as its incarceration rate, inmates locked up in prisons and jails only account for about 31% of all people under correctional supervision in the U.S.

rape; these latter cases are more likely to lead to prison or jail sentences. For every type of crime, people sentenced to probation generally receive shorter sentences than those sentenced to prison.

Given the media preoccupation with violent crime, it is understandable why the media generally ignore probationers. Exceptions include when a violent offender is sentenced to probation and when an offender on probation commits a heinous crime; these cases tend to attract media attention. A recent example is the robbery and murder of University of North Carolina (UNC) student body President Eve Carson; two men stand accused of her death. Both men were on probation for previous crimes at the time of the slaying, one for possessing a firearm as a felon and the other for larceny (and both were due in court for additional charges unrelated to this murder).[16] This crime, which was violent, random, and which involved a young white female victim and two black suspects, received enormous media attention in the state and in national news. It's relevant that the crime was interracial in nature because this type of crime tends to generate more media attention, as shown in Chapter 4.

Incarceration takes many forms, notably being sent to prison or jail. It involves having one's freedoms taken away while one is locked away from society. A *prison* is a state or federal correctional facility used to house those sentenced to more than one year of incarceration. A *jail* is a local correctional facility used to hold persons awaiting trial, awaiting sentencing, serving a sentence of less than one year, or awaiting transfer to another facility.[17] Incarceration is used more for violent criminals than for property criminals and is a sanction supposedly intended for more severe offenders.

A logical reason why the media are more focused on serious punishments such as imprisonment and the death penalty and less interested in probation is because the former are much rarer than the latter. They are also much harsher and violent in nature and are many times connected to crimes that also are heinous and violent in nature. Recall that the media tend to focus on events that are rare and violent.

Ignore That "Getting Tough on Crime" Does Not Work

Because of the massive criminal populations under its control, the U.S. criminal justice system is the largest in the world. Does this serve us well? And what do media images and stories tell us about this issue?

Primarily, punishment in the United States is aimed at two goals, incapacitation and deterrence. *Incapacitation* refers to taking away the freedom of offenders so that they cannot offend again. While typical forms involve probation (which limits freedom of movement), incarceration in jails and prisons, and numerous other forms like house arrest, the ultimate form is capital punishment. Unless you believe in reincarnation, you know that once an offender is dead, he or she cannot offend again.

Yet, the death penalty is not considered an effective form of incapacitation, simply because it is so rarely applied. Only about 1% of all murderers nationwide and only 2% of all murderers in death penalty states are sentenced to death. Further, far less than 1% of all killers have been executed in the United States since capital punishment was reinstated by the U.S. Supreme Court in 1976.[18] Stated simply, we do not kill enough people to meaningfully impact the number of killings that occur in society.

Deterrence is based on the logical notion that being punished for criminal activity will create fear in people so that they will not want to commit crime. There are two types of deterrence, special or specific deterrence and general deterrence. *Special or specific deterrence* means punishing an offender with the specific intent of instilling fear in that offender so that he or she will not commit crimes in the future. *General deterrence* involves punishing offenders in order to instill fear in society generally so that the rest of us will not want to commit crimes. Special or specific deterrence is aimed at stopping a known criminal offender from committing future crimes, whereas general deterrence is aimed at teaching the rest of us a lesson about what might happen to us if we were to commit crimes.

Deterrence as a justification for punishment is based on several assumptions:

- Offenders are *hedonistic* or pleasure-seeking (e.g., crime provides various pleasures).
- Offenders seek to minimize costs or pains associated with crimes (i.e., they do not want to get caught and be punished).
- Offenders are *rational* (i.e., they choose to commit crime after weighing the potential costs or punishments and benefits or rewards).

Many criminologists believe human beings are rational and motivated by desire for personal pleasure and want to avoid pain. Yet, numerous human behaviors seem quite irrational. Most forms of criminality, it has been argued, are impulsive, short-sighted, stupid, and risky behaviors. Many types of crimes are committed with only short-term gain in mind and with little or no thought of likely outcomes.[19] This is not consistent with the view of the rational criminal.

What many offenders do tell us is that long-term concern about potential punishment seems not to enter the minds of most offenders. If they thought there was a good chance of getting caught, after all, offenders would not likely engage in their criminal behaviors, especially if they are as rational as criminologists tell us. Further, there are numerous risk factors that increase the likelihood that individuals will choose crime. This suggests rationality is not something possessed equally by all.[20]

The majority of media depictions of criminals characterize offenders not as rational but instead as simply evil or deranged and mentally ill, as discussed in Chapter 4. Yet, dominant themes and narratives of criminality are consistent with the notion of hedonistic, rational offenders.

In the U.S., we assume that we can still deter offenders. In order to deter would-be offenders effectively, punishment must be certain (or at least likely), swift (or at least not delayed by months or years), and severe enough to outweigh the pleasures associated with crimes. Of these requirements, the most important is the *certainty of punishment*. The more likely that punishment is to follow a criminal act, the less likely the criminal act will occur.[21] Alfred Blumstein explains:

Research on deterrence has consistently supported the position that sentence 'severity' (that is, the time served) has less of a deterrent effect than sentence 'certainty' (the probability of going to prison). Thus, from the deterrence consideration, there is clear preference for increasing certainty, even if it becomes necessary to do so at the expense of severity.[22]

Punishment in the United States is far from certain, even for serious crime. Only about 40% of crimes are known to the police and only about 10% lead to an arrest. Further, only about 3% of all felonies lead to an incarceration. The only crime for which there exists a substantial risk of arrest, conviction, and imprisonment is murder and nonnegligent homicide. The risk of incarceration for murder and nonnegligent homicide is about 50%. Less than 10% of all other serious crimes lead to incarceration.

Offenders know this. They tell criminologists that they know from personal experiences and from the experiences of fellow criminals that their risks of being apprehended by the police and convicted in court are very low.[23] Since there are only about 3 police officers in the United States for every 1,000 citizens, it should not be surprising that the likelihood of apprehension is small.

Given all this, does sound, scientific evidence suggest that getting tough on crime (e.g., mass imprisonment) will work to make us safer? The answer is, "To a small degree, temporarily." In the wake of an explosion in imprisonment in the U.S. in the 1970s, 1980s, and 1990s, street crime did decline. Yet, it should be obvious that there is no single explanation for why crime fell in the U.S..[24] Factors such as economic improvement, an aging population, the stabilization of the illicit crack cocaine market, and increased use of other forms of criminal justice had significant effects.[25] Additionally, legalized abortion likely played some role, as millions of would-be children that would have been born in at-risk environments were not born.[26]

Simply stated, "no single factor can be invoked as *the* cause of the crime decline of the 1990s. Rather, the explanation appears to lie with a number of factors, perhaps none of which alone would have been sufficient and some of which might not have been of noticeable efficacy without reinforcement from others."[27] Prisons were likely only responsible for about one-fourth of the crime drop.[28]

⌁ For more information about what led to the declines in American crime rates, see the website for this book at: www.pscj.appstate.edu/media/crimedecline.html

---

If you compare these rising imprisonment rates to crime rate declines since the early 1970s, you might conclude that incarceration is an effective means of

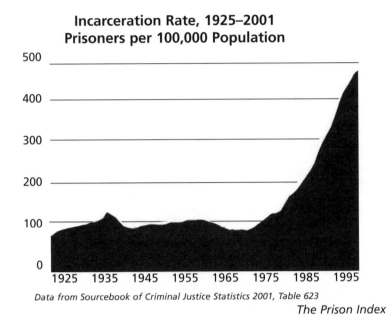

Incarceration Rate, 1925–2001
Prisoners per 100,000 Population

Data from Sourcebook of Criminal Justice Statistics 2001, Table 623

The Prison Index

The imprisonment boom depicted here started in 1973 and is unprecedented in U.S. history. http://www.prisonpolicy.org/prisonindex/graphs/incarceration rate.jpg.

reducing crime. But this conclusion would be at best, incomplete, and at worst, wrong. Todd Clear claims that the U.S. incarceration rate has little to do with crime rates in the United States: "prison populations continue to grow, despite five consecutive years of falling crime; indeed, since 1975, we have had 10 years of declining crime rates and then 13 years of increasing crime rates—but prison populations have gone up every year regardless."[29]

An analysis by Ryan King, Marc Mauer, and Malcom Young is particularly revealing. They note: "Advocates of increased use of incarceration have contended that the significant growth in incarceration has been the primary factor responsible for this reduction. The two-pronged approach of tougher sentences and restrictive release patterns are the primary cause, proponents claim, of this sustained crime drop."[30] For example, they point out that violent crime declined by 33% and property crime decreased by 23% between 1994 and 2004. During this same period, rates of incarceration increased by 24%. "Some commentators draw upon these two trends to support the conclusion that incarceration "works" to reduce crime. The reality is far more complex."[31]

An analysis of different time periods from 1984 to 1998 illustrates the less than clear relationship between incarceration and crime rates. From 1984–1998, "incarceration rates rose consistently, by 65% in the first seven-year period of 1984–91, and then by 47% from 1991–98. Yet crime rates fluctuated in this period, first increasing by 17% from 1984–91, then declining by 22% from 1991–98." Further, an analysis of the changes in incarceration and crime in all 50 states "reveals no consistent relationship between the rate at which incarceration increased and the rate at which crime decreased ... Between 1991 and 1998, those states that increased incarceration at rates that were *less* than the national average experienced a *larger* decline in crime rates than those states that increased incarceration at rates higher than the national average."[32]

The authors conclude:

> While incarceration is one factor affecting crime rates, its impact is more modest than many proponents suggest, and is increasingly subject to diminishing returns. Increasing incarceration while ignoring more effective approaches will impose a heavy burden upon courts, corrections and communities, while providing a marginal impact on crime. Policymakers should assess these dynamics and adopt balanced crime control policies that provide appropriate resources and support for programming, treatment, and community support."[33]

To whatever degree prisons reduce crime in the short run, it is also important to know that in the long run, higher imprisonment likely means more future crime.[34] For example, Todd Clear shows that America's practice of mass incarceration has significantly weakened both families and communities. Ironically, this increases crime in the neighborhoods from which the bulk of the inmates come. Perhaps it is not surprising that in many of the nation's large cities, up to 25% of all males in their 20s, 30s and 40s are incarcerated at any given time.[35]

Like with many realities of criminal justice, American citizens remain largely ignorant of the ineffectiveness of correctional punishment. This owes itself in part to the fact that the mainstream media do not often bring such issues to their attention. With the exception of a handful of media organizations, the inefficacy of correctional punishment is rarely addressed by the mainstream media. It is also true that decisions about punishment are often based not on evidence in the first place but instead are based on suppositions, personal opinions, and common sense (especially of the population who create the laws and policies that led to massive imprisonment).[36] So, a large portion of Americans are probably happy with punishing people who commit crimes based on the same rationale they use to justify spanking their kids for misbehaving, swat-

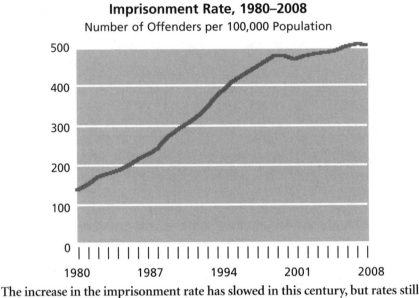

Imprisonment Rate, 1980–2008
Number of Offenders per 100,000 Population

The increase in the imprisonment rate has slowed in this century, but rates still continue to rise. http://bjs.ojp.usdoj.gov/content/glance/incrt.cfm.

ting their dogs with newspapers for peeing on the floor, and spraying their cats with water for clawing the furniture, whether or not it works to prevent future misbehavior. These approaches are logical and make sense on their face but may not be effective in the long run to reduce problem behaviors.

Ignore the Costs of Punishment

When was the last time you ever heard any person interviewed in the media about the costs of American punishment? Further, when have you ever seen the issue of the implications of these costs for society addressed in the media? As with the issue of the relatively ineffectiveness of punishment, the costs of punishment are also rarely addressed in the mainstream media.

According to the Pew Center on the States, the cost for imprisonment of each inmate each year was $23,876 in 2005.[37] Multiplying this by the 1,288,6900 inmates incarcerated in prisons in 2005, and the cost amounts to nearly $31 billion spent on prisons in 2005. In fact, the cost is much higher since these costs do not accurately capture how much it costs to build prisons, including interest on loans taken out by states to build prisons. Data from previous years show that roughly 77% of all corrections expenditures are for prisons.[38]

Since Americans spent roughly $68.8 billion on corrections in 2006, if we assume that 77% of this expense in for prisons, then we spent roughly $53 billion on prisons in 2006.[39] Even this figure masks much of the costs of imprisonment.

One reason punishment costs so much is that the U.S. leads the world in the size and scope of its criminal justice apparatus. For example, there are more people locked up in the U.S. than in any other country in the world.

At the end of the year in 2008, more than 7.3 million people were under some form of criminal justice supervision in the United States (i.e., probation, incarceration in jail or prison or on parole). This represents 3.2% of all U.S. adult residents. State and Federal prisons housed 1.6 million inmates (1.4 million in state custody and more than 200,000 in federal custody), and local jails housed more than 785,000 people either awaiting trial or serving a sentence (an additional 73,000 people were under jail supervision serving their sentence in the community). An additional 4.3 million adults were on probation and 825,000 were on parole.[40]

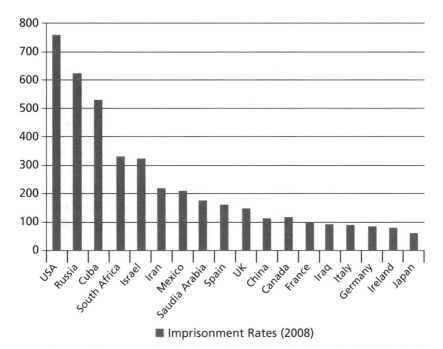

■ Imprisonment Rates (2008)

According to the International Centre for Prison Studies, the U.S. leads the world in its rate of imprisonment, at 760 inmates per 100,000 people. Other familiar countries are included in the chart to show scale relative to the U.S.

The rate of incarceration (prisons and jails) at the end of 2007 was 760 per 100,000 residents, number one in the world.[41] At present, the U.S. has roughly 5% of the world's population but houses 25% of its prisoners. The National Criminal Justice Commission writes: "Since 1980, the United States has engaged in the largest and most frenetic correctional buildup of any country in the history of the world."[42] While the increases slowed in the early 21st Century, they continue to slowly climb.

Think about the irony of this. Professor Todd Clear, an expert on corrections, writes:

> As Americans, we think of ourselves as a free people. And we think that our freedoms are central to what sets us apart from the rest of the world....
> It is ironic, then, that in America more people are denied these freedoms by law than in any other Western nation: we lock up more citizens per capita than any other nation that has bothered to count its prisoners.[43]

Much of the increase in prisons is due to drug convictions (including a 478% increase in drug offenders sentenced to state prisons and a 545% increase in drug offenders sentenced to federal prisons from 1985 to 1996). From 1980 to 1993, the percentage of prisoners in state prisons serving sentences for drug offenses more than tripled; in federal prisons, it more than doubled.[44] Drug offenders now make up about 20% of all people incarcerated in the U.S., including more than half of all federal inmates.[45] Given that when Americans think about crime, they think about violent crime, most would probably be surprised to learn that only about half of the increase of the prison population is because of violent offenders.

There are likely several reasons why costs of imprisonment rarely come to the attention of the media. First, since corrections is the least visible aspect of criminal justice, issues such as cost (as well as what happens to people once they are locked up) are often just not considered. Second, since the great majority of politicians have bought into the prison system as a legitimate means to deal with crime, it is very unlikely the issue of cost is even seen as relevant to them. Third, since the media rely on politicians and correctional personnel for information about correctional punishment, reporters are unlikely to ever hear the issue brought up in the first place. Finally, recall that the media are part of the dominant, status quo reinforcing institutions in society; thus they have little incentive to question the costs of the status quo. Some middle- and outer-ring media (second- and third-tier media) have extensively explained the issue of costs of incarceration, yet these analyses do not come to the attention of many citizens due to the limited reach of these media outlets. Major state level newspapers will occasionally address the issue of correctional costs as part of stories on state budget deficits, but you will almost never see officials question resources devoted to prisons.

Ignore the Pains of Imprisonment

Contrary to the mythical view of the comfortable prison, American prisons are terribly hot, loud, and violent places to live (and work—keep in mind that many people in prison simply work there). The myth of "country club" prisons has led state lawmakers to pass some laughable legislation and make startling threats. The National Criminal Justice Commission reports the following examples:

- A Mississippi law forbidding individual air conditioners, even though no inmate actually had an individual air conditioner;
- A Louisiana law forbidding inmates from taking martial arts classes, even though such classes were not currently available; and
- A complaint by the governor of Connecticut about the landscaping outside a prison, even though the plantings were made at the request of residential neighbors.[46]

Add to these examples efforts by state lawmakers to take away inmates' cigarettes (which contain the addictive drug nicotine and are used as a form of currency within prisons), other efforts to prevent inmates from lifting weights or watching television, the resurgence of chain gangs in many southern states, and other efforts to humiliate inmates by making them wear orange, pink, or striped jumpsuits. From all these efforts to make prison less pleasant, you might imagine that prison is a pretty nice place to be. According to Marian McShane and colleagues, part of the perception of prisons comes from media coverage: "Because of movies and television shows, the public is aware of recreation activities behind bars—there has even been a movie about a football game (*The Longest Yard*). Images of inmates working out with weight-training equipment are a mainstay of crime-related television series."[47]

In fact, because of the numerous *pains of imprisonment*, the typical prison is not anything like a country club. The major pains of imprisonment include:

- Loss of liberty;
- Loss of autonomy;
- Loss of security;
- Deprivation of heterosexual relationships; and
- Deprivation of goods and services.[48]

Additionally, inmates also suffer from:

- Loss of voting rights;
- Loss of dignity; and

- Stigmatization.

First and foremost, prisoners suffer from a *loss of* liberty. Many Americans seem to conceive of prisons as comfortable places where offenders watch television free of charge, eat three square meals per day at no cost, enjoy various extracurricular activities such as weight lifting and basketball, and get a free education. Most of these conceptions are false.

Some Americans might prefer to throw inmates into freshly dug holes in the ground and provide them with nothing but the bare minimum to survive. Others would like to "make 'em break rocks." Former Massachusetts governor William Weld publicly stated that life in prison should be "akin to walking through the fires of hell."[49] But these people misconceive the purpose of imprisonment. We send people to prison as punishment, not for punishment: "The incarceration itself [is] supposed to be the punishment, not an occasion for the state to arbitrarily inflict additional punishment."[50] In other words, the main part of the punishment is losing one's freedom. Individual freedom may be the most cherished part of being American. Prisoners, because they are locked up, away from friends and family, have lost their liberty. This means they are not free to do all the things you and I can do as they see fit. Their activities are decided by others.

Related to loss of freedom is the *loss of autonomy* that accompanies being incarcerated. Inmates do not decide for themselves when or where to sleep, wake up, shower, eat, engage in recreation, or live. They are told when and how to do virtually everything they do. Thus, prisoners lose the capacity and, some argue, the ability to govern their own lives and behaviors. What are the implications of this for society? If we want people to be responsible for themselves, their lives, their families, their children, wouldn't it make sense to equip them with the ability to live in the free world? Is our desire to make prisoners suffer more important than protecting us from their future acts of crime and violence?

Prisoners are subjected to numerous forms of victimization that are much more prevalent in correctional facilities than outside in the free world, and thus suffer from a *loss of security*. Prisoners are subjected to psychological victimization, economic victimization, social victimization, physical victimization, and sexual victimization. John May describes prisons this way:

> Prisons are violent places, and prisons teach violence. Anyone walking into a prison for the first time can feel the tension. The concrete and steel walls and floors serve to echo and intensify the noises of chains, steel doors slamming, yelling, cursing, and beatings. For an inmate who must make the prison his or her home, whether for months, years, or even a lifetime, avoiding a violent attack becomes

a daily concern. The need to maintain constant vigilance creates stress, tension, and chronic anxiety. Even in their sleep, they do not feel safe. They almost instinctively react to provocation with violence, as adjustments to this sense of vulnerability.[51]

JoAnne Page claims that "[v]iolence is a dominant and defining thread running through the fabric of jail and prison life" and describes facilities of incarceration as "factories of rage and pain."[52]

As explained by the National Criminal Justice Commission: "Inmates learn to strike first and seek strength in gangs often comprised of dangerous offenders. Sexual assaults are frequent and usually go unpunished."[53] Rather than being a deterrent to future criminality, the commission concludes that "the violent subculture of the correctional facility increasingly acts as a vector for spreading crime in our communities."[54] Ironically, then, imprisonment escalates the very behavior it is intended to deter because it increases violence instead of decreasing it.[55]

American criminals who are imprisoned are locked away in overcrowded warehouses and forced to live in closet-sized rooms.[56] Most are subjected to some type of physical abuse and many to sexual abuse.[57] Violence inflicted for the purpose of causing pain or as punishment is illegal and prohibited by the American Correctional Association.[58] Additionally, many of the inmates who become victims in prison were convicted of relatively minor acts—acts that many of us may have committed at one time in our lives. And remember, most of these inmates will one day get out of prison. Human rights violations are commonplace in prison. As examples, Michael Welch discusses chain gangs, inhumane prison conditions, and the use of political imprisonment in the United States. He writes: "American prisons are neither *civilized* nor *civilizing*. Simply put, inmates are subjected to a degrading prison environment, then returned to the community."[59]

Although not everyone is heterosexual, most Americans are. Incarceration means being forced to suffer from a *deprivation of heterosexual relationships*. This is likely worst for married couples who are separated by imprisonment. But, for any heterosexual person, being imprisoned generally means living without sexual contact with a member of the opposite sex. Consequently, heterosexuals may have to abstain completely from sexual encounters, turn to self-gratification, or engage in homosexual encounters. Even if a prisoner chooses to abstain, there is, of course, the risk of being forced to engage in homosexual relations because of the threat of rape in prison. And even though prison administrators know that rapes occur within the walls of American prisons, these attacks generally are not pursued or prevented.[60]

A growing number of American prisoners are being deprived of virtually all relationships, including contact with other people. One reason is that more and more prisons are being built in rural areas, far from the offenders' family members and significant others. Prisons are promoted in rural communities as a blessing—a source of jobs to boost the local economy. Another reason is that the United States has begun incarcerating some of its most dangerous offenders in *supermaximum* or *supermax* prisons. These facilities restrict inmate contact with other inmates and with correctional personnel. Many inmates are locked in their cells for most of the day, in stark cells with white walls. Cells have completely closed front doors, no windows, and bright lights on at all hours of day and night.

Examples of supermax facilities include Marion (Illinois) and Pelican Bay (California). Michael Welch describes the conditions in these prisons:

> [In Marion] all prisoners are confined to their cells for 23 hours per day, granted 1 hour of exercise outside of their cell, and allowed to shower 2 or 3 days a week. Handcuffs are fastened to inmates while they are transported within the facility ... [and they are chained] "long-term ... to their beds";
>
> [In Pelican Bay] [i]nmates are confined to their 8- by 10-foot cells, where the temperature registers a constant 85 to 90 degrees, for twenty-two and a half hours per day. The unrelenting heat produces headaches, nausea, and dehydration and drains the inmates of their mental and bodily energy.[61]

According to Jeffrey Ian Ross, there is a mass media silence of supermax prisons, including what transpires within the walls of these institutions and why they are needed in the first place.[62] Human rights violations in supermax facilities are hidden from the public. When abuses of prisoners in other types of prisons become known, Americans do not become concerned because state-controlled media outlets do not construct these harms as social problems.[63] The Pelican Bay facility in California was built at a cost of $278 million for 2,080 maximum security inmates. That's $134,000 per inmate! The organization Human Rights Watch calls these expensive facilities "a clear violation of human rights" and a breach of an international treaty implemented by the United States in 1992.[64] Yet, Americans are generally unaware or unconcerned over human rights violations against convicted criminals.

⌐🖰 For more information about the Jose Padilla case, see the website for this book at: www.pscj.appstate.edu/media/padilla.html

---

Another significant loss associated with imprisonment is the *deprivation of goods and services*. Imagine all of your worldly possessions being inacces-

Jose Padilla, who was born in New York City and who lived in Chicago, Illinois, was arrested in Chicago on May 8, 2002. He was first detained for a month as a material witness until President Bush declared him an enemy combatant, a status he held for more than four years. http://en.wikipedia.org/wiki/File:Jose_Padilla_at_the_Navy_Consolidated_Brig.jpg.

sible to you, along with virtually every service and product that a free person can enjoy. This would be a major loss associated with having your freedom taken away.

According to The Sentencing Project, 48 states and the District of Columbia prohibit inmates from voting while incarcerated for a felony offense; 35 states prohibit felons from voting while they are on parole (30 of these states also exclude felony probationers); 2 states deny the right to vote to all ex-offenders (including those who have completed their sentences); 9 states disenfranchise certain categories of ex-offenders and/or permit application for restoration of rights for specified offenses after a waiting period.[65]

In fact, all states impose some form of *collateral damage* on inmates. Although you may not consider the *loss of voting rights* an important loss, especially if you do not currently vote, it is inconsistent with the goal of integrating ex-convicts into free society. A member of free society has the right to vote and thus to help shape the direction of his or her life, as well as that of his or her family and community. In a representative democracy, when a person cannot vote, by definition, that person's voice cannot be heard and he or she is not represented.

According to The Sentencing Project, about 5.3 million Americans have lost their rights to vote because of felony convictions. In the United States, the loss of the right to vote is a burden disproportionately imposed on poor people and people of color. Statistics show that 1.4 million African American men (13% of all black men), are disenfranchised. The rate for black males is seven times the national average. The Sentencing Project reports that: "In five states that deny the vote to ex-offenders, one in four black men is *permanently* disenfranchised ... Given current rates of incarceration, three in ten of the next generation of black men can expect to be disenfranchised at some point in their lifetime ... In states that disenfranchise ex-offenders, as many as 40% of black men may permanently lose their right to vote."[66] About 5.3 million Americans have lost their rights to vote because of felony convictions, a burden disproportionately imposed on poor people and people of color: "This fundamental obstacle to participation in democratic life is exacerbated by racial disparities in the criminal justice system, resulting in an estimated 13% of Black men unable to vote."[67] Further, more than 2 million white Americans are disenfranchised, and more than 675,000 women currently cannot vote because of a felony conviction.

Associated with each of the losses described here is a *loss of dignity*. Prisoners are not treated as individual human beings, but as numbers. At worst, they lose respect for themselves because of this treatment. They come to be dependent on the government to live their lives. They are also subjected to various labels, such as "convict," "ex-convict," "criminal," "dangerous," "antisocial," etc. When prisoners are released, the pain of *stigmatization* (e.g., the "ex-con" label) makes it difficult for them to find places to live and work. This can actually increase the odds of re-offending upon release.[68] This is called the *self-fulfilling prophecy*, where we create the very thing we want to avoid, as predicted by labeling theory.

Labeling theory asserts that when people are labeled by the criminal justice network as "criminals," "convicts," or "offenders," the label can affect how these offenders view themselves, thus potentially changing their self-concepts. Once they begin to see themselves as "deviant" or "different," they will continue committing crime in order to live up to the expectations that society has set forth for them. Employers use the ex-con label as a warning against hiring former offenders.[69]

For the past several decades, U.S. prisons do little more than warehouse inmates. John Irwin and James Austin describe it this way:

> Convicted primarily of property and drug crimes, hundreds of thousands of prisoners are being crowded into human (or inhuman) warehouses where they are increasingly deprived, restricted, isolated, and consequently embittered and alienated from conventional worlds and where less and less is being done to prepare them for their eventual release. As a result, most of them are rendered incapable of returning to even a meager conventional life after prison.[70]

In spite of all these pains and losses, there is evidence that inmates do not view prison as the worse of all potential criminal sanctions.[71] John May claims that incarceration can "foster dependency" and, for some, actually "becomes a way of life—even a generational phenomenon." For them, the criminal justice network "becomes their only source of social support, structure, discipline, validation, and even power and respect." These people typically have family and friends who have been processed through the criminal justice agencies and live in communities where incarceration is simply an expected part of life.[72] Yet, this may because a great number of future inmates have already had experience in prison, and to some degree it has become an expected outcome for many people.

As with the other realities of punishment outlined in this chapter, Americans are mostly unaware of what goes on in the nation's prisons and jails. Since most of us do not end up incarcerated and we do not know anyone who does, without media attention to the issue, we will likely remain ignorant of it. We can only speculate what the effect would be on criminal justice practice generally and on imprisonment policy in particular if the media paid greater attention to prison conditions, especially given that many inmates are incarcerated for relatively petty crimes and that about half are inside for non-violent crimes. Recent television shows, such as MSNBC's "Lockup," attempt to bring the realities of imprisonment life to the American people. Unfortunately the show is not very realistic. The show is revisited in Chapter 8.

One thing is certain, the perception that prison inmates receive free educations paid for by tax payers is largely a myth. For example, data from the Sourcebook of Criminal Justice Statistics show that only about half of inmates are enrolled in some type of prison education program, and the vast majority of them are simply trying to earn their GEDs/high school diplomas or gain vocational skills that may serve them upon release from prison.[73] This rudimentary education will perhaps help the 90% of inmates who will be released from prison in the future.

Some scholars suggest that the media may help prevent criminality for prison inmates who will one day be released. For example, Heidi Vandebosch suggests that the media can assist with the process of re-entry to society by helping to normalize life in the penitentiary and keeping inmates informed about how society is changing. According to Vandebosch, the media

> can prevent, solve or at least soften the pains of imprisonment. Prisoners may, for instance, listen to the radio or watch television to banish disturbing noises and to get some privacy; use the media to pass time or to keep busy; follow news reports to stay in touch with the outside world and feel less isolated; listen to their 'own' music to strengthen their self image; consume erotic media contents to become sexually aroused; read exciting books to break down the monotony of their daily prison life; make use of the media to have a conversational topic or to banish loneliness; attend movies or go to the library to get out of their cell.[74]

While this is logical, it is still true that prisons do much more to foster dependency than they do to rehabilitate. For various reasons, though, this message has not been widely broadcast by the mainstream press.

Ignore the Mentally Ill in Criminal Justice

It is estimated that roughly one in ten of the nation's prisoners is mentally ill,[75] although some suggest that the figure may be more like 40%.[76] The Bureau of Justice Statistics (BJS) reports that in mid-year 2005, more than half of all inmates had a mental health problem of some kind, including 705,600 state prison inmates, 70,200 federal prisoners, and 479,900 local jail inmates. According to BJS, these estimates represented 56% of State prisoners, 45% of Federal prisoners, and 64% of jail inmates. The incidence of mental illness is even more pronounced for people spending life in prison.[77]

These numbers are of particular concern considering that correctional facilities are ill-equipped to provide safety and appropriate treatment for mentally ill persons. Prisons are dangerous and debilitating for inmates with mental illnesses, who often are victimized by other prisoners. Moreover, symptoms of mental illness are often misinterpreted by correctional staff as disruptive behavior, which can lead to additional punishment and disciplinary actions that may extend the length of an individual's sentence.[78]

The mentally ill are incarcerated largely because the nation's mentally ill populations were released from state hospitals in the expectation that they would be able to get treatment in their communities. But community treatment programs are not available in many communities; in places where such programs are available, systems are not in place to ensure that people who need them will obtain treatment. Over the past two decades, hundreds of new prisons have opened and nearly every state mental hospital was closed: "Jails and prisons have become the de facto providers of mental health services in this country."[79] In most states, the largest provider is the prison system; the nation's largest provider is the Los Angeles County Jail.

These outrageous conditions have been highlighted by groups such as the National Alliance for the Mentally Ill and thus have received some media attention.[80] Nevertheless, there has not been enough pressure mounted on our leaders to correct these outcomes. Senator Jim Webb (D-VA) has proposed the National Criminal Justice Commission Act of 2009 to "create a blue-ribbon commission to look at every aspect of our criminal justice system with an eye toward reshaping the process from top to bottom." According to Senator Webb, the legislation is needed because:

- With 5% of the world's population, our country now houses 25% of the world's reported prisoners.
- Incarcerated drug offenders have soared 1200% since 1980.

- Four times as many mentally ill people are in prisons than in mental health hospitals.
- Approximately 1 million gang members reside in the U.S., many of them foreign-based; and Mexican cartels operate in 230+ communities across the country.
- Post-incarceration re-entry programs are haphazard and often nonexistent, undermining public safety and making it extremely difficult for ex-offenders to become full, contributing members of society.
- America's criminal justice system has deteriorated to the point that it is a national disgrace. Its irregularities and inequities cut against the notion that we are a society founded on fundamental fairness. Our failure to address this problem has caused the nation's prisons to burst their seams with massive overcrowding, even as our neighborhoods have become more dangerous. We are wasting billions of dollars and diminishing millions of lives.[81]

This proposed reform was featured nationally in *Parade* magazine on March 29, 2009.[82] This is significant because *Parade* magazine is included in hundreds of Sunday newspapers and is thus the most widely read magazine in the United States. As of this writing, the bill has been passed by the U.S. House of Representatives.

Other than this one notable exception, the issue of mental illness in prisons and jails does not receive significant media attention, at least in the for-profit, mainstream media. Television stations such as PBS and radio stations such as NPR have focused on this issue, but these are non-profit media organizations with smaller audiences than the mainstream press.

Ignore Biases in Corrections

As surprising as it is given that images of the poor and minorities dominate media images of crime and punishment, the media rarely raise the issue of biases in American criminal justice and corrections. Yet, criminologists have outlined serious problems in criminal justice and punishment that explain these biases.

Some of the leading scholars in this area include Samuel Walker, Cassia Spohn, and Miriam DeLone. Their exhaustive analysis of the criminal justice process concludes that American criminal justice is characterized by what they refer to as contextual discrimination. These authors write: "After considering all the evidence, we conclude that the U.S. criminal justice system is characterized by *contextual discrimination*—that is, discrimination occurs in certain parts of the justice system but not necessarily all parts all the time."[83] Their analysis of policing shows evidence of biases based on race (and social class) when it comes to arrests and use of force. Their analysis of courts shows evidence of biases based on race (and social class) when it comes to decisions about bail, charges by the prosecution, plea bargaining, access to competent defense, peremptory challenges at trial, and sentencing outcomes especially in borderline cases where prosecutors have the most discretion about whether to press charges and which charges to press. Finally, there analysis of correctional punishment shows evidence of biases based on race (and social class) when it comes to the use of prison and the administration of capital punishment.

Contextual discrimination implies that there is discrimination based on race and/or ethnicity at some places and at some times under certain circumstances in the United States. Walker and his colleagues explain that contextual discrimination is different from *systematic discrimination*, which is defined as "discrimination at all stages of the criminal justice system, at all times, and all places" or *institutional discrimination*, defined as "racial and ethnic disparities in outcomes that are the result of the application of racially neutral factors such as prior criminal record, employment status, demeanor, etc." Note that the presence of contextual discrimination suggests that the problem is more complicated than discrimination resulting from behaviors of particular individuals, and that pure justice does not exist in the United States.

Examining correctional populations is quite useful in demonstrating the problems of bias in criminal justice. According to The Sentencing Project, the characteristics of those in incarcerated at the end of 2008 include the following: 93% were male; 40% were black; 20% were Hispanic; 82% of state prison inmates were sentenced to prison for non-violent crimes, including 34% for drug offenses and 29% for property offenses. Additionally, the typical prisoner has not completed high school; was underemployed (i.e., unemployed, employed part-time, or making very little money in a full-time job); was earning less than $1,000 per month at the time of arrest; and was under the influence of drugs at the time of their offenses.[84]

Black males are disproportionately likely to be under all forms of correctional supervision. According to The Sentencing Project, African American males have a 32% chance of serving time in prison at some point in their lives, versus 17% of Hispanic males and 6% of Caucasian males.[85]

The war on crime is clearly having its greatest effects on young black males. For example, the Bureau of Justice Statistics reports that at the end of 2008, one in ten (10.4%) black males aged 25–29 was in prison or jail, versus 1 in 26 (3.8%) Hispanic males and 1 in 59 (1.6%) white males. Thus, young black males are 6 times more likely than young Caucasian males and 2 times more likely than young Hispanic males to be in prison. Amazingly, black males in their 20s and

30s make up approximately 30% of all people locked up in America! Black men are overrepresented among jail inmates, probationers, and parolees as well.[86]

The result of such disparities is devastating. More than 1.4 million African American men (13% of all black men) cannot vote because of felony convictions. This is seven times higher than the national average. Additionally, about 80% of African American males can expect to have been arrested by age 18 years.

These outcomes have serious implications not only for blacks but for wider society as well. Just as one well-known example, the 2000 presidential election was decided in one state—Florida—where hundreds of thousands of blacks (who overwhelmingly vote democratic) were denied the right to vote based on a felony conviction.[87] Journalist Greg Palast studied this issue extensively and found that the great majority of people on a non-voting convicted felons list actually had not been convicted of any crime much less a felony. The votes they could not cast literally decided the election. Amazingly, this issue received very little attention from the mainstream press, even though the list was created by a company hired by the state of Florida with the instructions to be as broad as possible in order to deny as many people as possible the right to vote, and even though the final vote totals were certified by Secretary of State Kathleen Harris, who was George W. Bush's campaign co-director for the state of Florida.[88] Some middle- and outer-ring (second- and third tier) media outlets did cover this explosive story, along with other alleged malfeasance in the election, but for the most part the issue was ignored by the mainstream press.

This issue is important and probably would be of great interest to citizens, especially given that about half of people locked up for felonies in the nation's jails and prisons are not incarcerated for committing a violent crime. However, there has been little if any media attention placed on the issue. Recall that serious investigations into matters such as these are time-consuming and costly; thus, they are discouraged.

Women in Prison

Dawn Cecil suggests that in spite of an "ever growing institutional population," news stories rarely focus on prisons or prisoners: The scarcity with which these stories appear is likely due in part to the restrictions placed on media access to prisons and prisoners by administrators and/or state legislation ... When prisons are in the news it is due to rare events such as riots or escapes." Still even less common are stories featuring the experience of women in prisons.[89]

Dawn Cecil examined newspaper articles about Martha Stewart published in five top national newspapers between September 1, 2004 and March 31,

2005. Martha Stewart was imprisoned in 2004 to a five-month term for lying to investigators looking into her alleged insider trading activities. According to her article:

> America's domestic diva serving time in a federal prison was considered newsworthy. Journalists speculated about her impending prison sentence and provided details on the institution in which she would be incarcerated. Readers learned about the cells, the food (including holiday menus), and the activities of the prison camp in Alderson, West Virginia, which was referred to as "Camp Cupcake." Martha Stewart's release from prison received just as much fanfare from the media. What did she look like? What was she wearing? What was she looking forward to doing upon release? Had she changed for the better? And, what were the details of her impending house arrest on her 153-acre estate? The news media seemed fascinated by her incarceration, which is largely attributed to the fact that Martha Stewart is famous. It is also likely related to who she is beyond her fame. Martha Stewart sells an image of perfection and is also known as being a fairly aggressive female, thus the news media was able to tell a story of a woman whose downfall was drastic and in many people's minds may have gotten what she deserved. Each story became a lesson about the correctional system and more specifically about women in prison. With each story a very particular image of incarcerated women was being imprinted in the minds of the public.[90]

Martha Stewart was imprisoned for lying to investigators as part of their examination into her alleged insider trading activities. Her incarceration made national news, but shed almost no light onto the realities of life inside America's prisons. http://fullydevoted.blogspot.com/martha_sentencing.jpg.

Cecil concludes that the articles sent the main message that female offenders were not really being punished and that after release it was easy to smoothly transition back into functional life in society. Recall from Chapter 1 that Paris Hilton's short jail sentence also received a tremendous amount of mainstream media attention. It also showed how easy it is for the rich and powerful to transition back into society. What neither of these media stories examined, however, was the issue of incarceration itself, how many people are incarcerated in the U.S., what is really like in prison and jail, and how hard it is to make it in society upon release when one is not rich or powerful.

In reality, women now make up the fastest growing segment of the U.S. prison population, especially women of color. They also tend to be mothers[91] incarcerated for relatively minor drug offenses.[92] For the average incarcerated woman—who is nothing like Martha Stewart or Paris Hilton—life inside prison is a horrible experience. The transition to normal, free life upon release is also very difficult, unlike the experiences of Stewart and Hilton. The former receive little media attention whereas the latter received extensive coverage.

Death Sentences, Executions, and Exonerations

The death penalty, being the most severe of all criminal justice sanctions, is logically attractive to the media. The death penalty tends to make news when high profile murderers are sentenced to death, when inmates are executed, as well as when problems with capital punishment lead to wrongful convictions and exonerations.

A study of death sentences in two Ohio newspapers found that coverage varied between the papers, inconsistent with notion of a homogenization of coverage between similar sources.[93] Thus, the effects of such coverage on public opinion ought not to be so straight-forward.[94] Generally speaking, when killers are sentenced to death, it is deemed newsworthy. This is logical because death sentences are so rare. Specifically, only 1% of all killings nationwide lead to death sentences, and only 2% of killings in states with the death penalty lead to death sentences, as noted earlier.

Executions, too, are sometimes newsworthy, and they too are rare. Specifically, only 538 executions were carried out between 2000 and 2008, or 60 per year (or 5 per month). This is during a time when the nation experienced 147,499 murders, or an average of 16,389 murders per year (or 1,366 murders per month).[95]

The media are most interested in providing coverage of executions of widely known criminals such as serial killers like Ted Bundy or mass murderers like Timothy McVeigh. Given the major lessons of chapters 1 and 2, this is probably not surprising. Offenders like Ted Bundy, Timothy McVeigh and others committed high-profile crimes that themselves generated immense media coverage. In these cases (and almost only these cases), the news media follow the cases beyond the arrest and investigation through the courtroom process all the way until the final sentence is carried out. This allows the media to satisfy public demand to stay informed about these stories, and also to continue to satisfy advertisers and generate profit by continue to cover popular crime stories.

One of the most commonly discussed issues among students and some citizens is whether executions ought to be public.[96] It is possible that if executions were public, they might have a great crime preventive—or deterrent—effect. In fact, the U.S. has a long history of public executions. This history explains in large part why executions are now private events.

The last public execution in the U.S. occurred in Kentucky in August 1936. http://www.boston.com/news/globe/ideas/brainiac/Last%20Public%20 Execution.jpg.

✒️ For more information about public executions in the United States, see the website for this book at: www.pscj.appstate.edu/media/public executions.html

---

The last public execution in the United States was in 1936 in Owensboro, Kentucky.[97] Between ten and twenty thousand people turned out to witness this public hanging, which was described by the press as a carnival type atmosphere.[98] Decades after executions moved indoors, they still drew sizable crowds outside the jail. Eventually, however, the masses got their information from other sources, most notably the new "penny presses," which meant people no longer had to attend executions to experience the details.[99] However, some states even passed laws barring the press from attending executions and/or printing details about them in the papers.[100]

Banner explains the meaning of the shift from public to private executions:

Executions lost much of their symbolic meaning. The community no longer gathered to make its statement of condemnation. There was no more ritual to reinforce communal norms proscribing crime, no more ceremony at which to display one's participation in a collective moral order ... with executions conducted behind closed doors, before a small group of the well connected, out of the public eye, the *people* were no longer punishing the criminal. Now the government was doing the punishing, and the people were reading about it later.[101]

Johnson adds:

From this crucial transition—moving from passionate public executions to cold, clinical private ones—we can trace the beginnings of the bureaucratic regimen of modern private executions. Today, psychological dehumanization born of social isolation—on death row or in the death chamber—serves as the anesthetic that facilitates efficient, impersonal executions that are virtually devoid of human sentiment.[102]

Today, "executions could hardly be more different from executions in the past." They are:

always conducted in secluded areas within prisons. Only a limited number of spectators attend and most do so for professional reasons; these witnesses maintain a discreet silence, though many are reportedly shaken by what they see ... Neither death nor killing is any longer a familiar part of daily life for the population at large; killings by officials are especially rare events, and are drained of their emotional import by secrecy (hardly anyone sees them) and euphemism (hardly anyone calls an execution a killing).[103]

The outcome of this move to make executions private is our current system of executing inmates in the middle of the night and early morning hours. According to Bessler:

Executions in America, conducted behind prison walls, are cloaked in added secrecy because they frequently occur in the middle of the night. Of the 313 executions that took place in the United States from 1977 to 1995, over 82 percent of them were carried out between 11:00 pm and 7:30 am, and more than half of them happened between midnight and 1:00 am. Because television audiences are largest when people return home from work or school—viewership levels peak from 8:00 to 11:00 pm—many executions occur after most Americans are already sound asleep.[104]

It is state laws that typically require executions to be held at night. Yet, "[e]ven when executions are not mandated by statute, prison wardens or governmental officials frequently schedule executions for the middle of the night."[105] This is often done because midnight (and later) is the safest time in the prison where troublesome behaviors are least likely to occur. Further, midnight executions help "avoid unwanted protestors" and "ensure that enough time exists, because of possible last-minute stays and appeals, to carry out a death warrant—the legal document that lists a specific date on which the execution must occur."[106] Apparently, this practice started in 1885 in the state of Ohio.[107]

In the 20th and 21st centuries, almost all executions were invisible. David Dow and Bridget McNeese agree, writing: "Executions in American are typically invisible. High profile executions are the exceptions that demonstrate the rule. When a particularly infamous murderer is put to death, such as Timothy McVeigh or Ted Bundy, the execution receives significant attention. Yet, in nearly all other cases, executions are banal." [108]

Should American states resume public executions? Paul Leighton argues that executions should either be televised or else capital punishment should be abolished. His argument rests of the claim that the government must be accountable to the people for its actions carried out in their names.[109]

While some may argue that public executions—even if broadcast on television—would deter murder, there is literally no evidence that this is true.[110] Further, given the dominance of crime infotainment shown on television, we might expect executions to become seen as a form of entertainment alongside violent and gory movies.

A study by Jeremy Lipschultz and Michal Hilt of local television coverage of executions found that it tended to utilize powerful symbols (e.g., signs, candlelight vigils, heightened security, etc.) and "did not attempt to bridge the gap between proponents and opponents of capital punishment. Even in-studio experts focused on events at the prison scene, rather than the larger social issue of capital punishment."[111] According to the authors, capital punishment usually only makes the news when there is a horrible crime, during a trial, or when an execution occurs.

Joseph Jacoby and colleagues analyzed newspaper reports of executions imposed between 1977 and 2007 on network television, in national newspapers, and an in-state newspaper. The authors found that as executions became more common, coverage in the news became "less consistent, extensive, and prominent." In those states that had the most executions, newspapers regularly reported them, but the reports became shorter and less prominent even as executions increased. As for national news media coverage, "crimes with multiple victims, unusual offender characteristics, precedent-setting circumstances, unusual legal claims, or execution protocol violations" had the most coverage.[112]

Convicted Oklahoma City federal bomber Terry Nichols (who helped kill 168 people including 19 children) is in the news again after filing a lawsuit against prison officials for supposedly not providing him with healthy foods in prison. He wants "a high-fiber diet that includes whole grains along with fresh vegetables and fruit daily." http://dc-cdn.virtacore.com/5263eb68682c48cf84ab 37117a867cef.jpg.

Amazingly, less than 7% of the executions that took place between 1977 and 2007 were covered on national television news. According to the authors: "Executions have disappeared almost entirely from network TV news—between 2001 and 2007 only 14 [3%] of the 416 executions carried out in the U.S. was reported by *any* of the major TV networks. During the same period *USA Today* reported only [3%] of executions."[113]

Coverage in national newspapers was higher (*USA Today* and *New York Times* reported 20% and 48% of the executions, respectively). Further, while television news averaged only 15 reports per 100 executions, *USA Today* averaged 28 articles per 100 executions.

The average length of news reports was 140 seconds per execution. As for newspapers, reports were shorter in national newspapers than in newspapers with only coverage of in-state executions. Reports in the *New York Times* were longer than in the *USA Today* (366 words versus 37 words). Less than 5% of reports were reported on page 1.

The authors explain why executions are not a high priority for news sources. They point out that

> a single broadcast contains only 8–10 stories. A huge number of national and international events occur each day from which TV news

editors must chose no more than ten. Among these occurrences on a typical day would probably be bombings, accidents, or severe weather somewhere in the world resulting in many deaths, as well as political and economic events with important national and international consequences. In competition with news reports of such a large number of large-scale events, a news story about the death of a single criminal offender by lethal injection may, understandably, fail to survive an editor's cut. [114]

Further, consider that since the average execution occurs about 11 years after a crime, an execution following even a heinous crime will be of little interest to most people. The authors reason: "Stories that incorporate violent conflict, involve well-known persons, include graphic imagery, and allow for the reinforcement of traditional cultural values are preferred over more complex stories that may challenge the reader to reconsider widely held beliefs."[115]

Andy Hochstetler analyzed stories of executions in 50 large newspapers from January 1977 through February 1999. Of the 449 executions during this time, those who killed the most people received the greatest coverage. Further, sensational or unusual crimes received more attention.[116]

Another study examined 524 newspaper reports of 100 executions that occurred between January 1, 1990 and April 30, 2005.[117] The study found that defendant race had little effect on the mean articles per execution although executions of minority defendants received slightly more coverage. Finally, executions for crimes against white victims received more attention than those involving African-American victims.

According to the authors:

> Three factors had the largest impact on the number of reports. First, geography was a factor that influenced the coverage of an execution. Executions in non-southern states averaged 6.5 reports while those in southern states averaged 5.1. This is likely due to the fact that executions are more common in the south. Second ... the number of victims impacted the amount of coverage an execution received. Cases with multiple victims averaged 7 reports while those with a single victim averaged 5 ... Finally, the presence of some form of protest increased the number of reports. Executions that involved reports of collective protests averaged 6.2 articles per case while those without protest averaged 4.7.

Nearly two-thirds of the stories (65%) included a summary of the details of the crime that led to the convictions and executions. And most of the cases that were covered were atypical homicides that occurred between strangers.

Like telling a story, most of the reports began with the execution and then moved backwards to outline the original crime, the moving forward to explain the trial and appeals process that occurred prior to the execution. Included in most stories were details of the final hours and days of the condemned, including final appeals, final hours, and even the final meal. According to the authors, "final meals of the condemned were often described in great detail, with one newspaper even including an entire story about condemned inmates' last meals." Stories also tended to provide some details of the actual execution, including the "condemned's final statement, describing the execution scene, reporting someone's satisfaction with the event, mentions of on-site protests, and/or descriptions of the defendant's death."

David Niven examined newspaper coverage of 16 inmates released from death rows in three states. He found that executed inmates received more coverage than those exonerated. Further, coverage of exonerees suggested that isolated mistakes produce errors rather than systematic failure. The isolated mistake frame was more than twice as common as the systemic failure frame, and some of the articles even framed the exonerations themselves as proof that the system works. Finally, newspaper stories focused on life after release rather than experienced during incarceration, again by more than a two–to–one margin. According to Niven, "those who were executed received more than three times as much coverage as exonerated people on death row, which is akin to giving three times as much coverage to the planes that land safely compared to the ones that crash." Niven thus concludes: "Cumulatively, this pattern serves to minimize the seriousness of the innocent on death row situation, and is consistent with media theories suggesting political coverage is generally supportive of moderatism/mainstream elite political thinking."[118]

In the early 21st Century, the number of exonerees from death row grew, causing increased concern among many citizens, including death penalty opponents and activists. In Niven's study, there was "no significant increase in attention to the exonerated as their numbers have mounted ... the results suggest attention to each additional exoneration has been largely flat. Overall, the exonerated can expect just under 32 articles featuring their plight, placed on average on page 8 and just under 672 words long." [119]

Since 1976 through mid-2009, 129 people have been released from death row in the United States. These are people who have had their convictions overturned and who were either acquitted at re-trial, had all the charges dropped against them, or "they were given an absolute pardon by the governor based on new evidence of innocence."[120]

Although some may view these exonerations as proof that "the system works," in fact there is now overwhelming evidence that innocent people have

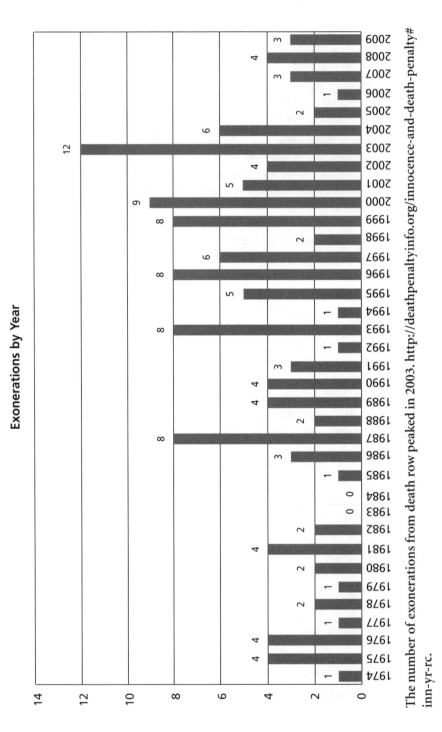

Exonerations by Year

The number of exonerations from death row peaked in 2003. http://deathpenaltyinfo.org/innocence-and-death-penalty#inn-yr-rc.

been executed in the United States. For example, consider the case of Cameron Willingham. Willingham was executed in the state of Texas in 2004 for starting a fire in his own home that killed his three children. Now, "four national arson experts have concluded that the original investigation of Willingham's case was flawed and it is possible the fire was accidental" ... finding "that prosecutors and arson investigators used arson theories that have since been repudiated by scientific advances.... Arson expert Gerald Hurst said, "There's nothing to suggest to any reasonable arson investigator that this was an arson fire. It was just a fire.' Former Louisiana State University fire instructor Kendall Ryland added, '[It] made me sick to think this guy was executed based on this investigation.... They executed this guy and they've just got no idea—at least not scientifically—if he set the fire, or if the fire was even intentionally set.'... Among the only other evidence presented by prosecutors during the trial was testimony from jailhouse snitch Johnny E. Webb, a drug addict on psychiatric medication, who claimed Willingham had confessed to him in the county jail.... Coincidentally, less than a year after Willingham's execution, arson evidence presented by some of the same experts who had appealed for relief in Willingham's case helped free Ernest Willis from Texas's death row. The experts noted that the evidence in the Willingham case was nearly identical to the evidence used to exonerate Willis."[121]

Recent articles published in the media have concluded that Willingham was innocent.[122] That major news entities (including an editorial in the *New York Times)* have covered this case is evidence that when a perceived wrong is serious enough, it will likely break into the mainstream press coverage (even in cases where it challenges mainstream institutions and practices like capital punishment).

⌨ **For more information about supposedly innocent individuals wo have been executed in recent U.S. history, see the website for this book at: www.pscj.appstate.edu/media/innocent.html**

Some cases of individuals who are now thought to be innocent after they were executed have also received media attention. As of now, none of the above individuals has been declared innocent by any state government.

Media coverage of the realities of capital punishment may help change opinions in the United States. For example, increased coverage of innocent people being released from death row has helped weaken support of the death penalty[123] Perhaps this is one reason media companies do not spend more time seriously challenging capital punishment; the media are vested in status quo approaches to fighting crime, as noted throughout this book.

Summary

Corrections is probably the least covered aspect of criminal justice by the media. Aside from documentaries and occasional stories of the nation's prisons, most Americans have no idea about the realities of American prisons, such as the enormous pains of imprisonment suffered each day by inmates. Corrections is the "last thought" of most Americans.

Historically, corrections has been less visible to Americans. Further, people tend to have direct experience with police officers and often with court personnel such as lawyers, but most people do not have direct experience with correctional facilities.

Prisons are also little covered in the news. Most corrections stories deal with cases as they progress through the different stages of criminal justice rather than dealing directly with correctional facilities. These are typically high profile cases that are followed by the media all the way to the point of correctional punishment. The most common news stories detail the discovery of crimes, the arresting of suspects, and the appearance of the accused in court.

Corrections is covered less because punishment is deemed less newsworthy than other aspects of criminal justice and less interesting to the public. Further, there is no corrections newsbeat that matches the police and court beats in journalism. Gaining access to inmates and correctional facilities is much more burdensome than accessing police and court personnel and procedures.

Like with crime, news coverage of corrections focuses on the extraordinary rather than the ordinary, events such as riots, escapes, executions, and so forth. Further, stories tend to be very negative in nature. Three types of negative stories dominate news coverage of corrections: stories about the failure of corrections to protect the public; stories about amenities of prisoners; and stories of corruption and misconduct. These cases are likely popular because they are negative in nature, involve conflict, are controversial, and can be used to generate profits for the mainstream press.

Probably the most well-known example of correctional failure to protect the public is the case of Willie Horton. The major lessons about winning and losing included: Don't be portrayed as being "soft on crime"; Portray your opponent as "soft on crime"; Simplify the crime issue; and Reinforce messages with emotional context. The mainstream media, with time constraints and budgetary needs, can be used by politicians to get these messages out to the public. This is precisely what happened in the Willie Horton case. Given the close connections between the media and law-makers, it is relatively easy to promote one's ideas about crime control, especially if they are consistent with the status quo approaches already being used.

The more common sanctions such as probation are given far less attention by the media. Probation, the least restrictive of punishments, is the most commonly used criminal sanction in the United States. Given the media preoccupation with violent crime, it is understandable why the media generally ignore probationers. Exceptions include when a violent offender is sentenced to probation and when an offender on probation commits a heinous crime; these cases tend to attract media attention.

A logical reason why the media are more focused on serious punishments such as imprisonment and the death penalty and less interested in probation is because the former are much rarer than the latter. They are also much harsher and violent in nature and are many times connected to crimes that also are heinous and violent in nature.

The majority of media depictions of criminals characterize offenders not as rational but instead as simply evil or deranged and mentally ill. Yet, dominant themes and narratives of criminality are consistent with the notion of hedonistic, rational offenders who can be deterred through tough punishment.

The U.S. leads the world in both the number of people it incarcerates as well as the incarceration rate. Much of the increase in prison inmates recently has been due to drug convictions. Given that when Americans think about crime, they think about violent crime, most would probably be surprised to learn that only about half of the increase of the prison population is because of violent offenders.

Imprisonment alone costs Americans tens of billions of dollars per year, a fact that is not known by many. There are likely several reasons why costs of imprisonment rarely come to the attention of the media. First, since corrections is the least visible aspect of criminal justice, issues such as cost (as well as what happens to people once they are locked up) are often just not considered. Second, since the great majority of politicians have bought into the prison system as a legitimate means to deal with crime, it is very unlikely the issue of cost is even seen as relevant to them. Third, since the media rely on politicians and correctional personnel for information about correctional punishment, reporters are unlikely to ever hear the issue raised in the first place. Finally, recall that the media are part of the dominant, status quo reinforcing institutions in society; thus they have little incentive to question the costs of the status quo.

Contrary to the mythical view of the comfortable prison, American prisons are terribly hot, loud, and violent places to live. In fact, because of the numerous pains of imprisonment, the typical prison is not anything like a country club. The major pains of imprisonment include: Loss of liberty; Loss of autonomy; Loss of security; Deprivation of heterosexual relationships; and

Deprivation of goods and services. Additionally, inmates also suffer from: Loss of voting rights; Loss of dignity; and Stigmatization.

More than half of all inmates had a mental health problem of some kind. The incidence of mental illness is even more pronounced for people spending life in prison. These numbers are of particular concern considering that correctional facilities are ill-equipped to provide safety and appropriate treatment for mentally ill persons. Prisons are dangerous and debilitating for inmates with mental illnesses, who often are victimized by other prisoners. Moreover, symptoms of mental illness are often misinterpreted by correctional staff as disruptive behavior, which can lead to additional punishment and disciplinary actions that may extend the length of an individual's sentence.

The issue of mental illness in prisons and jails does not receive significant media attention, at least in the for-profit media. Television stations such as PBS and radio stations such as NPR have focused on this issue, but these are non-profit media organizations with smaller audiences than the mainstream press.

As surprising as it is given that images of the poor and minorities dominate media images of crime and punishment, the media rarely raise the issue of biases in American criminal justice and corrections. Yet, criminologists have outlined serious problems in criminal justice and punishment that explain these biases.

The death penalty, being the most severe of all criminal justice sanctions, is logically attractive to the media. The death penalty tends to make news when high profile murderers are sentenced to death, when inmates are executed, as well as when problems with capital punishment lead to wrongful convictions and exonerations. The media are most interested in providing coverage of executions of widely known criminals such as serial killers like Ted Bundy or mass murderers like Timothy McVeigh.

Media coverage of the realities of capital punishment may help change opinions in the United States. For example, increased coverage of innocent people being released from death row has help weaken support of the death penalty. Perhaps this is one reason media companies do not spend more time seriously challenging capital punishment.

Discussion Questions

1) Why is corrections the least covered aspect of criminal justice by the media?
2) Under what circumstances do prisons get covered in the news?

3) In the book it is argued that news coverage of corrections focuses on the extraordinary rather than the ordinary. What does this mean?

4) Summarize the Willie Horton case. Why is this case significant for criminal justice?

5) How do politicians "use" the mainstream media to get their messages out to the public?

6) What is the most common criminal punishment used in the United States? Is this form of punishment commonly featured in the media? Explain.

7) Why are the media more focused on serious punishments such as imprisonment and the death penalty and less interested in probation?

8) What are the major goals of punishment in the United States? In your opinion, are these goals achieved?

9) What are the major assumptions underlying *deterrence*? Do you think people are deterred by the thought of major punishment?

10) Does getting "tough on crime" work to reduce crime? Explain.

11) Which country leads the world in incarceration? Why does this matter?

12) Outline all the costs of imprisonment. Why does this matter?

13) Identify and define the major pains of imprisonment.

14) What portion of people locked up in America suffers from mental illnesses? Is this largely known by Americans? Why?

15) Do the media raise the issue of biases in American criminal justice and corrections? Explain.

16) Under what conditions do death sentences and executions get covered by the media?

17) If more Americans learned of the realities of capital punishment from the media, do you think this would change people's opinions of the death penalty? Explain.

Chapter 8

How Entertainment and Infotainment Media Portray Crime: Unrealistic Violence on TV and in Film and Other Media

Learning Objectives

After reading this chapter, you will be able to:

1) Summarize the type of content you are likely to see on the television shows *To Catch a Predator* and *48 Hours Mystery*.
2) Discuss for how long crime and criminal justice shows have been popular on television and summarize the major types of shows being shown today as well as in the past.
3) Identify the main narratives promoted in entertainment today.
4) Explain what is meant by the "value free" nature of violence in entertainment media.
5) Explain to what degree violence is popular in film and music.
6) Explain to what degree violence is popular in comic books.
7) Discuss true crime novels.
8) Describe the popular television show *COPS* and identify major problems with it.
9) Describe the popular television show *Law & Order* and identify major problems with it.
10) Describe the popular television show *CSI* and identify major problems with it.
11) Discuss how modern coverage of trials in the media is inaccurate.

Introduction

In previous chapters, you've seen how the mainstream news media portray crime and efforts to reduce crime though the law, policing, courts and corrections. You've learned that the media generally ignore law-making, with the exception of some highly publicized crimes that lead to new laws. Further, most crime is ignored by the press; random, heinous, violent crimes committed by some types of offenders against certain types of victims are more likely to be featured.

You've also learned that the mainstream press rely heavily on official sources for information about crime, police, courts, and corrections, thereby limiting the breadth of issues explored and reinforcing status quo approaches to addressing crime. Finally, you've seen that media coverage of criminal justice agencies is highly inaccurate, thereby reinforcing major misconceptions about criminal justice practice (e.g., police spend most of their time fighting crime and are effective at it; most people charged with serious crimes receive trials; tough punishment is effective at reducing crime, etc.).

In this chapter, you will see how the entertainment and infotainment media deal with crime, police, courts, corrections. For the most part, you'll see great similarities in infotainment and entertainment coverage of these issues. The main difference is that infotainment and entertainment media are less accurate, owing in part to the fact that their main goal is to entertain rather than to inform.

Two Examples of Crime and Justice on TV: *To Catch a Predator* and *48 Hours Mystery*

To Catch a Predator

The television show, *To Catch a Predator*, is a good example of how crime has been featured in the mainstream press in an infotainment format. The show was first aired in November 2004 as a segment of the popular NBC newsmagazine show *Dateline NBC*. While the latter show started off with serious investigative journalism, it has slowly turned toward less serious, trivial, and at times salacious infotainment program that is easier and less expensive to produce.

To Catch a Predator features scenes filmed in real houses from real neighborhoods where a "sexual predator" (i.e., man willing to have sexual relations with an underage victim) has been lured to the home by NBC, in conjunction with the group "Perverted Justice." The purpose is to first interview the suspects on television and then to ultimately arrest them. The show features the usually shocked man being confronted by the host of the show, Chris Hanson, who confronts the suspect while he is being filmed by secret cameras. Hanson typically confronts the men with their own words (as well as images they have sent of themselves naked), captured from logs from actual online chats they have had with NBC's decoy who has pretended to be an underage girl. Then, an entourage of cameramen come out from behind hidden spaces and Hanson asks the men questions about their intentions with the underage girls. After his occurs, Hanson tells the men that if they have nothing else to say, they are "free to go."

The cameras then film the men walking outside to their cars to leave only to be arrested. NBC has its own website devoted to the show, where you can "meet the men" from the show; that is, meet the sex offenders who appeared and were arrested on the show.[1] The show's host, Chris Hanson also has his own book out about the show, which is also advertised on the web site. Since NBC owns the publishing house for the book, this is a good way to sell additional products to viewers, an example of *vertical integration* (see Chapter 1).

This show is a good example of crime and justice on television now because it accurately depicts how the mainstream media use crime to attract audiences. In the case of NBC's *To Catch a Predator*, viewers are shown "real events" as they occur in a format meant to entertain and thus hold viewers. Aside from increased awareness of "sexual predators" (which appear to be everywhere according to the show) and fear of crime (especially with those with young children), the educational value of the show is unclear.

48 Hours Mystery

The show *48 Hours Mystery* is broadcast by CBS. The show was first broadcast in 1986 as a serious investigation into the supposed "crack cocaine epidemic" of the 1980s. Starting in the 1990s, the serious investigative aspects of the show were abandoned in favor of its current "true crime" format. The latter format is easier, cheaper, and requires less staff than the show's original serious journalistic format.

Now the show *48 Hours Mystery* focuses on murders that occurred somewhere in the United States. The details of the crimes are recounted along with interviews and photos of victims, family members and ultimately the suspects. The show, in a one hour format (including many commercials) manages to summarize a crime, arrest and trial of a suspect in an effort to answer whatever questions led the producers of the show to classify the murder as a mystery or "whodunit" type case. This show also has its own web site where you can read about episodes of the show as well as watch full episodes. The web site also has a link titled "Crimesider" where visitors can visit to see the latest news and images pertaining to recent high profile crimes in the nation.[2] There, viewers can also buy books written by reporters affiliated with the show, detailing some of the cases featured on the show.

This show is another good example of crime and justice on television now because it also depicts how the mainstream media use crime to attract audiences. In the case of CBS' *48 Hours Mystery*, viewers are shown "real events" after they have occurred in a format meant to entertain and thus hold viewers. Unfortunately, this show is always focused on the crime of murder, which is the rarest of all crimes in any given year. This surely helps reinforce the myth that most crime is violent in nature as well as very serious.

The Prevalence of Crime and Justice on Television

It is obvious by now that crime sells. This is one major reason why crime is widely popular in all media forms of entertainment and infotainment. That is, crime is at the center of many TV shows, films, music and more.

Recall from Chapter 2 that infotainment refers to media that exist between the news and entertainment. Specifically, infotainment is intended for the purpose of entertaining audiences but has some basis in fact and is presented as reality. *TruTV*, formerly *Court TV*, is entirely dedicated to the infotainment format. They advertise their channel as "television's destination for real-life stories told from an exciting and dramatic first-person perspective and features high-stakes, action-packed originals that give viewers access to places and situations they can't normally experience."

Among the popular shows on this network are the police shows *Speeders*, *Hot Pursuit*, and *Forensic Files*. Christopher Wilson calls the increasing coverage of police in infotainment as the blurring between cop and pop.[3] The most successful and widely known infotainment show is *COPS*, which will be discussed later in this chapter.

According to Danielle Soulliere, crime and law enforcement programs "have virtually littered television programming for the past four decades." Among the programs noted by Soulliere include *The Avengers, Mod Squad, Kojak, Baretta, Hawaii Five-O, The Rockford Files, Dragnet, Starsky and Hutch, Columbo, Hill Street Blues, Magnum, P.I., Cagney and Lacy, Simon and Simon, Miami Vice, T.J. Hooker, In the Heat of the Night, Murder She Wrote, L.A. Law, The Commish, NYPD Blue, Walker: Texas Ranger, The X-Files, Homicide, Law and Order, The Practice, Nash Bridges, JAG, Judging Amy, The Fugitive, The District, Level-9, The Job* and *C.S.I: Crime Scene Investigation.*[4]

According to Gayle Rhineberger-Dunn, Nicole Rader, and Kevin Williams: "The popularity of crime-related television programming, both fiction and non-fiction, is well-established."[5] Even as far back as the 1976–1977 television season, 19 different crime dramas were on the air.[6] Since the mid-1980s, crime dramas have accounted for about one-third of prime-time television programming.[7] That one-third of television shows is about crime is a good indication of how much media companies know that crime sells.

In the late 1980s, contemporary infotainment programs like *Geraldo* and *Unsolved Mysteries* began to appear on television and the genre increased steadily in popularity. As a result of the blurring of the line between news and entertainment, it became more difficult for media consumers to identify what was news and what was entertainment.[8] Infotainment is now the most popular format of crime television.

Kenneth Dowler claims that in this century, "with the dawn of each new television season, several new programs that deal with crime and justice always commence. Even the casual television viewer is exposed to the frequent portrayals of crime and justice on television."[9] According to Dowler's research, popular shows from this decade include *CSI: Crime Scene Investigation* (2000–); *The District* (2000–2004); *Law and Order: Criminal Intent* (2001–); *Crossing Jordan* (2001–07); *24* (2001–); *CSI: Miami* (2002–): *Without a Trace* (2002–2009); *Cold Case* (2003–); *NCIS* (2003–); *CSI: NY* (2004–); *Numb3rs* (2005–); *Criminal Minds* (2005–); *Prison Break* (2005–2009); and *Bones* (2005–). Popular cable television shows include *The Sopranos* (1999–2007), *The Wire* (2002–), *The Shield* (2002–), *Dog the Bounty Hunter* (2004–), *Oz* (1997–2003), *Dallas SWAT* (2006–), *The First 48* (2004–), *Brotherhoods* (2006–) and *Dexter* (2006–).

A review of all the shows is beyond the scope of this book, but all of them share a focus on crime and crime-fighting. Most are pure entertainment rather than infotainment, meaning they are fictional and meant to entertain as opposed to inform.

According to Dawn Cecil, "the most consistent and ever-present crime format is the drama, usually an hour-long weekly program depicting some aspect of the criminal justice system and the people it pursues. Today's prime time line-up is filled with these crime dramas, which increased in number following the terrorist attacks of 2001 … For instance, nearly 41 percent of CBS's spring 2006 prime time line up consisted of crime dramas."[10]

Dowler identified and analyzed popular shows from the 1960s, 1970s, 1980s, and 1990s. Popular shows from the 1960s included *The Mod Squad* (1968–73); *Hawaii Five-O* (1968–80); *Ironside* (1967–75); *Dragnet* (1967–70); *Mannix* (1967–75); *The F.B.I.* (1965–74); *N.Y.P.D.* (1967–69); *Felony Squad* (1966–69); *The Fugitive* (1963–67); *The Defenders* (1961–65); *Adam 12* (1968–75); *Car 54, Where Are You?* (1961–63); and *The Andy Griffith Show* (1960–68).

Popular shows in the 1970s included *Charlie's Angels* (1976–81); *Vega$* (1978–1981); *Barney Miller* (1975–82); *Quincy M.E.* (1976–83); *Barnaby Jones* (1973–80); *Columbo* (1971–78); *The Rockford Files* (1974–80); *Hart to Hart* (1979–84); *CHiPs* (1977–83); *Cannon* (1971–76); *McLoud* (1970–77); *McMillan and Wife* (1971–77); *The Rookies* (1972–77); *The Streets of San Francisco* (1972–77); *Police Story* (1973–1978); *Kojak* (1973–78); *Police Woman* (1974–78); *Baretta* (1975–78); *Starsky and Hutch* (1975–79); and *S.W.A.T.* (1975–76).

Popular shows in the 1980s included *Simon and Simon* (1981–88); *The Fall Guy* (1981–86); *Magnum P.I.* (1980–88); *Hill Street Blues* (1981–87); *Matt Houston* (1982–85); *Cagney and Lacey* (1982–88); *Remington Steele* (1982–87); *Knight Rider* (1982–86); *T.J. Hooker* (1982–85); *Hardcastle and McCormick*

(1983–86); *Hunter* (1984–1991); *Miami Vice* (1984–89); *Murder She Wrote* (1984–1996); *Moonlighting* (1985–89); *Spencer For Hire* (1985–88); *Matlock* (1986–95); *The Equalizer* (1985–89); *L.A. Law* (1986–94); *Jake and the Fatman* (1987–1992); *Wiseguy* (1987–90); *21 Jump Street* (1987–91); *In the Heat of the Night* (1988–94); *America's Most Wanted* (1988–); *Unsolved Mysteries* (1987–2002); and *COPS* (1989–).

Popular shows in the 1990s included *Law and Order* (1990–); *The Commish* (1991–1995); *NYPD Blue* (1993–2005); *Walker, Texas Ranger* (1993–2001); *New York Undercover* (1994–1998); *Due South* (1994–1999); *Homicide: Life on the Streets* (1993–2000); *Diagnosis, Murder* (1993–2001); *Nash Bridges* (1996–2001); *Profiler* (1996–2000); *The Practice* (1997–2004); *Martial Law* (1998–2000); *Third Watch* (1999–2005); and *Law and Order: SVU* (1999–).

In 2005, there were 22 crime drama shows on network television and 9 on cable channels. Some of these shows included *CSI, CSI Miami, CSI: New York, Without a Trace, Cold Case, Bones, 48 Hours Mystery, Law & Order, Law & Order: SVU, The Closer, Crossing Jordan, Numb3rs, Medium,* and *Monk.*[11] In 2010, many shows in the fifty most watched shows dealt specifically with crime and criminal justice, including *NCIS, 24, Criminal Minds, Bones, Law & Order: SVU,* and *CSI: Miami.*[12] Many other top shows include acts of deviance and crime even though they are not the main focus of the programs.

The main themes of such crime and criminal justice oriented shows have changed across the decades. The earlier shows from the 1960s and 1970s were overwhelmingly pro-law enforcement and pro-criminal justice. That is, officers and criminal justice employees generally were depicted as honest, hard-working and clearly on "our side" in the "fight" against crime. In the 1980s, this was also generally true, but increasingly popular crime and criminal justice television shows depicted additional issues such as corruption, excessive use of force and the presence of vice (e.g., drugs) in communities and even among the police. Shows in the 1980s tended to be more complex than earlier shows and the line between the "good guys" and "bad guys" became harder to distinguish.

A good example comes from the show, *Hillstreet Blues.* This was one of the first widely watched police shows on television, and was about the daily life of officers in a police precinct. Although the individual characters had different views about what was right and acceptable police behavior, they all tended to be motivated by their desire to bring justice to the neighborhood and world. Many episodes featured the battles of Captain Frank Furillo and a lawyer from the Public Defender's office, Joyce Davenport (who were of course involved in a personal, intimate relationship), and every episode began with a roll call and the familiar words by Sergeant Phil, "Let's be careful out there."

The main themes of the show, as with many similar shows from the time period, were: it is acceptable and at times necessary to question authority and to resist bureaucracy as long as justice is achieved in the end; oppression in all its forms must be fought; justice demands standing up for what is right even when it is not popular; even though sometimes innocent people get caught up in the system we always get it right in the end; and sometimes the work of one person will bring about justice.[13]

In terms of popular television shows, "justice" most often means *corrective justice* or "justice as an outcome." This form of justice pertains to holding the guilty responsible for their crimes, and is most consistent with the crime control model of justice introduced earlier in the book.[14] Sarah Escholtz and colleagues agree, noting: "The dominant theme of all of these programs is 'justice,' brought about by an offender being caught and/or punished for a crime ... Each new television season offers a host of new programs that attempt to capture viewers hooked on this genre."[15] Perhaps it is not surprising then that exposure to such shows may increase support for capital punishment and handgun ownership. Further, people who believe such shows to be realistic are more likely to be afraid of crime.[16] Both of these outcomes drive support for crime control approaches.

Katherine Beckett and Theodore Sasson conclude that crime entertainment narratives tend to promote three related messages:

· Most offenders are professional criminals;
· Community safety is threatened by judges and defense attorneys who are too much concerned with offenders' rights; and
· Criminal justice personnel are out there every day, fighting the war on crime.[17]

These messages have the potential to be highly misleading to the general public. Therein lies the danger to doing justice, as well as to more honest crime control efforts. They also shift support toward a crime control model of criminal justice. Also notice how these characterizations of entertainment media are consistent with news media characterizations of crime and criminal justice.

Finally, it is important to understand that American popular culture—including television—influences not just the United States. According to Lane Crothers, American popular culture impacts the whole world, especially when it comes to entertainment media in the form of movies, television and music. Crothers says this is no accident, claiming that large multinational for-profit companies aim "to create as large and pervasive a consumer base for their products as possible."[18]

Crothers' research shows that American movies and DVDs dominate around the world, especially action adventure films (which he characterizes as all being exactly the same). Further, much of the dominant music in the world comes from America or owes itself to genres largely created in the U.S. and originally broadcast worldwide via MTV. Even American TV shows are highly popular around the world, most notably day time and night time soap operas.[19] Keep this in mind while reading this chapter.

Overemphasize Violence

It is probably not surprising that studies of entertainment and infotainment shows have consistently found that they tend to overemphasize violent crime. For example, an analysis of three contemporary prime-time justice shows (*Law and Order*, *The Practice* and *NYPD Blue*) was undertaken to discover the way in which crime and its participants are presented by entertainment television. The findings revealed an overrepresentation of violent crime and distorted images of offenders and victims.[20]

Focusing on the positive aspect of this, John Worrall suggests that policing infotainment programs "seem to quench Americans' voyeuristic thirsts for bloodshed, violence, and action even though these shows have few redeeming virtues." This is a recognition that, to some degree, we citizens and media consumers have some of the blame for the violence on television and in the media formats. Yet:

> these programs convey images of crime, criminals, law enforcement officials, and the criminal justice system which are incomplete, distorted, and inaccurate ... Viewers are led to believe policing is an action-packed profession, criminals frequently resist capture, crime is predominately violent, crime is the work of minorities, and the police regularly succeed in their endeavors to combat illicit activity.[21]

All of these messages are inaccurate, as shown in this book.

The Center for Media and Public Affairs (CMPA) regularly studies violence in various entertainment and infotainment media. One of these studies found:

- The top 50 big screen movies in 1998–1999 averaged 46 scenes of violence including 28 life-threatening types of violence.
- 25 made-for-broadcast TV movies in 1998–1999 averaged 5 violent scenes per episode.
- 25 made-for-cable TV movies in 1998–1999 averaged 15 violent scenes per episode.
- Popular television series in 1998–1999 averaged 6 violent scenes per episode.
- Music videos on MTV in 1998–1999 averaged 4 violent scenes, including 1 serious.[22]

In all, researchers identified 8,350 scenes of violence including 4,204 scenes of serious violence (i.e., murder, rape, kidnapping and assault) in the 100 movies, 284 episodes of television series and 189 music videos they studied.

After adjusting for the length of each show, movie and video, the following rates of violence per hour were determined:

- Broadcast TV series—18 per hour
- Movies in theaters—15 per hour
- Music videos—15 per hour
- Cable TV series—9 per hour
- TV movies—7 per hour.

In the past ten years since this study was published, it is likely that these numbers have increased, meaning that violence is even more widespread today than it was in the late 1990s. Unfortunately, at the time of this writing, CMPA has not replicated the study or updated these findings.

According to the authors of the study, violence in these forms of media tends to be "value free." That is, it is shown being used by both heroes and villains, it rarely causes physical or emotional harm, it rarely leads to any condemnation or punishment and it is sometimes depicted as laudable and even necessary. This is good evidence that violence in the entertainment and infotainment media lacks important context, just as it does in the news media. It also suggests the possibility that violence in the media may be repeated in the real world, particularly by those who are less able to differentiate between fact and fiction.

Finally, themes of drug use[23] and justice are common in films as well, even in action adventure and science fiction films.[24] Movies as varied as "The Green Mile," "Minority Report," and "Alien" present challenges related to crime and justice to the main characters who are forced to make vital decisions and struggle against immense odds to ultimately do the right thing. Other films center on major ethical struggles relevant for criminal justice, including "Mississippi Burning" and "The Road to Perdition."[25]

Film

If you've been to the movies lately, you are well aware that violence is prevalent in film. This is problematic because film is a primary source for people's ideas and perceptions about crime.[26]

A recent advertisement for the movie *Saw VI* suggested that this could very well be one of the most violent films ever made, at least when it comes to depicting gory murders and acts of graphic torture; some war movies such as *Saving Private Ryan* are more violent overall, but this film was meant to realistically show for the first time what the D-Day battle really looked like for those who were there in World War II.

A study by Wes Shipley and Gray Cavender analyzed the five top-grossing films in a one year period over each of the past four decades (i.e., 1964, 1974, 1984, and 1994).[27] The authors found that violence generally increased across the four decades. In 1964, the five top-grossing films contained a total of 144 violent acts (an average of 29 acts per film). In 1974, the five top-grossing films contained a total of 168 violent acts (an average of 34 acts per film). In 1984, the five top-grossing films contained a total of 307 violent acts (an average of 61 acts per film). In 1994, the five top-grossing films depicted a total of 223 violent acts (an average of 45 acts per film).

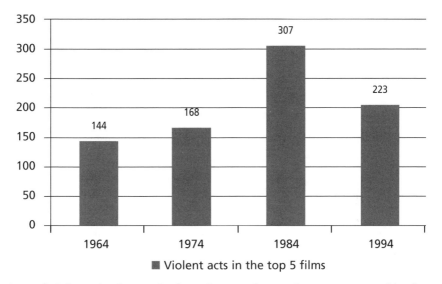

■ Violent acts in the top 5 films

Acts of violence in the movies have increased over time, as measured in the top five grossing films of each decade.

Instances of death also rose over time. In 1964, the five films showed a total of 41 deaths (an average of 8 deaths per film). In 1974, the five films showed a total of 44 deaths (an average of 9 deaths per film). In 1984, the five films showed 38 deaths (an average of 8 deaths per film). In 1994, the five films showed 76 deaths (an average of 15 deaths per film).

Graphic violence and graphic death also rose. Acts of graphic violence increased from 2 in 1964 to 12 in 1974 to 16 in 1984 to 64 in 1994. Graphic deaths increased from 0 in 1964 to 6 in 1974 to 10 in 1984 to 47 in 1994. This finding is consistent with claims that violence, graphic violence, and murder are becoming more common in the mainstream media. Potential implications

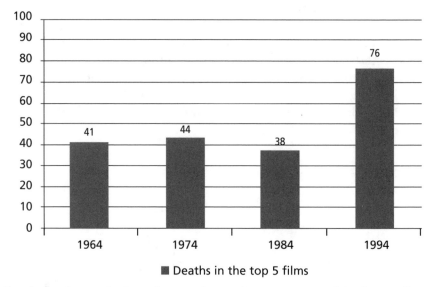

■ Deaths in the top 5 films

Deaths in the movies have increased over time, as measured in the top five grossing films of each decade.

for society, including increased violent behavior in society, are real possibilities.

However, acts of violence did not increase equally across all genres. Movies in two genres showed the most violence—action and disaster films. Another study of "slasher films" found that violent acts became more common, increasing from an average of 40 violent acts per film in 1980 to an average of 47 acts per film in 1985 to an average of 70 violent acts per film in 1989. Obviously, the violence in "slasher films" is graphic in nature, often showing very bloody attacks with major close-ups of injuries.[28] Popular "slasher films" feature gruesome killers like Freddie Kruger (pictured from "Nightmare on Elm Street"), Jason Voorhies (from "Friday the 13th"), Michael Myers (from "Halloween"), and so many others. Since the 1990s, it is certain that acts of violence and death have increased further. In fact, many of the best grossing films of today feature many acts of violence, including even the widely popular *Harry Potter* and *Twilight* series.

One study of intensely violent films included "The Matrix," "Reservoir Dogs," "Natural Born Killers" and "Elephant." Each film depicts numerous, very graphic

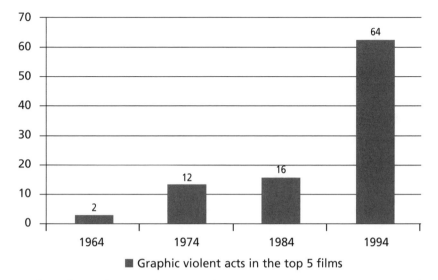

Acts of graphic violence in the movies have increased over time, as measured in the top five grossing films of each decade.

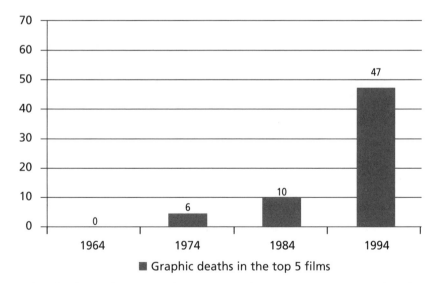

Graphic deaths in the movies have increased over time, as measured in the top five grossing films of each decade.

killings. Not surprisingly, each film has also been blamed as a cause of violence in the real world.[29]

Superhero movies are also quite violent. The most recent depictions of "The Joker" in the Batman series and the "Green Goblin" in the Spiderman series are very dark and disturbed figures—mentally ill, one is led to presume—who kill and injure many innocent civilians in very violent ways. The fact that each "bad guy" is framed as mentally ill—The Joker because of childhood abuse and the Green Goblin because of pressure from work which leads to a split personality—is consistent with the popular image of the criminal as mentally ill, as noted in Chapter 4.

Music

Themes of violence are also common in popular music. Lane Crothers provides the following as examples of violence in mainstream music:

- Jim Morrison imagines murdering his father and raping his mother in the song, "The End."
- Garth Brooks sings about a man killing his wife and her lover by driving his eighteen-wheel truck into a hotel room in the song, "Papa Loved Mama."
- The Dixie Chicks sing about murdering a man who beats his wife in a song called, "Goodbye Earl."

Another example is from the album "Appetite for Destruction" by Guns N' Roses (1987), which was criticized for depicting on the cover a woman appearing to have been raped. Importantly, these limited examples show that violent themes exists in multiple genres—in this case, rock and country. He also discussed numerous examples of violent lyrics from rappers like 50 Cent, Tupac Shakur, and Eminem.[30] The latter genre has probably received the most media attention.

Eric Armstrong analyzed lyrics from 490 rap songs produced by 13 different artists from 1987 to 1993. He found that 22% of gangsta rap music songs contain violent and misogynist lyrics. According to his study, the fastest selling rap album of all time—Eminem's *The Marshall Mathers LP*—contains 14 songs, and violent and misogynist lyrics are found in 11 (79%) of them: "Worse still, nine of the eleven songs depict killing women, with drowning becoming a new modus operandi. Comparing the lyric content of gangsta rap music's foundational period with that of Eminem shows the following: In terms of violent and misogynist lyrics, gangsta rap music (1987–1993) scores a 22 percent while Eminem (2000) reaches 78 percent."[31] Eminem's most recent album continues this approach. For example, the rapper ends one song singing about tying a woman to the bed and setting her house on fire to burn her alive.

Rap musicians have claimed that they merely reflect the reality of life out of which they arose and thus they should not be blamed or criticized for singing about where they came from. Additionally, rap music is often about a lot more than violence.[32] Some of it even contains very positive and uplifting messages as well as politically inspired themes.[33]

Violence in music is obviously not limited to only rap music. Rock 'n' Roll and several other genres of music like "Heavy Metal" have been criticized for violent themes and lyrics. One study found that, among a large sample of suburban high school young people, listening to heavy metal music was associated with an increased risk of delinquency when parental control was low.[34] Yet, Rock 'N Roll is also known for being explicitly anti-violence, especially when it comes to violence committed by the government. For example, numerous musicians became famous, at least in part, due to songs criticizing government actions in times of war and conflict, for example. Numerous artists are known widely for their impact on social justice. Examples include John Lennon, Bob Dylan, Johnnie Cash, Bruce Springstein, U2, Bob Marley and so many more.[35] Music also played a significant role in the civil rights movement, among many other important social movements.[36]

✓☝ For more informaton about music and crime, see the website for this book at: www.pscj.appstate.edu/media/music.html

---

Comic Books

Violence and crime is also common in comic books.[37] According to Bradford Wright: "Comic books are history. Emerging from the shifting interaction of politics, culture, audience tastes, and the economics of publishing, comic books have helped to frame a worldview and define a sense of self for the generations who have grown up with them."[38]

Scott Vollum and Cory Adkinson add:

> For decades, young Americans have looked to the world of comic book superheroes for a sense of justice. Since the 1930s the mythos of comic book superheroes has pervaded adolescents' sense of crime, justice and order. Whether it was through the weekly dose of comic book reading or, more contemporarily, through television and movie viewing, youths in America have been fixated on 'superheroes' and their battles for justice: good vs. evil, right vs. wrong.[39]

Mark Stoddart examined 52 comic books and graphic novels and found that "comic books reproduced a dominant discourse of negative drug use, which focused primarily on hard drugs such as heroin and cocaine." Further, images of "pleasurable or revelatory drug use existed only at the margins of comic book drug narratives." Just as in the case of violent crime, drug users were depicted as victims and drug dealers as predators: "Drug users were depicted as victims who may be saved rather than criminalized. At the same time, drug dealers were constructed as villains who were subjected to the justifiable violence of comic book heroes." Further, such images were commonly gendered, racialized, and depicted in class-based representations. Finally, issues such as managed or responsible drug use, decriminalization, and legalization "were rendered invisible."[40] Note how similar these findings are to those pertaining to the news media, discussed in Chapters 4 and 5.

Even though drugs like cocaine and heroin are rarely used in the United States (relative to more popular drugs such as marijuana), comic book depictions of drug use center around cocaine and heroin rather than marijuana. Additionally, depictions of illicit drugs were far more likely than of alcohol and tobacco, even though use of alcohol and tobacco is more common as well as more dangerous.

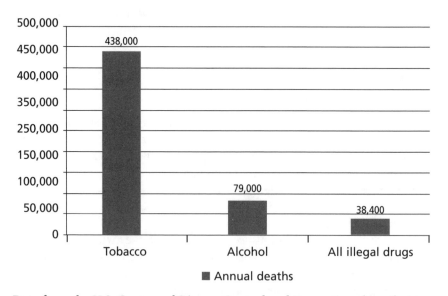

Data from the U.S. Centers of Disease Control and Prevention show that tobacco and alcohol kill far more people than all illegal drugs combined, yet the former are legal and there is far less media attention placed on the latter.

When alcohol use is depicted, it is generally negative in nature: "Problematic use was portrayed through recurring themes of denial, violence against others, and alcoholism as a permanent identity. Where alcohol differed from the depiction of illicit drugs was that discourses of normalized use were also admitted." [41]

Normal or pro-social use of drugs is not depicted in comic books. Instead, "addiction was a nearly universal outcome of drug use. The bulk of drug narratives adopted an addiction-sobriety dichotomy, where the user faced a binary choice between a moral sobriety and a morally degraded state of addiction, with little room for occasional drug use or managed dependency. Narratives repeatedly linked addiction with the impoverishment and sexual degradation of drug users." Other outcomes depicted in comic books were overdose and withdrawal.[42]

According to Stoddart's analysis, drug narratives in comic books are generally conservative in nature, reflective of the anti-drug discourses found among law enforcement agencies and other agencies of government:

> Here, morality is defined through abstinence. The good guys just say no. With the exception of a few deviant cases, alternative drug discourses of pleasurable drug use, or of spiritual drug use, are subsumed beneath dominant discourses that reproduce a law and order perspective on illicit drugs. Illicit drugs are defined as essentially bad substances, regardless of the social or historical context in which drug use occurs.[43]

Again, note how similar this finding is compared to the images of crime in the news media.

As for the issues of gender, race, and social class, women were more likely to appear as problematic drug users, in spite of the fact that men are more likely to use drugs than women. Further, women's drug use "was also generally linked with sexual degradation and exploitation by men, whether through involvement in the sex trade or through trading drugs for sexual access." Drug addicted characters were most often white; this may be due to the audience who reads the comic books. Blacks and Latinos more commonly made up "background characters" as part of "an impoverished inner city landscape."[44]

Perhaps not surprisingly given the fact that we are talking about comic books, the police, courts, and corrections are not widely featured. This helped justify violence of the superhero as "the dominant mechanism of punishment for drug criminals. Daredevil, Spider-Man, Green Arrow, Green Lantern, and Catwoman were among the heroic figures that repeatedly beat up drug dealers, without legal constraint or reprisal. Within these narratives, drug dealers received the same type of violent treatment that had been meted out to more exotic supervillains on a monthly basis." As such, vigilante justice is seen as normal.[45]

The Superhero

The most studied aspect of comic books is superheroes. Scholars have asserted that Superman is a symbol of both justice and power, whereas Batman represents vigilante justice.[46] Superman can also be seen as a protector of the status quo, for even though he inevitably captures "the bad guy," he never questions the structural conditions that produce him (or her). Instead, crime is depicted as a function of individual pathologies.[47]

As noted by Scott Vollum and Cary Adkinson:

> The messages portrayed in the comic book superhero mythos are clear. We are being told that we must preserve the status quo, or, as Superman might put it, "democracy and the American way;" threats to the status quo must be extinguished. We are presented with a world in which there is clearly right and wrong, good and evil. Good must prevail and social order must be maintained. The dominant hegemony is safe in the hands of the comic book superhero.[48]

This suggests comic books share one significant characteristic with news media when it comes to depictions of crime—a pro status quo message.

One of the most recent depictions of Batman, shown in movie theaters across the country, suggests to viewers that vigilantism is necessary because individual rights are dysfunctional and interfere with law and order.[49] Batman even goes as far to institute spying on all citizens in order to identify an enemy, but only temporarily and to prevent a major attack on citizens.[50]

Scott Vollum and Cary Adkinson add that Superman represents the "idealism of urban justice" whereas Batman represents the "realism of urban crime."[51] Further, according to depictions of Superman:

> law and the justice system are bright and shining examples of "the good guys." Law and justice must always prevail and are always to be respected ... For Batman, things are not so clear-cut. The line between good and evil is blurred. Those representing law and justice are not always the good guys ... there are corrupt officials and irresponsible law enforcement officers. It is no surprise that Batman feels compelled to work outside the confines of the law, while Superman works only within the bounds of the law.[52]

Part of these realities are due to the nature of the threats faced by each superhero. In the former case, they come from outside the community, whereas in the latter, they come from within:

Both superheroes contend with many of the same types of criminals, however. Faceless, nameless "thugs" and "hoodlums" are common in both Metropolis and Gotham City. Stereotypical gangsters and members of organized crime groups are also common foes. The difference is that in Superman's world such criminals are represented as outsiders who threaten the peace and social order in Metropolis. In Batman's world such criminals are depicted as *products* of Gotham City, part of the social fabric in which those on both sides of the law exist.[53]

Interestingly, both figures seem to favor a conservative view of the law, crime, and punishment. Common themes found in stories featuring these heroes include: the law is too lenient on criminals; the law favors the rights of criminals over the rights of victims; and society does not respect authority.[54] Again, each of these messages is commonly found in news media depictions of crime and criminal justice, as shown in the book.

True Crime

True crime refers to books about crime that "look[] like crime fiction. If one goes into a chain bookstore today, one will find a large section of books called 'crime' and a much smaller one called 'true crime.' The large section consists of crime fiction; the second consists of crime fact. This is crime fact of a specific kind: a species of paperback sociology that, for the most part, retells real-life cases of crime. However, these popular real-life case histories do their retelling by following the conventions of crime fiction."[55] While many specific true crime books are found across the nation's bookstores—especially when it comes to nationally known crimes committed by serial killers and mass murderers—others are unique to local bookstores because they depict local crimes that would be of interest to citizens in the area.

While it is not possible to summarize the nature of all true crime books, it is fair to say that the books tend to be focused on violent (and often especially heinous) crimes that were committed by a local person against another local person (or people). True crime books often start with the commission of the crime then work backwards to tell the story of what happened leading up to the crime (including the life stories of the offenders and victims) and then concluding with the outcome of the case (e.g., trial and punishment). The books are educational in the sense that they often report facts that have been widely reported in the media but are also meant to be entertaining and thus they often read like novels. Essentially, the true crime genre in books can be seen as infotainment TV (e.g., 48 Hours Mystery) for people who like to read rather than watch.

War as a Game

Roger Stahl suggests that America's war on terror has much in common with today's popular video games. He writes "the media paradigm by which we understand war is increasingly the video game. War is now a consumer commodity and video game players (gamers) can even take part in the war on terror in games."[56] Given what was noted earlier about how the first Gulf war was presented to Americans through the media, it is perhaps easy to understand how many citizens might see our real wars as not much more than what they see their children playing on many of today's popular video games.

Shooter games, like this one where the player takes on space aliens, are highly popular especially among young males. http://fsg-online.ucoz.de/.

There are literally thousands of so-called "shooter" games and games that simulate modern warfare. For example, web searches of "shooter games," "popular shooter video games," and "war video games" resulted in thousands of results. A complete summary of these games is beyond the scope of this book (and it is highly likely that the reader of this book has much more experience with these games since the author has none!), but these games share the elements of allowing the player to be in the shoes of a killer (e.g., a murderer, special agent, soldier, etc.) and to utilize various weaponry to kill other people (whether it be the enemy or just an innocent bystander).

These games have received enormous attention from parents and violence-prevention organizations over concern that playing these games may increase violence in those who play them. Given the research reviewed in Chapter 4, this seems like a legitimate concern.

It is hypothesized that being exposed to violent video games desensitizes people to violence—meaning diminished responsiveness to violence in the real world and possibly reduced inhibitions against aggressive behavior. The desensitization occurs because of changes to the brains of those being exposed to the violence, changes which are real and can be long-lasting.[57]

Whether violence in video games actually leads to violent behavior in the real world is debatable, but games like "Grand Theft Auto" (named after a felonious crime) that allow you to speed, crash, run over and kill people, shoot police officers, rape prostitutes, etc. are at the very least highly questionable forms of entertainment.

For more informaton about violence in video games, see the website for this book at: www.pscj.appstate.edu/media/videoviolence.html

---

COPS

As noted earlier, the television show *COPS* is perhaps the most successful infotainment show ever made. The show *COPS* has been produced since 1989 by the Fox Network. The show features police-approved selections of video showing incidents of police-citizen encounters. The show has been described as using a "highly stylized" manner[58] featuring a "truncated and sensationalized" process.[59] The show's content is controlled by the police because the agreement "to have cameras in the cruisers" means that the police have "full editorial control over the footage."[60]

As Mark Cavender and Gray Fishman note:

> The producers of *COPS* need permission to ride in patrol cars and to film in station houses. In order to get high-quality video or rich details in a pending case, cooperation between media and police is absolutely necessary. In exchange for this cooperation, those who produce

reality programs cannot or will not exercise independent and critical judgment of law enforcement agencies.[61]

Ryan Cotter, Willem de Lint, and Daniel O'Connor explain that *COPS* is so popular because "it functions to legitimate existing relations in which police retain a primary role in re-ordering strained and frayed edges of the social fabric."[62] To the producers of the show, it has the advantages of being cheap to produce as well as nicely adaptable to various situations.[63]

Although viewers likely believe what they are seeing is real (and it is in the sense that viewers are seeing something that actually happened), it is not realistic because it is more aimed at entertainment than providing information. Ray Surette explains that: "Despite their use of the trappings of traditional news and journalism, crime reality shows are thinly disguised entertainment, and the reality that they construct is not pretty. They mix reconstructions, actors, and interviews and employ camera angles, music, lighting, and sets to enhance their dramatic and entertainment elements."[64]

Robin Andersen explains that what makes such shows appear real is their formats, including "live action shots with extensive use of hand-held cameras, the absence of reenactment or dramatizations, and the lack of a narrative voice." Yet, these shows are partial and acontextual because we are not told of "what has come before or what will come later ... We are not ... privy to prior events, interior thoughts, or motivations; there are no second- or third-person perspective offered to provide a context for the action at hand." Further, the shows are expedited—they deny "enormous gaps in time and space—gaps that do not register consciously."[65] Even worse, according to Peter Manning, "the tapes are edited ... by the show's producers to heighten dramatic incidents; remove dubious violent, illegal, or racist incidents; and polish and create apparent continuity in the narrative."[66] To the degree that episodes are edited, then what viewers see is not real.

Others agree.[67] The show uses "live action shots with extensive use of hand-held cameras." Further, it does not include "reenactments or dramatizations" and does not use a narrative voice. However, these nightly representations of officers "pursuing drug dealers and other 'criminals' are social constructions. Masquerading as reality, these selected sequences drawn from the immediacy of live events form nothing more than stories."[68]

Of course, an obvious way in which shows like *COPS* are unreal is that they are condensed into very short time periods. *COPS* episodes run a mere 30 minutes (including commercials). In this time, several crimes are responded to, investigated, and solved. This creates the illusion of a highly effective police department. Other shows like *Law & Order* last only one hour (including commercials), and in this time, a crime occurs, is investigated, prosecuted all the way through trial, and it subsequently leads to some form of closure for all those involved. With regard to *COPS*, the "'crime' is condensed into mere minutes of soundbites ..."[69]

Such shows depict no boredom, which is a fundamental part of everyday policing, and also provide very little in the way of the context in which the crimes occur. Thus, the show helps reinforce misconceptions of policing created by news coverage of police, as shown in Chapter 5. According to Robin Andersen: "Instead of providing details, a contrived order provides plot progression and a seeming sense of resolution, even while the events themselves are usually left unresolved. The narrative is structured to provide a definite beginning and end, always opening with 'us' riding as passengers in a police patrol car and finishing with 'us' in the same position." As such, we are partners with the police and the criminal is "not us" but instead is "them," the enemy.

The very notion of "us versus them" is false. In fact, there is no such thing as a non-criminal. All of us are criminals. As noted in Chapter 3, some people start committing crimes earlier than others, some commit more serious crimes than others, and some persist in crime over their entire lives while most mature out of crime, but all of us are criminals.[70] The belief in a unique criminal population and a unique non-criminal population is a myth, what Matthew Robinson calls a "dualistic fallacy."[71]

Media coverage of crime, focused largely on street crime and on poor minorities, is a form of labeling whereby certain segments of the society are identified as bad, deviant, or immoral.[72] In this process, evil is dramatized, and the notion of "us" versus "them" is reinforced, because we tend to think of criminals as being different from us. When constantly shown images of crime and criminals in the media, viewers get the sense that "we" are different from "them." After all, we are part of the police force as viewers; we are in the car with the police, we are in the chase with police, and they talk to us as if we are part of the team. Offenders featured on such shows are the "them," not "us."

According to Gray Cavendar and Mark Fishman, *control talk* is a form of language used to typify crime and the policies that should be used to deal with it. "Control talk" seeks to make the criminals appear "different" from the rest of society. It seeks to portray an "us against them" model of crime in society.[73] Sarah Eschholz, Matthew Mallard, and Stacey Flynn add that control talk "works to portray our society as separated into good citizens and bad criminals."[74] Given that minorities and especially blacks and Hispanics are portrayed negatively, as offenders rather than victims, it is safe to assume that this serves to separate them from "good citizens."

Such shows also reinforce the belief that most offenders are black. For example, Robin Andersen writes: "Drug consumers and dealers are overwhelmingly white and middle class. But you wouldn't know this from watching reality cop shows."[75] Andersen evaluates the show *Night Beat* and finds that it regularly features predominantly white cops riding on city streets looking for poor, urban, black drug dealers.

The "them" is typically a minority, especially a black person. According to Ray Surette, "nonwhites account for more than half of all suspects shown, about two-thirds of police are white, and more than half of the victims shown are white ... the most typical police crime-fighting events are white police battling nonwhite criminals while protecting white victims."[76]

The television show *COPS* tends to focus more on blacks than any other groups. Andersen notes that this show and others like it involve citizens

> as police partners in an unwinnable war against the poor, seeing the 'mean streets' of unnamed cities through the eyes of hero cops who are seemingly incapable of doing anything but good, because they always 'get their man.' Never mind that their 'man' is always young and black and living in the poorest parts of the poorest cities in the country.[77]

Shows like *COPS* characterize criminals as minorities who are typified as more threatening or suffering from some form of insanity.[78] The shows also unfairly cover those with mental illness, especially shows like *World's Wildest Police Videos* where many drivers featured on the show are referred to as "deranged," "manic," "lunatic," and "crazy."[79] Recall that these findings hold true for news media coverage of crime as well.

A study of 60 episodes of the widely popular show *COPS* broadcast between May 16th and July 1st, 2005 included 231 incidents. Nearly three out of four (72%) of the incidents focused on violent crime.[80] Other studies of the program from different time periods found the show featured between 65% and 87% incidents of violent crime.[81] By comparison to earlier analyses of the show, the authors of the most recent study of *COPS* suggests that "representations of violent and victimless crime have decreased as a problem on *COPS*, while property crime incidents have more than doubled and domestic crimes have increased by more than 82 percent."[82]

Shows like COPS and others tend to focus on the most violent, random, and bizarre stories while ignoring more routine calls for service. Presentations of police are often over-dramatized and romanticized by fictional television crime dramas.[83]

The message of such shows is that offenders are quite dangerous, people who are best dealt with through aggressive or violent policing. Another study of *America's Most Wanted* found criminals were depicted as violent and intractable 77% of the time.[84]

When compared to the reality of street crime, as reflected in Uniform Crime Report (UCR) data, it is easy to see that the show is disproportionately focused on violent crime. This should not be surprising given the focus of the media on violent crime, as shown in Chapter 3. Recall that, according to the UCR, the vast majority of crime is committed against property.

The authors of the study on the show *COPS* write that "findings confirm the suggestion that minorities are disproportionately represented as responsible for the majority of index crimes (especially violent crimes) in the media, they also suggest a shift in representation whereby minorities are now more than twice as likely to be associated with drug offences."[85] This led the authors to conclude that the "representation of crime on *COPS* is an inverted, mirror image of the other reality-based encodings of crime, namely the official statistical representations of crime presented in the UCR."[86] This is the *law of opposites*— what we see in the media about crime is often the opposite of reality.[87]

The television show *COPS* also overrepresents clearance rates in comparison with actual UCR crime statistics. That is, in the show, police are far more likely than in reality to make an arrest after the occurrence of a crime. In reality, only about 40% of all crimes in the U.S. are even known to the police and only about 10% of all crimes will lead to an arrest.[88] The show thus creates the misperception that police are more effective than they really are.

Further, and perhaps more importantly, the authors assert that the show serves two very important functions for society:

> First, it serves to manage generalized anxieties about problems in the social order by steering the focus, repetitively, to select problems and their solutions. The focus is crimes of violence and vice, where violence is seen to stem from problems related to the character of domestic relations and vice is a problem of drugs associated with minority populations. We see in these associations larger political messages that define social problems in terms of declining family values. By folding back social and political anxieties on the presumed failing institutions of family and ethnic solidarity, *COPS* supports the ongoing legitimization of existing social and political relations. Second, *COPS* is proactive in presenting a pro-policing reality. Through their capacity to arrest crime by arresting criminals, police are seen to be highly effective instruments of social order. While predominantly white and male, they are also seen to successfully intervene in support of both the domestic sphere and minority groups. In this way police on *COPS* serve as heroic figures of the collectivity, representing support for the family, ethic solidarity, and hope for their reconstitution.[89]

The show *COPS* thus creates the perception that police officers are effective, controlled, non-corrupt, and fair, and that police generally solve crimes which tend to be overwhelmingly violent in nature.[90]

Night Beat

Robin Andersen provides another example of policing infotainment in her analysis of the prime-time news special called *Night Beat*. The show featured mostly white police officers

> cruising city streets in search of … dealers. The typical "*Night Beat*" scenario involves cops and camera crew suddenly charging out of a police van or cruiser in hot pursuit of young, black thugs. The daring foot chase usually ends with a flying leap as one of the pursuing cops tackles the young suspect to the ground, where his hands are wrestled behind his back and manacled. One or more young men lie cuffed on the street while the cop, panting heavily, begins to work off a little of the adrenaline accumulated from the chase.

As a result of such depictions of drug users, "the drug crisis came to be defined as a black, urban problem—even though white drug use continued to predominate. The official televisual icon of the war on drugs became the young, black, street-dealer 'thug.' "[91] Other research documents the stereotypical portrayals of blacks in television shows such as *COPS*.[92]

Data from the National Criminal Victimization Survey reflect the reality of criminal victimization (from street crime) in the United States. For example, in 2008, blacks suffered 26 violent victimizations per 1,000 people, versus only 18 per 1,000 for whites and 15 per 1,000 for people of other races. Rates of homicide are usually about six times higher for blacks than people of other races.[93] Rather than reflecting the reality that blacks are disproportionately likely to be victims of crime, shows like *Night Beat* and *COPS* help create the conception that blacks are more likely to be offenders; they are thus viewed as dangerous as opposed to endangered.

The show *Night Beat* regularly shows police officers being disrespectful even to law-abiding citizens and threatening and using excessive force. The show also creates disrespect for civil liberties. Andersen explains: "Constitutional assumptions about due process and civil liberties, such as protections against unwarranted search and seizure and the presumption of innocence, are antithetical to the crime-tabloid formula, which does not conceal its approval of the abuse of police power."[94] This is similar to news accounts of police, as shown in Chapter 5.

Given that television shows are more aimed at entertaining than informing, it is probably not surprising that television dramas tend to "provide viewers with an inaccurate representation of police work, overemphasizing sensational and dramatic activities while underemphasizing routine duties."[95] A study of children showed that police activities shown on television (e.g., using guns, engaging in high speed chases) were perceived by children to be accurate in terms of what police actually do. This suggests that the media are a major source of misconceptions of policing, just as they are of misconceptions of crime. Such findings also remind us how important the media can be for helping to inform people's *symbolic reality*, that reality learned through sources such as the media rather than directly experienced.

Law & Order

Another popular television show, like *COPS* in that it focuses on law enforcement (as well as prosecutors), but unlike *COPS* in that it is often based on actual events rather than being presented as "reality," is *Law & Order*. The show is both a policing show and a courts show because it focuses equally on these two components of criminal justice.

Law & Order aired first in 1990 and thus is now twenty years old. According to Gayle Rhineberger-Dunn, Nicole Rader, and Kevin Williams, the show was "the longest-running crime series and the second-longest-running drama series in the history of television. Only *The Simpsons* and *60 Minutes* have been on the air longer."[96] The show has only recently been cancelled, in 2010.

The show is divided roughly into two equal parts, the first focusing on the crime and investigation of the crime by the police, and the second part of the show on the prosecution at trial of the alleged offender. The opening audio of the show describes the nature of the show: "In the criminal justice system, the people are represented by two separate yet equally important groups, the police who investigate crime, and the district attorneys who prosecute the offenders. These are their stories." There are numerous problems with this introductory statement. First, there is actually no such thing as a criminal justice *system*. Criminal justice agencies, because they are not integrated, organized, and working harmoniously toward a shared goal, are better described as a *network*. Networks are separate parts (like police, courts, and corrections) of a whole that are interdependent but not well organized.[97] This may seem like a small difference, but actually it is quite significant. The notion of a *system* suggests a well functioning and effective whole; criminal justice agencies are nothing like this.

Second, police do not investigate crime but instead investigate alleged crime. Oftentimes, people call the police thinking they have been victimized by crime only to find out that a crime has not occurred. Third, district attorneys prosecute alleged offenders, not offenders. Recall that in America, suspects are supposedly presumed "innocent until proven guilty" in a court of law beyond a reasonable doubt. While this is just a subtle example of a problem with the show, the point is that it shows clearly that viewers of the show likely get the impression that people who are arrested and prosecuted are guilty, and that they will be processed in an effective, efficient way.

A major problem with shows like *Law & Order* is that they create misconceptions about what courtroom officers such as prosecutors are supposed to do. Attorneys depicted on television and in film are typically shown as only being concerned with fighting crime. The prosecutor is shown as fighting for the "people" in an effort to "get justice" for the crime victim and the community. His or her main job is to decide whether or not to press charges on the basis of the amount of quality evidence available to obtain a conviction. If the prosecution decides to press criminal charges, the next decision is to decide which charges to press. This role — *trial counsel for police* (fighting crime) — is common in the media. Another commonly depicted role in the media is *house counsel for police* (e.g., giving legal advice). Examples of the role of house counsel for the police include giving legal advice to the police, testifying in court, and so forth. In both cases, the prosecutor is shown as partner with the police in the fight against crime.[98]

Yet, prosecutors are also *representatives of the court* and thus they must be concerned with justice as a process. A prosecutor is thus "obliged to protect the rights of the defendant."[99] There is evidence, however, that many prosecutors ignore possible indications of innocence of defendants simply in order to gain convictions and clear cases.[100] Further, this role of the prosecutor is generally not very popular in the media.

The "dominant popular image" of the prosecutor and of courtroom activity comes from television and films. According to Ray Surette, the "soap opera format" has been applied to "TV courtroom dramas."[101] Not surprisingly, the show *Law & Order* is often quite dramatic and has successfully managed to weave into the show's plots personal stories about the main characters.

The show led to three spin-offs, two of which still air, including *Law & Order Criminal Intent* and *Law & Order Special Victims Unit*. A study of seasons 1 through 15 of the original series examined the way that juvenile offenders are depicted on the show. It found that *Law & Order usually* portrays the juvenile offenders as violent 16- to17-year-old white males who are "currently attending school and treated as an adult in the court process." Specifically, most offenders were in school (100%), white (91%), and male (81%). Further, of those where social class was apparent, the largest percentage was made up of lower to middle class status children (44%). When Blacks were (rarely) shown as offenders, they tended to be shown "as financially motivated, impoverished, and drug addicted offenders."[102] Interestingly, the general depiction of white offenders instead of black offenders is not consistent with news media coverage of crime, which tends to depict blacks as offenders more commonly, as shown in Chapter 4. This may be a function of who is viewing the show.

Perhaps not surprisingly, the crimes for which the juveniles were being tried were almost all murder, and almost all of them were tried in adult courts rather than juvenile courts. The authors conclude: "*Law & Order* does not appear to consider juvenile delinquency as an urgent social problem. While the most common motivations represent individual and rational-choice based theories, there is also a superficial discussion of sociological explanations for crime and delinquency." Specifically, four major motivation categories were found by the authors — financial gain, rational choice, emotional turmoil, and medical/psychological deficiencies.[103] These are consistent with the dominant motivations of offenders shown in the news media, as shown in Chapter 4.

Another study of the show examined evidence of how the mentally ill were depicted in *Law & Order*.[104] The study found that 7% of the 267 episodes studied included the element, "not guilty by reason of insanity." Compare this with the real world, where the plea is offered only between 0.9% and 1.5% of the time. With regard to the larger issue of how mental illness is characterized in the show, the authors found three major themes. They included: 1) personal responsibility and how it relates to criminal behavior; 2) human nature and good versus evil; and 3) problems with the legal and mental health systems when dealing with the mentally ill.

According to Rachel Gans-Boriskin and Claire Wardle, the most common depictions of the mentally ill on crime dramas "are that they lack social identity, are single, unemployed, dangerous, and unpredictable."[105] Further, they are depicted as violent, even when they generally are not. Recall from Chapter 3 that the mentally ill are no more violent than the rest of us, and that violence is only more likely when a person suffers from delusions, is abusing drugs, and is not being successfully treated.

A study of the spinoff show, *Law & Order Special Victims Unit*, examined the entire 2003–2004 season, including twenty-five one-hour episodes.[106] The study found that 48% of the programs did *not* focus on sex crimes, even though when the show started it was billed as a program that focused on these offenses in particular. Instead, "many of the programs focused on the murder of white males." Further, a large majority of the crimes on the show "are extremely brutal, and may serve to connect rape and murder in the viewer's mind. Almost 60% of the victims on 'SVU' were dead by the end of the program." In reality, most rape victims survive and do not require hospitalization for their injuries.[107]

However, as in reality, "the majority of criminal cases on 'SVU' did not involve strangers, but involved individuals who knew one another. Unlike reality, most rapes shown were not spousal or date rapes." [108]

About half of the victims on the show were under the age of 18 "compared to NCVS reports that suggest the actual figure is closer to one-quarter or all victims." Further, nearly two-thirds of the crimes on the show featured white victims, "while in Manhattan the majority of victims are minorities." Further, black females "were almost completely missing as rape victims on 'SVU,' despite the fact that they are the group most at risk for sexual assault."[109]

Recall from Chapter 1 that the main goal of the media is to make a profit. Perhaps those who write and cast for these shows know that since black females do not make up a sizeable portion of the audience, it is acceptable to exclude them from roles on the show and target the shows to the largest portion of the audience, whites (and especially young white males). Yet, ignoring minority victims—who make up the largest portion of street crime victims—does a disservice to those victims as well as anyone else who wants to understand the realities of crime in America.

As for offenders, women were overrepresented as offenders on the show. For example, in reality, "females commit just 5% of the sexual assaults and murders in Manhattan, [but] on 'SVU' females commit more than one-third of these offenses. Men on the other hand commit 95% of the rapes, murders and manslaughters in Manhattan, NY, but only 63% of similar crimes on 'SVU.'" Not only were women shown as more likely to be offenders than in reality, when featured, they were "particularly manipulative and cruel in their planning and execution of violent crimes. For example, one mother hired a man to kill her future son-in-law's ex-girlfriend and her unborn baby, so that her daughter would not have to compete with a baby and an ex-girlfriend for attention in her new marriage." Similarly, "female juvenile offenders were brutal, vindictive, petty and manipulative, where as the two juvenile male offenders were shown as victims of their circumstances."[110] These depictions serve as good examples of the *evil woman* hypothesis, introduced in Chapter 4.

As in the study of the original series, offenders on the show "are always identified, and almost always punished by the criminal justice system for their offenses."[111] In reality in Manhattan, NY less than one-half of murder and rape reports are cleared by arrest, only one-half of those lead to convictions. Yet, on the show, all of the crimes are cleared by arrest and 92% of the arrests result in a conviction. The authors thus conclude: "Combine this with the fact that the program exaggerates crimes against young white victims and the viewer is left with a vision of an efficient criminal justice system that fights for justice for stereotypical 'special' victims.[112]

Similar to other shows, such as COPS, the SVU program regularly featured civil rights violations "as part of doing business with heinous criminals." The authors note: "The importance of civil rights to the United States justice system are almost never mentioned on 'SVU,' instead violations of these rights are normalized and the implicit message is that suspects and offenders have too many rights. Combine this with frequent control talk, which implies an 'us' versus 'them' mentality, from police officers and the impression you are left with is that police officers need to resort to any means necessary to protect 'us' from 'them.' "[113] All of this is consistent with news media coverage of crime, as shown in Chapters 3 and 4.

NYPD Blue

The television show *NYPD Blue* was broadcast on ABC from 1993 until 2005. The show was created by Steven Bochco, who also brought forth the shows *Hill Street Blues*, and *L.A. Law*, among others. A study of *NYPD Blue* and *Law & Order* examined 44 one-hour episodes, with 20 episodes from *NYPD Blue* and 24 from *Law & Order*. The authors explain the significance of their study: "While these programs are fictional, they frequently borrow and sensationalize story lines from newspaper and television news headlines across the country. This blurring of fiction and reality may influence viewers' perceptions of the criminal justice system and criminal justice problems in the United States."[114]

One major finding of the study pertains to race. Whites were over-represented in all categories of characters on the show when compared to actual data from New York City, while Hispanic and other races were under-represented. Interestingly, the greatest disparity existed for criminal justice personnel where only 5% of criminal justice personnel on *NYPD Blue* and 2% of criminal justice personnel on *Law & Order* were non-white.

Additionally:

> African Americans and 'others' have a statistically significant higher ratio than Whites of being portrayed as offenders to other character roles in six and seven (respectively) out of the ten comparisons. On *NYPD Blue*, African Americans have a higher ratio of being portrayed as an offender than a victim, CJ personnel, police or attorney, than their White counterparts. On *Law & Order*, African Americans have a higher

ratio of handcuffed offender to offender (with handcuffed offenders appearing more dangerous), offender to victim, and offender to attorney than their White counterparts. In four of these cases for Blacks and seven of these cases for Hispanics, minorities are at least twice as likely to be shown as offenders than in other roles than their White counterparts. Neither program showed a single Hispanic attorney with a speaking role during their 2000 seasons.[115]

Both of these shows are set in New York City. According to the U.S. Census, as of 2008, blacks make up 17% of the population, and Hispanics also make up 17% of the population.[116] These groups are vastly underrepresented on these shows.

Men were most shown in all roles and especially as offenders. As for females, they were most likely to be depicted in "positive and sympathetic roles, such as victim or CJ personnel including police officers and lawyers, than as offenders, compared to their male counterparts."

Both *NYPD Blue* and *Law & Order* tended to focus on homicide (79% and 92%, respectively), which exaggerates how common homicide is in New York City. The shows also focus on unique kinds of murders. For example, 50% of murders on *NYPD Blue* and 46% of murders on *Law & Order* were committed with firearms, even though about 60% of real murders are committed with guns: "Alternatively, knives and cutting instruments are overrepresented on *NYPD Blue* (21% compared to UCR's 13%), blunt objects are overrepresented on *Law & Order* (17% compared to UCR's 5%) and personal weapons (hands, feet, etc.) are disproportionately shown on both *NYPD Blue* (23%) and *Law & Order* (17%) compared to UCR (7%)." This can lead to misconceptions of murder among viewers.

Both shows also depict police officers and prosecuting attorneys as more likely to close cases and obtain convictions than in reality, just as with other popular shows discussed earlier. Further, "civil rights violations are often used to obtain evidence and confessions, including no Miranda warning, physical abuse, forced confessions, and promises of leniency." This may reinforce the belief among viewers that the Miranda warnings, the exclusionary rule, and other protections granted to suspects are unnecessary (which would logically reinforce support for the crime control model). The *exclusionary rule*, applied to the states in the 1961 Supreme Court case, *Mapp v. Ohio*, states that any evidence obtained illegally by the police is not admissible into criminal proceedings against suspects. Yet, as our nation's wars on crime, drugs and terrorism have intensified, numerous exceptions have been created that allow police to get around the exclusionary rule.

🖰 For more informaton about the exclusionary rule, see the website for this book at: www.pscj.appstate.edu/media/exclusionaryrule.html

---

Physical brutality was especially prevalent on *NYPD Blue*. Officers frequently shoved suspects, and in some cases witnesses and informants, into walls and onto police cruisers, and punched or kicked suspects in the course of an arrest."[117] Finally, insulting language was prevalent in both programs. As explained by the author, these findings are significant: "The 'us' against 'them' mentality pervading the programs often depicted the criminals as less than human, where any means necessary was appropriate for the their capture" ... implying "that incarceration is the only way to deal with these offenders. Treatment, probation and parole are rarely addressed as options, and their occasional mention is usually in a negative light."[118] These findings help reinforce the dualistic fallacy created by the news media that was noted in Chapter 4, the notion that criminals are different than non criminals.

Another analysis of the television show *NYPD Blue* suggested that the show depicted some Constitutional protections (such as the Fifth Amendment right to freedom from self-incrimination) as unnecessary. Christopher Wilson writes:

> To many, of course, that *Miranda* is habitually circumvented on TV is hardly a secret. Even New York Police Commissioner William Bratton ... has voiced his concern over *N.Y.P.D. Blue*'s apparent indifference to due process. Like Constitutional experts and police analysts, media scholars have long been (and rightly) concerned about the presence of coercion in interrogations, and whether cop shows' indifference to these matters undermine public respect for law. Because these shows present due process rights as technicalities hampering police work.[119]

This is significant because the show was quite popular in the 1990s, won Emmy awards, and was even popular among police officers.

Interestingly, in the case of *U.S. v. Dickerson* (2000), the U.S. Supreme Court upheld the *Miranda* requirements by a vote of 7–2. At issue was a 1968 federal law that allowed voluntary confessions by suspects to be admitted into court even if the defendant had not been read his or her rights. This law conflicted with the Supreme Court's decision in *Miranda v. Arizona* (1966). Chief Justice William Rehnquist (quite the conservative) wrote the majority opinion of the Court, in which he stated: "We hold that *Miranda*, being a constitutional decision of this Court, may not be ... overruled by an Act of Congress, and we decline to overrule *Miranda* ourselves. We therefore hold that *Miranda* and its progeny in this Court govern the admissibility of statements made during custodial interrogation in both state and federal courts."

Rehnquist added that because the "advent of modern custodial police interrogation brought with it an increased concern about confessions obtained by
coercion," *Miranda* requirements were considered more important than ever by
the Court. Rehnquist wrote, for example, that being questioned by the police places
a "heavy toll on individual liberty and trades on the weakness of individuals."

Ironically, the appeal of the original 1966 *Miranda* decision did not come
from a law enforcement agency. In fact, most police administrators have always believed that *Miranda* provides an important protection for all Americans. They recognize that reading *Miranda* warnings to suspects is part of their
professional responsibility of upholding the Constitutional right of suspects
not to incriminate themselves. Because police have always been able to use
strategies to convince suspects to waive their right not to incriminate themselves, *Miranda* is not and never has been a major impediment to effective
policing.

Edward Lazarus, wrote (about three weeks before the decision came down):

> As matters currently stand, when police officers fail to observe *Miranda*,
> judges almost always limit themselves ... to finding "technical" violations
> of *Miranda*, thereby allowing prosecutors to use evidence derived from
> challenged confessions and to keep defendants from testifying in their
> own defense. Judges almost never take the extra step of finding a con-
> fession to be actually involuntary—which would deprive the prosecu-
> tion of any evidence obtained as a resulted of the tainted confession.[120]

Indeed, in practice, and wholly apart from the much-debated issue of whether
Miranda inhibits police from obtaining confessions, the ruling has become
largely symbolic. It allows judges to scold police for misbehavior and pay lip
service to the right against self-incrimination, while minimizing the actual effect on police and prosecutors.

In 2000, the Court ruled that *Miranda* warnings have become intertwined
with the fabric of American society. That is, *Miranda* protects a right that is
crucial to being free from unwarranted government interference into our lives,
a right that is so cherished by Americans that it cannot be eliminated by Court
order. Unfortunately, popular crime television shows threaten the value of Miranda warnings and other Constitutional protections.

CSI

The show, *CSI: Crime Scene Investigation* (*CSI*), is among the most popular shows on television each year. Further, it has generated two successful spin-

offs, including *CSI: Miami* and *CSI: NY*. More than forty million people watch *CSI* every week in the United States.[121]

Aside from the interest it has generated in criminal justice and forensics among college and university students,[122] it has created the illusion in citizens that "science and the police are virtually infallible." According to Sarah Deutsch and Gray Cavender: "*CSI* constructs the illusion of science through its strategic web of forensic facticity. Ironically, although *CSI* depicts unrealistic crimes in a melodramatic fashion, this crime drama does so in a manner that suggests that its science is valid, that the audience understands science and can use it to solve crimes."[123] As noted by Thomas Hughes and Megan Magers: "The captivating television shows focused on criminal investigations and forensic techniques may not only be providing viewers with entertainment but may also be leading them to have certain expectations about criminal cases and the administration of justice."[124]

Hughes and Magers assert that shows like *CSI*

> may create expectations in minds of jurors regarding the use and necessity of forensic evidence. In reaction to these media-generated beliefs, courtroom actors create practices designed to cater to a jury member's expectations of best practices rather than the actual logical dictates of a case. The potential impact of *CSI* has not escaped the show's creator, Anthony E. Zuiker, who observes, 'The CSI Effect is, in my opinion, the most amazing thing that has ever come out of the series. For the first time in American history, you're not allowed to fool the jury anymore.

Deutsch and Cavender studied the 23 episodes of the 2000–2001 season, which included 74 unique cases. Of these cases, 72% were violent in nature, and the most common crime depicted was murder. As with all other significant criminal justice shows on television, *CSI* helps create the misconception that most crime is violent.

Of the murders, 77% were committed by males, 19% by females, and 4% by unknown offenders. 87% of the murderers were White, 6% were Black, and 6% were unknown. And 91% of murder victims were White. This finding likely reflects the audience that watches the show. Males made up 66% of murder victims, versus 32% female victims. Further, 62% of murder victims knew their attackers, and in 36% of the murders, victims were murdered by strangers. This is, again, not consistent with reality. In reality, males are about four times more likely than women to be murdered. Further, in reality, only 14% of people murdered in 2005 were killed by strangers while the largest portion (45%) it was not known who committed the murders.[125]

Lane Crothers describes the nature of violence on *CSI* as both graphic and dehumanizing. He notes that "through computer animation the audience sees bullets penetrate skin, shatter bones, and slice through arteries, leading to arcs of blood spurting across the screen and splattering across walls."[126] Such depictions are unnecessary aside from their entertainment value; they place the show in the same genre as some slasher films that depict violence for the mere sake of showing blood and gore.

Like with the other popular policing shows, in the *CSI* episodes virtually every crime was solved. According to Deutsch and Cavender: "These media presentations provide a kind of ideological closure that cloaks the infallibility of the police with the mantle of science. Such closure tends to forestall critical questions about policing in the United States."[127]

Images of policing have increasingly become unrealistically scientific, captured best in the CSI effect. Marcia Mardis summarizes the meaning of this term, writing: "The *CSI: Crime Scene Investigation* television series has become a pop culture juggernaut. It has spawned what many scientists and lawyers call 'The CSI Effect,' in which forensic science is seen as fascinating, exhaustive, and infallible."[128] The majority of research onto the impact of television shows such as CSI have been conducted with regard to the impact of the depiction of forensic sciences in crime scene investigations on the courts (e.g., on its impact on prosecutors and jurors). This research was reviewed in Chapter 6.

In terms of public perceptions, it is clear that shows such as *CSI* tend to create misconceptions about policing in the minds of the public. Most police work does not deal with criminality; that portion that does rarely leads to meaningful forensic investigations. The myth is that most crimes are solved with science. In fact, most crimes are never solved. The relatively few crimes that are solved (about 20 percent of those reported to the police) owe their solution to human evidence and mundane investigative work more often than to science.[129]

The popular show *Forensics Files* also helps create the false perception that forensic sciences are usually involved in solving crimes (when in fact they seldom are). Other shows that have a similar theme include *Body Of Evidence: From the Case Files of Dayle Hinman*, *Cold Case Files*, *The New Detectives*, and *American Justice*. Fictional series such as *Cold Case* and *Cold Squad* also drive home the perception that forensics are the gold standard for solving crime.

Cops in the media almost always solve their cases, when in reality there are many unsolved cases by police. In fact, the percentage of violent crimes cleared by arrest fell from 50% in 1999 to 44% in 2006.[130] Cases also tend to be solved quickly, when in reality even when crimes lead to an arrest, investigations often take a great deal of time and resources and the criminal justice process takes months if not years.

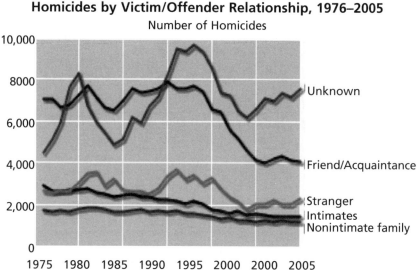

Homicides by Victim/Offender Relationship, 1976–2005

Number of Homicides

Over time, homicides by friends and acquaintances have generally fallen, meaning more homicides go unsolved by the police. This reality is not reflected in fictional crime dramas. http://ojp.usdoj.gov/bjs/homicide/relationship.htm.

Dawn Cecil analyzed 90 episodes of *CSI*, *Law & Order*, *Law & Order: Criminal Intent*, and *Without a Trace* and found that 43% of the episodes featured female offenders. This is similar to previous studies that found that women made up between 6 and 25% of offenders.[131] None of the programs studied by Cecil accurately depict the prevalence of female offenders. For example, women make up only a small portion of people arrested, convicted and incarcerated in prison in the United States. Further, the female offenders "are primarily shown as white, violent and driven by greed, revenge, and most commonly, love.[132] Cecil speculates that such portrayals are more supportive of punishment rather than rehabilitation.

According to Cecil:

> the reality of female offenders is missing from these crime dramas. For the most part these characters do not appear to suffer from real

problems. Instead these women are demonized. This demonization sends the message that these females are completely responsible for their criminal behavior, which over-endows them with agency. Furthermore, it ignores the social context in which female crime occurs, making it highly unlikely that the public will understand the role society plays in the creation of female criminality.[133]

An earlier analysis of the show *America's Most Wanted* found that female offenders tended to be older, diverse in terms of ethnicity, and greedy. According to Lisa Bond-Maupin: "These women were seductive, preoccupied with sex, and sexually manipulative. Their male victims were unable or unwilling to resist their sexual advances."[134] Once again, these depictions reinforce conservative, status quo, get tough on crime approaches. Further, the women were shown to be dangerous and in need of apprehension, which is consistent with the main purpose of the show.

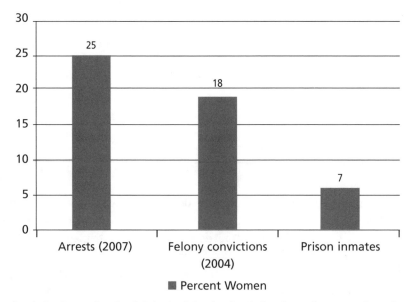

Data from the Sourcebook of Criminal Justice Statistics show that even though women make up more than half of the U.S. population, they make up only 25% of people arrested by the police, 18% of those convicted of felonies in state courts, and only 7% of those incarcerated in state and federal prisons.

The Practice

The television show, *The Practice*, was about a Boston law firm that ran on ABC from 1997 to 2004. A study examined murder in *Law and Order*, as well as *NYPD Blue* and *The Practice*.[135] The authors conclude: "The findings suggest that murder is presented fairly accurately such that viewers should come away with a basic understanding of the nature and circumstances surrounding murder, although they are likely to be somewhat misled that violence is common." In these shows, murder made up 63% of all crimes depicted, consistent with the notion that murder is overrepresented on such shows. On *Law and Order*, 75% of murders were committed by offenders against victims they knew while 25% involved strangers. According to the authors: "The largest category for known relationships was familial (42%) involving spouses, siblings, a parent killing a child, or a child killing a parent, followed by acquaintance (33%) including lovers." On *The Practice* 81% of murders involved known offenders and 19% involved strangers: "Both familial (35%) and acquaintance (35%) relationships were featured slightly more prominently than other known relationships (30%) such as doctor-patient, police-suspect and teacher-student." On *NYPD Blue*, 84% of murders involved people who knew each other versus 16% stranger murders: "acquaintance relationships emerged as the most common (48%) of the known relationships, followed by familial relationships (33%)."

Also consistent with the facts of most murders, the typical murder was male perpetrated, intraracial, and frequently committed in the home. Further, "television murders also highlight the use of handguns as the murder weapon of choice, although they under-represent knives and other cutting instruments as alternative weapon choices, instead emphasizing the use of body parts such as hands, feet and fists which are, in reality, less likely to be lethal." However, "television crime dramas tend to give the impression that most murders are meticulously planned. Indeed, the over-emphasis on planned murders on television masks the spontaneity of real-life murder, which is often the result of an argument or dispute or fuelled by alcohol and/or drugs."[136]

In terms of what motivated the murders on these shows, more than half (56%) of the murders occurred due to "emotive responses such as jealousy, anger, frustration, or fear. This bodes well with the research literature which emphasizes a predominance of expressive motives for real-life murder."[137] Also, 16% of the murders resulted from mental illness or defect, a gross misrepresentation of reality. Although sociologically-based explanations did exist in the shows, the explanations tended to be "fairly unsophisticated, simply blaming society for the individual offender's actions, or were somewhat obscure so that they were likely to go unnoticed by the average (non-criminology trained) viewer."[138]

Police in Film

There have been several analyses of action cop films and corrupt cop films.[139] The action films are probably best known and include the very popular *48 Hours, Beverly Hills Cop, Die Hard,* and *Lethal Weapon.* Although some of the earliest police films debuted in the 1940s and 1950s, the action cop films were probably most common in the 1980s and 1990s. An examination of popular films analyzed martial arts films "as a sub-genre of action-cop films."[140] The action-cop genre is typically portrayed in three acts; the first introduces the major players; the second shows the plot highlighted by conflict, and the third shows the resolution to the conflict, achieved through violence.[141] According to Robert Schehr, the final act is the "hero's redemption." This is when the hero "systematically eliminates the villain and his cohorts, each of whom suffers a unique and excessively violent death."[142] This is much like the plot of your typical comic book, discussed earlier.

Violent, vigilante type cops were more commonly depicted in film in the 1970s. The prime example is *Dirty Harry* starring Clint Eastwood. In the 1971 film, the character Harry Callahan uses violence and breaks the rules of due process to pursue criminals including a serial killer. Dirty Harry Callahan returns in this role in the films *Magnum Force* (1973), *The Enforcer* (1976) and *Sudden Impact* (1983). As the series progresses, the films get more violent, extreme, and unrealistic in their depictions of law enforcement.

Actor Clint Eastwood is depicted as vigilante cop, Dirty Harry, in this U.S. postal stamp. http://farm4.static. flickr.com/3278/2493132526_f687dd2811.jpg.

Films depicting corruption in law enforcement go back at least to the 1950s. Among the most well-known corruption films include *The Big Heat* (1953),

Magnum Force (1973), *Serpico* (1973), *Witness* (1985), *The Big Easy* (1987), *The Untouchables* (1987), *The Glass Shield* (1994), *L.A. Confidential* (1997), and *Training Day* (2001).

Joseph Gustafson examined several films depicting corruption in policing. According to Gustafson: "The typical corrupt cop film presents an honest or repentant cop as its protagonist. He is confronted with individual-level, small group, or systemic corruption within his department and offered an opportunity by his crooked peers to share in the spoils.[143] Typically, in films, he usually wins, but attaining victory is not easy and requires great sacrifice. Gustafson suggests that a common scene in such films is of the corrupt cop "reflecting on the reasons he became a cop or the expectations he had when he first came on the job." It is often this idealism that is pitted against higher-ups in the department and local politicians who are shown to be facilitating corruption. Interestingly, corruption is often shown to be emanating from efforts to assure public safety, and the corrupt are simply willing to do whatever it takes to bring about their crime control goals, consistent with the crime control model of criminal justice.

Timothy Lenz analyzed two classic crime-related films—*Dirty Harry* and *Death Wish*—as examples of films that depict the shift in the United States from liberal to conservative thinking about crime.[144] According to Lenz, "*Dirty Harry* is a classic cop film starring Clint Eastwood as Inspector Harry Callahan, a San Francisco homicide detective assigned the case of a serial killer named Scorpio." In the film, various "legal technicalities" are confronted by the lead character that frustrate his efforts to bring a killer to justice. The film *Death Wish* is a vigilante film where the lead character, Paul Benjamin, a New York City accountant, "becomes a vigilante after young thugs murder his wife and seriously injure his daughter." According to Lenz, "Kersey's personal journey from a bleeding-heart liberal, who sympathizes with the underprivileged who were driven by poverty to lives of crime, to a crime control conservative, who advocates vigilantism as a response to street crime, mirrors the nation's political transformation from liberalism to conservatism" or the shift from a due process model to a crime control model of criminal justice.[145]

According to Lenz, these two films "portray the problem of street crime as a manifestation of a broader political problem—the breakdown of social order caused by liberal ideas and legal policies. The solution, according to the conservative approach to crime control, is solving problems through violence and even vigilantism, stress the importance of order, and weakening individual rights if necessary.[146]

Court TV/truTV

There has been far less analysis of courts as a mechanism of infotainment. Modern coverage of trials in the media started with the O.J. Simpson murder case in 1995. The trial was shown virtually in its entirety on television. According to Surette, since this time, "the infotainment format has been incorporated into a number of contemporary media court-based productions. Currently, the social construction of the courts is rendered through a triumvirate of trial and law films, infotainment style pseudojudicial programs, and heavily publicized media co-opted live cases."[147] These media programs tend to focus on the most uncommon crimes (e.g., homicide) and the rare events (e.g., trials). This is, of course, very similar to the news media's coverage of crime.

The infotainment media portrayals of courts will necessarily be different than factual, objective accounts of court activity, for their goal is to entertain not inform. As such portrayals of courts in these media tend to be brief, time-limited, dramatic, and focused on elements such as random violence, sex, and cases involving celebrities.

A good example of this type of coverage comes from *truTV*, which was originally referred to as *Court TV*. *Court TV* was a popular network that hosted many crime- and criminal justice-themed shows. Recently, *Court TV* partnered with CNN to form *truTV* "to deliver online live trial coverage and the best crime and justice reporting and analysis anywhere."[148] Among the shows now featured on the network are *Disorder in the Court, Forensic Files, Hot Pursuit, Inside American Jail, Most Daring, Most Shocking, Speeders*, all of which pertain to police, courts, and corrections. On the network's website, there are additional links for videos of "naughty girls" (including bad girls, girls gone wild, wild women, catfights, prostitutes, hookers, biker chicks, jersey girls, psycho, deranged, angry ladies, drunk co-eds, and bridezillas).[149] Also on the website are links to videos titled "Dumbest,"[150] "Fights and brawls,"[151] "Chases,"[152] and "Car crashes."[153] Clearly, these are meant to be entertaining, to satisfy what is our perceived pleasure from voyeurism, and nothing more.

Before offering the wide variety of infotainment choices to viewers that are now available through *truTV, Court TV* originally focused on high profile trials and/or trials that network executives thought would be of great interest to viewers. Thus, the network was in the habit of broadcasting trials live as they occurred. While this has tremendous potential for education of viewers, most citizens do not have the time to sit through entire trials. Further, this coverage logically reinforced the myth that trials are the norm in American justice even though they are quite rare.

⌂ For other examples of the courts on TV, including *The People's Court*, *Judge Judy*, and more, see the website for this book at: www.pscj.app state.edu/media/courtTV.html

---

Courts in Film

While coverage of trials is popular in the news media, they are far less common in film relative to the emphasis on police in film. It is true that, just like news media, films tend to create the illusion that trials are the norm in criminal court processing. The American Bar Association created a list of the top 12 trial films. They include:

- *The Passion of Joan of Arc* (1928)—about the trial of Joan of Arc after being captured by the English
- *M* (1931)—about a psychopathic child killer in Germany
- *Twelve Angry Men* (1957)—about a murder trial in New York involving a Puerto Rican youth facing the death penalty
- *The Wrong Man* (1957)—about a man arrested for a crime he did not commit
- *Paths of Glory* (1958)—about three soldiers accused of cowardice during a time of war in France
- *Anatomy of Murder* (1959)—about a defense attorney defending a man accused of murdering the man who supposedly raped his wife
- *Inherit the Wind* (1960)—a fictionalized account of the famous Scopes monkey trial
- *Judgment at Nuremberg* (1961)—about Nazi war crimes
- *The Trial* (1962)—about a man facing death about being arrested for a sexual crime
- *To Kill a Mockingbird* (1963)—about a small town white defense attorney defending a black man accused of rape in 1932 Alabama
- *A Man for All Seasons* (1966)—about a man, living in England in the 16th Century, sentenced to imprisonment and then death for treason against his King
- *The Verdict* (1982)—about an alcoholic attorney pursuing justice in a medical malpractice case.[154]

Further, the American Film Institute created its own top 10 list of films related to courtroom drama. They include:

- *To Kill a Mockingbird* (1963)—about a small town white defense attorney defending a black man accused of rape in 1932 Alabama, as noted above

- *12 Angry Men* (1957)—about a murder trial in New York involving a Puerto Rican youth facing the death penalty, as noted above
- *Kramer v Kramer* (1979)—about a custody battle between two parents
- *The Verdict* (1982)—about an alcoholic attorney pursuing justice in a medical malpractice case, as noted above
- *A Few Good Men* (1992)—about a Navy lawyer defending two Marines involved in the death of a fellow Marine
- *Witness for the Prosecution* (1958)—about a murder case set in England
- *Anatomy of a Murder* (1959)—about a defense attorney defending a man accused of murdering the man who supposedly raped his wife, as noted above
- *In Cold Blood* (1967)—about the murder of four members of a family in 1959 Nebraska by two convicts
- *A Cry in the Dark* (1988)—about a woman in Australia whose child went missing while camping that is charged in his death
- *Judgment at Nuremburg* (1961)—about Nazi war crimes, as noted above.[155]

In addition to perhaps creating the illusion that trials are a common way to settle meaningful disputes and solve serious issues of power and injustice, notice that the overwhelming majority of the top courts films deal with violent crime. This is probably not surprising given that all forms of media are so highly focused on acts of violence. Yet, such shows are also involved in reinforcing myths of crime.

Oz

Generally, the entertainment media have paid the least amount of attention to corrections, just as with the news media (see Chapter 7). Recently, there have been popular television shows that focus on corrections, especially prison life. Media depictions of prisons show them to be violent, harsh, and ineffective at rehabilitation.[156] While these depictions are largely accurate, prisons can also be effective at rehabilitation.

One recently popular show on cable television was the show *Oz*. There were six seasons of the show between 1997 and 2003. The show focused on the fictional maximum security New York prison called the Oswald State Correctional Facility. Many of the episodes focused on the experimental unit in the prison called Emerald City where rehabilitation and personal responsibility were emphasized.

The show was unique not only for the style of how stories were presented, but also because of the types of issues depicted on the show (e.g., bad language, violence and rape, drug use, homosexuality). Episodes focused on the nature of crimes for which inmates were incarcerated, as well as their struggles to live life behind bars. Common themes focused on gang activity, violence in the prison, retribution and revenge, plots to attack staff and escape from the facility.

Lockup

The television show *MSNBC Investigates—Lockup* focuses on specific prisons around the country and on particular issues during each episode. For example, episodes focus on weapons in prisons, gangs in prisons, dealing with boredom in prisons, juveniles in prison and so forth. Although everything on the show is real, one study of the show found that it tends to show the "extreme institutions and the most violent inmates" which ultimately justifies mass imprisonment policies.[157] The introduction to a recent episode of the show where the introduction indicated that the filming team spent "months" at the prison. Yet, what was shown amounted to only a one-hour segment (including commercials). This is evidence that the show only features a tiny portion of what was filmed.

The producers of the show do a good job of interviewing a wide variety of correctional personnel as well as inmates to show as many different aspects of prison life as they can as part of the continuing series. This makes the show educational even if partial and incomplete. Yet, the goal of the show is to entertain the viewer; hence much of the show focuses on gangs, weapons, drugs, sex, and violence in prison. One study of the show suggests that it "presents tales of some of the most extreme institutions and the most violent inmates. By using violence as the main frame," the show "sends messages that support the United States' current use of imprisonment."[158] That what is featured in the show is not representative of real life in prison should not be surprising; the primary goal of the show is to entertain. A recent episode of the show dealt with extreme situations of violence in prison. The producer of the show explained at the beginning that there were, "of course," boring moments in prison but then went on to explain that at any time violence can erupt. The show, unfortunately, tends to focus on the unusual instances as opposed to the normal, routine, monotony of prison life.

Similar shows include *Jail* and *Inside American Jail* which obviously focus on jails rather than prisons. A study of these shows illustrated that both programs offered only "a selective look into the jail system." According to the author: "Whether depicting the largest jails in the country or focusing exclusively on the areas of the jail where inmate outbursts are most likely to take place, these programs offer a sensationalized view of jail that supports current crime control policies."[159]

Prisons in Film

There have also been numerous popular films focused on life in prison.[160] According to Jamie Bennett:

> Generally, people have low levels of exposure to prisons through personal experience and therefore the media plays an important role in informing beliefs and actions. In particular prison films are an important and extensive form of media depiction. However, media depiction of crime and imprisonment has been criticised on ethical, political and social grounds.[161]

Paul Mason notes that "discourses around the futility and inhumanity of incarceration are scant, replaced by scenes of prison violence; rape and death appear, which appear to exist purely for the pleasure of the spectator." As for prisoners themselves, they are shown to be "an inhuman other: a danger to society and deserving for harsh punishment."[162] Violence in prison is depicted acontextually, and media depictions suggest it occurs frequently. Mason agrees that the media help create the belief that prisons are "the only process for crime control and reduction." This is ironic given how violent prisons are shown to be in the media. One study of prison films found that rape in prison is overrepresented in the media. Specifically, prison films found that 50% of the films included an attempted or completed rape and almost 75% mentioned rape.[163]

Derral Cheatwood identified four narratives in prison films:

- *The nature of confinement*—These are films focused on life inside correctional institutions. Inmates are shown as victims of injustice up against corrupt and/or brutal correctional facilities. An example of a film in the genre is *The Big House*.
- *The pursuit of justice*—These are films focused on guilty offenders deservedly locked up. Inmates are not victims of injustice but rather deserve punishment. An example of a film in the genre is *The Birdman of Alcatraz*.
- *Authority and control*—These are films focused on offenders who may or may not be guilty but who are locked up for relatively minor offenses and/or for butting up against powerful interests. Inmates are showing struggling against typically unjustified correctional authority and control figures. An example of a film in the genre is *Cool Hand Luke*.

- *Freedom and release*—These are often films about the future where prisons are extremely violent and unable to rehabilitate offenders. Inmates are humanized and shown as struggling to survive or escape. An example of a film in the genre is *Escape from New York*. [164]

The latter type of prison film tends to focus on redemption.[165] A highly successful and recent example of this type of film is "The Shawshank Redemption" which tells the story of a man who is wrongly imprisoned for a crime he did not commit and his years long struggle to gain his release, which ultimately only is possible with an elaborate escape plan.

According to Ray Surette, popular images of prison movies include "convict buddies, evil wardens, cruel guards, craven snitches, bloodthirsty convicts, and inmate heroes."[166] While these images are to some degree descriptive of conditions that do exist inside America's correctional facilities, each creates false conceptions of what life is really like on the inside.

Robert Freeman analyzes Hollywood portrayals of prisons and identifies two major stereotypes that dominate: the "smug hack" and "country club." The "smug hack" stereotype is much more common and features the tyrannical correctional employee. The "country club" stereotype is less common but portrays inmates living comfortable lives with numerous luxuries.[167] Neither of these depictions is realistic.

According to Marsha Clowers, the typical image of female prisoners comes from films.[168] As noted by Cecil: "Since the 1950s films about women in prison have focused on girls-gone-bad plots using exploitation-style filmmaking." These films "reinforce society's stereotypes about female prisoners: that they are violent, worthless, sex-crazed monsters totally unworthy of humane treatment, much less educational programs."[169] A vast literature shows these images to be false.[170]

Summary

Crime and criminal justice shows have been popular on television since the earliest days of television. The main themes of such crime- and criminal justice-oriented shows have changed across the decades. The earlier shows from the 1960s and 1970s were overwhelmingly pro-law enforcement and pro-criminal justice. That is, officers and criminal justice employees generally were depicted as honest, hard-working and clearly on "our side" in the "fight" against crime. In the 1980s, this was also generally true, but increasingly popular crime and criminal justice television shows depicted additional issues such as corruption, excessive use of force and the presence of vice (e.g., drugs) in communities and among the police. Shows in the 1980s tended to be more complex than earlier shows and the line between the "good guys" and "bad guys" became harder to distinguish.

Crime entertainment narratives promote three related messages: Most offenders are professional criminals; Community safety is threatened by judges and defense attorneys who are too much concerned with offenders' rights; and criminal justice personnel are out there every day, fighting the war on crime. These messages have the potential to be highly misleading to the general public.

Studies of entertainment and infotainment shows have consistently found that they tend to overemphasize violent crime. Further, the incidence of violence has grown over time and is typically depicted as "value free." That is, it is shown being used by both heroes and villains, it rarely causes physical or emotional harm, it rarely leads to any condemnation or punishment and it is sometimes depicted as laudable and even necessary. This is good evidence that violence in the entertainment and infotainment media lacks important context, just as it does in the news media.

Violence is also prevalent in film. Further, it has increased over time, as has graphic violence and graphic death, especially in action and disaster films. Themes of violence are also common in popular music. Violent themes exists in multiple genres, although the rap genre has probably received the most media attention.

Violence and crime are also common in comic books, as are negative portrayals of some forms of drug use. Normal or pro-social use of drugs is not depicted in comic books. Nor is legalization as an alternative to the drug war. In comic books, the police, courts, and corrections are not widely featured, whereas violence of the superhero is very common.

True crime refers to books about crime that look like crime fiction but are based on real cases. These books tend to be focused on violent (and often especially heinous) crimes that were committed by a local person against another local person (or people). True crime books often start with the commission of the crime then work backwards to tell the story of what happened leading up to the crime (including the life stories of the offenders and victims) and then conclude with the outcome of the case (e.g., trial and punishment). The books are educational in the sense that they often report facts that have been widely reported in the media but are also meant to be entertaining and thus they often read like novels.

The television show *COPS* is perhaps the most successful infotainment show ever made. The show features police-approved selections of video showing incidents of police-citizen encounters. The show is presented as real even though it is highly stylized, condensed, edited, and meant to entertain.

The show reinforces the notion of "us versus them" which drives current status quo approaches to fighting crime. Media coverage of crime, focused largely on street crime and on poor minorities, is a form of labeling whereby certain segments of the society are identified as bad, deviant, or immoral. In this process, evil is dramatized, and the notion of "us" versus "them" is reinforced, because we tend to think of criminals as being different from us. When constantly shown images of crime and criminals in the media, viewers get the sense that "we" are different from "them." After all, we are part of the police force as viewers; we are in the car with the police, we are in the chase with police, and they talk to us as if we are part of the team. Offenders featured on such shows are the "them," not "us." Such shows also reinforce the belief that most offenders are black. The "them" is typically a minority, especially a black person.

Shows like *COPS* tend to focus on the most violent, random, and bizarre stories while ignoring more routine calls for service. Presentations of police are often over-dramatized and romanticized by fictional television crime dramas. The message of such shows is that offenders are quite dangerous people who are best dealt with through aggressive or violent policing.

The television show *COPS* also overrepresents clearance rates in comparison with actual UCR crime statistics. That is, in the show, police are far more likely than in reality to make an arrest after the occurrence of a crime. In reality, only about 40% of all crimes are even known to the police and only about 10% of all crimes will lead to an arrest. The show thus creates the misperception that police are more effective than they really are.

Law & Order is divided roughly into two equal parts, the first focusing on the crime and investigation of the crime by the police, and the second part of the show on the prosecution at the trial of the alleged offender. The show led to three spin-offs, two of which still air, including *Law & Order Criminal Intent* and *Law & Order Special Victims Unit*. Studies of these shows demonstrate major misconceptions created by the way the show depicts crime and delinquency.

The show, *CSI: Crime Scene Investigation* (*CSI*), is among the most popular shows on television each year. Further, it has generated two successful spin-offs, including *CSI: Miami* and *CSI: NY*. The show has created the illusion in citizens that science and the police are virtually infallible. Further, it creates the misconception that forensics are typically the way crimes are solved, which is simply not true. Further, the nature of violence on *CSI* is both graphic and dehumanizing.

When it comes to criminal justice in film, action films are probably best known and include the very popular *48 Hours*, *Beverly Hills Cop*, *Die Hard*, and *Lethal Weapon*. Although some of the earliest police films debuted in the

1940s and 1950s, the action cop films were probably most common in the 1980s and 1990s. Violent, vigilante type cops were more commonly depicted in film in the 1970s. The prime example is *Dirty Harry* starring Clint Eastwood. In the 1971 film, Harry Callahan uses violence and breaks the rules of due process to pursue criminals including a serial killer. Dirty Harry Callahan returns in this role in the films *Magnum Force* (1973), *The Enforcer* (1976) and *Sudden Impact* (1983). As the series progresses, the films get more violent, extreme, and unrealistic in their depictions of law enforcement.

Modern coverage of trials in the media started with the O.J. Simpson murder case in 1995. Media programs tend to focus on the most uncommon crimes (e.g., homicide) and the rare events (e.g., trials). The infotainment media portrayals of courts will necessarily be different than factual, objective accounts of court activity, because their goal is to entertain not inform. As such, portrayals of courts in these media tend to be brief, time-limited, dramatic, and focused on elements such as random violence, sex, and cases involving celebrities.

A good example of this type of coverage comes from *TruTV*, which was originally referred to as *Court TV*. *Court TV* was a popular network that hosted many crime- and criminal justice-themed shows.

Cameras have long been in America's courts. For example, the popular show, *The People's Court*, daily features courtroom television. Yet, this is small-claims civil court rather than criminal court and litigants in the cases agree to have the cases broadcast on television. Other popular shows on network and cable television include *Judge Judy* and *Judge Joe Brown* among many others. These shows likely create misconceptions of the kinds of cases that are actually handled in civil courts given that the cases are likely selected for inclusion on the show based on their potential to titillate and entertain. Yet, they do offer the opportunity to witness "real" courtroom procedures without having to travel down to the local courthouse of one's city or county.

While coverage of trials is popular in the news media, they are far less common in film relative to the emphasis on police in film. It is true that, just like news media, films tend to create the illusion that trials are the norm in criminal court processing. In addition to perhaps creating the illusion that trials are a common way to settle meaningful disputes and solve serious issues of power and injustice, the overwhelming majority of the top courts films deal with violent crime. This is probably not surprising given that all forms of media are so highly focused on acts of violence.

Generally, the entertainment media have paid the least amount of attention to corrections, just as with the news media. Recently, there have been popular television shows that focus on corrections, especially prison life. Media depictions of prisons show them to be violent, harsh, and ineffective at rehabilitation. While these depictions are largely accurate, prisons can also be effective at rehabilitation.

One recently popular show on cable television was the show *Oz*. The show focused on the fictional maximum security New York prison called the Oswald State Correctional Facility. Many of the episodes focused on the experimental unit in the prison called Emerald City where rehabilitation and personal responsibility were emphasized.

The show was unique not only for the style of how stories were presented, but also because of the types of issues depicted on the show (e.g., bad language, violence and rape, drug use, homosexuality). Episodes focused on the nature of crimes for which inmates were incarcerated, as well as their struggles to live life behind bars. Common themes focused on gang activity, violence in the prison, retribution and revenge, plots to attack staff and escape from the facility.

The television show *MSNBC Investigates — Lockup* focuses on specific prisons around the country and on particular issues on each episode. For example, episodes focus on weapons in prisons, gangs in prisons, dealing with boredom in prisons, juveniles in prison and so forth. Although everything on the show is real, one study of the show found that it tends to show the "extreme institutions and the most violent inmates" which ultimately justifies mass imprisonment policies.

There have also been numerous popular films focused on life in prison. There are four narratives in prison films: the nature of confinement; the pursuit of justice; authority and control; and freedom and release.

Discussion Questions

1) Summarize the type of content you are likely to see on the television shows, *To Catch a Predator* and *48 Hours Mystery*.
2) Discuss for how long crime and criminal justice shows have been popular on television. Summarize the major types of shows being shown today as well as in the past.
3) What are the main narratives promoted in crime entertainment today?
4) What does it mean that studies of entertainment and infotainment show them to depict violence in a "value free" manner.
5) Explain to what degree violence is popular in film and music. Provide examples.
6) Explain to what degree violence is popular in comic books. Provide examples.

7) What is true crime?

8) Describe the popular television show "COPS." What are some of the major problems with the show identified in the chapter?

9) Describe the popular television show "Law & Order." What are some of the major problems with the show identified in the chapter?

10) Describe the popular television show "CSI." What are some of the major problems with the show identified in the chapter?

11) Discuss how modern coverage of trials in the media is inaccurate.

12) In your opinion, why are the types of shows broadcast on TruTV so popular?

13) In your opinion, why have the entertainment media generally paid the least amount of attention to corrections?

Chapter 9

Summary, Conclusions, and Reform

Learning Objectives

After reading this chapter, you will be able to:

1) Summarize major problems with the media generally and with media coverage of crime and criminal justice.
2) Compare and contrast the three major explanations or models for the news media's inaccuracy in covering crime, criminal justice and related topics.
3) Explain which of the three major models meant to explain what the media cover and do not cover is most accurate, and why.
4) Discuss how the inaccuracies and problems of coverage of topics by the media stem from the organizational nature of the media.
5) Illustrate how the media benefit from intense coverage of violent crime.

6) Illustrate how the media benefit from inaccurate coverage of crime and criminal justice.
7) Explain how imitation and a lack of criminal justice education help explain inaccuracies in media coverage.
8) Discuss how the media frame crime as a failure of criminal justice agencies.
9) Identify and discuss the major effects of consuming media (e.g., watching television) on consumers (e.g., viewers).
10) Outline major reforms aimed at changing the way media operate in the United States.

Introduction

In this book, the following facts have been established:

- The major news media are owned and thus controlled by major corporations.
- Mainstream media outlets have been consolidated into fewer and fewer hands, each of which is part of the corporate system.
- Inner-ring or upper tier media outlets have grown larger and more influential through horizontal and vertical integration.
- Agenda setting media serve in numerous ways with other corporations including interlocking directorates.
- The media are mainly concerned with profit, particularly advertising dollars.
- The media rely heavily on information provided by government sources.
- The powerful have greater ability to produce "flak" in order to influence media coverage.
- Problems of crime and criminal justice are typified in media coverage using frames and narratives that have proven effective in the past. These frames and narratives, though effective for the media, do not accurately depict the realities of crime and criminal justice.
- Although the media attempt to remain neutral on issues, present balanced perspectives, and maintain reliability by consulting and presenting official sources, subjectivity creeps into media stories; further, false conceptions of issues are created when the media present only two sides and rely so heavily on government sources of information.
- Decisions of newsworthiness (deciding which stories to cover and which to ignore), decisions of priority (deciding where to run a story), decisions of framing (deciding how to tell a story), and decisions of mar-

ketability (deciding between conflicting demands of the public and advertisers) allow potential biases and subjectivity to impact the media.

· For the most part, the media tend to ignore the law-making process, with the exception of laws that are considered and created in the wake of a widely publicized crime and those laws that are perceived as highly controversial or that will bring sweeping change to society's institutions or practices (e.g., health care reform).

· Even highly controversial laws such as the USA PATRIOT Act that seriously threaten citizens' civil liberties tend not to be covered in great depth in the mainstream press.

· The vast majority of crime receives no attention in the media. Generally speaking, violent crimes receive far more media attention than property crimes, especially when they are random in nature, committed against children, and involve white victims and minority offenders.

· The media overemphasize crimes like homicide, serial killing and rape, focusing especially on the most extreme and rare of these cases.

· Media coverage of crime tends not to provide any context; instead it tends to be sensationalistic and fails to help citizens understand their true risks of victimization.

· Acts of crime tend to be framed in terms of the impact on the innocent victims by violent, deranged offenders.

· Media coverage of crime tends to be suggestive of individual motives for criminality (including mental illness) while generally ignoring structural sources of crime.

· Media coverage of crime is associated with fear of crime, at least in some consumers.

· Exposure to violence in the media is associated with greater violence in society; one way this occurs is that the media desensitize us to violence.

· Corporate and white-collar crimes are generally ignored in the press in spite of the enormous harm they cause to society (which vastly dwarf the harms caused by street crime).

· Even when corporate and white-collar crimes are covered, oftentimes the most important elements of the stories are downplayed or ignored (e.g., structural sources of the behaviors).

· The media rely on official sources for information about crime, thereby reinforcing status quo approaches to "fighting" these social problems.

· Media coverage of criminal justice is front-end loaded, meaning the early stages of policing (e.g., arrest) receive far more attention than the latter stages of courts and corrections.

· The media are disproportionately focused on local cops and street crime as opposed to state and federal police and white-collar and corporate crime.
· The media overemphasize the law enforcement role of policing and suggest that the police are effective in reducing crime even though the least amount of policing is devoted to law enforcement and policing has only a modest impact on crime.
· There are positive and negative images of policing in the media; positive images dominate but negative images associated with police profiling, brutality, and corruption are also common.
· Most courtroom activity is ignored by the media, as the focus is mostly on trial procedures (especially involving high profile cases) which are quite rare relative to the mostly invisible process of plea bargaining.
· Most media activity is focused on state court activity and street crime rather than on federal court activity and white-collar and corporate crime.
· There is a disproportionate focus by the media on the poor and people of color when it comes to coverage of courts.
· Sentencing is largely ignored by the media except in cases where crimes have been tracked by the press all the way through the criminal justice process.
· The least visible component of criminal justice is corrections due to limited media coverage.
· Media coverage of corrections misrepresents the true nature of American punishment, suggesting that the typical form of punishment is incarceration when in fact it is probation.
· The media generally fail to shed sufficient light on issues such as that getting "tough on crime" does not work, that punishment is enormously costly in the U.S., that prison is a horrible place, that the largest provider of mental health services is the criminal justice system, and that there are serious biases in correctional punishment based on social class and race.
· Media coverage of criminal justice tends to reinforce crime control values over due process values.
· Entertainment and infotainment media are less accurate than the news media in their presentations of crime and criminal justice; this should be expected given that these media sources are meant to entertain rather than to inform.
· Crime and criminal justice are popular on television, in films, music, and movies. Crime has long held a place on television and remains popular today. Other forms of media (including comic books and true crime novels) are also highly focused on crime.
· Entertainment and infotainment media are disproportionately focused on violent crime which is typically depicted in a "value free" manner.

· The poor and minorities, especially black men, are the focus of many "reality" television shows such as *COPS*. In other popular crime dramas, such as *Law & Order*, blacks are underrepresented on the show, especially as victims.

· Television dramas, movies, and other forms of media focused on crime and criminal justice, create major misconceptions not only about criminals and victims, but also about the (in)effectiveness of criminal justice to deal with crime. They also help create the misconception that crime is often solved using forensics rather than normal, everyday police techniques such as interviewing witnesses and suspects.

This final chapter explains more fully why the media are so inaccurate when it comes to crime and criminal justice. Considered in this chapter are factors that tend to be ignored by other media scholars.

Explanations of Media Inaccuracy

There are two major, competing explanations for the news media's inaccuracy in covering crime, criminal justice and related topics.[1] According to one explanation—the *market model*—crime is considered newsworthy because of the public interest in it, and thus it is covered. In this model, newsworthiness is determined by consumers; thus we are to blame for the way the media operate. The market model also assumes that facts are objectively reported and are often realistically portrayed.

According to the other explanation—the *manipulative model*—crime is of interest to the owners of the media and is purposefully distorted to shape public interests in line with those of the owners of the media. In this model, newsworthiness is determined by news agency owners based on concerns about marketability and profitability; thus we are not to blame for the way the media operate. The manipulative model also assumes that facts are subjectively reported (i.e., distorted) and unrealistically portrayed.

Ray Surette describes both models as simplistic and inadequate, and puts forth an alternative explanation, the *organizational model*. This model contains elements of the market and manipulative models but is more similar to the manipulative model than the market model. According to the organizational model, content is selected based on the needs of the media rather than the demands of the public; thus the blame lies more on the media for how the media operate. Specifically, whether and how stories get covered depends on the periodicity of the stories and how well they match the needs of the media; *peri-*

odicity pertains to the timing of a story. Whether and how stories get covered also depends on the consonance of the stories to previously covered themes and narratives; *consonance* pertains to how well a story fits previously covered stories. To the degree that stories fit a routine pattern of media coverage (*routinization*), they are more likely to be covered.[2]

A safe conclusion about stories pertaining to crime and criminal justice is that the periodicity or timing of these stories is always right; these stories are always popular with consumers and always profitable for media corporations. Further, it is fair to say that the media have perfected various themes and narratives through which to tell these stories; thus, new acts of crimes are relatively easy to connect to previous stories (consonance). We might conclude that stories about crime and criminal justice are routinely covered in the media because they work.

Proponents of the organizational model do not see the media as intentionally distorting content and thus aimed at manipulating public opinion. Rather, they see the media as simply responding to organizational factors. Since crime is popular, always timely (periodicity), easy to connect to previously depicted themes and narratives (consonance), and routinely covered (routinization), crime news will make up a large part of all news.

The organizational model offers a reasonable explanation that does not go as far as the media critics introduced in Chapter 1 who argue that the media are intentionally biased for the purpose of spreading propaganda. Yet, it acknowledges the reality that most of the problems with media coverage are organizational in nature. It also acknowledges that objective reporting about issues such as crime and criminal justice simply does not exist, as noted in Chapter 2. The organizational model also assumes that we consumers share some of the blame for media practices; after all, if we didn't consume the news, entertainment, and infotainment they produced, the media would not continue to produce it.

This is a good starting point. In examining the literature in this area, however, there are other reasons that the media focus on crime and tend to be inaccurate in their coverage of it. Each of these reasons is discussed next, beginning with a discussion of organizational factors. This amounts to a summary of the main argument of the first two chapters of the book.

Organizational Factors: Entertainment for Profit

Reporters do not deserve all or even most of the blame for providing inaccurate coverage of crime and criminal justice. Most are simply following orders of their superiors. Instead, blame resides in "the moguls, stockholders, owners, and publishers ..."[3] Those who set the agenda for the media are the most to blame for

Market	Organizational	Manipulative
• Crime covered because of public interest	• Crime covered mostly due to organizational needs of media	• Crime covered because of owner interest
• Newsworthiness determined by consumers	• Newsworthiness determined by both media and consumers	• Newsworthiness determined by marketability, profitability
• Coverage is objective and realistic	• Coverage fits previous patterns of coverage	• Coverage is subjective and unrealistic

Of the three models of media behavior, the organizational model is probably most accurate. It acknowledges that the media generally determine what is counted as news and entertainment, and thus they are largely responsible for media content. Yet, consumers share some of the blame too, for we help determine what is profitable based on what we consume.

inaccuracies about crime and criminal justice in the media. These are the folks that are interested in profit before and above everything else, including accuracy. As citizens, we now know who these companies are, who owns them, what their goals are, and why it matters. These issues were discussed in Chapters 1 and 2.

Media inaccuracies and problems of coverage of crime and criminal justice stem, first and foremost, from the organizational nature of the media. Mainstream media are owned by corporations and will inevitably cover stories in a way that serves their own interests (including ignoring stories that call their interests into question). The media also attempt to give us what they think will help sell the products that they advertise on their stations and in their newspapers. Since violence is so important and even celebrated in America, stories about crime fit our preoccupation with violence nicely. It even fits well when the stories are inaccurate and/or result in misinformation. David Altheide says much of this "misinformation is quite intentional. This does not mean that everyone in the mass media lies … Rather … it is the emphasis on entertainment and making profits that leads to the major distortions."[4] Altheide's statement is important because it reminds us that, to a significant degree, the nature of reporting about any issue is determined by structural or organizational factors related to the corporate media system.

Recalling a major lesson of this book, Ben Bagdikian asserts that crime coverage is inexpensive, captivating and mostly "socially trivial filler." This helps explain its popularity among companies interested in making a profit. Further, coverage is almost always divorced from any social context or public policy concerns and, if anything, it serves to enhance popular paranoia about crime waves and prod political support for tough-talking 'three strikes and you're out' programs."[5] It also tends not to "enmesh the parent corporation in controversy."[6] Again, there are structural or organizational reasons for this.

As shown throughout this book, crime is almost always the top story in the news. Specifically, studies of news by the Center for Media and Public Affairs (CMPA) show that crime is usually the top story in any given year, and at no time in the 1990s did it drop below the top 5 stories. Recall that, in 2008, crime was the fifth most popular story in the news. Part of the reason that crime is so newsworthy and that violence is so prevalent in entertainment media, is apparently because Americans like to watch it. As shown in Chapter 8, studies of American television shows, movies, and music illustrate that violence is a main theme. In fact, shows about crime are some of the most popular on TV.

Crime has been the most popular story in the fifty year history of U.S. television, "with crime-related shows regularly accounting for one-fourth to one-third of all the three major networks' prime time shows" from the 1960s to the 2000s.[7] Robert Bohm and Jeffery Walker suggest that programs about crime and criminal justice account for as much as 30% to 80% of programming on television.[8] Why is this so? Since the media are businesses, economic factors are inherently involved in selecting content. The content of the media is shaped in line with the economic interests of the organization that owns the media outlet.[9]

Given the finite resources of reporters and news space, the fact that crime is so prominent in the news means that other issues, such as international affairs, are not adequately addressed. Is this intentional? According to David Krajicek: "The process of journalism—collecting, organizing, and disseminating information—happens in a series of priority-setting decisions about how to use ... resources."[10] Those that prioritize crime over other vexing social problems are the most accountable.

Who decides, then, what will be newsworthy? As shown throughout the book, decisions about newsworthiness are made by the leaders of corporate media. First and foremost, these leaders are concerned with profit. Thus, news becomes anything that generates audiences, ratings, sales, and advertising dollars; this includes the routine (e.g., crime, which is covered every day) and the extraordinary (e.g., unusual crimes and terrorism that rarely occur but that always receive extensive media coverage).[11]

As one example, a recent lead story on the national news was of a home-made hot air balloon in the shape of a flying saucer which a six-year-old boy supposedly climbed into and somehow managed to fly up into the sky; the mainstream television news provided live coverage for more than three hours.[12] As it turned out, the whole story was a hoax, fabricated by a father that was seeking a starring role in a reality television show. The original event was deemed newsworthy (for the whole nation, thus it was covered live) probably because it was so unusual and also because a young boy was supposedly imperiled inside; subsequent stories about the hoax also received extensive coverage, probably because Americans were outraged at the father and wanted to see him punished for the hoax. Subsequently, the father both admitted to and denied the hoax.

Only a few weeks after the balloon story, a disgruntled soldier (an Army Major, no less) went on a shooting rampage at Fort Hood in Texas, killing twelve soldiers and one security guard. This event led to very intense media coverage for days related to the actual shooting; subsequent coverage focused on what motivated the attacks and whether it was best described as an act of mass murder or terrorism or both. Then, only a couple of days later, another man went to his former office in Orlando, Florida and sought revenge for being fired by shooting people there. Sadly, similar events have occurred elsewhere since, each of which received significant media attention.

The latter stories were of great interest to the media because they were random and excessively violent. The Fort Hood shooting is still being discussed, mostly because some members of Congress and certain talk show hosts on TV and the radio continue to discuss it as part of the "war on terror." The organizational model suggests that these stories are covered because they are profitable, and because we want to see them. Whether we as consumers get an accurate or truthful perspective on such events is debatable.

Here are some responses to the Fort Hood shooting. First, former spokeswoman for President Bush Dana Perino called the Fort Hood shooting a "terrorist attack on U.S. soil" and then stated: "We did not have a terrorist attack on our country during President Bush's term." Former New York City Mayor Rudy Giuliani also stated: "We had no domestic attacks under Bush; we've had one under Obama." And Fox News contributor Monica Crowley asserted that: "After 9/11, President Bush and Vice President Cheney had a 100 percent perfect track record in keeping the homeland safe from an Islamic terrorist attack."

In fact, during President Bush's time in office (January 20, 2001, to January 19, 2009), the following terrorist attacks were committed or attempted in the United States:

- the anthrax attacks, which killed five people (September 2001—8 months after Bush took office).
- the attempted attack on an airplane by Richard Reid, the "shoe bomber" (December 2001—11 months after Bush took office).
- the shooting by Hesham Mohamed Hadayet at a ticket counter at LAX airport, which killed two people, an act that has been officially labeled terrorism by the U.S. government due to its political motivation, (July 2002—18 months after Bush took office).
- the "Beltway sniper" attacks by John Allen Muhammad and Lee Boyd Malvo, which killed ten people, acts which are considered terrorism by many experts as well as at least one of the courts that handled these cases (October 2002—21 months after Bush took office).
- The injury of nine people by Mohammed Reza Taheri-Azar who intentionally drove his SUV into a crowd of people at UNC-Chapel Hill to "avenge the deaths of Muslims worldwide" in honor of one of his role models, Mohammad Atta, the ringleader of the 9/11 hijackers (March 2006—63 months after Bush took office).

And of course, there is 9/11 itself, the largest terrorist attack ever committed on U.S. soil occurred during the Bush Administration, which killed 2,973 people (September 2001—8 months after Bush took office). These examples demonstrate clearly one problem with relying on inner-ring (or first-tier) media sources for information; oftentimes, the information being presented is debatable if not simply false. According to Rosyln Muraskin and Shelly Domash, stories about crime and related phenomena may not be about truth anyway, but rather about exciting people and selling the news.[13]

✓🖰 For more information about how terrorism is treated in entertainment media, see the website for this book at: www.pscj.appstate.edu/media/terrorentertainment.html

---

Recall that television programming is aimed at attracting and keeping large audiences because the "larger the audience, the more that sponsors are willing to spend for advertising and the greater the profits."[14] Given the organizational needs of the media, including profit-generating news,[15] crime is valuable because it attracts viewers and because it is relatively easy to write about given the abundance of official sources of information in law enforcement and politics.[16] These officials are considered legitimate, authoritative, reliable, and consistently available, as shown throughout the book.[17]

When it comes to entertainment and infotainment media, they are obviously profiting immensely from crime and violence; it forms the basis for popular movies, music, and television shows. Clearly, profit-seeking is the culprit here; crime and violence sell, so the media continue to produce it.

Because of the focus on violence and unusual events, even television news comes to be seen as a form of entertainment, whereby the media are highly selective in what they broadcast. Violence is more "sellable" than the mundane aspects of theft and other forms of property crime. This explains what Ray Surette calls the recent blurring of news and entertainment in media outlets.[18]

A recent attempted rape, covered on a local television station, serves as a good example of the blurring between the news and entertainment. Although the original story was likely meant not at all to be entertaining, the brother of the victim appeared on camera and went on a tirade against the alleged offender. His tirade immediately became a YouTube sensation and within days, parts of his tirade were turned into a hip hop song using special computer software. This led to even more media attention of the brother, including follow-up stories by the local news.

Some go further and claim that media are organized to promote fear. David Altheide refers to the combination of news and entertainment as a "fear-generating machine."[19] The result is a *visual reality* that parallels actually reality; the visual reality is what affects people's perceptions of crime in the United States.[20]

And who benefits from this visual reality? According to Altheide

> many businesses provide services and products to help solve or reduce the alleged sources of fear ... There is a massive home protection and security industry; the gun industry has fired up many neighborhoods to get involved in personal security and home protection by buying weapons and taking weapons training and has spawned numerous hobbies involving firearms ... Businesses also use security services that are very visible to customers in banks, offices, retail outlets, schools, and even places of worship.[21]

Ironically, the academic field of criminal justice benefits enormously from fear and our fascination with crime and violence. Criminal justice is one of the more popular majors in the United States. Unfortunately, our academic discipline "tends to focus on police, courts, and correctional operations and procedures ... much of the curriculum concerns straightforward descriptions, evaluations, models, and recommendations for the organization of criminal justice agencies and the role that its workers ... play in keeping crime under control and keeping us all safe."[22] Both the security and criminology industries thus benefit from crime and violence.

Peer Culture

Another part of the organizational nature of the media that often does not get much attention is the peer culture that permeates the media. The "peer culture among journalists is as intense as that at any junior high school. Reporters and editors look to one another—both colleagues and competitors—to determine what is appropriate. If everyone else is doing it, that deserves an affirmation."[23] Consistent with *social learning theories* of crime, the media imitate what others in the business are doing and are likely to continue to cover it when the coverage is positively reinforced.[24]

Simple *imitation* plays a role.[25] Once a news agency picks up on a crime story or theme, other news organizations are likely to pick it up as well, especially when the original source is an inner-ring or first-tier source, as discussed in Chapter 1. When the theme runs throughout the media industry as a whole or through the mainstream media discussed earlier, it can lead to a "media crime wave" or "moral panic." As noted earlier, the inner circle/first-tier media — who are owned by large corporations — are the ones that determine what is newsworthy. Yet, more than imitation is involved. When media coverage of crime and terrorism is reinforced (e.g., with higher ratings and higher income), it is likely to be repeated, as predicted by *differential reinforcement theory*. Further, when reporters, editors and other media personnel associate with others who are already promoting crime and terrorism through their media work, it is likely that this will impact other media outlets, as predicted by *differential association theory*.[26]

Finally, to some degree, the issue of pack journalism is relevant here. *Pack journalism* refers to the process whereby dozens of reporters flock to a scene (e.g., a crime scene or press conference) en masse to cover the same story in essentially the same way.[27] The concept of pack journalism is similar to the notion of a "feeding frenzy" put forth by Larry Sabato whereby the press flock to the scene like sharks to blood in the water; such reporting is intense yet not necessarily justified by the story being covered.[28]

Lack of Criminal Justice Education

Another factor that helps us understand inaccuracy in the press is a lack of education on the part of media personnel. Stated simply, few media owners, editors, and even reporters have expertise about crime, criminal justice, as well as other topics they routinely cover. If media owners, reporters, and editors do not understand basic facts of crime, criminal justice, and related topics, they will merely report what they are told by official sources. For example, you have likely seen headlines and stories about rising and falling crime rates that base their arguments on rising or falling arrest rates. Arrest rates are not valid measures of crime rates, but instead are a function of what police are doing. It is doubtful that many in the media understand the difference.

Drug Arrests, 1970–2005

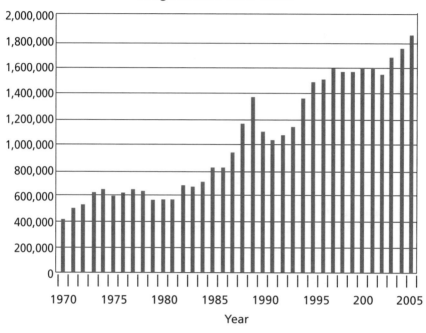

This figure shows trends in arrests for drug-related offenses. The untrained reporter, editor as well as consumer of media information might see such data and assume that drug use trends or drug selling trends must be increasing. In fact, about 80% of arrests in any given year are for simple possession of drugs, and drug use trends are, for the most part, stable. http://www.sentencing project.org/doc/publications/dp_drugarrestreport.pdf.

The journalist writes crime stories to get on the front page much as the academic criminologist or criminal justice professor writes articles to get published in the best journals. The goal of each is not necessarily to make an actual difference in criminal justice policy but, rather, to play the game successfully within the rules laid out by the discipline. Ultimately, personal and even financial reward may be gained by each, as well as by their respective employers.

While academics practice "real criminology" and have been highly critical of recent criminal justice policy, their findings rarely inform criminal justice policy. Politicians practice "kindergarten criminology," and reporters have not held politicians or criminal justice policy makers accountable for it.[29]

The Role of Politics in the "Framing" of Crime

The media, by reporting what such official sources report, create perceptions of the crime problem in viewers, thereby also creating support for particular crime control policies.[30] Because government sources are typically cited in crime reports, it is not surprising that Americans support "more police, more arrests, longer sentences, more prisons, and more executions."[31] State managers cited in media reports about crime also tend to emphasize a crime control perspective over a due process model of criminal justice.[32]

Logically, as news becomes routinized—as it follows similar formats to those proven acceptable to owners of the media and news consumers and to what has evolved in line with needs of advertisers[33]—sources that have been relied on in the past are relied on regularly. This makes getting the news relatively easy. Government sources can be also be cited as "official" and thus reliable.[34] The problem is that the media and government are so close now, it is at times easy to see the institutions as on the same team or same side, as opposed to a separate, independent media acting as a watchdog for the good of the nation's democracy.

Given that the media are dominant institutions in society, they share similar characteristics with other dominant institutions, such as the state and corporations.[35] They reproduce the status quo, which is beneficial to them.[36] An example can be characterized as a form of media inbreeding. Given that "media professionals are trained, educated, and socialized in a way as to internalize the values and norms of the dominant, mainstream culture ... [they will] interpret or mediate news, information, and complex issues in a way that is usually consistent with the dominant culture and with the interests of powerful groups."[37]

The media will also amplify viewpoints of the powerful, especially when these views are already shared by members of society because they appeal to our "common sense." Anything offensive to consumers, advertisers, or owners will be discouraged.[38] News stories about crime and criminal justice also often include "commentary from public officials"[39] or "state managers,"[40] which supposedly provide expert opinion about crime-related problems. Thus, politicians attempt to "capitalize on the news to further support their political agendas and to gain support of voters."[41]

The best of these politicians—the most effective claims-makers about crime and criminal justice—have their views of crime turned into media coverage;

thus, they determine the focus of the coverage of the media.[42] Strangely enough, politicians then see media coverage of crime problems as evidence of heightened public concern over crime.[43] Yet, most scholars posit that political action often occurs before public concern and that public concern stems from actions of politicians, rather than the other way around.

In the media, one common way in which crime is framed is as a failure of criminal justice agencies, as shown in Chapter 2.[44] For example, misleading and misinforming media coverage of crime highlights the failures of criminal justice agencies and characterizes the justice network as inefficient and soft on crime.[45] This is one of the paradoxes of news coverage of criminal justice. Although the media depict the criminal justice network as ineffective, "the cumulative effect of these portraits appears to be increased support for more police, more prisons, and more money for the criminal justice system."[46]

In other words, media coverage of criminal justice advances the status quo of big government when it comes to fighting crime by reinforcing the dominant ideology in American criminal justice.[47] That is, discourse on crime control is limited to present, get-tough policies.[48] Given that the media focus disproportionately on law enforcement crime-fighting activities, the end result is increased support for a crime control model rather than a due process model.[49] As if due process rights were the cause of crime in the United States, politicians have made us all less free in an effort to fight a crime problem that is actually less problematic today than it has been in a long, long time.[50]

Studies of people who watch crime shows on television illustrate that regular viewers of crime shows are more likely to oppose gun control and believe that firearms prevent crime.[51] For example, Kenneth Dowler examined public opinion data and found that regular viewers of shows such as *COPS, Real Stories of the Highway Patrol, Justice Files,* and *America's Most Wanted* were more likely to oppose gun control efforts.[52]

Exposure to media also has been found to increase support for the death penalty, especially in simplistic media (e.g., tabloids and TV news magazines).[53] Exposure to more complex media (i.e., newspapers and TV news about government and politics) moderates views toward death penalty. Exposure to more complex media formats is related to more complex thinking. While the hard news format aims to utilize balanced coverage of diverse viewpoints that may provide a better understanding of complex issues, the infotainment format focuses on drama and emotion rather than information. Television news magazine shows tend to overdramatize and oversimplify issues of crime, leading to broader support for "get tough" measures of crime.

Even as the United States has been cast by "get tough" politicians as "a victim of its own liberty"—that "U.S. society is too free for its own good and insufficiently fearful of authority"[54]—the media have not alerted citizens to how their Constitutional protections have been eroded in the move toward a crime control model of criminal justice. As explained by David Krajicek, "the media have uncritically reproduced official, conservative, 'law-and-order' perspectives with little fundamental analysis of their success or failure."[55] This should not be surprising given the facts of the mainstream media laid out in Chapters 1 and 2.

The media tend to amplify the claims of politicians about crime.[56] Theodore Sasson states the dominant claim this way: "People do crimes because they know they can get away with them. The police are handcuffed by liberal judges. The prisons, bursting at their seams, have revolving doors for serious offenders."[57] Thus, the way to reduce crime is to reduce "loopholes and technicalities that impede the apprehension and imprisonment of offenders" and increase the "swiftness, certainty and severity of punishment"—in other words, to erode due process protections that interfere with the crime-fighting capacity of our criminal justice network.[58]

The term *politics of fear* refers to "decision makers' promotion and use of audience beliefs and assumptions about danger, risk, and fear in order to achieve certain goals."[59] It relies on "nationalism and perceived consensus against an enemy."[60] Generally, the politics of fear correlates with the amount of social control in society, meaning the more prevalent the politics of fear the more repressive criminal justice. It results when "social control is perceived to have broken down and/or [when] a higher level of control is called for by a situation or events, such as a 'terrorist attack.'"[61]

The politics of fear begins with a definition of the situation and then a justification of it through propaganda "or the manipulation of information for a specific purpose."[62] Fear is "socially constructed and managed by political actors to promote their own goals," meaning it is ideological in nature.[63] It is most effective "when the messages and meanings are part of the broader culture and are recognized and taken for granted by a mass audience."[64] In the case of crime, Americans generally agree that crime is bad; that is something that is taken for granted. So, any policy that claims to be anti-crime is easily sellable as a good thing. The most effective messages are simple and often repeated.

So What Can Be Done?

Given all the problems about the media identified in the book, at least some effort should be made to consider what can be done to reform the media. Our concern is what can be done to help make media coverage of crime, criminal justice and related topics better match the empirical realities of these phenomena.

Two Outlandish Possibilities?

Ray Surette offers two future possibilities for media evolution. In the first, media have evolved further toward infotainment, "reality programs" abound, and media coverage of crime and criminal justice has expanded and become more intrusive. As one example, picture television shows where real inmates are executed live on TV. Given the long evolution of American media toward more violence, more graphic violence, more death, more graphic death, and so forth, this may very well be where we are heading.

In the second, media have been greatly restricted and thus have much more difficulty covering crime and criminal justice. As one example, imagine the news unable to provide any coverage of crime at all due to public concern about past coverage.[65] This second possibility would occur if our nation's leaders placed additional constraints on the media aimed at restricting access to crime and criminal justice events in order to protect society from the kind of reporting we are seeing now. It is unlikely this will occur in a society that values freedom of the press, but it is possible that greater caution will be shown by media organizations in their coverage of crime and terrorism when citizens (and advertisers) withdraw their support of such programs.

Surette concludes that neither of these possibilities is particularly attractive. You may concur. Can you imagine living in a nation where citizens pay to watch crime victims, criminal offenders, and the administration of criminal punishment, sold to them for profit? Can you imagine living in a nation where the media are more restricted by law and thus are less free to investigate stories related to crime, criminal justice and so forth?

Instead, perhaps it is easier to imagine that citizens and media consumers will one day demand that the media lay off of crime and criminal justice stories a bit—i.e., cover some but only those that are actually important and cover them in a responsible way that reflects reality. You can probably simultaneously imagine that eventually there will be a natural blowback against violence in infotainment and entertainment media; in the near future it is likely that there will still be a strong focus on violence and crime yet just not as strong as we see today. The question is how will we get there?

Media Reforms Being Pursued Now

Most major reforms aimed at the media are based on the assumption that the major problem with the mainstream media is that they are owned by large for-profit corporations, as shown in this book. The principles of "StopBig-Media" include that a free and vibrant media full of diverse, local and competing voices is the lifeblood of America's democracy. Massive consolidation of media ownership has dangerously reduced the number of voices in our nation's media. Today, the vast majority of popular news, entertainment and information is controlled by a handful of giant media conglomerates. These corporations seek to minimize competition and maximize profits rather than inform, enlighten, and promote the public interest. The FCC and Congress must ensure that our media system is, in the words of the Supreme Court, "an uninhibited marketplace of ideas in which truth will prevail."[66]

Given these realities, the most significant reforms underway now are aimed at breaking up corporate owned media and/or restricting their power. These are reforms aimed at breaking up the highly consolidated companies that own the great bulk of media today, at loosening the vertical and horizontal connections between media companies, at empowering non-profit news agencies, and so forth.

One example comes from the group called "Save the News," a project of the Free Press. According to Save the News: "Newsrooms are failing. Investigative journalism is disappearing. Reporters are losing their jobs. Vital stories are not being told. Real journalism gives communities the information they need to understand our world, hold our leaders accountable and participate in our democracy."[67] In their view, this is why media reform is so essential.

Save the News offers the following as its principles:

· *Protect the First Amendment*—Freedom of speech and freedom of the press are essential to a free society and a functioning democracy.
· *Produce quality news coverage*—To self-govern in a democratic society, the public needs in-depth reporting on local issues as well as national and international affairs that is accurate, credible and verifiable. Journalism should be animated by a multitude of voices and viewpoints.
· *Provide adversarial perspectives*—Reporting should hold the powerful accountable by scrutinizing the actions of government and corporations. Journalism should foster genuine debate about important issues.
· *Promote public accountability*—Newsrooms should serve the public interest, not private or government aims, and should be treated as a public service, not a commodity. Journalism should be responsive to the needs of changing communities.
· *Prioritize innovation*—Journalists should utilize new tools and technology to report and deliver the news. The public needs journalism that crosses traditional boundaries and is accessible to the broadest range of people across platforms.[68]

Most would probably agree that these principles are appropriate for the media. Yet, the question remains, how do you assure these principles are put into place? More specifically, what reforms are needed to get from where we are now to where Save the News says we need to go? After reviewing several possibilities, Save the News notes: "One conclusion is incontrovertible: To support new forms of reporting and new methods of distribution, we must think outside of current structures and beyond the current system. We cannot fix this problem by simply subsidizing or propping up old business models."[69]

Save the News considers six categories of reforms. The first is called "Public Subsidies and Policy Changes" and consists of efforts by the government to break up media monopolies and oligopolies through measures such as bankruptcies and to assist alternative media through subsidies.[70] These reforms are unlikely to succeed given that the media monopolies and oligopolies are powerful and will resist such change. The second set of reforms is called "Public and Government Models" and is made up of more direct government intervention such as investing in public media and helping train a whole new batch of journalists.[71] The goal here would be the realization of additional media outlets similar to the Public Broadcasting System (PBS) and National Public Radio (NPR). The third set of reforms is called "Nonprofit, Low-Profit and Cooperative Models" and is comprised primarily of different forms of media ownership, forms that are interested less in profit and more in news[72] This approach is now being embraced by some media outlets, including newspapers, around the country. The fourth set of reforms is called "Community and Municipal Models" and suggests the best way to promote independent media is through local ownership.[73] This approach is also started to be adopted but only sporadically so. The fifth set of reforms is called "Foundation and Endowment Models" and is made up of efforts to fund the media through alternative sources of money including foundations and public endowments.[74] The media organization, ProPublica, introduced in Chapter 5, is a good example of this model. The sixth set of reforms is called "New Commercial Models" and consists of a wide variety of proposed changes to the existing structures of the media.[75] The last model includes ending media consolidation, empowering consumers to choose and pay for the news they want to see, and more. As one example, picture paying for the news and entertainment you want to see, hear, or read, and nothing more.

⌂ **For more information about these proposed media reforms, see the website for this book at: www.pscj.appstate.edu/media/mediareform. html**

Other Possible Reforms

Additional recommendations for media reform are called for, based on the assumption that major corporations will strongly resist reforms like those discussed above. Thus, assuming that the mainstream media continue to be operated for-profit, here are some additional recommendations for helping the media get stories about crime, criminal justice and related phenomena right:

- *Educate the media about crime and criminal justice through planned workshops.*

The nation's crime experts can no longer afford to sit on the sidelines, watching the media continue to get it wrong. We seem to know how and why the media are misinforming citizens about the true nature of crime and criminal justice in the United States. It is our responsibility to ensure that this misinformation stops, especially given that most Americans get their information from media outlets. Although part of the educational effort might be aimed at separating mainstream media from corporate ownership, it also makes sense to simply educate the media about the realities of crime and criminal justice, and then expect the media to get it right when they are reporting. This is especially true for the news media whose job it is to be accurate and objective. It will remain our job to call them on it when they make mistakes.

- *Develop a network of contacts between criminal justice scholars and the media.*

Every expert owes it to the nation to insert himself or herself into the media when stories about their areas of expertise are discussed. We cannot afford to allow politicians and the police to be the primary sources of information about crime and criminal justice in the United States, given their clear biases in favor of the status quo, and because we study crime and criminal justice for a living. We can write letters to the editor as well as opinion editorials to newspapers. This is but one way to demand the truth (and present the truth) to news consumers when the media get it wrong. We can also create and maintain blogs, websites, Facebook pages and so forth to correct the record when it needs to be corrected.

- *Utilize, advertise, and celebrate independent media outlets.*

One thing we can all do is use independent media outlets that are not privately owned and that operate with the interests of the people in mind.

We ought to tell our colleagues and students and every day people to turn off the television and radio unless they are watching public television and listening to public radio, or to at least boycott television shows and networks that sell us harmful stories about crime and related phenomena and harm the nation in so doing. We can do the same with movies, music, books, and more.

• *Insist that the media get it right by reducing consumer demand for sleazy news.*

We must encourage citizens to pursue alternative forms of education and news rather than crime shows and sensational news. Research shows that crime entertainment and news promote a "siege mentality" among some viewers, who become more likely to stay inside and to fear the poor and people of color rather than wanting to help them have good lives. The news media should develop and broadcast clear statements reflecting their intention to cease broadcasting sleazy, sensationalized crime stories. As for the entertainment and infotainment media, a great deal of this is focused exclusively on sleaze; we ought to tell the companies that we do not value this; perhaps the best way to do this is to withhold our dollars from their products. This part of reform is up to us, the consumers.

Ray Surette offers another interesting idea, suggesting that if crime was covered like sports, people would have a much better understanding of the realities of crime: Sports coverage stands as a model for reporting on individual events, supplemented by statistics, trend analysis, forecasts, commentary, and discussion. Sporting events are consistently placed by the media in their larger social context … and constructed in a way that provides historical understanding and current comprehension."[76] If crime was covered this way, at least more context would be provided in the news.

We as consumers can demand a change in the content of the news, as well as in infotainment and entertainment media. First, we can demand that the news media tell us the truth about crime. For example, we can insist that the media focus more of their attention on those acts that cause the most harm to society—white-collar and corporate crime—and spend far less time focused on relatively harmless street crimes. We can also demand the news media provide better context for crime whenever it is covered. Second, we can also demand the news media stop covering bad news exclusively. For example, as a citizen living in North Carolina, do I need to know about a high speed police chase in Los Angeles, California? Is there *ever* a reason to cover this event live, aside from alerting people in the nearby area to avoid that particular road? There is so much good in our community, state, region and country that we never hear about because the news media tend not to focus on good news. As consumers, it may be up to us to insist that the media cease with their depressing formula of crime, crime, crime, other bad news, followed by weather and sports, and tell us more about the good things that do exist and that can inspire other good behavior.

When it comes to the infotainment and entertainment media, we as consumers ultimately decide what television shows, movies and music are successful based on what we buy. While we have little to no impact on what content is initially produced by such media companies, it is a fact that if we don't watch or buy violent television, movies and music, media companies will stop producing it; after all, they are in the business of making money not losing it. So, to a large extent, media reform is up to us.

Summary

This chapter summarized the entire book, laying out the major problems with the media and its coverage of crime and criminal justice. There are two major, competing explanations for the news media's inaccuracy in covering crime, criminal justice and related topics, including the market model and the manipulative model. An alternative explanation—the organizational model—contains elements of the market and manipulative models but is more similar to the manipulative model than the market model. It is the most accurate of the three models. According to the organization model, content is selected based on the needs of the media rather than the demands of the public; thus the blame lies more on the media for how the media operate. Specifically, whether and how stories get covered depends on the periodicity of the stories and how well they match the needs of the media; periodicity pertains to the timing of a story. Whether and how stories get covered also depends on the consonance of the stories to previously covered themes and narratives; consonance pertains to how well a story fits previously covered stories. To the degree that stories fit a routine pattern of media coverage (routinization), they are more likely to be covered.

Proponents of the organizational model do not see the media as intentionally distorting content and thus aimed at manipulating public opinion. Rather, they see the media as simply responding to organizational factors. Since crime is popular, always timely (periodicity), easy to connect to previously depicted themes and narratives (consonance), and routinely covered (routinization), crime news will make up a large part of all news.

Media inaccuracies and problems of coverage of crime and criminal justice stem, first and foremost, from the organization nature of the media. Mainstream media are owned by corporations and will inevitably cover stories in a way that serves their own interests (including ignoring stories that call their interests into question). The media also attempt to give us what they think will help us sell the products that they advertise on their stations and in their newspapers. Since violence is so important and even celebrated in America, stories about crime fit our preoccupation with violence nicely. It even fits well when the stories are inaccurate and/or result in misinformation.

Decisions about newsworthiness are made by the leaders of corporate media. First and foremost, these leaders are concerned with profit. Thus, news becomes anything that has generates audiences, ratings, sales, and advertising dollars; this includes the routine (e.g., crime, which is covered every day) and the extraordinary (e.g., unusual crimes that rarely occur but that always receive extensive media coverage).

Given the organizational needs of the media, including profit-generating news, crime is valuable because it attracts viewers and because it is relatively easy to write about given the abundance of official sources of information in law enforcement personnel and politicians. These officials are considered legitimate, authoritative, reliable, and consistently available, as shown throughout the book.

When it comes to entertainment and infotainment media, they are obviously profiting immensely from crime and violence; it forms the basis for popular movies, music, and television shows. Clearly, profit-seeking is the culprit here; crime and violence sell, so the media continue to produce them.

Because of the focus on violence and unusual events, even television news comes to be seen as a form of entertainment, whereby the media are highly selective in what they broadcast. Violence is more "sellable" than the mundane aspects of theft and other forms of property crime. Another part of the organizational nature of the media that often does not get much attention is the peer culture that permeates the media.

Other factors that help us understand inaccuracy in the press are a lack of education, the peer culture that is prevalent in the media, and politicians framing crime and similar social problems in the media.

Most major reforms aimed at the media are based on the assumption that the major problem with the mainstream media is that they are owned by large for-profit corporations, as shown in this book. The most significant reforms underway now are aimed at breaking up corporate owned media and/or restricting their power. These are reforms aimed at breaking up the highly consolidated companies that own the great bulk of media today, at loosening the vertical and horizontal connections between media companies, at empowering non-profit news agencies, and so forth.

Discussion Questions

1) Of all the problems with the media summarized in this chapter, which are the most important? Why?
2) Compare and contrast the three major explanations or models for the news media's inaccuracy in covering crime, criminal justice and related topics.
3) Which of the three major models for the news media's inaccuracy in covering crime, criminal justice and related topics is most accurate? Explain.
4) In the chapter, it was stated that "inaccuracies and problems of coverage of crime and criminal justice stem, first and foremost, from the organization nature of the media." Do you agree? Why or why not?
5) How do the mainstream media benefit from intense coverage of violent crime?
6) How do the mainstream media benefit from inaccurate coverage of crime and criminal justice?
7) Explain how imitation and a lack of criminal justice education help explain the inaccuracies in media coverage presented in this book.
8) Discuss how the media frame crime as a failure of criminal justice agencies. And what are the implications for criminal justice practice?
9) Identify and discuss the major effects of consuming media (e.g., watching television) on consumers (i.e., viewers).
10) Outline the major reforms aimed at the way media operate in the United States.

Activities

Investigate your local newspapers. Who owns them? How well do they cover local stories versus national stories? It this newspaper doing an adequate job informing citizens of relevant local matters?

What types of stories are covered in the paper? What percentage of the stories are about crime? What percentage of the stories are about criminal justice? What are the dominant themes and narratives used to depict crime and criminal justice?

Identify the number of local channels on television in your area. What types of stories do they cover and how do they cover them? What percentage of the stories are about crime? What percentage of the stories are about criminal justice? What are the dominant themes and narratives used on these channels to depict crime and criminal justice?

Find a recent example of a crime problem that received objective coverage in the news. Discuss how this example fits with the main premise or argument of the book.

Find a recent example of a crime problem that received subjective coverage in the news. Discuss how this example fits with the main premise or argument of the book.

Find a recent example of a crime problem that was turned into a moral panic in the news. Discuss how this example fits with the main premise or argument of the book.

Identify recent television shows about crime and/or criminal justice. Discuss the way crime and/or crime fighting is depicted on these shows.

Design a more realistic fictional television program about crime or criminal justice. Create the characters and story-lines that could be shown in order to more accurately reflect the realities of crime or criminal justice.

Identify recent movies about crime and/or criminal justice. Discuss the way crime and/or crime fighting is depicted in these movies.

Create a plot for a movie about crime and/or criminal justice that would be entertaining but also informative of facts of crime and/or criminal justice.

Identify popular music artists and their songs. Analyze the content of their songs/lyrics relative to the major findings of the book.

Write a letter or op-ed to your local, regional, or a national newspaper to lay out the major problems with the media that concern you the most.

Discuss the major media reforms you would support to make the media more accurate and reliable.

Identify blogs, websites, and YouTube channels for information about crime and criminal justice.

Identify major sources of information from "alternative" media sources. Which are your favorite? Why? What can you do to support these alternative media?

Find and summarize recent scholarly articles about crime or criminal justice in the media.

Visit the website for this book (www.pscj.appstate.edu/media) and read additional information about the media and how they cover crime and criminal justice, as well as terrorism and the war on terrorism.

Endnotes

Preface

1. Wykes, M. (2001). *News, crime and culture.* New York: Pluto Press.
2. Robinson, M. (2009). *Justice blind? Ideals and realities of American criminal justice* (3rd Ed.). Upper Saddle River, New Jersey: Prentice Hall.
3. Robinson, M.(2007). Freedom in an era of terror: A critical analysis of the USA PATRIOT Act. *Justice Policy Journal 4* (1), 1–48.
4. Surette, R. (2007). *Media, crime, and criminal justice.* Belmont, CA: Wadsworth, p. 2.

Chapter 1

1. Dictionary.com (2008). Entry for medium. Retrieved November 24, 2008, from http://dictionary.reference.com/browse/medium.
2. Dictionary.com (2008). Entry for media. Retrieved November 24, 2008, from http://dictionary.reference.com/browse/media.
3. Surette, R. (1992). *Media, crime, and criminal justice: Images and realities.* Pacific Grove: Brooks/Cole, p. 10.
4. Altheide, D. (2006). *Terrorism and the politics of fear.* Lanham, MD: AltaMira Press, p. 48.
5. Merriam Webster (2009). Entry for "infotainment." Retrieved August 18, 2009, from: http://www.merriam-webster.com/dictionary/infotainment.
6. Hess, S. (1981). *The Washington reporters.* Washington, DC: Brookings Institution.
7. Lewis, D. (1981). Crime in the media: Introduction. In D. Lewis (Ed.), *Reactions to crime.* Beverly Hills, CA: Sage Publications; Marion, N. (1995). *A primer in the politics of criminal justice.* Albany, NY: Harrow and Heston.
8. Merlo, A., & Benekos, P. (2000). *What's wrong with the criminal justice system: Ideology, politics and the media.* Cincinnati, OH: Anderson.
9. Center for Media and Public Affairs. (2000). The media at the millennium. Retrieved November 25, 2008, from http://www.cmpa.com/files/media_monitor/00julaug.pdf.
10. Dowler, K. (2003). Media consumption and public attitudes toward crime and justice: The relationship between fear of crime, punitive attitudes, and perceived police effectiveness. *Journal of Criminal Justice and Popular Culture, 10*(2): 109–126. http://www.albany.edu/scj/jcjpc/vol10is2/dowler.pdf, p. 109.

11. Robinson, M. (2009). *Justice blind? Ideals and realities of American criminal justice* (3rd Ed.). Upper Saddle River, NJ: Prentice Hall.

12. Krajicek, D. (1998). *Scooped! Media miss real story on crime while chasing sex, sleaze, and celebrities.* New York: Columbia University Press, p. 139.

13. Harrigan, J. (2000). *Empty dreams, empty pockets: Class and bias in American politics.* New York: Addison-Wesley Longman, p. 120.

14. Weaver, D., & Wilhoit, G. (1986). *The American journalist: A portrait of U.S. news people and their work.* Bloomington: Indiana University Press.

15. Krajicek, D. (1998).

16. Chomsky, N. (1997). What makes mainstream media mainstream. Retrieved January 13, 2009, from: http://www.chomsky.info/articles/199710—.htm.

17. Parenti, M. (1993). *Inventing reality: The politics of the news media.* New York: St. Martin's Press, p. 26.

18. Bagdikian, B. (2004). *The new media monopoly.* Boston, MA: Beacon Press.

19. Bagdikian (2004), p. 3.

20. Ownership chart: The big six. Retrieved September 21, 2009, from: http://www.free press.net/ownership/chart/main.

21. McChesney, R. (2004). *The problem of the media.* New York: Monthly Review Press, p. 17.

22. McChesney (2004), p. 57.

23. Montross Jr., W., & Mulvaney, P. (2009). Virtue and vice: Who will report on the failings of the American criminal justice system? *Stanford Law Review, 61*(6), 1429–1461, p. 1444.

24. Chomsky, N. (1997).

25. Bagdikian (2004), p. 1.

26. Bagdikian (2004), pp. 2–3.

27. Common Dreams (2004). More than 100 Clear Channel stations to get Fox newscasts. Retrieved February 24, 2009, from: http://www.commondreams.org/headlines04/1207-12.htm.

28. Greenwald, R. (2004). *Outfoxed: Rupert Murdoch's war on journalism.* New York: The Disinformation company.

29. Bagdikian (2004), p. 15.

30. Shah, A. (2009). Media conglomerates, mergers, concentration of ownership. Retrieved January 13, 2009, from: http://www.globalissues.org/article/159/media-conglomerates-mergers-concentration-of-ownership.

31. Bagdikian, B. (2004).

32. McChesney, R. (1999). *Rich media poor democracy.* New York: The New Press, p. 16.

33. McChesney (1999), p. 177.

34. McChesney (1999), p. 178.

35. McChesney (1999), p. 16.

36. Federal Trade Commission (2009). Maintaining or creating a monopoly. Retrieved February 24, 2009, from: http://www.ftc.gov/bc/compguide/maintain.htm.

37. Bagdikian, B. (2004).

38. Bagdikian (2004), p. 185.

39. Bagdikian (2004), pp. 196–198.

40. Bagdikian (2004), p. 105.

41. Montross Jr., W., & Mulvaney, P. (2009). Virtue and vice: Who will report on the failings of the American criminal justice system? *Stanford Law Review, 61*(6), 1429–1461, p. 1444.

42. Bagdikian (2004), p. 196.

43. McChesney (1999), p. 180.

44. Bagdikian, B. (2004), p. 31.

45. Crothers, L. (2007). *Globalization & American culture*. Lanham, MD: Rowman & Littlefield, p. 30.

46. McChesney (2004), p. 184.

47. McChesney (2004), p. 21.

48. Reck, G. (2008). Globalization, resistance, and the new empire of capital. Retrieved November 3, 2009, from: http://www.justiceblind.com/globalization.doc.

49. Bagdikian (2004), p. 51.

50. Bagdikian (2004), p. 9.

51. Herman & Chomsky (2002), p. 10.

52. Robinson (2009).

53. Herman & Chomsky (2002), p. 13.

54. Bagdikian (2004), p. 4.

55. Bagdikian (2004), p. 6.

56. Federal Trade Commission (2009). FTC guide to the antitrust laws. Retrieved February 24, 2009, from: http://www.ftc.gov/bc/antitrust/index.shtm.

57. McChesney (2004), p. 28.

58. McChesney (2004), p. 9.

59. Bagdikian, B. (2004), p.

60. McChesney (2004), p. 4.

61. McChesney (2004), p. 6.

62. McChesney (2004), pp. 29–30.

63. Free Press (2009). About us. Retrieved September 21, 2009, from: http://www.free press.net/about_us.

64. Free Press (2009). Media consolidation. Retrieved September 21, 2009, from: http://www.freepress.net/node/71.

65. Free Press (2009). Media consolidation. Retrieved September 21, 2009, from: http://www.freepress.net/node/71.

66. McChesney (2004), p. 93.

67. Williams, J. (2008). The lessons of 'Enron': Media accounts, corporate crimes, and financial markets. *Theoretical Criminology, 12*(4), 471.

68. Lynch, M., Stretesky, P., & Hammond, P. (2000). Media coverage of chemical crimes, Hillsborough County, Florida, 1987–97. *The British Journal of Criminology, 40*(1), 112–126; McMullan, J. (2006). News, truth, and the recognition of corporate crime. *Canadian Journal of Criminology and Criminal Justice, 48*(6), 905–939.

69. Evans, S. & Lundman, R. (1983). Newspaper coverage of corporate price-fixing. *Criminology 21*, 529–541, p. 539.

70. Bagdikian (2004), p. 161.

71. Pew Research Center for the People and the Press (2005). Public sours on government and business. Retrieved April 23, 2009, from: http://people-press.org/report/261/public-sours-on-government-and-business.

72. Pew Research Center for the People and the Press (2002). News media's improved image proves short-lived. April 23, 2009 from: http://people-press.org/report/?pageid=629

73. Hitchens, C. (2001). *The trial of Henry Kissinger*. Brooklyn, NY: Verso.

74. Bagdikian (2004), p. 209.

75. Woodward, B. (2006). *State of denial.* New York: Simon and Schuster.

76. McChesney (2004), p. 73.

77. McChesney (2004), p. 74.

78. Harrigan, J. (2000), p. 124.

79. Bagdikian (2004), p. xiii.

80. McChesney (2004), p. 17.

81. Herman, Edward, & Chomsky, Noam (2002). *Manufacturing consent: The political economy of mass media.* New York: Pantheon Books, p. lix.

82. Herman & Chomsky (2002), p. lix.

83. Herman & Chomsky (2002), p. 1.

84. Herman & Chomsky (2002), p. xi.

85. Herman & Chomsky (2002), p. 298.

86. Herman & Chomsky (2002), p. 2.

87. Herman & Chomsky (2002), pp. 4–5.

88. Herman & Chomsky (2002), p. 5.

89. McChesney (2004), p. 186.

90. McChesney (2004), p. 189.

91. McChesney (2004), p. 8.

92. McChesney (2004), p. 19.

93. Herman & Chomsky (2002), p. xvii.

94. Herman & Chomsky (2002), p. 14.

95. Herman & Chomsky (2002), p. 5.

96. McChesney (2004), p. 14.

97. McChesney (2004), pp. 72–73.

98. McChesney (2004), pp. 143–144.

99. Herman & Chomsky (2002), p. 303.

100. Herman & Chomsky (2002), p. 16.

101. Herman & Chomsky (2002), p. 17.

102. Herman & Chomsky (2002), p. 18.

103. McChesney (2004), p. 144.

104. Surette, R. (2006). *Media, crime, and criminal justice.* Belmont, CA: Wadsworth, p. 25.

105. Bagdikian (2004), p 242.

106. Herman & Chomsky (2002), p. 18.

107. McChesney (2004), p. 144.

108. Bagdikian (2004), p. 225.

109. Bagdikian (2004), p. 234.

110. Bagdikian (2004), pp. 235–239.

111. McChesney (2004), p. 59.

112. Crothers, L. (2007). *Globalization & American culture.* Lanham, MD: Rowman & Littlefield, pp. 10–11.

113. Herman & Chomsky (2002), pp. 18–19.

114. McChesney (2004), p. 68.

115. McChesney (2004), p. 69.

116. Bagdikian (2004), p. 19.

117. McChesney (2004), p. 70.

118. McChesney (2004), p. 82.

119. McChesney (2004), pp. 21–22.

120. McChesney (2004), p. 22.

121. Herman & Chomsky (2002), p. 23.

122. Miller, R. (1996). *Drug warriors and their prey.* New York: Praeger.

123. Robinson, M, & Scherlen, R. (2007). *Lies, damned lies, and drug war statistics.* Albany, NY: State University of New York Press.

124. Gray, J. (2001). *Why our drug laws have failed and what we can do about it.* Philadelphia, PA: Temple University Press; Miron, J. (2004). *Drug war crimes.* Washington, DC: Independent Institute.

125. Herman & Chomsky (2002), p. 26.

126. Herman & Chomsky (2002), p. 26.

127. Herman & Chomsky (2002), p. 29.

128. Bagdikian (2004), p. 85.

129. Goldberg, B. (2003). *Bias.* New York: Harper.

130. Alterman, E. (2004). *What liberal media.* New York: Basic Books.

131. Ackerman, S. (2001). The most biased name in news. Fairness and Accuracy in Reporting. Retrieved February 25, 2009, from: http://www.fair.org/index.php?page=1067.

132. Lewis, C., & Reading-Smith, M. (2008). False pretenses. The Center for Public Integrity. Retrieved February 25, 2009, from: http://projects.publicintegrity.org/WarCard/.

133. Media Matters for America (2007). Black and white and re(a)d all over: The conservative advantage in syndicated op-ed columns. Retrieved September 18, 2009, from:http://mediamatters.org/reports/oped/?f=h_top.

134. Media Matters for America (2007), p. 1.

135. Pew Center for Excellence in Journalism (2009). Talk radio. Retrieved September 18, 2009, from: http://www.stateofthemedia.org/2009/narrative_audio_talkradio.php?cat=6&media=10.

136. Altheide, D. (2006). *Terrorism and the politics of fear.* Lanham, MD: AltaMira Press.

137. Herman & Chomsky (2002), p. 31.

138. Herman & Chomsky (2002), p. 302.

139. Herman & Chomsky (2002), p. 306.

140. Herman & Chomsky (2002), p. xi.

141. Herman & Chomsky (2002), p. xii.

142. Bagdikian (2004), p. xvii.

143. Herman & Chomsky (2002), p. xiii.

144. McChesney (2004), p. 73.

145. McChesney (2004), p. 81.

146. http://www.propublica.org/about/.

147. McChesney (1999), p. xviii.

148. Crothers, L. (2007). *Globalization & American culture.* Lanham, MD: Rowman & Littlefield, p. 68.

149. McChesney (1999), p. xix.

150. Hsieh and Pugh (1993); Fowles & Merva, 1996; Hagan & Peterson, 1994; Land, McCall, & Cohen, 1990; Messner & Tardiff, 1986; Sampson, 1995.

151. Vieraitis (2000).

152. McCall, Parker, & MacDonald (2007).

153. McChesney (1999), pp. xviii–xix.

154. Robinson, M. (2009). *Justice blind? Ideals and realities of American criminal justice* (3rd Ed.). Upper Saddle River, NJ: Prentice Hall.

155. McChesney (1999), p. xxi.

Chapter 2

1. Potter, G., & Kappeler, V. (1998). *Constructing crime: Perspectives on making news and social problems*. Prospect Heights, IL: Waveland Press.

2. Bennett, L. (1980). *Public opinion in American politics*. New York: Harcourt Brace Jovanovich.; Iyengar, S., & Kinder, D. (1987). *News that matters: Television and American opinion*. Chicago: University of Chicago Press; McCombs, M., & Shaw, D. (1972). The agenda setting function of the mass media. *Public Opinion Quarterly 36*, 176–187; Muraskin, R., & Domash, S. (2006). *Crime and the media: Headlines vs. reality*. Upper Saddle River, NJ: Prentice Hall; Sacco, V. (2005). *When crime waves*. Thousand Oaks, CA: Sage.

3. Sotirovic, M. (2003). How individuals explain social problems: The influences of media use. *Journal of Communication, 53*(1), 122–137.

4. Edy, J., & Meirick, P. (2007). Wanted, dead or alive: Media frames, frame adoption, and support or the war in Afghanistan. *Journal of Communication, 57*, 119–141, p. 120.

5. Altheide, D. (2006), p.61.

6. Altheide (2006), p.78.

7. Hollinger, R., & Lanza-Kaduce, L. (1988). The process of criminalization. *Criminology, 26*, 101–126; Muraskin & Domash, 2006; Sacco, 2005)

8. Surette, R. (1992), p. 2.

9. Ferrell, J., & Websdale, N. (1999). *Making trouble: Cultural constructions of crime, deviance, and control*. New York: Aldine De Gruyter; Mason, P. (2004) *Criminal Visions: Media Representations of Crime and Justice*. Uffculme, Devon, UK: Willan.

10. Potter, G., & Kappeler, V. (1998, p. 7).

11. Marion, N. (1995). *A primer in the politics of criminal justice*. Albany, NY: Harrow and Heston; Van Horn, C., Baumer, D., & Gormley, Jr., W. (1992). *Politics and public policy*. Washington, DC: CQ Press.

12. Herman & Chomsky (2002), p. xix.

13. Bagdikian (2004).

14. McChesney (2004), p. 9.

15. McChesney (1999), p. 108.

16. McChesney (2004), p. 86.

17. McChesney (2004), p. 200.

18. Bagdikian (2004), p. 241.

19. Crothers, L. (2007). *Globalization & American culture*. Lanham, MD: Rowman & Littlefield, p. p. 94.

20. Crothers, L. (2007). *Globalization & American culture*. Lanham, MD: Rowman & Littlefield, p. 66.

21. McChesney (1999), p. 33.

22. Sacco, V. F. (2005). *When crime waves*. Thousand Oaks, CA: Sage.

23. McChesney, 1999, p. 34.

24. McChesney R. (2004). *The problem of the media.* New York: Monthly Review Press, pp. 86–87.

25. McChesney (2004), pp. 194–195.

26. Crothers, L. (2007). *Globalization & American culture.* Lanham, MD: Rowman & Littlefield, p. 100.

27. Surette, R. (1992), p. 4; also see Altheide, D. (1984). TV news and the social construction of justice: Research issues and policy. In R. Surette (Ed.), *Justice and the media.* Springfield, IL: Charles C Thomas; Quinney, R. (1970). *The Social reality of crime.* New Brunswick, NJ: Transaction Publishers; Tuchman, G. (1978). *Making news: A study in the social construction of reality.* New York: The Free Press.

28. Cohen, S., Young, J. (1981). *The manufacture of news.* Newbury Park, CA: Sage Publications; Lichter, S. (1988). Media power: The influence of media on politics and business. *Florida Policy Review, 4,* 35–41.

29. Barkan, S. (1997). *Criminology: A sociological understanding.* Englewood Cliffs, NJ: Prentice Hall; Kappeler & Potter (2004).

30. Potter, G., & Kappeler, V. (1998).

31. Barak, G. (1994). *Media, process, and the social construction of crime.* New York: Garland; Ericson, R., Baranek, P., & Chan, J. (1989). *Negotiating control: A study of news sources.* Toronto: University of Toronto Press; Graber, D. (1980). *Crime news and the public.* Westport, CT: Praeger.

32. Entman, R. (1989). *Democracy without citizens: Media and the decay of American politics.* New York: Oxford University Press; Nelkin, D. (1987). *Selling science: How the press covers science and technology.* New York: WH Freeman & Co.

33. Merriam Webster's Dictionary (2009). Entry for "objective." Retrieved February 26, 2009, from: http://www.merriam-webster.com/dictionary/objective

34. White, R. (2000). Media objectivity and the rhetoric of news story structure. In E. Ventola (Ed.), *Discourse and community.* Narr.

35. Davis, J. (2007). News: Beyond the myth of objectivity. Retrieved February 28, 2009, from: http://www.medialit.org/reading_room/article48.html.

36. Dedman. B. (2007). Journalists dole out cash to politicians (quietly). Retrieved May 19, 2009, from: http://www.msnbc.msn.com/id/19113485/; Media Research Center (2009). Media bias basics. Retrieved May 19, 2009, from: http://www.mediaresearch.org/biasbasics/bias basics1.asp.

37. Alterman, E. (2003). *What liberal media? The truth about bias and the news.* New York: Basic Books.

38. Surette, R. (2007). *Media, crime, and criminal justice.* Belmont, CA: Wadsworth, p. 37.

39. Lee, M., & Solomon, N. (1990). *Unreliable sources: A guide to detecting bias in news media.* New York: Carol Publishing Group, p. 16.

40. McNair, B. (1994). *News and journalism in the UK.* New York: Routledge.

41. Robinson, M. (2009). *Justice blind? Ideals and realities of American criminal justice.* Upper Saddle River, NJ: Prentice Hall.

42. Rockler-Gladen, N. (2008). Does media objectivity exist? Retrieved February 28, 2009, from: http://media-bias.suite101.com/article.cfm/does_media_objectivity_exist.

43. Beder, S. (2009). The media. Retrieved February 28, 2009, from: http://homepage.mac.com/herinst/envcrisis/media/contents.html.

44. Lee, M., & Solomon, N. (1990). *Unreliable sources: A guide to detecting bias in news media.* New York: Carol Publishing Group, p. 16.

45. Media Owners (2009). Washington Post Company. Retrieved February 28, 2009, from: http://www.mediaowners.com/company/washingtonpost.html.

46. Thomas, E. (2008). The myth of objectivity. *Newsweek* March 10. Retrieved February 27, 2009, from: http://www.newsweek.com/id/117850.

47. Mauss, A. (1975). *Social problems as social movements.* New York: J. B. Lippincott.

48. Jensen, E., Gerber, J., & Babcock, G. (1991). The new war on drugs: Grass roots movement or political construction? *Journal of Drug Issues, 21*(3), 651–667.

49. Mauss (1975), p. 62.

50. Mauss (1975), p. 63.

51. Jensen, Gerber, & Babcock (1991).

52. PBS (2009). Marijuana timeline. Retrieved March 3, 2009, from: http://www.pbs.org/wgbh/pages/frontline/shows/dope/etc/cron.html.

53. Robinson, M., & Scherlen, R. (2007). *Lies, damned lies, and drug war statistics.* Albany, NY: State University of New York Press.

54. Merriam Webster's Dictionary (2009). Entry for "subjective." Retrieved February 26, 2009, from: http://www.merriam-webster.com/dictionary/subjective.

55. Surette (2007), p. 39.

56. Surette (2007), pp. 39–41.

57. Surette (2007), p. 206.

58. Surette (2007), pp. 42–43.

59. Spitzberg, B., & and Cadiz, M. (2002). The media construction of stalking stereotypes. *Journal of Criminal Justice and Popular Culture, 9*(3), 128–149. http://www.albany.edu/scj/jcjpc/vol9is3/spitzberg.pdf, p. 128.

60. Robinson & Scherlen (2007).

61. Boyd, S. (2004). *From witches to crack moms: Women, drug law, and policy.* Durham, NC: Carolina Academic Press.

62. Surette (2007), p. 3.

63. Surette (2007), pp. 32–34.

64. Surette (2007), p. 35.

65. Mauss (1975); Mauss, A. (1989). Beyond the illusion of social problems theory. In J. Holstein & G. Miller (Eds.), *Perspectives on social problems* (Vol. 1). Greenwich, CT: JAI Press; Spector, M., & Kitsuse, J. (1987). *Constructing social problems.* Hawthorne, NY: Aldine de Gruyter.

66. Cohen, S. (1972). *Folk devils and moral panics: The creation of the Mods and the Rockers.* London: MacGibbon and Kee, p. 9.

67. Escholtz, S. (1997). The media and fear of crime: A survey of research. *University of Florida Journal of Law and Public Policy, 9*(1), 48.

68. Suratt, H., & Inciardi, J. (2001). Cocaine, crack, and the criminalization of pregnancy. In J. Inciardi & K. McElrath (Eds.), *The American drug scene.* Los Angeles, CA: Roxbury.

69. Jensen, E., & Gerber, J. (1998). *The new war on drugs: Symbolic politics and criminal justice policy.* Cincinnati, OH: Anderson, p. ix.

70. Robinson (2005).

71. Best (1989).

72. Jensen & Gerber (1998). p. 5.

73. See Office of National Drug Control Policy (2004). Ad gallery. Retrieved February 17, 2005, from http://www.mediacampaign.org/mg/.

74. Jensen & Gerber (1998), p. 8.

75. Quoted in Bonnie, R., & Whitebread, C. (1974). Marihuana conviction: A history of Marihuana prohibition in the United States. Charlottesville, VA: University of Virginia, p. 109.

76. Kappeler, V., Blumberg, M., & Potter, G. (2000). *The mythology of crime and criminal justice* (3rd ed.). Prospect Heights, IL: Waveland Press, p. 9.

77. See Vankin J., & Whalen, J. (2004). *The 80 greatest conspiracies of all time.* New York, NY: Citadel Press; J. Herer (1998). *The emperor wears no clothes: The authoritative historical record of cannabis and the conspiracy against marijuana* (11th ed.). Van Nuys, CA: Ah Ha Publishing Company.

78. See Anslinger, H., & Cooper, C. (2001). Marijuana: assassin of youth. In J. Inciardi & K. McElrath (Eds.), *The American drug scene.* Los Angeles, CA: Roxbury.

79. Webb, G., & Brown, M. (1998). United States drug laws and institutionalized discrimination. In E. Jensen & J. Gerber (Eds.), *The new war on drugs: Symbolic politics and criminal justice policy.* Cincinnati, OH: Anderson, p. 45.

80. Jensen & Gerber (1998).

81. Sandor, S. (1995). Legalizing/decriminalizing drug use. In R. Coombs & D. Zeidonis (Eds.), *Handbook on drug abuse prevention: A contemporary strategy to prevent the abuse of alcohol and other drugs.* Boston, MA: Allyn & Bacon, p. 48.

82. Belenko, S. (1993). *Crack and the evolution of the anti-drug policy.* Westport, CT: Greenwood Press, p. 9.

83. Becker, H. (1963). *Outsiders.* New York: Free Press.

84. Beckett, K., & Sasson, T. (2000). *The politics of injustice: Crime and justice in America.* Thousand Oaks, CA: Pine Forge Press, p. 37.

85. Jenkins, P. (1998). *Moral panic: changing concepts of the child molester in modern America.* New Haven, CT: Yale University Press.

86. Spitzberg, B., & and Cadiz, M. (2002). The media construction of stalking stereotypes. *Journal of Criminal Justice and Popular Culture, 9*(3), 128–149. http://www.albany.edu/scj/jcjpc/vol9is3/spitzberg.pdf, p. 133.

87. Glassner, B. (1999). *The Culture of Fear.* New York: Basic Books.

88. Reinarman, C., & Levine, H. (1989). Crack in context: Politics and media in the making of a drug scene. *Contemporary Drug Problems, 16,* 116–129.

89. Beckett, K. (1997). *Making crime pay: Law and order in contemporary American politics.* New York: Oxford University Press.

90. Potter, G., & Kappeler, V. (1998). *Constructing crime: Perspectives on making news and social problems.* Prospect Heights, IL: Waveland Press.

91. Beckett (1997).

92. Reinarman, C. (1995). Crack attack: America's latest drug scare, 1986–1992. In J. Best (Ed.), *Typifying contemporary social problems.* New York: Aldine de Gruyter.

93. Robinson (2005).

94. Cobbina, J. (2008). Race and class differences in print media portrayals of crack cocaine and methamphetamine.*Journal of Criminal Justice and Popular Culture, 15*(2), 145–167. http://www.albany.edu/scj/jcjpc/vol15is2/Cobbina.pdf, p.145.

95. Cobbina (2008), p. 161.

96. Cobbina (2008), p.145.

97. Reinarman & Levine (1989), pp. 541–542.

98. Orcutt, J., & Turner, J. (1993). Shocking numbers and graphic accounts: Quantified images of drug problems in print media. *Social Problems, 6,* 217–232; Walker, S. (1998). *Sense and nonsense about crime and drugs, A policy guide* (4th ed.). Belmont, CA: Wadsworth.

99. Jensen & Gerber (1998), p. 14.

100. U.S. Department of Health and Human Services. (2000). 1999 National Household Survey on Drug Abuse. Table 4.2a. Estimated numbers (in thousands) of persons who first used cocaine during the years 1965 to 1999, their mean age at first use, and annual age-specific rates of first use (per 1,000 person-years of exposure): Based on 1999 and 2000 NHSDAs. Retrieved February 20, 2005, from http://oas.samhsa.gov/nhsda/2kdetailedtabs/Vol_1_Part_3/sect3_5v1.htm#4.2a.

101. U.S. Department of Health and Human Services. (2000). 1999 National Household Survey on Drug Abuse. Table 4.3a. Estimated numbers (in thousands) of persons who first used crack during the years 1965 to 1999, their mean age at first use, and annual age-specific rates of first use (per 1,000 person-years of exposure): Based on 1999 and 2000 NHSDAs. Retrieved February 10, 2005, from http://oas.samhsa.gov/nhsda/2kdetailedtabs/Vol_1_Part_3/sect3_5v1.htm#4.3a.

102. Beckett & Sasson (2000), p. 28.

103. Reinarman (1995).

104. Brownstein, H. (2006). The myth of drug users as violent offenders. In R. Bohm & J. Walker (Eds.), *Demystifying crime and criminal justice*. Los Angeles, CA: Roxbury, p. 45.

105. Jensen & Gerber (1998), p. 17.

106. Clymer, A. (1986). Public found ready to sacrifice in drug fight. *New York Times* September 2, A1, D 16.

107. Sourcebook of Criminal Justice Statistics (2005). Table 2.1. Attitudes toward the most important problem facing the country." Retrieved March 30, 2005, from http://www.albany.edu/sourcebook/pdf/t21.pdf.

108. Goode, D., & Nachman, B. (1994). The American drug panic of the 1980s. Retrieved May 19, 2009, from: http://www.psychedelic-library.org/panic.htm.

109. Jensen, Gerber, & Babcock (1991).

110. Bagdikian, Ben (2004). *The new media monopoly*. Boston, MA: Beacon Press, pp. xii.

111. Pew Project for Excellence in Journalism (2009). *The State of the News Media*. Retrieved September 18, 2009, from: http://www.stateofthemedia.org/2009/index.htm.

112. Pew Project for Excellence in Journalism (2009). *The State of the News Media*. Exectuive summary. Retrieved September 18, 2009, from:http://www.stateofthemedia.org/2009/chapter% 20pdfs/COMPLETE%20EXEC%20SUMMARY%20PDF.pdf.

113. German, D., & Lally, C. (2007). A profile of Americans' media use and political socialization effects: Television and the Internet's relationship to social connectedness in the USA. *Policy Futures in Education, 5*(3), 327–344.

114. Pew Research Center for the People and the Press (2006). State of the American News Media, 2007: Mainstream Media Go Niche. Retrieved January 10, 2009, from: http://pewresearch.org/pubs/428/state-of-the-american-news-media-2007-mainstream-media-go-niche.

115. Beckett, K., & Sasson, T. (2003). *The politics of injustice: Crime and punishment in America* (2nd Edition). Thousand Oaks, CA: Sage.

116. Tunnell, K. (1992). Film at eleven: Recent developments in the commodification of crime. *Sociological Spectrum, 12,* 295.

117. Fields, C., & Jerin, B. (1999). The media and the criminal justice system. In R. Muraskin and A. Roberts (Eds). *Visions for change: Justice and the twenty-first century*. Upper Saddle River, NJ: Prentice Hall, p. 94.

118. Angolabahere, S., Behr, R., & Iyengar, S. (1993). *The media game: American politics in the television age.* New York: Macmillan; Pew Research Center for the People and the Press (2006).

119. Dong, L., Block, G., & Mandel, S. (2004). Activities contributing to total energy expenditure in the United States: Results from the NHAPS study. *International Journal of Behavioral Nutrition and Physical Activity 1, 4.*

120. American Academy of Pediatrics (2002). Online: www.aap.org; Center for Media Education. (2000). Online: www.cme.org.

121. Altheide, D. (2006), p. 53.

122. Surette, R. (1992).

123. Pew Project for Excellence in Journalism (2009). *The State of the News Media.* Public attitudes. Retrieved September 18, 2009, from: http://www.stateofthemedia.org/2009/narrative_overview_publicattitudes.php?media=1&cat=3.

124. Pew Research Center for the People and the Press (2006).

125. Robinson, M. (2009).

Chapter 3

1. Center for Responsive Politics (2010). Communications/electronics: Long-term contribution trends. Retrieved February 15, 2010, from: http://www.opensecrets.org/ industries/ indus.php?ind=B.

2. About.com (2010).Salaries and benefits of U.S. Congress members. Retrieved February 15, 2010, from: http://usgovinfo.about.com/od/uscongress/a/congresspay.htm.

3. Center for Responsive Politics (2010). Personal finances: Overview. Retrieved February 15, 2010, from: http://www.opensecrets.org/pfds/index.php#avg.

4. Robinson, M. (2009). *Justice blind? Ideals and Realities of American Criminal Justice* (3rd Ed.). Upper Saddle River, NJ: Prentice Hall.

5. Robinson (2009).

6. Robinson (2009).

7. Robinson (2009).

8. Center for Responsive Politics (2009). TV/Movies/Music: Top contributors to federal candidates and parties. Retrieved September 29, 2009, from: http://www.opensecrets.org/industries/contrib.php?ind=B02&cycle=2008.

9. Robinson (2009).

10. Schmalleger, F. (2006). *Criminal Justice Today* (9th Edition). Upper Saddle River, NJ: Prentice Hall.

11. Balkin, J. (2000).*Bush v. Gore*and the Boundary between Law and Politics. *The Yale Law Journal,110.* Retrieved May 19, from: http://findarticles.com/p/articles/mi_qa3975/is-_200304/ai_n9221306/; Neumann, R. (2003). Conflicts of interest in Bush v. Gore: Did some justices vote illegally?*The Georgetown Journal of Legal Ethics*, Spring.

12. Kritzer, H. (2001). The impact of Bush v. Gore on public perceptions and knowledge of the Supreme Court. *Judicature*, 85(1), 32–38.

13. Baird, V., & Gangl, A. (2006). Shattering the myth of legality: The impact of the media's framing of Supreme Court procedures on perceptions of fairness. *Political Psychology*, 27(4), 597–614.

14. Robinson, M. (2007). Freedom in an era of terror: A critical analysis of the USA PATRIOT Act. *Justice Policy Journal*, 4(1): 1–48.

15. Abdolian, L., & Takooshian, H, (2003). The USA PATRIOT Act: Civil liberties, the media, and public opinion. *Fordham Urban Law Journal*. Retrieved March 26, 2009, from: http://goliath.ecnext.com/coms2/summary_0199-3081499_ITM#readmore.

16. Hart, P. & Coen, R. (2003). John Ashcroft needs help. Attorney general seeks media's aid in selling Patriot Act. Extra! Update. Retrieved March 26, 2009, from: http://www.fair.org/extra/0308/ashcroft.html.

17. Finnegan, L. (2006). *No questions asked: News coverage since 9/11*. New York: Praeger, p. 55.

18. Hart, & Coen (2003).

19. Herman, Edward, & Chomsky, Noam (2002). *Manufacturing Consent: The Political Economy of Mass Media*. New York: Pantheon Books, p. lix.

20. Finnegan (2006), p. 55.

21. Finnegan (2006).

22. Abdolian, L., & Takooshian, H, (2003). The USA PATRIOT Act: Civil liberties, the media, and public opinion. *Fordham Urban Law Journal*. Retrieved March 26, 2009, from: http://goliath.ecnext.com/coms2/summary_0199-3081499_ITM#readmore.

23. Abdolian, L., & Takooshian, H, (2003). The USA PATRIOT Act: Civil liberties, the media, and public opinion. *Fordham Urban Law Journal*. Retrieved March 26, 2009, from: http://goliath.ecnext.com/coms2/summary_0199-3081499_ITM#readmore.

24. Abdolian, L., & Takooshian, H, (2003). The USA PATRIOT Act: Civil liberties, the media, and public opinion. *Fordham Urban Law Journal*. Retrieved March 26, 2009, from: http://goliath.ecnext.com/coms2/summary_0199-3081499_ITM#readmore.

25. Abdolian, L., & Takooshian, H, (2003). The USA PATRIOT Act: Civil liberties, the media, and public opinion. *Fordham Urban Law Journal*. Retrieved March 26, 2009, from: http://goliath.ecnext.com/coms2/summary_0199-3081499_ITM#readmore.

26. Robinson (2007).

27. See Bill of Rights Defense Committee (2009). Resolutions passed. http://bordc.org/resolutions.php.

28. Fairness in Accuracy and Reporting (2003). Media advisory: Muted response to Ashcroft's sneak attack on liberties . Retrieved March 26, 2009, from: http://www.fair.org/press-releases/patriot-sequel.html.

29. Muraskin, R., & Domash, S. (2007). *Crime and the Media: Headlines vs. Reality*. Upper Saddle River, NJ: Prentice Hall.

30. Surette (2007), p. 16.

31. Chermak, S. (1995a). Predicting crime story salience: The effects of crime, victim, and defendant characteristics. *Journal of Criminal Justice, 26*, 61–70; Chermak, S. (1995b). *Victims in the News: Crime and the American Media*. Boulder, CO: Westview Press.

32. Becker-Blease, K., Finkelhor, D., & Turner, H. (2008, June). Media Exposure Predicts Children's Reactions to Crime and Terrorism. *Journal of Trauma & Dissociation, 9*(2), 225–248.

33. Bohm, R., & Walker, J., (2006). *Demystifying Crime and Criminal Justice*. Los Angeles, CA: Roxbury, (p. xxi).

34. For an excellent summary of classic and contemporary self-report studies, see Terence Thornberry and Marvin Krohn (2003). Comparison of self-report and official data for measuring crime (43–94). In John V. Pepper and Carol V. Petrie (eds.), *Measurement Problems in Criminal Justice Research*. Washington, DC: National Academies Press.

35. O'Connor, Tom (2005). Crime data. Retrieved August 1, 2007, from faculty.ncwc. edu/toconnor/111/111lect02.htm.

36. Farrington, David (2005). *Integrated Developmental and Life-Course Theories of Offending*. Newark, NJ: Transaction; John Laub and Robert Sampson (2006). *Shared Beginnings, Divergent Lives: Delinquent Boys to Age 70*. Boston, MA: Harvard University Press; Terrie Moffitt (1993). Adolescent-limited and life-course-persistent antisocial behavior: A developmental taxonomy. *Psychological Review* 100:674–701; Terrie Moffitt (1997). Adolescent-limited and life-course-persistent offending: A complementary pair of developmental theories (11–54). In T. Thornberry (ed.), *Developmental Theories of Crime and Delinquency, Advances in Criminological Theory*. Newark, NJ: Transaction; Robert Sampson and John Laub (2005). *Crime in the Making: Pathways and Turning Points through Life*. Boston, MA: Harvard University Press.

37. Durkheim, Emile (1895, 1982). *Rules of the Sociological Method*. New York: Free Press, 65.

38. Sutherland, Edwin (1973). Crime of corporations. In Schuessler, Karl (ed.), *On Analyzing Crime*. Chicago: University of Chicago Press.

39. Clinard, Marshall, and Peter Yeager (1980). *Corporate Crime*. New York: The Free Press.

40. Sourcebook of Criminal Justice Statistics (2010). Retrieved February 15, 2010, from http://www.albany.edu/sourcebook/pdf/t31062008.pdf.

41. U.S. Department of Justice, Office of Justice Programs, Bureau of Justice Statistics. Criminal victimization. Retrieved July 30, 2007, from www.ojp.usdoj.gov/bjs/cvictgen.htm.

42. U.S. Department of Justice, Office of Justice Programs, Bureau of Justice Statistics. Criminal victimization in the United States, 2005, statistical tables. Table 1: Number, percent distribution, and rate of victimizations, by type of crime. Retrieved July 30, 2007, from www.ojp.usdoj.gov/bjs/pub/pdf/cvus05.pdf.

43. Kappeler, Victor, and Gary Potter (2004). *The Mythology of Crime and Criminal Justice* (4th ed.). Long Grove, IL: Waveland Press.

44. Reiman, Jeffrey (2006). *The Rich Get Richer and the Poor Get Prison* (8th ed.). Boston, MA: Allyn & Bacon; Matthew Robinson (forthcoming). *Justice Blind? Ideals and Realities of American Criminal Justice* (3rd ed.). Upper Saddle River, NJ: Prentice Hall.

45. Simon, David (2005). *Elite Deviance* (8th ed.). Boston, MA: Allyn & Bacon.

46. Sutherland, Edwin (1977a, 1977b). White-collar criminality. In Gilbert Geis and Robert Meier (eds.), *White-Collar Crime: Offenses in Business, Politics, and the Professions*. New York: The Free Press.

47. Clinard, Marshall, and Peter Yeager (2005).*Corporate Crime*. Edison, NJ: Transaction.

48. Frank, Nancy, and Michael Lynch (1992). *Corporate Crime, Corporate Violence*. Albany, NY: Harrow and Heston.

49. Blount, Ernest (2002).*Occupational Crime: Deterrence, Investigation, and Reporting in Compliance with Federal Guidelines*. New York: CRC.

50. Erman, David, and Richard Lundman (2001). *Corporate and Governmental Deviance: Problems of Organizational Behavior in Contemporary Society* (6th ed.). New York: Oxford University Press.

51. Michalowski, Raymond, and Ronald Kramer (2006). *State-Corporate Crime: Wrongdoing at the Intersection of Business and Government*. Camden, NJ: Rutgers.

52. Shover, Neil, and John Wright (2000). *Crimes of Privilege: Readings in White-Collar Crime*. New York: Oxford University Press.

53. Rosoff, Stephen, Henry Pontell, and Robert Tillman (2006). *Profit Without Honor: White-Collar Crime and the Looting of America* (4th ed.). Upper Saddle River, NJ: Prentice Hall.

54. Reiman, *The Rich Get Richer*.

55. Friedrichs, David (2006). *Trusted Criminals: White Collar Crime in Contemporary Society* (3rd ed.). Belmont, CA: Wadsworth.

56. Reiman, *The Rich Get Richer*.

57. Altheide, D. (2002) *Creating fear: News and the construction of crisis*. New York: Aldine Transaction.

58. Garnder, Dan (2009).*Risk: Why We Fear the Things We Shouldn't – and Put Ourselves in Greater Danger*. New York: Emblem Editions.

59. Bishop, D. (2006). The myth that harsh punishments reduce juvenile crime. In R. Bohm & J. Walker (Eds.), *Demystifying crime and criminal justice*. Los Angeles, CA: Roxbury, p. 144.

60. Chermak, S., & Chapman, N. (2007). Predicting crime story salience: A replication. *Journal of Criminal Justice, 35*(4), 351.

61. Federal Bureau of Investigation. Uniform Crime Reports. Retrieved July 29, 2009, from: http://www.fbi.gov/ucr/ucr.htm.

62. Brezina, T., & Kaufman, J. (2008). What really happened in New Orleans? Estimating the threat of violence during the Hurricane Katrina disaster. *Justice Quarterly, 25*(4), 701.

63. Landy, M. (2008). A failure of initiative: Final report of the elect bipartisan committee to investigate the preparation for and response to Hurricane Katrina/The federal response to Hurricane Katrina lesons learned. *Publius: The Journal of Federalism, 38*(1), 152–165.

64. Federal Bureau of Investigation (2006). Crime in the United States. Retrieved February 15, 2010, from: http://www.fbi.gov/ucr/05cius/.

65. Ruiz, J., & Treadwell, D. (2002). The perp walk: Due process v. freedom of the press. *Criminal Justice Ethics, 21*(2), 44–56.

66. Greer, C. (2006). Delivering death: capital punishment, botched executions, and the American news media. In: P. Mason (Ed.), *Captured by the Media: Prison Discourse in Popular Culture*. Devon, U.K.: Willan Publishing.

67. Meyers, M. (1997). News coverage of violence against women: Engendering blame. Thousand Oaks, CA: Sage.

68. Bohm, & Walker (2006), p. xxii.

69. Potter, G., & Kappeler, V. (1998). *Constructing Crime: Perspectives on Making News and Social Problems*. Prospect Heights, IL: Waveland Press.

70. Chiricos, T. (1995). The moral panic of the drug war. In M. Lynch (Ed.), *Race and Criminal Justice*. Albany, NY: Harrow and Heston; Kooistra, P., Mahoney, J., & Westervelt, S. (1999). The world of crime according to "COPS." In G. Cavender & M. Fishman (Eds.), *Entertaining Crime: Television Reality Programs*. Hawthorne, NY: Aldine de Gruyter.

71. Merlo, A., & Benekos, P. (2000). *What's Wrong with the Criminal Justice System: Ideology, Politics and the Media*. Cincinnati, OH: Anderson, p. 5.

72. Sacco, V. (1995). Media constructions of crime. *Annals of the American Academy of Political and Social Science, 539,* 141–154.

73. Dowler, K. (2004). Comparing American and Canadian local television crime stories: A content analysis. *Canadian Journal of Criminology and Criminal Justice, 46*(5), 573–596.

74. Heide, K., & Boots, D. (2007). A Comparative analysis of media reports of U.S. parricide cases with officially reported national crime data and the psychiatric and psychological literature. *International Journal of Offender Therapy and Comparative Criminology, 51*(6), 646.

75. Krajicek (1998), p. 95.

76. Muraskin & Domash (2007), p. 1.

77. Platt, L. (1999). Armageddon—live at 6! In R. Hiebert (Ed.), *Impact of Mass Media: Current Issues* (4th Ed). New York: Longman.

78. Newman, G. (1990). Popular culture and criminal justice: A preliminary analysis. *Journal of Criminal Justice, 18,* 261–274.

79. Krajicek (1998), p. 4.

80. Soothill, K., Peelo, M., Francis, B. Pearson, J., & Ackerley, E. (2002). Homicide and the media: Identifying the top cases in The Times. *The Howard Journal of Criminal Justice, 41*(5), 401–421.

81. Kappeler, V., Blumberg, M., & Potter, G. (2000). *The Mythology of Crime and Criminal Justice* (3rd Ed). Prospect Heights, IL: Waveland Press, p. 42.

82. Center for Media and Public Affairs. (1997). Media monitor. Washington, DC: Center for Media and Public Affairs.

83. Center for Media and Public Affairs. (2000). Online: www.cmpa.com/factoid/agenda.htm.

84. Marsh, H. (1991). A comparative analysis of crime coverage in newspapers in the United States and other countries from 1960–1989: A review of the literature. *Journal of Criminal Justice, 19,* 67–80.

85. Chermak, S. (1994). Crime in the news media: A refined understanding of how crime becomes news. In G. Barak (Ed.), *Media, Process, and Social Construction of Crime: Studies in News Making Criminology.* New York: Garland, p. 580.

86. Potter & Kappeler (1998), p. 7.

87. Tunnell, K. (1998). Reflections on crime, criminals, and control in newsmagazine television programs. In F. Bailey & D. Hale (Eds.) Popular culture, crime and justice (pp. 111–122). Belmont, CA: West/Wadsworth.

88. Maguire, B., Sandage, D., & Weatherby, G. (1999). Crime stories as television news: A content analysis of national, big city, and small town newscasts. *Journal of Criminal Justice and Popular Culture, 7*(1):1–14. http://www.albany.edu/scj/jcjpc/vol7is1/maguire.pdf.

89. Surette, R. (1992). *Media, Crime, and Criminal Justice: Images and Realities.* Pacific Grove: Brooks/Cole, p. 68.

90. Paulsen, D. (2000). Murder in black and white: The newspaper coverage of homicide in Houston, 1986–1994. PhD dissertation, Sam Houston State University.

91. Buckler, K., & Travis, L. (2005). Assessing the newsworthiness of homicide events: An analysis of coverage in the Houston Chronicle. *Journal of Criminal Justice and Popular Culture, 12*(1) 1–25. http://www.albany.edu/scj/jcjpc/vol12is1/buckler.pdf.

92. Pollak, J., & Kubrin, C. (2007). Crime in the news: How crimes, offenders and victims are portrayed in the media. *Journal of Criminal Justice and Popular Culture, 14*(1), 59–83. http://www.albany.edu/scj/jcjpc/vol14is1/pollak.pdf, p. 59.

93. Boulahanis, J.G. & Heltsley, M.J. (2004). Perceived fears: The reporting patterns of juvenile homicide in Chicago newspapers. *Criminal Justice Policy Review, 15*(2),132–160.

94. Pizarro, J., Chermak, S., & Gruenewald, J. (2007). Juvenile "super-predators" in the news: A comparison of adult and juvenile homicides. *Journal of Criminal Justice and Popular Culture, 14* (1), 84–111. http://www.albany.edu/scj/jcjpc/vol14is1/pizarro.pdf.

95. Pizarro, Chermak, & Gruenewald (2007), p. 105.

96. Sorensen, S., Manz, J., & Berk, R. (1998). News media coverage and the epidemiology of homicide. *American Journal of Public Health, 88*(10), 1510–1514.

97. Sorensen, Manz, & Berk (1998), p. 1514.

98. Bohm, & Walker (2006), p. xxii.

99. Bohm, & Walker (2006), p. xxii.

100. Bohm, & Walker (2006), p. xxiv.

101. Oleson, J. (2005). King of killers: The criminological theories of Hannibal Lector, part one. *Journal of Criminal Justice and Popular Culture*, *12*(3), 186–210. http://www.albany.edu/scj/jcjpc/vol12is3/special%20feature%202.pdf, p. 186.

102. Montaldo, C. (2009). The myths about serial killers. Retrieved August 19, 2009, from: http://crime.about.com/od/serial/a/serial_myths.htm.

103. Gibson, D. (2006, March). B.T.K. Strangler versus Wichita Police Department: The significance of serial murder media relations. *Public Relations Review*, *32*(1), 58–65.

104. Conway, M. (2006, April). Terrorism and the Internet: New Media—New Threat?. *Parliamentary Affairs*, *59*(2), 283–298.

105. Merlo & Benekos (2000).

106. Cherbonneau, M., & Copes, H. (2003). Media construction of carjacking: A content analysis of newspaper articles from 1993–2002. *Journal of Crime & Justice*, *26*(2), 1–21.

107. U.S. Department of Education (2009). Indicators of school crime and safety, 2008. Retrieved July 29, 2009, from: http://nces.ed.gov/programs/crimeindicators/crime indicators2008/key.asp.

108. Lawrence, R., & Mueller, D. (2003). School shootings and the man-bites-dog criterion of newsworthiness. *Youth Violence and Juvenile Justice*, *1*(4), 330–345.

109. Glassner, B. (1999). *The Culture of Fear: Why Americans Are Afraid of the Wrong Things*. New York: Basic Books.

110. Victor. J. (2006). Why the terrorism scare is a moral panic. *The Humanist*. July 1. Retrieved August 1, 2006, from: http://www.encyclopedia.com/doc/1G1-148674633.html.

111. Killingbeck, (2001), p. 195.

112. Killingbeck, (2001), p. 197.

113. Killingbeck (2001), p. 186.

114. Cullen, D. (2009). *Columbine*. New York: Twelve.

115. Center for Media and Public Affairs (1999). Violence goes to school: How TV news covered school shootings. Retrieved September 19, 2009, from: http://www.cmpa.com/files/media_monitor/99julaug.pdf.

116. Robinson, M. (2002). Crime prevention through environmental design in schools. In Robinson, D. (Ed.), *Police and Crime Prevention*. Upper Saddle River, NJ: Prentice-Hall.

117. Kolenic, A. (2009). Madness in the making: Creating and denying narratives from Virginia Tech to Gotham City. *Journal of Popular Culture*, *42*(6), 1023–1039, p. 124.

118. Best, J. (1999). *Random Violence: How We Talk about New Crimes and New Victims*. Berkeley, CA: University of California.

119. Best (1999), p. xiii.

120. Escholtz, S. (1997). The media and fear of crime: A survey of research. *University of Florida Journal of Law and Public Policy*, *9*(1), 48.

121. Robinson, M. (2002). Crime prevention through environmental design in schools. In D. Robinson (Ed.), *Police and Crime Prevention*. Upper Saddle River, NJ: Prentice-Hall.

122. Ardovini- Brooker, J., Caringella-Macdonald, S. (2002). Media attributions of blame and sympathy in ten rape cases. *The Justice Professional*, *15*, 3–18; Bufkin, J. & Eschholz, S. (2000) Images of sex and rape. *Violence Against Women*, *6*(12), 1317–1344; Meyers, M. (2004). African American women and violence: Gender, race, and class in the news. *Criminal Studies in Media Communication*, *21*(2) 95–118.

123. Best, J. (1987). Rhetoric in claims-making: Constructing the missing children problem. *Social Problems*, *34*(2), 101–121; Finkelhor, D., Hotaling, G., & Sedlak, A. (1992).

The abduction of children by strangers and non-family members: Estimating the incidence using multiple methods. *Journal of Interpersonal Violence, 7*(2), 226–243.

124. Benedict, H. (1992). *Virgin or Vamp: How the Press Covers Sex Crimes.* New York: Oxford University Press; Hirsch, S. (1994). Interpreting media representations of a "right of madness": Law and culture in the construction of rape identities. *Law and Social Inquiry, 19*, 1023–1056; Meyers, M. (1997). *News Coverage Against Violence and Women: Endangering Blame* . Newbury Park, CA: Sage.

125. Adelman, S. (1989). Representations of violence against women in mainstream film. *Resources for Feminist Research, 18*, 21–26.

126. Bufkin, J. & Eschholz, S. (2000) Images of sex and rape. *Violence Against Women, 6*(12), 1317–1344, p. 1337.

127. Rafter, N. (2006). *Shots in the Mirror: Crime Films in Society.* New York: Oxford University Press.

128. Dowler, K. (2006). Sex, lies, and videotape: The presentation of sex crime in local television news. *Journal of Criminal Justice, 34*(4), 383–392.

129. Cheit, Ross E. (2003). What hysteria? A systematic study of newspaper coverage of accused child molesters. *Child Abuse & Neglect, 27*(6), pp. 607–623.

130. Horowitz, E. (2007). Growing media and legal attention to sex offenders: More safety or more injustice? *Journal of the Institute of Justice and International Studies, 7*, 143–158.

131. Bureau of Justice Statistics (2006). Key facts at a glance. Violent crime trends. Retrieved July 5, 2009, from: http://ojp.usdoj.gov/bjs/glance/tables/viortrdtab.htm.

132. Lotke, E. (2006). Sex offenses: Facts, fictions, and policy implications. National Center on Institutions and Alternatives. Retrieved June 1, 2006, from http://66.165.94.98/stories/SexOffendersReport.pdf.

133. U.S. Department of Justice Office of Justice Programs. (2000). Sexual assault of young children as reported to law enforcement: victim, incident, and offender characteristics (NCJ Publication No. 182990). Washington, DC: Bureau of Justice Statistics.

134. Spitzberg, B., & and Cadiz, M. (2002). The media construction of stalking stereotypes. *Journal of Criminal Justice and Popular Culture, 9*(3), 128–149. http://www.albany.edu/scj/jcjpc/vol9is3/spitzberg.pdf, p. 137.

135. Spitzberg, B., & and Cadiz, M. (2002). The media construction of stalking stereotypes. *Journal of Criminal Justice and Popular Culture, 9*(3), 128–149. http://www.albany.edu/scj/jcjpc/vol9is3/spitzberg.pdf, p. 139.

Chapter 4

1. Muraskin & Domash (2007).

2. McChesney (2004), p. 71.

3. Harrigan, J. (2000). *Empty dreams, empty pockets: Class and bias in American politics.* New York: Addison-Wesley Longman, p. 130.

4. Krajicek (1998), p. 7.

5. Zuckerman, M. (1994). The limits of the TV lens. *U.S. News & World Report*, July 25, p. 64.

6. Grossman, L. (1997). Why local TV news is so awful. *Columbia Journalism Review* November/December 21.

7. Harrigan (2000)

8. Krajicek (1998), pp. 6–7.

9. Immarigeon, R. (2006). The myth that public attitudes are punitive. In R. Bohm & J. Walker (Eds.), *Demystifying crime and criminal justice.* Los Angeles, CA: Roxbury, p. 153.

10. Surette, R. (1992), pp. 86–87.

11. Muraskin & Domash (2007), p. 8.

12. McChesney (2004), p. 87.

13. Mayhew, P., & Van Dijk, J. (1997). Criminal victimization in eleven industrialized countries: Key findings from the 1996 International Crime Victims Survey. The Hague: Dutch Ministry of Justice.

14. Chermak, S., Bailey, F., & Brown, M. (2003). *Media representations of September 11.* New York: Praeger.

15. Krajicek (1998) p. 12.

16. Beckett & Sasson (2003).

17. Kappeler, V., & Potter, G. (2004). *The mythology of crime and criminal justice* (4th Ed.). Prospect Long Grove, IL: Waveland.

18. Barak (1995), p. 133.

19. Chiricos, T., Eschholz, S., & Gertz, M. (1997). Crime, news and fear of crime: Toward an identification of audience effects. *Social Problems, 44,* 342–357.

20. Potter & Kappeler (1998), p. 3.

21. Barkan, S. (1997). *Criminology: A sociological understanding.* Englewood Cliffs, NJ: Prentice Hall; Jackson, D. (1994). Politician crime rhetoric. *Boston Globe,* October 21, 15.

22. National Center on Institutions and Alternatives. (1999). What every American should know about the criminal justice system. Retrieved January 20, 2000, from: www.ncianet.org/ncia/facts.html.

23. Killingbeck, D. (2001). The role of television news in the construction of school violence as a "moral panic."*Journal of Criminal Justice and Popular Culture, 8*(3), 186–202. http://www.albany.edu/scj/jcjpc/vol8is3/killingbeck.pdf, p. 191.

24. MacCoun, R., & Reuter, P. (2000). *Drug war heresies: Learning from other vices, times, and places.* New York: Cambridge University Press.

25. Ericson, R., Baranek, P., & Chan, J. (1989). *Negotiating control: A study of news sources.* Toronto: University of Toronto Press; Surette (1998).

26. Altheide (2006), p. 75.

27. Project for Excellence in Journalism (2005). The state of the news media. Retrieved June 10, 2006, from: http://www.stateofthemedia.org/2005/narrative_localtv_intro.asp?cat+1$media=6.

28. Altheide (2006), p. 167.

29. Altheide (2006), p. 74.

30. Altheide (2006), p. 76.

31. Krajicek (1998), p. 4.

32. David Krajicek (1998). *Media miss real story on crime while chasing sex, sleaze, and celebrities.* New York: Columbia University Press, p. 180.

33. Krajicek (1998), p. 111.

34. Reiman, J. (2006). *The rich get richer and the poor get prison.* Boston, MA: Allyn & Bacon.

35. Dixon, T. (2007). Black criminals and white officers: The effects of racially misrepresenting law breakers and law defenders on television news. *Media Psychology, 10,*

270–291; Dixon, T. (2008). Crime News and Racialized Beliefs: Understanding the Relationship Between Local News Viewing and Perceptions of African Americans and Crime. *Journal of Communication, 58*(1), 106–125; Johnson, J., Bushman, B., & Dovidio, J. (2008). Support for harmful treatment and reduction of empathy toward blacks: "Remnants" of stereotype activation involving Hurricane Katrina and "Lil' Kim." *Journal of Experimental Social Psychology, 44*(6), 1506–1513; Johnson, K., & Dixon, T. (2008). Change and the Illusion of Change: Evolving Portrayals of Crime News and Blacks in a Major Market. *Howard Journal of Communications, 19*(2), 125–143.

36. Wilcox, P. (2005). Beauty and the beast: Gendered and raced discourse in the news. *Social & Legal Studies, 14*(4), 515–532.

37. Dowler, K. (2004). Dual realities? Criminality, victimization, and the presentation of race on local television news. *Journal of Crime & Justice, 27*(2), 79–100.

38. Crothers, L. (2007). *Globalization & American culture.* Lanham, MD: Rowman & Littlefield, pp. 103–104.

39. Russell-Brown, K. (2006). The myth of race and crime. In R. Bohm & J. Walker (Eds.), *Demystifying crime and criminal justice.* Los Angeles, CA: Roxbury, p. 29.

40. Russell-Brown (2006), p. 29.

41. Bishop (2006), p. 145.

42. German, D., & Lally, C. (2007). A profile of Americans' media use and political socialization effects: Television and the Internet's relationship to social connectedness in the USA. *Policy Futures in Education, 5*(3), 327–344.

43. Russell, K. (1998). *The color of crime: Racial hoaxes, white fear, black protectionism, police harassment, and other macroaggressions.* New York: New York University Press.

44. National Public Radio (2009). Racial hoaxes: Black men and imaginary crimes. June 8. Retrieved September 29, 2009, from: http://www.npr.org/templates/story/story.php?storyId=105096024&ft=1&f=1003&sc=YahooNews.

45. Perry, B., & Sutton, M. (2006). Seeing red over black and white: Popular and media representations of inter-racial relationships as precursors to racial violence. *Canadian Journal of Criminology & Criminal Justice, 48*(6), 887–904.

46. Wilcox, Paula (2005). Beauty and the beast: Gendered and raced discourse in the news. *Social Legal Studies, 14*(4), 515–532.

47. Dixon, T. (2007). Black criminals and white officers: The effects of racially misrepresenting law breakers and law defenders on television news. *Media Psychology, 10,* 270–291.

48. Gilliam, F., & Iyengar, S. (2000). Prime suspects: The influence of local television news on the viewing public. *American Journal of Political Science, 44,* 560–573.

49. Dixon (2007), p. 168.

50. Dixon, T. (2007), p. 239.

51. Dixon, T., & Azocar, C. (2007). Priming crime and activating blackness: Understanding the psychological impact of the overrepresentation of blacks as lawbreakers on television news. *Journal of Communication, 57,* 229–253.

52. Dixon, T., Azocar, C., & Casas, M. (2003). The portrayal of race and crime on television network news. *Journal of Broadcasting & Electronic Media, 47*(4), 498–523.

53. Krajicek (1998), p. 4.

54. McChesney (2004), p. 87.

55. Huhns III, J., & Coston, C. (2006). The myth that serial murderers are disproportionately white. In R. Bohm & J. Walker (Eds.), *Demystifying crime and criminal justice.* Los Angeles, CA: Roxbury.

56. Walsh, A. (2005). African Americans and serial killing in the media: The myth and the reality. *Homicide Studies, 9*(4), 271–291.

57. Mastro, D., Lapinski, M., Kopacz, M., & Behm-Morawitz, E. (2009). The influence of exposure to depictions of race and crime in TV news on viewer's social judgments. *Journal of Broadcasting & Electronic Media, 53*(4), 615–635.

58. Belknap, J. (1995). *Invisible woman: Gender, crime, and justice.* Belmont, CA: Wadsworth, pp. 69–70.

59. Berrington, E., & Honkatukia, P. (2002). An evil monster and a poor thing: Female violence in the media. *Journal of Scandinavian Studies in Criminology & Crime Prevention, 3*(1), 50–72.

60. Morgan-Sharp, E. (1999). The administration of justice based on gender and race. In R. Muraskin & A. Roberts (Eds.), *Visions for change: Crime and justice in the 21st century.* Upper Saddle River, NJ: Prentice Hall, p. 384.

61. Chesney-Lind, M., & Pasko, L. (2004). *The female offender: Girls, women, and crime.* Thousand Oaks, CA: Sage Publications.

62. Cecil, D. (2008). From *Heathers* to Mean *Girls*: An examination of relational aggression in film. *Journal of Criminal Justice and Popular Culture, 15*(3), 262–276. http://www.albany.edu/scj/jcjpc/vol15is3/Cecil.pdf, p. 268.

63. Cecil, D. (2006). Violence, privilege and power: Images of female delinquents in film. *Women and Criminal Justice, 17*(4), 63–84.

64. Chesney-Lind, M. & Irwin, K. (2004). From badness to meanness: Popular constructions of contemporary girlhood. In A. Harris (ed.) *All About the Girl: Culture, Power, and Identity* (pp. 45–56). New York: Routledge.

65. Berns, N. (2004). *Framing the victim: Domestic violence, media, and social problems.* New York: Aldine Transaction.

66. Taylor, R. (2009). Slain and slandered: A content analysis of the portrayal of femicide in crime news. *Homicide Studies, 13*(1), 21.

67. Ryan, C., Anastario, M., & DaCunha, A. (2006). Changing coverage of domestic violence murders: A longitudinal experiment in participatory communication. *Journal of Interpersonal Violence, 21*(2), 209–228.

68. Pizarro, J., Chermak, S., & Gruenewald, J. (2007). Juvenile "super-predators" in the news: A comparison of adult and juvenile homicides. *Journal of Criminal Justice and Popular Culture, 14* (1), 84–111. http://www.albany.edu/scj/jcjpc/vol14is1/pizarro.pdf.

69. Bishop (2006), pp. 140–141.

70. Bishop (2006), p. 141.

71. Bishop (2006), p. 141.

72. Bishop (2006), p. 142.

73. Boulahanis, J., & Heltsley, M. (2004). Perceived fears: The reporting patterns of juvenile homicide in Chicago newspapers. *Criminal Justice Policy Review, 15*(2), 132-160; Yanich, D. (2004). Crime creep: Urban and suburban crime on local TV news. *Journal of Urban Affairs, 26*(5), 535–563.

74. Center for Media and Public Affairs (2000). What's the matter with kids today? Images of teenagers on local and national TV news. Retrieved September 19, 2009, from: http://www.cmpa.com/files/media_monitor/00sepoct.pdf.

75. Yanich, D. (2005). Kids, crime, and local television news. *Crime & Delinquency, 51*(1), 103–132.

76. Howell, J. (2007). Menacing or mimicking? Realities of youth gangs. *Juvenile & Family Court Journal, 58*(2), 39.

77. Esbensen, F., & Tusinski, K. (2007). Youth gangs in the print media. *Journal of Criminal Justice and Popular Culture, 14*(1), 21–38. http://www.albany.edu/scj/jcjpc/vol14is1/esbensen.pdf, p. 21.

78. Payne, B., Appel, J., & Kim-Appel, D. (2008). Elder abuse coverage in newspapers: Regional differences and its comparison to child-abuse coverage. *Journal of Elder Abuse & Neglect, 20*(3), 265.

79. Griffin, T., & Miller, M. (2008). Child abduction, AMBER alert, and crime control theater. *Criminal Justice Review, 33*(2), 159.

80. Cavender, Gray and Lisa Bond-Maupin. 1993. "Fear and Loathing on Reality Television: An Analysis Of *America's Most Wanted* and *Unsolved Mysteries*". Sociological Inquiry. 63(3): 20 –30.

81. Bohm, & Walker (2006), p. xxi.

82. Surette (2007), p. 209.

83. Surette (2007), p. 230.

84. Dowler, K. (2004). Comparing American and Canadian local television crime stories: A content analysis. *Canadian Journal of Criminology and Criminal Justice, 46*(5), 573–596.

85. Sourcebook of Criminal Justice Statistics (2009). Table 2.0013. Attitudes toward approaches to lowering the crime rate in the United States. Retrieved March 31, 2009, from: http://www.albany.edu/sourcebook/pdf/t200132006.pdf.

86. Surette (2007), pp. 39–41.

87. Robinson and Murphy (2008).

88. Merton, R. (1957). *Social theory and social structure* Glencoe, IL: The Free Press.

89. Cloward, R., & Lloyd, O. (1961). *Delinquency and opportunity: A theory of delinquent gangs.* New York: The Free Press.

90. Messner, S., & Rosenfeld, R. (1994). *Crime and the American dream.* New York: Wadsworth.

91. Chamlin, M., & Cochran, J. (2007). An evaluation of the assumptions that underlie institutional anomie theory. *Theoretical Criminology, 11*(1); Maume, Michael, and Lee, Matthew (2003). Social institutions and violence: A sub-national test of Institutional Anomie Theory. *Criminology, 41,* 1140; Messner, S. (2003). An institutional-anomie theory of crime: Continuities and elaborations in the study of social structure and anomie, *Cologne Journal of Sociology and Social Psychology, 43*(1); Savolainen, J. (2000). Inequality, welfare state, and homicide: Further support for the Institutional Anomie Theory. *Criminology, 38,* 1022.

92. Dowler, K. (2004). Comparing American and Canadian local television crime stories: A content analysis. *Canadian Journal of Criminology and Criminal Justice, 46*(5), 573–596.

93. Surette (2007), p. 218.

94. Bullock, J., & Arrigo, B. (2006). The myth that mental illness causes crime. In R. Bohm & J. Walker (Eds.), *Demystifying crime and criminal justice.* Los Angeles, CA: Roxbury, p. 12.

95. Kendell, R. (2001). Media madness: Public images of mental illness. Criminal behaviour and mental health. *Special Book Reviews, 11*(1), S139.

96. Bullock, & Arrigo (2006), p. 16.

97. Wahl, O. (1997). *Media madness: Public images of mental illness.* Newark NJ: Rutgers University Press.

98. Robinson, M., & Beaver, K. (2009). *Why crime? An interdisciplinary approach to explaining criminal behavior*. Durham, NC: Carolina Academic Press.

99. Weitzer, R., & Kubrin, C. (2004). Breaking news: How local TV news and real-world conditions affect fear of crime. *Justice Quarterly, 21*(3), 497–520, p. 499.

100. Nabi, R., & Riddle, K. (2008). Personality traits, television viewing, and the cultivation effect. *Journal of Broadcasting & Electronic Media, 52*(3), 327–348, p. 328.

101. Nabi & Riddle (2008), p. 328.

102. Weitzer, & Kubrin (2004), p. 500.

103. Weitzer, & Kubrin (2004), p. 500.

104. Weitzer, & Kubrin (2004), p. 512.

105. Weitzer, & Kubrin (2004), p. 515.

106. Murray, J. (2008, April). Media violence: The effects are both real and strong. *American Behavioral Scientist, 51*(8), 1212–1230.

107. Coyne, S. (2007). Does media violence cause violent crime? *European Journal on Criminal Policy and Research,13* (3–4), 205–211.

108. Livingston, J. (1996). *Crime and criminology* (2nd Ed.). Upper Saddle River, NJ: Prentice Hall.

109. Cohen, S., & Solomon, S. (1995). How *Time* magazine promoted a cyberhoax. *Media Beat*. Retrieved January 16, 2006, from http://www.fair.org/fair/media-beat/950719. html.

110. Uribe, R., & Gunter, B. (2007). Are 'sensational' news stories more likely to trigger viewers' emotions than non-sensational news stories?. *European Journal of Communication, 22*(2), 207–228.

111. Krajicek (1998, p. 7.

112. Donziger, S. (1996). *The Real War on Crime: the Report of the National Criminal Justice Commission*. New York: HarperPerennial, p. 9.

113. Davis, R., & Meddis, S. (1994). Random killing hit a high. *USA Today*, December 5: 1a.

114. Kappeler et al. (2000), p. 39.

115. Gerbner, G., et al. (1980). The mainstreaming of America: Violence profile No. 11. *Journal of Communications, 30*, 10–29; Morgan, M., & Signorielli, N. (1990). *Cultivation Analysis: New Directions in Media Effects Research*. Newbury Park, CA: Sage Publications).

116. Altheide (2006), p. 62.

117. Dowler, K. (2003). Media consumption and public attitudes toward crime and justice: The relationship between fear of crime, punitive attitudes, and perceived police effectiveness. *Journal of Criminal Justice and Popular Culture, 10*(2): 109–126. http://www.albany.edu/scj/jcjpc/vol10is2/dowler.pdf

118. Gerbner, G. (1994). Television voice: The art of asking the wrong question. Currents in *Modern Thought, July*, 385–397.

119. Harrigan (2000), p. 131.

120. Eschholz, S., Chiricos, T., & Gertz, M. (2003). Television and fear of crime: Program types, audience traits, and the mediating effect of perceived neighborhood racial composition. *Social Problems, 50*(3), 395–415.

121. Chiricos, Eschholz, & Gertz (1997).

122. Marsh (1991).

123. Diefenbach, D., & West, M. (2001). Violent crime and Poisson regression: A measure and a method for cultivation analysis. *Journal of Broadcasting & Electronic Media, 45*(3), 432.

124. Smolej, M., & Kivivuori, J. (2006). The relation between crime news and fear of violence. *Journal of Scandanavian Studies in Criminology and Crime Prevention 7*(2), 211–227.

125. Altheide (2006), p. 6.

126. Heath, L., & Gilbert, K. (1996). Mass media and fear of crime. *American Behavioral Scientist 39,* 379–386.

127. Chiricos, Eschholz, & Gertz (1997).

128. Tunnell, K. (1992). Film at eleven: Recent developments in the commodification of crime. *Sociological Spectrum* 12: 293–313, p. 300.

129. Eschholtz, S. (1997). The media and fear of crime: A survey of research. *University of Florida Journal of Law and Public Policy, 9*(1), p. 50.

130. Kappeler & Potter (2004)

131. Culverson, D. (1998). Stereotyping by politicians: The welfare queen and Willie Horton. In C. Mann & M. Zatz (Eds.), *Images of color, images of crime.* Los Angeles: Roxbury; Rome, D. (1998). Stereotyping by the media: Murderers, rapists, and drug addicts. In C. Mann & M. Zatz (Eds.), *Images of color, images of crime.* Los Angeles: Roxbury.

132. Krajicek (1998), p. 4.

133. National Institute on Media and the Family (2008). Children and media violence. Retrieved December 21, 2008, from http://www.mediafamily.org/facts/facts_vlent.shtml.

134. American Academy of Pediatrics (1998). *Caring for your baby and young child: Birth to age 5.* New York: Bantam Books, p. 512.

135. Pruitt, D. (1998). *Your child: What every parent needs to know: What's normal, what's not, and when to seek help. Emotional, behavioral and cognitive development from infancy through preadolescence.* New York: HarperCollins, p. 154.

136. Surette, R. (2002). Self-reported copycat crime among a population of serious and violent juvenile offenders. *Crime and Delinquency, 48*(1), 46–69.

137. Brown, M.(2007). Beyond the requisites: Alternative starting points in the study of media effects and youth violence.*Journal of Criminal Justice and Popular Culture, 14* (1), 1–20. http://www.albany.edu/scj/jcjpc/vol14is1/brown.pdf.

138. Altheide, D. (2006). *Terrorism and the politics of fear.* Lanham, MD: AltaMira Press, p. 63.

139. McChesney (2004), p. 203.

140. Perry, D. (2007). Does television kill? Testing a period-characteristic model. *Media Psychology, 9*(3), 567–594.

141. Altheide, D. (2006), p. 75.

142. Callanan, V (2005). *Feeding the fear of crime: Crime-related media and support for three strikes.* El Paso, TX: LFB Scholarly Publishing LLC.

143. Krajicek (1998), pp. 5–6.

144. Krajicek (1998), pp. 5, 17.

145. Meloy, J., & Mohandie, K. (2001). Investigating the role of screen violence in specific homicide cases. *Journal of Forensic Sciences, 46*(5), 1113–8.

146. Surette, R. (1992), p. 87.

147. Robinson, M. (1999). What you don't know *Can* hurt you: Perceptions and misconceptions of harmful behaviors among Criminology and Criminal Justice students. *Western Criminology Review, 2*(1). Retrieved January 10, 2009, from: http://wcr.sonoma.edu/v2n1/robinson.html.

148. Potter & Kappeler (1998); Surette (1992); Evans, S., & Lundman, R. (1987). Newspaper coverage of corporate crimes. In M. Erdman & R. Lundman (Eds.), *Corporate and*

government deviance: Problems of organizational behavior in contemporary society. New York: Oxford University Press; Randell, D. (1995). The portrayal of business malfeasance in the elite and general media. In G. Geis, R. Meier, & L. Salinger (Eds.), *White-collar crime: Classic and contemporary views.* New York: The Free Press.

149. Robinson and Murphy (2008).

150. Friedrichs, D. (2006). The myth that white-collar crime is only about financial loss. In R. Bohm & J. Walker (Eds.), *Demystifying crime and criminal justice.* Los Angeles, CA: Roxbury, p. 20.

151. Levi, M. (2006). The media construction of financial white-collar crimes. *The British Journal of Criminology, 46*(6), 1037–1057.

152. Muraskin & Domash (2007), p. 19.

153. Griffin, S. (2002). Actors or activities? On the social construction of "white-collar crime" in the United States. *Crime, Law and Social Change, 37*(3), 245–276.

154. Dubois, J. (2002). Media coverage of organized crime—Police managers survey. *Trends in Organized Crime, 7*(4), 29–54.

155. Conrad, C. (2004). The illusion of reform: Corporate discourse and agenda denial in the 2002 "corporate meltdown." *Rhetoric & Public Affairs, 7*(3), 311–338.

156. Potter and Kappeler (1998), p. 15, citing Mintz, M. (1992). Why the media cover up corporate crime: A reporter looks back in anger. *Trial, 28,* 72–77.

157. Barak, G. (1994). *Media, process, and the social construction of crime.* New York: Garland.

158. McChesney (2004), p. 73.

159. Bagdikian (2004), p. 131.

160. Center for Media and Public Affairs (2002). Scandalous business: TV news coverage of the corporate scandals. Retrieved September 21, 2009, from: http://www.cmpa.com/files/media_monitor/02sepoct.pdf.

161. McChesney (2004), p. 94.

162. McChesney (2004), p. 86.

163. Beckett, K., & Sasson, T. (2003). *The Politics of injustice: Crime and punishment in America* (2nd Ed,). Thousand Oaks, CA: Sage.

Chapter 5

1. Simons, H. (1999). Media, police, and public information: From confrontation to conciliation. *Communications and the Law,70,* 69–93.

2. Leishman, F., & Mason, P. (2003). *Policing and the media: Facts, fictions and factions.* Uffculme, Devon, UK: Willan.

3. Perlmutter, D. (2000). *Policing the media.* Belmont, CA: Sage.

4. Bohm, & Walker, p. xxii.

5. Dowler, K. (2003). Media consumption and public attitudes toward crime and justice: The relationship between fear of crime, punitive attitudes, and perceived police effectiveness. *Journal of Criminal Justice and Popular Culture, 10*(2): 109–126. http://www.albany.edu/scj/jcjpc/vol10is2/dowler.pdf, p. 111.

6. Marion, N. (1995). *A primer in the politics of criminal justice.* Albany, NY: Harrow and Heston.

7. Surette, R. (2007). *Media, crime, and criminal justice.* Belmont, CA: Wadsworth, p. 94.

8. Bureau of Justice Statistics (2009). Expenditure and employment statistics. Retrieved April 6, 2009, from http://ojp.usdoj.gov/bjs/eande.htm.

9. Bureau of Justice Statistics. (2009). Law enforcement statistics. Retrieved March 30, 2009, from: http://ojp.usdoj.gov/bjs/lawenf.htm; Federal Bureau of Investigation (2007). Table 74. Full time law enforcement employees. Retrieved February 17, 2010 from: http://www. fbi.gov/ucr/cius2007/data/table_74.html.

10. Robinson, M. (2009). *Justice blind? Ideals and realities of American criminal justice* (3rd Ed.). Upper Saddle River, NJ: Prentice Hall.

11. Robinson (2009).

12. Shukovsky, P., Johnson, T., & Lathrop, D. (2007). The FBI's terrorism trade-off Focus on national security after 9/11 means that the agency has turned its back on thousands of white-collar crimes.*Seattle PI*, April 11. Retrieved May 2, 2007, from:http://seattlepi. nwsource.com/national/311046_fbiterror11.html.

13. Feinberg, S. (2002). Media effects: The influence of local newspaper coverage on municipal police size. *American Journal of Criminal Justice, 26*(2), 249–268.

14. Feinberg, Seth L. (2002). Media Effects: The Influence of Local Newspaper Coverage on Municipal Police Size. *American Journal of Criminal Justice, 26*(2), 249–268.

15. Wrobleski, H. (2006). *Introduction to law enforcement and criminal justice* (8th Edition). Beverly Hills, CA: Wadsworth.

16. Fyfe, J., Greene, J., Walsh, W., Wilson, O., & McLaren, R. (1997). *Police administration* (5th Ed). New York: McGraw-Hill.

17. Barlow & Barlow (2006).

18. Bayley, D. (1994). *Police for the future.* New York: Oxford University Press.

19. Cox, S., & Wade. J. (1998). *The criminal justice network: An introduction.* New York: McGraw-Hill.

20. Manning, P. (1997). *Police work: The social organization of policing* (2nd Ed.). Prospect Heights, IL: Waveland Press, p. 93.

21. Robinson (2009).

22. Barlow, D., & Barlow, M. (2006). The myth that the role of police is to fight crime. In R. Bohm & J. Walker (Eds.), *Demystifying crime and criminal justice.* Los Angeles, CA: Roxbury, p. 73.

23. Barlow, D., & Barlow, M. (2006). The myth that the role of the police is to fight crime. In R. Bohm & J. Walker (Eds.), *Demystifying crime and criminal justice.* Los Angeles, CA: Roxbury, p. 73.

24. Hess, K. (2008). *Introduction to law enforcement and criminal justice* (9th Ed.). Belmont, CA: Wadsworth.

25. Loewen. J. (2007).*Lies my teacher told me: Everything your American history textbook got wrong.* New York: Touchstone.
Zinn, H. (2005). *A people's history of the United States: 1492 to present.* New York: Harper.

26. Chermak, S., & Weiss, A. (2005). Maintaining legitimacy using external communication strategies: An analysis of police-media relations. *Journal of Criminal Justice, 33*(5), 501–512.

27. . Donahue, A., & Miller, J. (2005). Citizen preferences and paying for police. *Journal of Urban Affairs, 27* (4), 419–435.

28. Montross Jr., W., & Mulvaney, P. (2009). Virtue and vice: Who will report on the failings of the American criminal justice system? *Stanford Law Review, 61*(6), 1429–1461, p. 1447.

29. Klockars, C. (1991). The rhetoric of community policing. In J. Greene & S. Mastrofski (Eds.). *Community policing: Rhetoric and reality*. New York: Praeger, p. 250.

30. Sherman, L., Gottfredson, D., MacKenzie, D., Eck, J., Reuter, P. & Bushway, S. (1997). Preventing crime: What works, what doesn't, what's promising. Washington, DC: U.S. Department of Justice, Office of Justice Programs, National Institute of Justice.

31. Robinson (2009).

32. Sherman, L. (1997). Policing for crime prevention. Retrieved April 2, 2009, from: http://www.ncjrs.gov/works/chapter8.htm.

33. Robinson, M., & Beaver, K. (2009). *Why crime? An interdisciplinary approach to explaining criminal behavior*. Durham, NC: Carolina Academic Press.

34. Sherman (1997).

35. Goldstein, H. (2001) Reported in Center for Problem-Oriented Policing. Retrieved April 2, 2009, from: http://www.popcenter.org/about-whatisPOP.htm.

36. Goldstein (2001).

37. Andersen, R. (1994). "Reality" TV and criminal injustice. *Humanist, 54*(5), 8–13.

38. Surette (2007), p. 108.

39. Bohm, & Walker (2006), p. xxii.

40. Packer, H. (1968). *The limits of the criminal sanction*. Stanford, CA: Stanford University Press.

41. Ruiz, J., & Treadwell, D. (2002). The perp walk: Due process v. freedom of the press. *Criminal Justice Ethics, 21*(2), 44–56.

42. Ruiz, J., & Treadwell, D. (2002). The perp walk: Due process v. freedom of the press. *Criminal Justice Ethics, 21*(2), 44–56.

43. Michalowski, R. (2006). The myth that punishment reduces crime. In R. Bohm & J. Walker (Eds.), *Demystifying crime and criminal justice*. Los Angeles, CA: Roxbury.

44. Robinson, M. (2009). *Justice blind? Ideals and realities of American criminal justice* (3rd Ed.). Upper Saddle River, NJ: Prentice Hall.

45. Surette (2007), pp. 101–104.

46. Lovell, J. (2003). *Good cop/Bad cop: Mass media and the cycle of police reform*. St. Louis, MO: Willow Tree Press.

47. Surette (2007), p. 93.

48. Surette (2007), p. 93.

49. Surette (2007), p. 219.

50. Greene, J. (1999). Zero tolerance: A case study of police policies and practices in New York. *Crime & Delinquency* 45(2), 171–187; McArdle, A., & Erzen, T. (2001). *Zero tolerance. Quality of life and the new police brutality in New York City*. New York: New York University Press.

51. Harris, D. (1999). Driving while black: Racial profiling on our nation's highways. New York: American Civil Liberties Union; Roberts, D. (1993). Crime, race and reproduction. *Tulane Law Review 1945*, 1; Son, I., Davis, M., & Rome, D. (1998). Race and its effect on police officers' perceptions of misconduct. *Journal of Criminal Justice, 26*(1), 21–28.

52. Buerger, M. (2006). The myth of racial profiling. In R. Bohm & J. Walker (Eds.), *Demystifying crime and criminal justice*. Los Angeles, CA: Roxbury.

53. Lundman, R., & Kaufman, R. (2003). Driving while black: Effects of race, ethnicity, and gender on citizen self-reports of traffic stops and police encounters. *Criminology, 41*(1),195–220.

54. Barlow, D., & Barlow, M. (2002). Racial profiling: A survey of African American police officers. *Police Quarterly, 5*(3), 334–358; Batton, C. & Kadleck, C. (2004). Theoretical and methodological issues in racial profiling research. *Justice Quarterly, 7*, 30–64; Bostaph, L. (2007). Race and repeats: The impact of officer performance on racially biased policing. *Journal of Criminal Justice, 35*(4), 405–417; Buerger, M., & Farrell, A. (2002). The evidence of racial profiling: Interpreting documented and unofficial sources. *Police Quarterly, 5*(3), 272; Engel, R., & Calnon, J. (2004). Examining the influence of drivers' characteristics during traffic stops with police: Results from a national survey. *Justice Quarterly, 21*, 49–90; Gross, S., & Barnes, K. (2002). Road word: Racial profiling and drug interdiction on the highways. *Michigan Law Review, 101*(3), 653; Langan, P., Greenfeld, L., Smith, S., Durose, M., & Levin, D. (2001). Contacts between the police and the public: Findings from the 1999 National Survey (No. NCJ184957). Washington, DC: Bureau of Justice Statistics, U.S. Department of Justice; Lundman, R. (2004). Driver race, ethnicity, and gender and citizen reports of vehicle searches by police and vehicle search hits: Towards a triangulated scholarly understanding. *Journal of Criminal Law & Criminology, 94*, 309–349; Meehan A.J. & Ponder, M.C. (2002). Race and place: The ecology of racial profiling African American motorists. *Justice Quarterly, 19*, 399–430; Peruche, B., & Plant, E. (2006). The correlates of law enforcement officers' automatic and controlled race-based responses to criminal suspects. *Basic & Applied Social Psychology, 28*(2), 193–199; Petrocelli, M., Piquero, A., & Smith, M. (2003). Conflict theory and racial profiling: An empirical analysis of police traffic stop data. *Journal of Criminal Justice, 31*(1), 1; Romero, M. (2006). Racial profiling and immigration law enforcement: Rounding up of usual suspects in the Latino community. *Critical Sociology, 32*(2/3), 447–473; Schafer, J., Carter, D., Katz-Bannister, A., & Wells, W. (2006). Decision making in traffic stop encounters: A multivariate analysis of police behavior. *Police Quarterly, 9*(2), 184–209; Tomaskovic-Devey, D., Wright, C., Czaja, R., & Miller, K. (2006). Self-reports of police speeding stops by race: Results from the North Carolina reverse record check survey. Journal of *Quantitative Criminology, 22*(4), 279–297; Warren, P., Tomaskovic-Devey, D., Smith, W., Zingraff, M., & Mason, M. (2006). Driving while black: Bias processes and racial disparity in police stops. *Criminology, 44*(3), 709–738.

55. Robinson (2009).

56. Robinson (2009).

57. Reiman, J. (1998). *The rich get richer and the poor get prison* (6th Ed.). Boston, MA: Allyn & Bacon, p. 55.

58. Kappeler, V., Blumberg, M., & Potter, G. (2000). *The mythology of crime and criminal justice* (3rd Ed). Prospect Heights, IL: Waveland Press, p. 221.

59. Robinson (2009).

60. Geller, W., & Toch, H. (1995). *And justice for all*. Washington, DC: Police Executive Research Forum.

61. Geller, W., & Scott, M. (1992). *Deadly force: What we know*. Washington, DC: Police Executive Research Forum.

62. Ross, J. (2000) *Making news of police violence: A comparative study of Toronto and New York City*. New York: Praeger.

63. Lawrence, R. (2000). *The politics of force: Media and the construction of police brutality*. Berkeley, CA: University of California Press.

64. International Association of Chiefs of Police (2002). *Police use of force in America, 2001*. Retrieved March 10, 2003, from: http://www.theiacp.org/documents/pdfs/Publications/2001useofforce%2Epdf.

65. Pate, T., & Fridell, L. (1994). Police use of force: Official reports, citizen complaints, and legal consequences, 1991–1992. Ann Arbor, MI: Interuniversity Consortium for Political and Social Research.

66. Ross, D. (1999). Assessing the patterns of citizen resistance during arrests. *FBI Law Enforcement Bulletin, 68*(6), 5–11; Walker, S., Delone, M., & Spohn, C. (2007). *The color of justice* (3rd Ed.). Beverly Hills, CA: Wadsworth.

67. Robinson (2009).

68. Dowler, K., & Zawilski, V. (2007). Public perceptions of police misconduct and discrimination: Examining the impact of media consumption. *Journal of Criminal Justice, 35*(2), 193.

69. Chermak, S., McGarrell, E., & Gruenewald, J. (2006). Media coverage of police misconduct and attitudes toward police. *Policing, 29*(2), 261–281; Weitzer, R., & Tuch, S. (2005). Racially biased policing: Determinants of citizen perceptions. *Social Forces, 83*(3), 1009–1030.; Weitzer, R., & Tuch, S. (2004, August). Race and Perceptions of Police Misconduct. *Social Problems, 51*(3), 305–325.

70. Escholz, S., Blackwell, B., Gertz, M. & Chiricos, T. (2002), Race and attitudes toward the police: assessing the effect of watching "reality" police programs. *Journal of Criminal Justice, 30*, 327–341; Huebner, B., Schafer, J., & Bynum, T. (2004). African American and White perceptions of police services: Within- and between-group variation. *Journal of Criminal Justice, 32*(2), 123–135; Weitzer, R. & Tuch, S. (2005). Determinants of public satisfaction with the police. *Police Quarterly, 8*, 279–297.

71. Chermak, S., McGarrell, E., & Gruenewald, J. (2006). Media coverage of police misconduct and attitudes toward police. *Policing, 29*(2), 261–281.

72. TASER (2009). Overview. Retrieved June 19, 2009, from: www.taser.com/products/law/Pages/TASERX26.aspx.

73. Ready, J., White, M., & Fisher, D. (2008). Shock value: A comparative analysis of news reports and official police records on TASER deployments. *Policing, 31*(1), 148–170.

74. Ready, J., White, M., & Fisher, D. (2008). Shock value: A comparative analysis of news reports and official police records on TASER deployments. *Policing, 31*(1), 148–170.

75. Ready, J., White, M., & Fisher, D. (2008). Shock value: A comparative analysis of news reports and official police records on TASER deployments. *Policing, 31*(1), 148–170.

76. Manning, P. (2001). Policing and reflection. In Dunham, R. & Alpert, G. (Eds). *Classical Issues in Policing.* Prospect Heights, IL: Waveland, pp. 149–57, p. 153.

77. Chermak, S. (1995). Image control: how police affect the presentation of crime news. *American Journal of Police, 14*(2), 21–43, p. 21.

78. Hallett, M. (2007). COPS and CSI: Reality television? In White, M (Ed.). *Current Issues and Controversies in Policing.* Boston, MA: Allyn & Bacon.

79. Donziger, S., (1996). *The real war on crime: The report of the National Criminal Justice Commission.* New York: Harper Perennial.

80. The Mollen Commission. (1994). Police brutality and excessive force in the New York City Police Department. New York: The Mollen Commission.

81. Harriston, K., and M. P. Flaherty. (1994). Law and disorder—the District's troubled police. *Washington Post,* August 28–31.

82. Christopher, W. (1991). Report of the Independent Commission on the Los Angeles Police Department. Los Angeles: The Commission.

83. Robinson (2009).

84. Gray, J. (2001). *Why our drugs laws have failed and what we can do about it.* Philadelphia: University of Temple Press; Kellner, L. (1988). Narcotics-related corruption. In U.S. Department of Justice (Ed.). *Prosecution of public corruption cases.* Washington, DC: U.S. Department of Justice.

85. Drug Policy Alliance (2007). Police corruption. Retrieved July 3, 2008, from: http://www.drugpolicy.org/law/police/.

86. Niederdeppe, J., Kuang, X., Crock, B., & Skelton, A. (2008, November). Media campaigns to promote smoking cessation among socioeconomically disadvantaged populations: What do we know, what do we need to learn, and what should we do now?. *Social Science & Medicine, 67*(9), 1343–1355; Self-Brown, S., Rheingold, A., Campbell, C., & De Arellano, M. (2008, June). A Media Campaign Prevention Program for Child Sexual Abuse: Community Members' Perspectives. *Journal of Interpersonal Violence, 23*(6), 728–743; Slater, M., Hayes, A., & Ford, V. (2007, August). Examining the Moderating and Mediating Roles of News Exposure and Attention on Adolescent Judgments of Alcohol-Related Risks. *Communication Research, 34*(4), 355–381.

87. Robinson, M., & Scherlen, R. (2007). *Lies, damned lies, and drug war statistics: A critical analysis of claims made by the Office of National Drug Control Policy.* Albany, NY: SUNY Press.

88. Centers for Disease Control and Prevention (2007). Fact sheet. Health effects of cigarette smoking. Retrieved November 8, 2007, from http://www.cdc.gov/tobacco/data_statistics/Factsheets/health_effects.htm.

89. Centers for Disease Control and Prevention. PERLINK"http://www.cdc.gov/mmwr/preview/mmwrhtml/mm5114a2.htm"Annual Smoking-Attributable Mortality, Years of Potential Life Lost, and Productivity Losses—United States, 1997–2001. Morbidity and Mortality Weekly Report [serial online]. 2002;51(14):300–303 [cited 2006 Dec 5]. Available from: http://www.cdc.gov/mmwr/preview/mmwrhtml/mm5114a2.htm; Centers for Disease Control and Prevention. Health United States, 2003, With Chartbook on Trends in the Health of Americans. (PDF–225KB) Hyattsville, MD: CDC, National Center for Health Statistics; 2003 [cited 2006 Dec 5]. Available from: http://www.cdc.gov/nchs/data/hus/tables/2003/03hus031.pdf.

90. U.S. Department of Health and Human Services. Reducing the Health Consequences of Smoking—25 Years of Progress: A Report of the Surgeon General. Atlanta, GA: U.S. Department of Health and Human Services, CDC; 1989. DHHS Pub. No. (CDC) 89–8411 [cited 2006 Dec 5]. Available from: http://profiles.nlm.nih.gov/NN/B/B/X/S/.

91. Centers for Disease Control and Prevention. Annual Smoking-Attributable Mortality, Years of Potential Life Lost, and Productivity Losses—United States, 1997–2001. Morbidity and Mortality Weekly Report [serial online]. 2002;51(14):300–303 [cited 2006 Dec 5]. Available from: http://www.cdc.gov/mmwr/preview/mmwrhtml/mm5114a2.htm; McGinnis J, Foege WH. Actual Causes of Death in the United States. Journal of the American Medical Association 1993;270:2207–2212.

92. Novotny TE, Giovino GA. Tobacco Use. In: Brownson RC, Remington PL, Davis JR (Eds.). Chronic Disease Epidemiology and Control. Washington, DC: American Public Health Association; 1998;117–148 [cited 2006 Dec 5].

93. Centers for Disease Control and Prevention. Annual Smoking-Attributable Mortality, Years of Potential Life Lost, and Productivity Losses—United States, 1997–2001. Morbidity and Mortality Weekly Report [serial online]. 2002;51(14):300–303 [cited 2006 Dec 5]. Available from: http://www.cdc.gov/mmwr/preview/mmwrhtml/mm5114a2.htm.

94. U.S. Department of Health and Human Services. Tobacco Use Among U.S. Racial/Ethnic Minority Groups—African Americans, American Indians and Alaska Natives, Asian Americans and Pacific Islanders, and Hispanics: A Report of the Surgeon General. Atlanta, GA: U.S. Department of Health and Human Services, CDC; 1998 [cited 2006 Dec 5]. Available from: http://www.cdc.gov/tobacco/data_statistics/sgr/sgr_1998/index.htm.

95. U.S. Department of Health and Human Services. Tobacco Use Among U.S. Racial/Ethnic Minority Groups—African Americans, American Indians and Alaska Natives, Asian Americans and Pacific Islanders, and Hispanics: A Report of the Surgeon General. Atlanta, GA: U.S. Department of Health and Human Services, CDC; 1998 [cited 2006 Dec 5]. Available from: http://www.cdc.gov/tobacco/data_statistics/sgr/sgr_1998/index.htm.

96. U.S. Department of Health and Human Services. Reducing the Health Consequences of Smoking—25 Years of Progress: A Report of the Surgeon General. Atlanta, GA: U.S. Department of Health and Human Services, CDC; 1989. DHHS Pub. No. (CDC) 89–8411 [cited 2006 Dec 5]. Available from: http://profiles.nlm.nih.gov/NN/B/B/X/S/.

97. Centers of Disease Control and Prevention (2007). Percentage of adults* who were current, former, or never smokers,† overall and by sex, race, Hispanic origin, age, education, and poverty status. Retrieved November 9, 2007, from: http://www.cdc.gov/tobacco/data_statistics/tables/adult/table_2.htm.

98. Rosoff, Stephen, Pontell, Henry, and Tillman, Robert (2002). *Profit Without Honor: White-Collar Crime and the Looting of America* (2nd Ed.). Upper Saddle River, NJ: Prentice Hall, p. 91.

99. Rosoff, Stephen, Pontell, Henry, and Tillman, Robert (2002). *Profit Without Honor: White-Collar Crime and the Looting of America* (2nd Ed.). Upper Saddle River, NJ: Prentice Hall, p. 149.

100. University of California, San Francisco (2009). Hearing on the regulation of tobacco products House Committee on Energy and Commerce Subcommittee on Health and the Environment. April 14, 1994. Retrieved February 17, 2010, from: http://senate.ucsf.edu/tobacco/executives1994congress.html.

101. Herman, Edward, & Chomsky, Noam (2002). *Manufacturing consent: The political economy of mass media.* New York: Pantheon Books, p. lix.

102. Herman & Chomsky (2002), p. lix.

103. McMullan, J. (2006). News, truth, and the recognition of corporate crime. *Canadian Journal of Criminology and Criminal Justice, 48*(6), 905–939.

104. International Center for the Prevention of Crime (2008). The media, crime prevention and urban safety: A brief discussion on media influence and areas for further exploration. Retrieved September 14, 2009, from: http://www.crime-prevention-intl.org/publications/pub_212_1.pdf.

105. Mendelsohn, H., & O' Keefe, G. (1982). Media campaigns and crime prevention: An executive summary. Washington DC: National Institute of Justice.

106. Lurigio, A., & Rosenbaum, D. (1991). The effects of mass media on crime prevention awareness, attitudes, and behavior: The case of crime stoppers. *American Journal of Criminal Justice, 15*(2), 82–105.

107. Clarke, R. (1992). *Situational crime prevention: Successful case studies.* New York: Harrow and Heston, pp. 3–4).

108. Robinson, M. (2010). Crime prevention through environmental design (CPTED) and related approaches in the United States. *Community Safety and Environmental Design, 1.*

Chapter 6

1. Surette, R. (2007). *Media, crime, and criminal justice.* Belmont, CA: Wadsworth, p. 118.

2. Surette (2007), p. 120.

3. Vinson, C., & Ertter, J. (2002, Fall). Entertainment or education: How do media cover the courts?. *Harvard International Journal of Press/Politics, 7*(4), 80.

4. Gaines, L., Kaune, M., & Miller, R. (2000). *Criminal justice in action.* Belmont, CA: Wadsworth, p. 270.

5. Peoples, E. (2000). *Basic criminal procedures.* Upper Saddle River, NJ: Prentice Hall; Stuckey, G., Robertson, C., & Wallace, H. (2001). *Procedures in the justice system* (6th Ed.). Upper Saddle River, NJ: Prentice Hall.

6. Donziger, S. (1996). *The real war on crime: The report of the National Criminal Justice Commission.* New York: Harper Perennial, p. 181.

7. Yanus, A. (2009). Full-court press: An examination of media coverage of state Supreme courts. *Justice System Journal, 30*(2), 180-196.

8. Vinson, D., &; Ertter, J. (2002). Entertainment or education: how do media cover the courts? *Harvard International Journal of Press/Politics, 7*(4), 80-97.

9. Surette, R. (2007). *Media, crime, and criminal justice.* Belmont, CA: Wadsworth, p. 118.

10. Robinson, M. (2010). Review of *Citizens United v. Federal Election Commission* 588 US **** (2010) [No. 08-205]. Retrieved February 18, 2010, from: http://www.justiceblind.com/citizensunited.html.

11. Robinson, M. (2009). *Justice Blind? Ideals and realities of American criminal justice.* Upper Saddle River, NJ: Prentice Hall.

12. Cox, S., & Wade, J. (1998). *The criminal justice network: An introduction.* New York: McGraw-Hill, p. 130.

13. Sourcebook of Criminal Justice Statistics (2009). Table 5.44. Felony convictions in state courts. Retrieved April 8, 2009, from: http://www.albany.edu/sourcebook/pdf/t544 2004.pdf.

14. Sourcebook of Criminal Justice Statistics (2009). Table 5.17. Disposition of cases terminated in U.S. District courts. Retrieved April 8, 2009, from: http://www.albany.edu/sourcebook/pdf/t5172004.pdf.

15. Sourcebook of Criminal Justice Statistics (2009). Table 5.46. Percent distribution of felony convictions in state courts. Retrieved April 8, 2009, from: http://www.albany.edu/sourcebook/pdf/t5462004.pdf

16. Sourcebook of Criminal Justice Statistics (2009). Table 5.17. Disposition of cases terminated in U.S. District courts. Retrieved April 8, 2009, from: http://www.albany.edu/sourcebook/pdf/t5172004.pdf.

17. Haltom, W. (1998). *Reporting on the courts: How the mass media cover judicial elections.* Chicago: Nelson-Hall, p. 157.

18. Sourcebook of Criminal Justice Statistics (2009). Table 5.45. Percent distribution of characteristics of felony offenders convicted in state courts. Retrieved April 8, 2009, from: http://www.albany.edu/sourcebook/pdf/t5452004.pdf.

19. Sourcebook of Criminal Justice Statistics (2009). Table 5.18. Federal defendants convicted in U.S. district courts. Retrieved April 8, 2009, from: http://www.albany.edu/sourcebook/pdf/t5182003.pdf.

20. National Center for State Courts (2003). Indigent defense. Retrieved April 8, 2009, from: http://www.ncsconline.org/WC/CourTopics/FAQs.asp?topic=IndDef.

21. Bureau of Justice Statistics (2009). Indigent defense statistics. Retrieved April 8, 2009, from: http://ojp.usdoj.gov/bjs/id.htm.

22. Bonsignore, J., Katsh, E., D'Errico, P., Pipkin, R., Arons, S., & Rifkin, J. (1998). *Before the law: An introduction to the legal process* (6th Ed.). Boston: Houghton Mifflin; Spire, R. (1990). Breaking up the old boy network. *Trial, 26*(2), 57–58.

23. Graham, B. (2000). Judicial recruitment and racial diversity on state courts: An overview. In G. Mays & P. Gregware (Eds.), *Courts and justice: A reader* (2nd Ed.). Prospect Heights, IL: Waveland Press.

24. Death Penalty Information Center (2009). The death penalty in black and white: Who lives, who dies, who decides. Retrieved April 8, 2009 from: http://deathpenalty info.org/death-penalty-black-and-white-who-lives-who-dies-who-decides.

25. Cole & Smith (2006); Schmalleger (2006).

26. Neubauer, D. (2007). *America's courts and the criminal justice system* (9th Ed.). Beverly Hills, CA: Wadsworth, p. 113.

27. Gaines et al. (2000), p. 271.

28. Merlo, A., & Benekos, P. (2000). *What's wrong with the criminal justice system: Ideology, politics and the media.* Cincinnati, OH: Anderson, p. 57.

29. Walker, S. (1998). *Sense and nonsense about crime and drugs: A policy guide* (4th Ed.). Belmont, CA: West/Wadsworth, p. 13.

30. Walker (1998), pp. 51–52.

31. Feeley, M. (1992). *The process is the punishment: Handling cases in a lower criminal court.* New York: Russell Sage Foundation Publications.

32. Nardulli, P., Eisenstein, J., & Flemming, R. (1988). *The tenor of justice: Criminal courts and the guilty plea process.* Urbana: University of Illinois Press.

33. Davis, A. (2007). *Arbitrary justice: The power of the American prosecutor.* New York: Oxford University Press.

34. Albonetti, C. (1987). Prosecutorial discretion: The effects of uncertainty. *Law and Society Review, 21*, 291–313.

35. Marion (1995).

36. Grace, N., & D. Clehane (2006). *Objection! How high-priced defense attorney's, celebrity defendants, and a 24/7 media have hijacked our criminal justice system.* New York: Hyperion.

37. Montross Jr., W., & Mulvaney, P. (2009). Virtue and vice: Who will report on the failings of the American criminal justice system? *Stanford Law Review, 61*(6), 1429-1461, p. 1451.

38. Cole & Smith (2006).

39. Surette, R. (1992). *Media, crime, and criminal justice: Images and realities.* Pacific Grove: Brooks/Cole, p. 40.

40. Blumberg, A. (1967). The practice of law as confidence game: Organizational cooptation of a profession. *Law and Society Review, 4*, 115–139; Casper, J. (1972). *American criminal justice: The defendant's perspective.* Englewood Cliffs, NJ: Prentice Hall.

41. Gaines et al. (2000), p. 294.

42. Gorr, M. (2000). The morality of plea bargaining. *Social Theory and Practice, 26*(1), 129–151; Kaminer, W. (1999). Games prosecutors play. *American Prospect, 46*, 20–26; Palermo, G., White, M., & Wasserman, L. (2998). Plea bargaining: Injustice for all? *International Journal of Offender Therapy and Comparative Criminology, 42*(2), 111–123.

43. Quoted in Herbert, B. (1998). Cheap justice. *New York Times*, March 1, p. 15.

44. Miller, R. (1997). Symposium on coercion: An interdisciplinary examination of coercion, exploitation, and the Law: III. Coerced confinement and treatment: The continuum of coercion: constitutional and clinical considerations in the treatment of mentally disordered persons. *Denver Law Review, 74,* 1169–1214.

45. Weitzer, R. (1996). Racial discrimination in the criminal justice system: Findings and problems in the literature. *Journal of Criminal Justice, 24,* p. 313.

46. Langbein, J. (2000). On the myth of written constitutions: The disappearance of criminal jury trial. In G. Mays & P. Gregware (Eds.)., *Courts and justice: A reader* (2nd Ed). Prospect Heights, IL: Waveland Press, p. 227.

47. Cox & Wade (1998), p. 149.

48. Reiman, J. (1998). *The rich get richer and the poor get prison: Ideology, class, and criminal justice* (5th Ed.). Boston: Allyn and Bacon, p. 118.

49. Langbein (2000), p. 31.

50. Walker (1998), p. 153.

51. Grochowski, T. (2002). The "tabloid effect" in the O.J. Simpson case: The National Enquirer and the production of crime knowledge. *International Journal of Cultural Studies, 5*(3), 336; Sellers, D. (2008). The circus comes to town: The media and high-profile trials. *Law & Contemporary Problems, 71*(4), 181-199.

52. Hannaford-Agor, P. (2008). When all eyes are watching: Trial characteristics and practices in notorious trials. *Judicature, 91*(4), 197-201.

53. Fox, R., Van Sickel, R., & Steiger, T. (2007). *Tabloid justice: Criminal justice in an age of media frenzy* (2nd Ed.). Boulder, CO: Lynne Rienner.

54. Surette (2007), p. 125.

55. Gibeaut, J. (2005). Celebrity justice. *ABA Journal, 91,* 42-49.

56. McKenzie, M. (2009). The criminal justice system. Retrieved August 24, 2009, from: http://personal.uncc.edu/mfmckenz/Socy3173.The%20Criminal%20Justice%20System.htm.

57. McKenzie (2009).

58. Shelden, R. (2009). What does the criminal justice system look like? Retrieved August 24, 2009, from: http://www.sheldensays.com/Res_nine.htm.

59. Shelden (2009).

60. Surette (2007), p. 128.

61. Surette (2007), p. 130.

62. Carpenter, S., Lacy, S., & Fico, F. (2006). Network news coverage of high-profile crimes during 2004: A study of source use and reported context. *Journalism & Mass Communication Quarterly, 83*(4), 901-916.

63. Pogorzelski, W., & Brewer, T. (2007). Cameras in court: How television news media use courtroom footage. *Judicature, 91*(3), 124-134.

64. Pogorzelski and Brewer (2007).

65. Pogorzelski and Brewer (2007).

66. Surette (2007), p. 127.

67. Pogorzelski and Brewer (2007).

68. Entman, R., & Gross, K. (2008). Race of judgment: Stereotyping media and criminal defendants. *Law & Contemporary Problems, 71*(4), 93-133.

69. Kovera, M. (2002). The effects of general pretrial publicity on juror decisions: An examination of moderators and mediating mechanisms. *Law and Human Behavior: Empirical and Legal Perspectives on the Impact of Pretrial, 26*(1), 43-72.

70. CNN (1996). I am not the Olympic park bomber. Retrieved May 11, 2009, from: http://www.cnn.com/US/9610/28/jewell.presser/.

71. Rush, G. E. (2000). *The dictionary of criminal justice* (4th Ed.). Boston: Dushkin/McGraw-Hill.

72. Robinson, M. (2009). *Justice blind? Ideals and realities of American criminal justice* (3rd Ed.). Upper Saddle River, NJ: Prentice Hall.

73. Walker, S. (2005). *Sense and nonsense about crime and drugs* (6th Ed.). Beverly Hills, CA: Wadsworth.

74. Donziger, S. (1996). *The real war on crime: The report of the National Criminal Justice Commission.* New York: Harper Perennial, p. 25.

75. Gray, J. (2001). *Why our drugs laws have failed and what we can do about it.* Philadelphia: University of Temple Press; Sileo, C. (1993). Sentencing rules that shackle justice. *Insight 11.*

76. Beckett, K., and T. Sasson. (2000). *The politics of injustice: Crime and punishment in America.* Thousand Oaks, CA: Pine Forge Press, p. 180.

77. Brown, B., & Jolivette, G. (2005). A primer—three strikes. Retrieved April 10, 2009, from: http://www.lao.ca.gov/2005/3_Strikes/3_strikes_102005.htm; Ehlers, S. Schiraldi, V., & Lotke, E. (2004). Racial divide. Retrieved April 10, 2009 from: http://www.justicepolicy.org/images/upload/04-10_TAC_CARacialDivide_AC-RD.pdf; Ehlers, S., Schiraldi, V., & Ziedenberg, J. (2004). Still striking out. Retrieved April 10, 2009, from: http://www.soros.org/initiatives/usprograms/focus/justice/articles_publications/publications/still_striking_20040305/threestrikes_press.pdf; Schiraldi, V., Colburn, J., & Lotke, E. (2004). Three strikes and you're out. Retrieved April 10, 2009, from: http://www.soros.org/initiatives/usprograms/focus/justice/articles_publications/publications/threestrikes_200 40923/three_strikes.pdf.

78. Brunner, J. (2000). Crime laws bear names of young victims. *The Seattle Times,* March 31. Retrieved October 10, 2009, from: http://community.seattletimes.nwsource.com/archive/?date=20000331&slug=4012908.

79. Kappeler et al. (2000), p. 228.

80. Kappeler et al. (2000), p. 28.

81. Walker, S., Spohn, C., & Delone, M. (2006). *The color of justice: Race, ethnicity, and crime in America* (4th Edition). Beverly Hills, CA: Wadsworth, p. 280.

82. For examples, see Death Penalty Information Center (2009). Race and the death penalty. http://www.deathpenaltyinfo.org/race-and-death-penalty.

83. Department of Health and Human Services, Substance Abuse and Mental Health Services Administration, Office of Applied Studies.

(2007). National survey on drug use and health. Figure 2.9 Past month illicit drug use among persons aged 12 or older, by race/ethnicity: 2007. Retrieved April 11, 2009, from: http://www.oas.samhsa.gov/NSDUH/2k7NSDUH/2k7results.cfm#Fig2-9.

84. Sourcebook of Criminal Justice Statistics (2009). Table 4.10. Arrests. Retrieved April 11, 2009, from: http://www.albany.edu/sourcebook/pdf/t4102007.pdf.

85. For example, see Albonetti, C. (1997). Sentencing under the federal sentencing guidelines: Effects of defendant characteristics, guilty pleas, and departures on sentencing outcomes for drug offenses, 1991–1992. *Law and Society Review, 31,* 789–822.

86. Robinson (2009).

87. Reeves, J., & Campbell, R. (1994). Cracked coverage: Television news, the anti-cocaine crusade, and the Reagan legacy. Durham, NC: Duke University Press.

88. Kennedy, R. (1997). *Race, crime and the law*. New York: Vintage.

89. Haltom (1998), p. 157.

90. Cavender, G. (2004). Media and crime policy: A reconsideration of David Garland's *The Culture of Control. Punishment and Society 6*, 335-348; Ericson (1995) Garland, D. (2001). *The culture of control: Crime and social order in contemporary society*. Chicago, IL: University of Chicago Press; Surette (1998).

91. Altheide (2006), p. 212.

92. Altheide (2006), p. 30.

93. Haltom (1998), p. 158.

94. Schlesinger, P., & Tumber, H. (1994). *Reporting crime: The media politics of criminal justice*. Oxford: Clarendon.

95. Haltom (1998), p. 158.

96. Dreschel, R. (1983). *News making in the trial court*. New York: Longman.

97. Haltom (1998), p. 165.

98. Surette (2007), p. 120.

99. Project for Excellence in Journalism (2001). The look of local news. Retrieved January 16, 2006, from: http//www.journalism.org/resources/research/reports/localTV/2001/look.asp.

Chapter 7

1. Kalman, G. (2001). Avoiding prison policy by sound bite. *Corrections Today, June*, 1.

2. Surette (2007), p. 151.

3. Surette (2007), p. 152.

4. Welch, M., Weber, L., & Edwards, W. (2000). "All the news that's fit to print": A content analysis of the correctional debate in the *New York Times. The Prison Journal, 80*(3), 245–264.

5. Doyle, A., & Ericson, R. (1996). Breaking into prison: News sources and correctional institutions. *Canadian Journal of Criminology, April*, 155–190, p. 156.

6. Chermak, S. (1998). Police, courts, and corrections in the media. In F. Bailey and D. Hale (Eds.), *Popular Culture, Crime and Justice*. Belmont, CA: Wadsworth.

7. Mason, P. (2005) *Captured by the media: Prison discourse in popular culture*. Uffculme, Devon, UK: Willan.

8. Surette (2007), p. 160.

9. Montross Jr., W., & Mulvaney, P. (2009). Virtue and vice: Who will report on the failings of the American criminal justice system? *Stanford Law Review, 61*(6), 1429–1461, p. 1460.

10. Surette (2007), p. 162.

11. Freeman, R. (2000). *Popular culture and corrections*. Lanham, MD: American Correctional Association.

12. Surette (2007), p. 162.

13. Merlo, A., & Benekos, P. (2000). *What's wrong with the criminal justice system: Ideology, politics and the media*. Cincinnati, OH: Anderson, p. 14.

14. Bureau of Justice Statistics (2009). Probation and parole statistics. Retrieved April 9, 2009, from: http://ojp.usdoj.gov/bjs/pandp.htm.

15. Petersilia, J., & Turner, S. (1986). Prison versus probation? in California: Implications for crime and offender recidivism. Santa Monica, CA: Rand Corporation.

16. WRAL (2009). Captured: Eva Carson murder suspects. Retrieved October 12, 2009, from: http://www.ncwanted.com/ncwanted_home/story/2568746/.

17. Robinson (2009).

18. Robinson, M. (2008). *Death nation: The experts explain American capital punishment.* Upper Saddle River, NJ: Prentice Hall.

19. Robinson, M., & Beaver, K. (2009). *Why crime? An interdisciplinary approach to explaining criminal behavior.* Durham, NC: Carolina Academic Press.

20. Robinson, M. (2004). *Why crime? An integrated systems theory of antisocial behavior.* Upper Saddle River, NJ: Prentice Hall.

21. Mendes, S. (2004). Certainty, severity , and their relative deterrent effects: Questioning the implications of the role of risk in criminal deterrence policy. *Policy Studies Journal, 32*(1), 59–74; Nagin, D., & Pogarsky, G. (2001). Integrating celerity, impulsivity, and extralegal sanction threats into a model of general deterrence: Theory and evidence. *Criminology, 39*(4), 865–891; Pogarsky, G., KiDeuk, K., & Paternoster, R. (2005). Perceptual change in the national youth survey: Lessons for deterrence theory and offender decision-making. *Justice Quarterly, 22*(1), 1–9; Yu, J., & Liska, A. (1993). The certainty of punishment: A reference group effect and its functional form. *Criminology, 31*(3), 447–464.

22. Blumstein, A. (1995). Prisons. In J. Wilson & J. Petersilia (Eds.), *Crime.* San Francisco: San Francisco Institute for Contemporary Studies, pp. 408–409.

23. Cromwell, P. (1995). *In their own words.* Los Angeles: Roxbury.

24. Conklin, J. (2002). *Why crime rates fell.* Boston, MA: Allyn & Bacon.

25. Zimring, F. (2006) *The great American crime decline.* New York: Oxford University Press.

26. Levitt, S., & Dubner, S. (2005). *Freakonomics.* New York: William Morrow.

27. Blumstein, A., & Wallman, J. (2000). *The crime drop in America.* New York: Cambridge University Press, p. 11.

28. Spelman, W. 2000. The limited importance of prison expansion. In A. Blumstein & J. Wallman (Eds.), *The crime drop in America.* New York: Cambridge University Press.

29. Clear, T. (1999). Foreword to Welch, M. (1999). *Punishment in America: Social control and the ironies of imprisonment.* Thousand Oaks, CA: Sage Publications, p. ix).

30. King, R., Mauer, M., and M. Young (2005). Incarceration and crime: a complex relationship. [Online]. Available: http://www.sentencingproject.org/Admin/Documents/publications/inc_iandc_complex.pdf.

31. King et al. (2005), p. 3.

32. King et al. (2005), p. 3.

33. King et al. (2005), p. 8.

34. May, J., ed. (2000). *Building violence: How America's rush to incarcerate creates more violence.* Thousand Oaks, CA: Sage Publications.

35. Clear, T. (2009). *Imprisoning communities: How mass incarceration makes disadvantaged neighborhoods worse.* New York: Oxford University Press.

36. Welsh, W., & Harris, P. (2008). *Criminal justice policy and planning* (3rd Ed.). Cincinnati, OH: Lexis/Nexis.

37. Pew Center on the States (2009). One in 100: Behind bars in America. Retrieved April 9, 2009, from: http://www.pewcenteronthestates.org/uploadedFiles/8015PCTS-_Prison08_FINAL_2-1-1_FORWEB.pdf.

38. Stephan, J. (2004). State prison expenditures, 2001. Washington, DC: Bureau of Justice Statistics. Retrieved April 9, 2009, from: http://www.ojp.usdoj.gov/bjs/pub/pdf/ spe01.pdf.

39. Bureau of Justice Statistics (2009). Key facts at a glance. Retrieved April 9, 2009, from: http://ojp.usdoj.gov/bjs/glance/tables/exptyptab.htm.

40. Bureau of Justice Statistics (2009). Corrections statistics. Retrieved April 10, 2009, from: http://ojp.usdoj.gov/bjs/correct.htm.

41. King's College of London (2008). Prison brief—highest to lowest rates. Retrieved April 10, 2009, from: http://www.kcl.ac.uk/depsta/law/research/icps/worldbrief/wpb_stats.php?area=all&category=wb_poprate.

42. Donziger (1996), p. 31.

43. Clear, T. (1997). Forward. In J. Irwin, & J. Austin. *It's about time: America's imprisonment binge*. Belmont, CA: Wadsworth.

44. Welch, M. (1999). *Punishment in America: Social control and the ironies of imprisonment*. Thousand Oaks, CA: Sage Publications, p. 52.

45. Robinson, M., & Scherlen, R. (2007). *Lies, damned lies, and drug war statistics*. Albany, NY: State University of New York Press.

46. Donziger (1996), p. 45.

47. McShane, M. Williams III, F., & Pelz, B. (2006). The myth of prisons as country clubs. In R. Bohm & J. Walker (Eds.), *Demystifying crime and criminal justice*. Los Angeles, CA: Roxbury, p. 202.

48. Sykes, G. (1958). *The society of captives: A study of a maximum-security prison*. Princeton, NJ: Princeton University Press.

49. McGinnis, K. (2000). Make 'em break rocks. In J. May (Ed.), *Building violence: How America's rush to incarcerate creates more violence*. Thousand Oaks, CA: Sage Publications, p. 35.

50. Ingley, S. (2000). Corrections without corrections. In J. May (Ed.), *Building violence: How America's rush to incarcerate creates more violence*. Thousand Oaks, CA: Sage Publications, p. 20.

51. May (2000), p. 134.

52. Page, J. (2000). Violence and incarceration: A personal observation. In J. May (Ed.), *Building violence: How America's rush to incarcerate creates more violence*. Thousand Oaks, CA: Sage Publications, pp. 138, 141.

53. Donziger (1996), p. 43.

54. Donziger (1996), p. 44.

55. Welch, M. (1999). *Punishment in America: Social control and the ironies of imprisonment*. Thousand Oaks, CA: Sage Publications.

56. Clark, C. (1994). Prison overcrowding. Congressional Quarterly Researcher 4 (February): 100.

57. Donaldson, S. (1995). Rape of incarcerated prisoners: A preliminary statistical look. New York: Stop Prison Rape, Inc.

58. Martin, S. (2000). Sanctioned violence in American prisons. In J. May (Ed.), *Building violence: How America's rush to incarcerate creates more violence*. Thousand Oaks, CA: Sage Publications.

59. Welch (1999), p. 199.

60. Mariner, J. (2000). Body and soul: The trauma of prison rape. In J. May (Ed.), *Building violence: How America's rush to incarcerate creates more violence*. Thousand Oaks, CA: Sage Publications, p. 129.

61. Welch (1999), p. 200.

62. Ross, Jeffrey Ian (2007). Supermax prisons. *Society, 44*(3), 60–64.

63. Welch (1999), p. 208.

64. Weinstein (2000), p. 120.

65. The Sentencing Project (2007). Felony disenfranchisement. Retrieved April 11, 2009, from: http://www.sentencingproject.org/IssueAreaHome.aspx?IssueID=4.

66. The Sentencing Project (2007).

67. Sentencing Project (2009). Felony disenfranchisement. Retrieved September 10, 2009, from: http://www.sentencingproject.org/template/page.cfm?id=133.

68. Robinson (2004).

69. Sampson R., & Laub, J. (1997). A life-course theory of cumulative disadvantage and the stability of delinquency. In T. Thornberry (Ed.), *Developmental theories of crime and delinquency*. New Brunswick, NJ: Transaction.

70. Irwin, J., & Austin, J. (1997). *It's about time: America's imprisonment binge*. Belmont, CA: Wadsworth, p. 162.

71. Wood, P. (2006). The myth that imprisonment is the most severe form of punishment. In R. Bohm & J. Walker (Eds.), *Demystifying crime and criminal justice*. Los Angeles, CA: Roxbury.

72. May, J. (2000). *Building violence: How America's rush to incarcerate creates more violence*. Thousand Oaks, CA: Sage Publications, p. xvii.

73. Sourcebook of Criminal Justice Statistics (2008). Table 6.46. Participation in education programs for those in State and Federal prisons, in local jails, and on probation. Retrieved November 11, 2009, from: http://www.albany.edu/sourcebook/pdf/t646.pdf.

74. Vandebosch, H. (2005). The perceived role of mass media use during incarceration in light of prisoner re-entry into society. *Journal of Criminal Justice and Popular Culture*, 12 (2), 96–115. http://www.albany.edu/scj/jcjpc/vol12is2/vandebosch.pdf, p. 99.

75. Weisman, A. (2000). Mental illness behind bars. In J. May (Ed.), *Building violence: How America's rush to incarcerate creates more violence*. Thousand Oaks, CA: Sage Publications.

76. Torrey, E., Steiber, J., Ezekiel, J., Wolfe, S., Sharftein, J., Noble, J., & Flynn, L. (1992). Criminalizing the seriously mental ill: The abuse of jails as mental hospitals. Washington, DC: National Alliance for the Mentally Ill and Public Citizens Health Research Group.

77. James, D., & Glaze, L. (2006). Mental health problems of prison and jail inmates. Washington, DC: Bureau of Justice Statistics. Retrieved April 11, 2009, from: http://www.ojp.usdoj.gov/bjs/pub/pdf/mhppji.pdf.

78. Mauer, M., King, R., & Young, M. (2004). The meaning of "life": Long prison sentences in context. Washington DC: The Sentencing Project.

79. Weisman (2000), p. 106.

80. National Alliance for the Mentally Ill (2009). The criminalization of people with mental illness. Retrieved October 12, 2009, from: http://www.nami.org/Content/Content Groups/Policy/WhereWeStand/The_Criminalization_of_People_with_Mental_Illness ___WHERE_WE_STAND.htm.

81. Senator Jim Webb (2009). National Criminal Justice Commission Act of 2009. Retrieved October 12, 2009, from: http://webb.senate.gov/email/criminaljusticereform.html.

82. Parade (2009). What's wrong with our prisons? March 29. Retrieved October 12, 2009, from: http://webb.senate.gov/email/incardocs/parade_jimwebb.pdf.

83. Walker, S., Delone, M., & Spohn, C. (2007). *The color of justice* (3rd Ed.). Beverly Hills, CA: Wadsworth, p. 419.

84. The Sentencing Project (2010). Facts about prison and prisoners. Retrieved February 18, 2010, from: http://sentencingproject.org/doc/publications/publications/inc_facts aboutprisons_Dec2009.pdf.

85. The Sentencing Project (2007).

86. Robinson (2009); the Sentencing Project (2010).

87. Dershowitz, A. (2002). *Supreme injustice: How the high court hijacked election 2000.* New York: Oxford University Press.

88. Palast, G. (2004). *The best democracy money can buy.* New York: Plume.

89. Cecil, D. (2007). Doing time in "Camp Cupcake:" Lessons learned from newspaper accounts of Martha Stewart's incarceration. *Journal of Criminal Justice and Popular Culture, 14*(2), 142–160. http://www.albany.edu/scj/jcjpc/vol14is2/cecil.pdf, p. 142.

90. Cecil (2007), p. 143.

91. Honderich, K. (2003). The real cost of prisons for women and their children. Retrieved February 18, 2010, from: http://www.realcostofprisons.org/rcpp_background_women.pdf.

92. ACLU (2010). Caught in the net. Retrieved February 18, 2010, from: http://www.aclu.org/FilesPDFs/caught%20in%20the%20net%20-%20report.pdf.

93. Williams, M. (2007). How coverage of death sentences vary: A study of two Ohio newspapers. *Journal of Crime & Justice, 30*(2), 53.

94. Dardis, F., Baumgartner, F., Boydstun, A., De Boef, S., & Shen, F. (2008, Spring2008). Media Framing of Capital Punishment and Its Impact on Individuals' Cognitive Responses. *Mass Communication & Society, 11*(2), 115–140.

95. Death Penalty Information Center (2009). Executions by year. Retrieved November 11, 2009, from: http://deathpenaltyinfo.org/executions-year; and Federal Bureau of Investigation (2009). Uniform Crime Reports, Crime in the United States. Table 1. Retrieved November 11, 2009, from: http://www.fbi.gov/ucr/cius2008/data/table_01.html.

96. Hochstetler, D..(2001). Reporting of executions in U.S. newspapers. *Journal of Crime & Justice, 24*(1), 1–13.

97. Ryan, P. (1992). *The Last Public Execution in America.* [Online]. Available: http://www.geocities.com/lastpublichang.

98. Banner (2003), p. 156.

99. Banner (2003), p. 162.

100. Bessler (1997).

101. Banner (2003), p. 168.

102. Johnson (1998), p. 31.

103. Johnson (1998), p. 41.

104. Bessler (1997), p. 81.

105. Bessler (1997), p. 82.

106. Bessler (1997), p. 82.

107. Bessler (1997), p. 84.

108. Dow, D, & McNeese, B. (2004). Invisible executions: A preliminary analysis of publication rates in death penalty cases in selected jurisdictions. *Texas Journal of Civil Liberties & Civil Rights, 8*(2), 149–173, p. 149.

109. Leighton, P. (2009). Televising executions: An overview of the arguments. Retrieved October 12, 2009, from: http://paulsjusticepage.com/cjethics/6-emergingissues/tvexecutions.htm.

110. Robinson, M. (2008). *Death nation: The experts explain American capital punishment.* Upper Saddle River, NJ: Prentice Hall.

111. Lipschultz, J., & Hilt, M. (1999). Mass media and the death penalty: Social construction of three Nebraska executions. *Journal of Broadcasting & Electronic Media, 43*(2), 236–253, p. 250.

112. Jacoby, J., Bronson, E., Wilczak, A., Mack, J., Suter, D., Xu, Q., & Rosenmerkel, S. (2008). The newsworthiness of executions. *Journal of Criminal Justice and Popular Culture, 15*(2), 168–188. http://www.albany.edu/scj/jcjpc/vol15is2/Jacoby_et_al.pdf, p. 169.

113. Jacoby et al., (2008), p. 184.

114. Jacoby et al., (2008), pp. 184–185.

115. Jacoby et al., (2008), p. 169.

116. Hochstetler, A. (2001). Reporting of executions in U.S. newspapers. *Journal of Crime and Justice.* 24:1–13.

117. Miller, K., & Hunt, S. (2008). Exit stage left: A dramaturgical analysis of media accounts of executions in America. *Journal of Criminal Justice and Popular Culture, 15*(2), 189–217. http://www.albany.edu/scj/jcjpc/vol15is2/MillerHunt.pdf.

118. Niven, D. (2004). Southern newspaper coverage of exonerations from death row. *Journal of Criminal Justice and Popular Culture, 11(1),* 20–31. http://www.albany.edu/scj/jcjpc/vol11is1/niven.pdf, p. 20.

119. Niven, D. (2004). Southern newspaper coverage of exonerations from death row. *Journal of Criminal Justice and Popular Culture, 11(1),* 20–31. http://www.albany.edu/scj/jcjpc/vol11is1/niven.pdf, p. 24.

120. Death Penalty Information Center (2009). The innocence list. Retrieved September 10, 2009, from: http://deathpenaltyinfo.org/innocence-list-those-freed-death-row.

121. Death Penalty Information Center (2006). Additional innocence information, Executed but possibly innocent. [Online]. Available: http://www.deathpenaltyinfo.org/article.php?scid=6&did=111#executed.

122. Grann, D., (2009).Trial by fire: Did Texas execute an innocent man? *The New Yorker*, September 7; Mills, S. (2009), Cameron Todd Willingham case: Expert says fire for which father was executed was not arson. *Chicago Tribune*, August 25.

123. Fan, D., Keltner, K., & Wyatt, R. (2002) A matter of guilt or innocence: How news reports affect support for the death penalty in the United States. *International Journal of Public Opinion Research, 14,* 439–452.

Chapter 8

1. NBC (2009). Dateline NBC: To catch a predator. Retrieved October 26, 2009, from: http://www.msnbc.msn.com/id/10912603/.

2. CBS (2009). 48 Hours Mystery. Retrieved October 26, 2009, from: http://www.cbsnews.com/sections/48hours/main3410.shtml.

3. Wilson, C. (2000). *Cop knowledge: Police power and cultural narrative in twentieth century America.* Chicago, IL: University of Chicago Press.

4. Soulliere, D. (2003). Prime-time crime: Presentations of crime and its participants on popular television justice programs. *Journal of Crime & Justice, 10*(1), 12–38, p. 12.

5. Rhineberger-Dunn, G., Rader, N., & Williams, K. (2008). Constructing juvenile delinquency through crime drama: An analysis of Law & Order. *Journal of Criminal Justice and Popular Culture, 15* (1), 94–116. http://www.albany.edu/scj/jcjpc/vol15is1/Rhineberger_Raider_Williams.pdf.

6. Pandiani, J. (1978). Crime time TV: If all we knew is what we saw. *Contemporary Crises, 2,* 437–458.

7. Estep, R., & Macdonald, P. (1983). How prime time crime evolved on TV, 1976–1981. *Journalism Quarterly, 60*(2), 293–300.

8. Surette, R., & Otto, C. (2002). A test of a crime and justice infotainment measure. *Journal of Criminal Justice, 30*(5), 443–453.

9. Dowler, K. (2007). Introduction: Media criminology in the television world. *Journal of Criminal Justice and Popular Culture, 14* (3) 237–242. http://www.albany.edu/scj/jcjpc/vol14is3/Dowler_Intro.pdf.

10. Cecil, D. (2007). Dramatic portrayals of violent women: Female offenders on prime time crime dramas. *Journal of Criminal Justice and Popular Culture, 14*(3), 243–258. http://www.albany.edu/scj/jcjpc/vol14is3/Cecil.pdf, p. 243.

11. Hughes, T., & Magers, M. (2007). The perceived impact of crime scene investigation shows on the administration of justice. *Journal of Criminal Justice and Popular Culture, 14*(3), 259–276. http://www.albany.edu/scj/jcjpc/vol14is3/HughesMagers.pdf, p. 260.

12. TV Guide (2010). TV Guide's most popular TV shows. Retrieved February 19, 2010, from: http://www.tvguide.com/top-tv-shows.

13. Robinson, M. (2003). Justice as freedom, fairness, compassion, and utilitarianism: How my life experiences shaped my views of justice. *Contemporary Justice Review, 6*(4), 329–340.

14. Robinson, M. (2009). *Justice blind? Ideals and realities of American criminal justice* (3rd Ed.). Upper Saddle River, NJ: Prentice Hall.

15. Eschholz, S., Mallard, M., & Flynn, S. (2004). Images of prime time justice: A content analysis of "NYPD Blue" and "Law & Order." *Journal of Criminal Justice and Popular Culture, 10*(3), 161–180. http://www.albany.edu/scj/jcjpc/vol10is3/eschholz.pdf.

16. Holbert, L., Shah, D., & Kwak, N. (2004). Fear, authority, and justice: Crime-related TV viewing and endorsements of capital punishment and gun ownership. *J&MCQ, 51*(2), 343–363.

17. Beckett & Sasson (2000), p. 118.

18. Crothers, L. (2007). *Globalization & American culture.* Lanham, MD: Rowman & Littlefield, p. 8.

19. Crothers, L. (2007). *Globalization & American culture.* Lanham, MD: Rowman & Littlefield, pp. 56–62.

20. Soulliere, D. (2003). Prime-time crime: Presentations of crime and its participants on popular television justice programs. *Journal of Crime & Justice, 10*(1), 12–38.

21. Reality based shows and civil liberties — Worrall, J. (2000). Constitutional issues in reality-based police television programs: Media ride-alongs. *American Journal of Criminal Justice, 25*(1), 41–64, p. 41.

22. Center for Media and Public Affairs (1999). Merchandizing mayhem: Violence in popular entertainment 1998–1999. Retrieved September 24, 2009, from: http://www.cmpa.com/files/media_monitor/99sepoct.pdf.

23. Boyd, S..(2010). Reefer Madness and beyond. *Sociology of Crime, Law and Deviance: Popular Culture, Crime and Social Control, 14,* 3.

24. Campbell, E. (2010). The future(s) of risk: Barthes and Baudrillard go to Hollywood. *Crime, Media, Culture, 6*(1), 7.

25. Pino, N., Brunson, R., & Stewart, E. (2009). Using movies to illustrate ethical dilemmas in undergraduate criminal justice classes. *Journal of Criminal Justice Education, 20*(2), 194.

26. Rafter, N. (2007). Crime, film and criminology: Recent sex-crime movies. *Theoretical Criminology, 11*(3), 403.

27. Shipley, W., & Cavender, G. (2001). Murder and mayhem at the movies. *Journal of Criminal Justice and Popular Culture, 9*(1): 1–14. http://www.albany.edu/scj/jcjpc/vol9 is1/shipley.pdf.

28. Molitor, F., & Sapolsky, B. (1993). Sex, violence, and victimization in slasher films. *Journal of Broadcasting & Electronic Media 37*, 233–242.

29. Young, A. (2009). The screen of the crime: Judging the affect of cinematic violence. *Social & Legal Studies, 18*(1), 5.

30. Crothers, L. (2007). *Globalization & American culture.* Lanham, MD: Rowman & Littlefield, p. 96.

31. Armstrong, E. (2001). Gangsta misogyny: A content analysis of the portrayals of violence against women in rap music, 1987–1993. *Journal of Criminal Justice and Popular Culture,* 8(2) 96–126. http://www.albany.edu/scj/jcjpc/vol8is2/armstrong.pdf, pp. 105–106

32. Kubrin, C., & Weitzer, R. (2010). Rap music's violent and misogynistic effects: Fact of fiction? *Sociology of Crime, Law and Deviance: Popular Culture, Crime and Social Control, 14,* 121.

33. Saleh-Hanna, V. (2010). Crime, resistance and song: Black musicianship's black criminology. *Sociology of Crime, Law and Deviance: Popular Culture, Crime and Social Control, 14,* 145.

34. Singer, Simon I, Levine, Murray, & Jou, S. (1993). Heavy metal music preference, delinquent friends, social control, and delinquency. *The Journal of Research in Crime and Delinquency, 30*(3), 317.

35. For example, see Hemmens, C. (2009). A community under siege: Bruce Springstein and social justice. *Journal of the Institute of Justice and International Studies (9),* 19–37.

36. Leichtman, E. (2010). The different sounds of American protest: From freedom songs to punk rock. *Sociology of Crime, Law and Deviance: Popular Culture, Crime and Social Control, 14,* 173.

37. Kirsh, S., & Olczak, P. (2002). The effects of extremely violent comic books on social information processing. *Journal of Interpersonal Violence, 17*(11), 1160–1178.

38. Wright, B. W. (2001). *Comic book nation: The transformation of youth culture in America.* Baltimore: The Johns Hopkins University Press, p. xiii.

39. Vollum, S., & Adkinson, C. (2003). The portrayal of crime and justice in the comic book superhero mythos. *Journal of Criminal Justice and Popular Culture, 10*(2), 96–108. http://www.albany.edu/scj/jcjpc/vol10is2/vollum.pdf, p. 96.

40. Stoddart, M. (2006). "They say it'll kill me ... but they won't say when!" Drug narratives in comic books. *Journal of Criminal Justice and Popular Culture,* 13 (2), 66–95. http://www.albany.edu/scj/jcjpc/vol13is2/Stoddart.pdf, pp. 66–67.

41. Stoddart (2006), p. 75.

42. Stoddart (2006), p. 75.

43. Stoddart (2006), p. 82.

44. Stoddart (2006), p. 78.

45. Stoddart (2006), p. 81.

46. Walker, E. (2004). Suffragettes, vigilantes and superheroes: One girl's guide to chicks in comics. In E. Pohl-Weary (Ed.), *Girls who bite back: Witches, mutants, slayers and freaks* (pp. 209–222). Toronto, Ontario: Sumach Press.

47. Eagan, P. L. (1987). A flag with a human face. In D. Dooley & G. Engle (Eds.), *Superman at fifty! The persistence of a legend!* (pp. 88–95). Cleveland, OH: Octavia Press.

48. Vollum, S., & Adkinson, C. D. (2003). The portrayal of crime and justice in the comic book superhero mythos. *Journal of Criminal Justice and Popular Culture, 10*, 96–108, p. 105.

49. Blackmore, T. (1991). The dark knight of democracy: Tocqueville and Miller cast some light on the subject. *Journal of American Culture, 14*, 37–56.

50. Phillips, N. (2010). The Dark Knight: Constructing images of good vs. evil in an age of anxiety. *Sociology of Crime, Law and Deviance: Popular Culture, Crime and Social Control, 14*, 25.

51. Vollum & Adkinson (2003), p. 98.

52. Vollum & Adkinson, p. 100.

53. Vollum & Adkinson, p. 100.

54. Stoddart (2006), p. 78.

55. Seltzer, M. (2008). Murder/media/modernity. *Canadian Review of American Studies, 38*(1), 11–41, p. 26.

56. Stahl, R. (2006). Have you played the war on terror? *Critical Studies in Media Communication, 23*(2), 112–130, p. 112.

57. Schwartz, K. (2007). Chronic violent video game exposure and desensitization to violence Behavioral and event-related brain potential data. *Journal of Youth Ministry, 5*(2), 95–98.

58. Hallett, M., & Powell, D. (1995). Backstage with "COPS": The Dramaturgical Reification of Police Subculture in American Crime "Info-tainment". *American Journal of Police, 14*(1), 101–129.

59. Mastro, D.E., & Robinson, A.L. (2000). Cops and crooks: Images of minorities on primetime television. *Journal of Criminal Justice, 28*, 385–396.

60. Hallett, M. (1994). Why We Fail At Crime Control. In Elias, R. (ed.), *Declaring Peace on Crime (Special Issue). Peace Review, 6*(2), 177–181.

61. Cavender G. & Fishman, M. (1998). Television Reality Crime Programs: Context and History. In Fishman, M. & Cavender, G. (eds), *Entertaining Crime* (pp. 3–15). New York: Aldine De Gruyter, p. 11.

62. Cotter, R., de Lint, W., & O'Connor, D. (2008). Ordered images: cooking reality in *Cops. Journal of Criminal Justice and Popular Culture, 15*(3), 277–290. http://www.albany.edu/scj/jcjpc/vol15is3/CotterdeLintOConnor.pdf, p. 277.

63. Fishman, M. (1998). Ratings and reality: The persistence of the reality crime genre. In M. Fishman & G. Cavender (Eds), *Entertaining Crime*. New York: Aldine De Gruyter.

64. Surette (2007), p. 21.

65. Andersen, R. (1994). "Reality" TV and criminal injustice. *The Humanist, September/October*, 8–13, p. 8.

66. Manning, P. (1998). Media loops. In F. Bailey & D. Hale (Eds.). *Popular culture, crime, and justice* (pp. 25–39). Belmont, CA: Wadsworth.

67. Hallett, M., & Powell, D. (1995). Backstage with "Cops:" The dramaturgical reification of police subculture In American crime "info-tainment." *American Journal of Police, 14*(1), 101.

68. Andersen, R. (1994). "Reality" TV and criminal injustice. *Humanist, 54*(5), 8–13.

69. Andersen (1994).

70. Farrington, David (2005). *Integrated Developmental and Life-Course Theories of Offending*. Newark, NJ: Transaction; John Laub and Robert Sampson (2006). *Shared Beginnings, Divergent Lives: Delinquent Boys to Age 70*. Boston, MA: Harvard University Press; Terrie Moffitt (1993). Adolescent-limited and life-course-persistent antisocial behavior: A developmental taxonomy. *Psychological Review* 100:674–701; Terrie Moffitt (1997). Adolescent-limited and life-course-persistent offending: A complementary pair of developmental theories (11–54). In T. Thornberry (ed.), *Developmental Theories of Crime and Delinquency, Advances in Criminological Theory*. Newark, NJ: Transaction; Robert Sampson and John Laub (2005). *Crime in the Making: Pathways and Turning Points through Life*. Boston, MA: Harvard University Press.

71. Robinson, M. (2004). *Why Crime? An integrated systems theory of antisocial behavior*. Upper Saddle River, NJ: Prentice Hall.

72. Gans, H. (1995). *The war against the poor*. New York: Basic Books.

73. Cavender, G., & Fishman, M. (1998). Television reality crime programs: Context and history. In M. Fishman & G. Cavendar (Eds.), *Entertaining Crime*. New York, NY: Aldine De Gruyter.

74. Eschholz, S., Mallard, M., & Flynn, S. (2004). Images of prime time justice: A content analysis of "NYPD Blue" and "Law & Order." *Journal of Criminal Justice and Popular Culture, 10*(3), 161–180. http://www.albany.edu/scj/jcjpc/vol10is3/eschholz.pdf.

75. Andersen (1994), p. 9.

76. Surette (2007), pp. 106–107.

77. Andersen, R. (1994). "Reality" TV and criminal injustice. *Humanist, 54*(5), 8–13.

78. Chiricos, T., & Eschholtz, S. (2002). The racial and ethnic typification of crime and the criminal typification of race and ethnicity in local television news. *Journal of Research in Crime and Delinquency, 39*(4), 400–420; Perlmutter, D. (2001). Before rushing to judge cops for their actions. *Law Enforcement News, 27*(557), 11.

79. Chong Ho Shon, P., & Arrigo, B. (2006). Reality-based television and police-citizen encounters. *Punishment & Society, 8*(1), 59–85.

80. Cotter, R., de Lint, W., & O'Connor, D. (2008). Ordered images: cooking reality in *Cops. Journal of Criminal Justice and Popular Culture*, 15(3), 277–290. http://www.albany.edu/scj/jcjpc/vol15is3/CotterdeLintOConnor.pdf, p. 277.

81. Oliver, M (1994). Portrayals of crime, race, and aggression in "reality-based" police shows: A content analysis. *Journal of Broadcasting & Electronic Media*, 38(2), 179–92; Kooistra, P, Mahoney, J., & Westervelt, S. (1998). The world of crime according to "Cops." In M. Fishman & G. Cavender (Eds), *Entertaining Crime*. New York: Aldine De Gruyter; Carmody, D. (1998). Mixed messages: Images of domestic violence on "reality" television. In M. Fishman & G. Cavender (Eds), *Entertaining Crime*. New York: Aldine De Gruyter.

82. Cotter et al (2008), pp. 281–282.

83. Mawby, R. (2002). *Policing images: Policing, communication, and legitimacy*. Uffculme, Devon, UK.

84. Lavender, G., & Bond-Maupin, L. (1993). Fear and loathing on reality television: An analysis of America's most wanted and unsolved mysteries. *Sociological Inquiry, 63*, 305–317.

85. Cotter et al (2008), p. 283.

86. Cotter et al (2008), p. 284.

87. Surette, R. (2007).

88. Robinson, M. (2009). *Justice Blind? Ideals and Realities of American Criminal Justice* (3rd Ed.). Upper Saddle River, NJ: Prentice Hall.

89. Cotter et al (2008), p. 285.

90. Donovan, P. (1998). Armed with the power of television: Reality crime programming and the reconstruction of law and order in the United States. In M. Fishman & G. Cavendar (Eds.), *Entertaining crime*. New York: Aldine de Gruyter; Doyle, A. (1998). Cops: Television policing as policing reality. In M. Fishman & G. Cavendar (Eds.), *Entertaining crime*. New York: Aldine de Gruyter.

91. Andersen (1994).

92. Oreb, M. (2008). Representations of race in reality TV: Watch and discuss. *Studies in Media Communication, 25*(4), 345–352.

93. Bureau of Justice Statistics (2009). Criminal victimization 2008. Retrieved February 15, 2010, from: http://bjs.ojp.usdoj.gov/content/pub/pdf/cv08.pdf.

94. Andersen (1994), p. 12.

95. Low, J, & Durkin, K. (2001). Children's conceptualization of law enforcement on television and in real life. *Legal and Criminological Psychology, 6*, 197–214, p. 197.

96. Rhineberger-Dunn, G., Rader, N., & Williams, K. (2008). Constructing juvenile delinquency through crime drama: An analysis of Law & Order. *Journal of Criminal Justice and Popular Culture, 15* (1), 94–116. http://www.albany.edu/scj/jcjpc/vol15is1/Rhineberger_Raider_Williams.pdf.

97. Robinson (2009).

98. Robinson (2009).

99. Cox & Wade (1998), p. 148.

100. Stevens, D. (2011).*Media and criminal justice: The CSI effect*. New York: Jones and Bartlett.

101. Surette (2007), p. 121.

102. Rhineberger-Dunn, G., Rader, N., & Williams, K. (2008). Constructing juvenile delinquency through crime drama: An analysis of Law & Order. *Journal of Criminal Justice and Popular Culture, 15* (1), 94–116. http://www.albany.edu/scj/jcjpc/vol15is1/Rhineberger_Raider_Williams.pdf.

103. Rhineberger-Dunn, G., Rader, N., & Williams, K. (2008). Constructing juvenile delinquency through crime drama: An analysis of Law & Order. *Journal of Criminal Justice and Popular Culture, 15* (1), 94–116. http://www.albany.edu/scj/jcjpc/vol15is1/Rhineberger_Raider_Williams.pdf

104. Gans-Boriskin, R., & Wardle, C. (2005). Mad or bad? Negotiating the boundaries of mental illness on *Law & Order. Journal of Criminal Justice and Popular Culture, 12* (1) 26–46. http://www.albany.edu/scj/jcjpc/vol12is1/gans-boriskin.pdf.

105. Gans-Boriskin, R., & Wardle, C. (2005). Mad or bad? Negotiating the boundaries of mental illness on *Law & Order. Journal of Criminal Justice and Popular Culture, 12* (1) 26–46. http://www.albany.edu/scj/jcjpc/vol12is1/gans-boriskin.pdf, p. 29.

106. Britto, S., Hughes, T., Saltzmann, K., & Stroh, C. (2007). Does "special" mean young, white and female? Deconstructing the meaning of "special" in Law & Order: Special Victims Unit. *Journal of Criminal Justice and Popular Culture, 14* (1), 39–57. http://www.albany.edu/scj/jcjpc/vol14is1/britto.pdf.

107. Britto et al, (2007).

108. Britto et al, (2007).

109. Britto et al, (2007).

110. Britto et al, (2007).

111. Britto et al, (2007).

112. Britto et al, (2007), p. 49.

113. Britto et al, (2007), p. 49.

114. Eschholz, S., Mallard, M., & Flynn, S. (2004). Images of prime time justice: A content analysis of "NYPD Blue" and "Law & Order." *Journal of Criminal Justice and Popular Culture*, 10 (3) 161–180. http://www.albany.edu/scj/jcjpc/vol10is3/eschholz.pdf.

115. Eschholz, S., Mallard, M., & Flynn, S. (2004). Images of prime time justice: A content analysis of "NYPD Blue" and "Law & Order." *Journal of Criminal Justice and Popular Culture*, 10 (3) 161–180. http://www.albany.edu/scj/jcjpc/vol10is3/eschholz.pdf, p. 168.

116. U.S. Census (2009). State and county QuickFacts. New York. Retrieved August 21, 2009, from: http://quickfacts.census.gov/qfd/states/36000.html.

117. Eschholz, S., Mallard, M., & Flynn, S. (2004). Images of prime time justice: A content analysis of "NYPD Blue" and "Law & Order." *Journal of Criminal Justice and Popular Culture*, 10 (3) 161–180. http://www.albany.edu/scj/jcjpc/vol10is3/eschholz.pdf, p. 172.

118. Eschholz et al. (2004), p. 173.

119. Wilson, C. (2005). "Let's work out the details:" Interrogation and deception in prime time. *Journal of Criminal Justice and Popular Culture,* 12 (1) 47–64. http://www.albany.edu/scj/jcjpc/vol12is1/wilson.pdf, p. 48.

120. Lazarus. E. (2000). How Miranda really works and why it matters. *CNN*, June 7. Retrieved August 2, 2009, from: http://archives.cnn.com/2000/LAW/06/columns/lazarus. 06.07/.

121. Cohen, A. (2006). The CSI effect. Retrieved on February 19, 2006, from http://wtnh.com/Global/story.asp?S=4446803.

122. Fradella, H. Owen, S., & Burke, T. (2007). Building bridges between criminal justice and the forensic sciences to create forensic studies programs. *Journal of Criminal Justice Education, 18*(2), 261—282.

123. Deutsch, S., & Cavender, G. (2008). CSI and forensic realism. *Journal of Criminal Justice and Popular Culture 15*(1), 34–53. http://www.albany.edu/scj/jcjpc/vol15is1/Deutsch_Cavender.pdf, p. 34.

124. Hughes & Magers (2007), p. 259.

125. Bureau of Justice Statistics (2007). Homicide trend in the United States. Retrieved November 12, 2009, from: http://ojp.usdoj.gov/bjs/homicide/homtrnd.htm.

126. Crothers, L. (2007). *Globalization & American culture*. Lanham, MD: Rowman & Littlefield, p. 96.

127. Deutsch & Cavender (2008), p. 48.

128. Mardis, M. (2006). It's not just whodunnit, but how: THE CSI effect. *Knowledge Quest, 35*(1), 12–17.

129. Cordner, G., & Scarborough, K..(2006). The myth that science solves crime. In R. Bohm & J. Walker (Eds.), *Demystifying crime and criminal justice*. Los Angeles, CA: Roxbury, p. 104.

130. Sourcebook of Criminal Justice Statistics (2009). Table 4.20. Offenses known to the police and cleared by arrest. Retrieved April 6, 2009, from: http://www.albany.edu/sourcebook/pdf/t4202006.pdf.

131. Escholz, S., Mallard, M. & Flynn, S. (2004). Images of prime time justice: A content analysis of "NYPD Blue" and "Law & Order". *Journal of criminal justice and popular*

culture, 10(3): 161–180; Sumser, J. (1996). *Morality and social order in television crime drama.* Jefferson, NC: McFarland & Company, Inc., Publishers.

132. Cecil (2007), p. 243.

133. Cecil (2007), p. 253.

134. Bond-Maupin, L. (1998). "That wasn't even me they showed" Women as criminals on America's Most Wanted. *Violence against women, 4*(1): 30–44, p. 36.

135. Soulliere, D. (2003). Prime-time murder: Presentations of murder on popular television justice programs. *Journal of Criminal Justice and Popular Culture*, 10 (1): 12–38. http://www.albany.edu/scj/jcjpc/vol10is1/soulliere.pdf.

136. Soulliere, D. (2003). Prime-time murder: Presentations of murder on popular television justice programs. *Journal of Criminal Justice and Popular Culture*, 10 (1): 12–38. INK"http://www.albany.edu/scj/jcjpc/vol10is1/soulliere.pdf"http://www.albany.edu/scj/jcjpc/vol10 is1/soulliere.pdf, p. 25.

137. Soulliere, D. (2003). Prime-time murder: Presentations of murder on popular television justice programs. *Journal of Criminal Justice and Popular Culture*, 10 (1): 12–38. http://www.albany.edu/scj/jcjpc/vol10is1/soulliere.pdf, p. 27.

138. Soulliere, D. (2003). Prime-time murder: Presentations of murder on popular television justice programs. *Journal of Criminal Justice and Popular Culture*, 10 (1): 12–38. http://www.albany.edu/scj/jcjpc/vol10is1/soulliere.pdf, p. 30.

139. Brown, J.A. (1993). "Bullets, buddies, and bad guys: The 'action-cop' genre". *Journal of Popular Film and Television*, 21, 79–87; Gates, P. (2004). *Cop Action Films.* Retrieved December 13, 2005, from http://www.crimeculture.com/Contents/80sCopFilms.html; King, N. (1999). *Heroes in Hard Times: Cop Action Movies in the U.S.* Philadelphia, PA: Temple.

140. Schehr, R. (2000). Martial arts films and the action-cop genre: Ideology, violence, and spectatorship. *Journal of Criminal Justice and Popular Culture, 7*(3), 102–118. http://www.albany.edu/scj/jcjpc/vol7is3/schehr.pdf.

141. Brown, J. (1993). Bullets, buddies and bad guys: The action cop genre. *Journal of Popular Film and Television, 21* (2): 79–87.

142. Schehr (2000), p. 82.

143. Gustafson, J. (2007). A descriptive analysis of police corruption in film. *Journal of Criminal Justice and Popular Culture, 14*(2), 161–175. http://www.albany.edu/scj/jcjpc/vol14is2/gustafson.pdf, p. 163.

144. Lenz, T. (2005). Conservatism in American crime films. *Journal of Criminal Justice and Popular Culture, 12*(2), 116–134. http://www.albany.edu/scj/jcjpc/vol12is2/lenz.pdf

145. Lenz (2005), p. 117.

146. Lenz (2005), p. 130.

147. Surette (2007), p. 121.

148. http://www.cnn.com/CRIME/.

149. http://www.trutv.com/video/cats/naughty-girls.html.

150. http://www.trutv.com/video/cats/dumbest.html.

151. http://www.trutv.com/video/cats/fights-and-brawls.html.

152. http://www.trutv.com/video/cats/high-speed-chases.html.

153. http://www.trutv.com/video/cats/car-crashes.html.

154. Patrone, V. (1989). The 12 best trial movies. Retrieved October 19, 2009, from: http://www.supremecourt.ne.gov/students-teachers/movies.shtml.

155. American Film Institute (2009). Top 10 courtroom drama. Retrieved October 19, 2009, from: http://www.afi.com/10top10/crdrama.html.

156. Surette (2007), p. 157.

157. Cecil, D. & Leitner, J. (2009). Unlocking the gates: An examination of MSNBC Investigates—Lockup. *The Howard Journal of Criminal Justice, 48*(2), 184–199.

158. Cecil, D., & Leitner, J. (2009). Unlocking the gates: an examination of MSNBC Investigates—Lockup. *Howard Journal of Criminal Justice, 48*(2), 184–199.

159. Cecil, D..(2010). Televised images of jail: Lessons in controlling the unruly. *Sociology of Crime, Law and Deviance: Popular Culture, Crime and Social Control, 14,* 67.

160. O'Sullivan, S. (2001, November). Representations of prison in nineties Hollywood cinema: From Con Air to The Shawshank Redemption. *Howard Journal of Criminal Justice, 40*(4), 317.

161. Bennett, J. (2006). The good, the bad and the ugly: The media in prison films. *The Howard Journal of Criminal Justice, 45*(2), 97–115, p. 97.

162. Mason. P. (2006). Prison decayed: Cinematic penal discourse and populism. *Social Semiotics, 16*(4), 607–626, p. 607.

163. Eigenberg, H., & Baro, A. (2003). If you drop the soap in the shower you are on your own: Images of male rape in selected prison movies. *Sexuality & Culture, 7*(4), 56–89.

164. Cheatwood, D. (1998). Prison movies: Films about adult, male, civilian prisons: 1929–1995, In F. Bailey & D. Hale (Eds.), *Popular culture, crime, and justice* (3rd Ed.). Belmont, CA: Wadsworth.

165. Nellis, M. (2009). The aesthetics of redemption: Released prisoners in American film and literature. *Theoretical Criminology, 13*(1), 129.

166. Surette (2007), p. 153.

167. Freeman, R. (2000). *Popular culture and corrections.* Lanham, MD: American Correctional Association.

168. Clowers, M. (2001). Dykes, gangs, and danger: Debunking popular myths about maximum-security life. *Journal of criminal justice and popular culture, 9*(1): 22–30.

169. Clowers (2001), p. 27.

170. Talvi, S. (2007). *Women behind bars: The crisis of women in the U.S. prison system.* New York Seal Press; Zaitzow, B., & Thomas, J. (2003). *Woman in prison: Gender and social control.* Boulder, CO: Lynne Rienner.

Chapter 9

1. Cohen, S., and Young, J. (1981). *The manufacture of news.* Newbury Park, CA: Sage Publications.

2. Surette (1992), p. 57.

3. Krajicek (1998), p. 5.

4. Altheide (2006), pp. 18–19.

5. Bagdikian (2004), p. xxi.

6. Bagdikian (2004), p. 54.

7. Surette (1992), pp. 22, 32.

8. Bohm, & Walker (2006), p. xxii.

9. Potter & Kappeler (1998), p. 19.

10. Krajicek (1998), p. 13.

11. Beckett & Sasson (2000; Ericson et al. (1989).

12. Fox News (2009). Officials race to save little boy trapped in flying balloon. October 15. Retrieved October 15, 2009, from: http://www.foxnews.com/story/0,2933,567041,00.html.

13. Muraskin and Domash, p. 2.

14. Surette (1992), p. 31.

15. Beckett, K., & Sasson, T. (2003). *The politics of injustice: Crime and punishment in America* (2nd Edition). Thousand Oaks, CA: Sage; Marion, N. (1995). *A primer in the politics of criminal justice.* Albany, NY: Harrow and Heston.

16. Fishman, M. (1978). Crime waves as ideology. *Social Programs 25,* 531–543; Sherizen, S. (1978). Social creation of crime news: All the news that's fitted to print. In C. Winick (Ed.), *Deviance and the mass media.* Beverly Hills, CA: Sage Publications.

17. Beckett, K. (1997). *Making crime pay: Law and order in contemporary American politics.* New York: Oxford University Press; Gans, H. (1979). *Deciding what's news.* New York: Vintage Books; Schlesinger, P., & Tumber, H. (1994). *Reporting crime: The media politics of criminal justice.* Oxford: Clarendon; Sigal, L. (1973). *Reporters and officials: The organization and politics of newsmaking.* London: D. C. Heath.

18. Surette (1992), p. 14.

19. Altheide (2006), p. 61.

20. Altheide (2006), p. 67.

21. Altheide (2006), pp. 34–35.

22. Altheide (2006), p. 36.

23. Krajicek (1998), p. 35.

24. Akers, R., & Jensen, G. (2007). *Social learning theory and the explanation of crime.* Edison, NJ: Transaction.

25. Fishman (1978).

26. Robinson & Beaver (2009).

27. Stevens, S. (2009). *Media and criminal justice: The CSI effect.* Sudbury, MA: Jones & Bartlett.

28. Sabato, L. (2000). *Feeding frenzy: Attack journalism and American politics.* Baltimore, MD: Lanahan.

29. Krajicek (1998), p. 5.

30. Roberts, J., & Doob, A. (1990). News media influences on public views of sentencing. *Law and Human Behavior 14,* 451–468; Roberts, J., & Edwards, D. (1992). Contextual affects in judgements of crime, criminals, and the purpose of sentencing. *Journal of Applied Social Psychology 19,* 902–917.

31. Potter & Kappeler (1998), p. 3.

32. Welch, M., Fenwick, M., & Roberts, M. (1998). State managers, intellectuals, and the media: A content analysis of ideology in experts' quotes in feature newspaper articles on crime. *Justice Quarterly 15*(2), 219–241.

33. Potter & Kappeler (1998), p. 19.

34. Surette (1992).

35. Potter & Kappeler (1998), p. 17.

36. Alvarado, M., & Boyd-Barrett, O. (1992). *Media education: An introduction.* London: Milton Keynes; Gurevitch, M., et al. (1982). *Culture, society, and the media.* London: Methuen; Lapley, R., & Westlake, M. (1988). *Film theory: An introduction.* Manchester, England: Manchester University Press; McQuail, D. (1994). *Mass communication theory* (3rd Ed.). London: Sage; Stevenson, N. (1995). *Understanding media culture: Social theory*

and mass communication. London: Sage; Strinati, D. (1995). *An introduction to theories of popular culture.* London: Routledge.

37. Potter & Kappeler (1998), p. 18.

38. Potter & Kappeler (1998), p. 18.

39. Merlo & Benekos (2000), p. 2.

40. Welch et al. (1998).

41. Merlo & Benekos (2000), p. 2.

42. Edelman, M. (1988). *Constructing the political spectacle.* Chicago: University of Chicago Press; Gusfield, J. (1967). Moral passage: The symbolic process in public designations of deviance. *Social Problems 15,* 175–188; Hilgartner, S., and C. Bosk. (1988). The rise and fall of social problems: A public arenas model. *American Journal of Sociology 94,* 53–78; Kitsuse, S., & Spector, M. (1973). Toward a sociology of social problems: Social condition, value judgments, and social problems. *Social Problems 20,* 407–419.

43. Beckett & Sasson (2003).

44. Beckett & Sasson (2003).

45. Roberts, J. (1992). Public opinion, crime, and criminal justice. In M. Tonry (Ed.), *Crime and justice: A review of research* (Vol. 16). Chicago: University of Chicago Press; Roberts, J., & Doob, A. (1990). News media influences on public views of sentencing. *Law and Human Behavior 14,* 451–468.

46. Surette, R. (1992), p. 14.

47. Fishman (1978) Graber, D. (1980). *Crime news and the public.* Westport, CT: Praeger.

48. Potter & Kappeler (1998).

49. Surette (1992).

50. Schattenberg, G. (1981, January). Social Control Functions of Mass Media Depictions of Crime. *Sociological Inquiry, 51*(1), 71–77.

51. Holhert, B., Shah, D., & Kwak, N. (2004). Fear, authority, and justice: Crime-related TV viewing and endorsements of capital punishment and gun ownership. *J&MC Quarterly, 81*(2), 343–363.

52. Dowler, K. (2002). Media influence on attitudes toward guns and gun control. *American Journal of Criminal Justice, 26*(2), 235–247.

53. Fan, D., Kelner, K., & Wyatt, R. (2002). A matter of guilt or innocence: How news reports affect support for the death penalty in the United States. *International Journal of Public Opinion Research, 14*(4), 439–452.

Sotirovic, M. (2001). Effects of media use on complexity and extremity of attitudes toward the death penalty and prisoners' rehabilitation. *Media Psychology, 3,* 1–24.

54. Krajicek (1998), p. 16.

55. Krajicek (1998), p. 139.

56. Beckett & Sasson (2003).

57. Sasson (1995), p. 13.

58. Surette (1992), p. 14.

59. Altheide (2006), p. 15.

60. Altheide (2006), p. 39.

61. Altheide (2006), p. 15.

62. Altheide (2006), p. 17.

63. Altheide (2006), p. 18.

64. Altheide (2006), p. 47.

65. Surette (2007), p. 238.

66. StopBigMedia (2009). Coalition principles. Retrieved September 21, 2009, from: http://www.stopbigmedia.com/=principles.

67. Save the News (2009). Homepage. Retrieved September 21, 2009, from: http://www.savethenews.org/what_we_stand_for.

68. Save the News (2009). What we stand for. Retrieved September 21, 2009, from: http://www.savethenews.org/what_we_stand_for.

69. Save the News (2009). Evaluating the new models. Retrieved October 27, 2009, from: http://www.savethenews.org/new_models.

70. http://www.savethenews.org/new_models/subsidies_and_policies.

71. http://www.savethenews.org/new_models/public_and_government.

72. http://www.savethenews.org/new_models/nonprofit_and_lowprofit.

73. http://www.savethenews.org/new_models/community_and_municipal.

74. http://www.savethenews.org/new_models/foundation_and_endowment.

75. http://www.savethenews.org/new_models/new_commercial.

76. Surette (2007), p. 219.

Index